DATE DUE

#47-0108 Peel Off Pressure Sensitive

CULTURES OF CITIZENSHIP IN POST-WAR CANADA,
1940–1955

Cultures of Citizenship in Post-war Canada, 1940–1955

Edited by

NANCY CHRISTIE and
MICHAEL GAUVREAU

McGill-Queen's University Press
Montreal & Kingston · London · Ithaca

Legal deposit fourth quarter 2003
Bibliothèque nationale du Québec

Printed in Canada on acid-free paper that is 100% ancient forest free
(100% post-consumer recycled), processed chlorine free.

This book has been published with the help of a grant from the
Humanities and Social Sciences Federation of Canada, through the
Aid to Scholarly Publications Programme, using funds provided by
the Social Sciences and Humanities Research Council of Canada.

McGill-Queen's University Press acknowledges the support of the
Canada Council for the Arts for our publishing program. We also
acknowledge the financial support of the Government of Canada
through the Book Publishing Industry Development Program (BPIDP)
for our publishing activities.

National Library of Canada Cataloguing in Publication

Cultures of citizenship in post-war Canada, 1940– 1955 / edited by
Nancy Christie and Michael Gauvreau.

Includes bibliographical references and index.
ISBN 0-7735-2608-0

1. Family – Canada – History.   2. Family – Canada – Historiography.
I. Gauvreau, Michael, 1956–   .   II. Christie, Nancy, 1958–   .

HQ559.C84 2003   306.85'0971'09044   C2003–902958–1
F1021.2.F72 2003

Typeset in 10/12 Sabon by True to Type

Contents

Acknowledgments

This book brings together the efforts of a number of researchers currently investigating aspects of Canada's post-war culture and institutional life, who were approached by the editors in the fall of 1999 with the idea of situating both English-speaking Canada and Quebec within a growing body of international literature on postwar social and cultural history.

Over the course of this project, we have incurred many debts. Our thanks go to Don Akenson, senior editor of McGill-Queen's University Press, who from the outset expressed a firm and enthusiastic support for the idea of a volume on post war Canadian society. We would also like to state our gratitude to John Fraser, the master of Massey College at the University of Toronto, who generously provided us with facilities to hold a one-day workshop in December 2000, where a number of contributors were able to meet and discuss preliminary versions of the essays. As the manuscript moved towards publication, Roger Martin and Joan Harcourt at McGill-Queen's University Press were constantly available to answer our numerous telephone inquiries with patience, and to provide sound advice on the publishing process itself. Together with Don Akenson, this first-rate editorial team continues to make McGill-Queen's a welcoming environment for scholarly endeavours. At the production stage, Joan McGilvray's discerning care eased the transition from manuscript to book. To Elizabeth Hulse, our copy editor, we owe considerable thanks for a superb editorial mastery of a work involving two languages and for smoothing the edges of a multi-author, collective work.

Finally, as editors, we would like to thank the participants in this endeavour for their consistent intellectual contribution to elaborating a new concept of the Canadian postwar cultural experience.

Contributors

DENYSE BAILLARGEON is associate professor of history at the Université de Montréal. She has published numerous articles in women's and family history and is the author of *Ménagères au temps de la crise* (Remue-ménage, 1991 and 1993), translated as *Making Do: Women, Family and Home in Montreal during the Great Depression* (Wilfrid Laurier University Press, 1999). She is currently writing a book on infant mortality and the medicalization of motherhood in Quebec between 1910 and 1970.

P.E. BRYDEN is an associate professor of history at Mount Allison University and the author of *Planners and Politicians: Liberal Politics and Social Policy, 1957–1968* (McGill-Queen's University Press, 1997).

NANCY CHRISTIE is the author of two prize-winning monographs, *Engendering the State: Family Work and Welfare in Canada* (2000) and *A Full-Orbed Christianity: The Protestant Churches and Social Welfare in Canada, 1900–1940* (1996). She has edited *Households of Faith: Family, Gender, and Community in Canada, 1760–1969* (2002) and, with Michael Gauvreau, is editor of a forthcoming volume that reconceptualizes the nature of the Canadian family, *Discordant Kin: Mapping Marginality in the Canadian Family* (McGill-Queen's University Press).

MICHAEL GAUVREAU teaches history at McMaster University and is author of *The Evangelical Century: College and Creed in English*

Canada from the Great Revival to the Great Depression (1991) and, with Nancy Christie, *A Full-Orbed Christianity: The Protestant Churches and Social Welfare in Canada, 1900–1940* (1996). He has recently completed a cultural history of the relationship between Catholicism and Quebec's Quiet Revolution.

KARINE HÉBERT holds a postdoctoral fellowship at Carleton University and a fellowship from the FQRSC. Her doctoral thesis, completed at the Université du Québec à Montréal, is entitled "La construction d'une identité étudiante montréalaise, 1895–1960." She is a member of the Montreal History Group, her articles have appeared in *Revue d'histoire de l'Amérique française*, *Bulletin d'histoire politique*, and *Mens*.

LEN KUFFERT holds a SSHRCC post-doctoral fellowship in history at Carleton University and is a fellow of the University of Manitoba Institute for the Humanities. He is the author of *A Great Duty: English-Canadian Responses to Modern Life and Mass Culture, 1939–1967* (forthcoming from McGill-Queen's University Press). His current research involves the concept of taste and its role in the development of Canadian radio.

PETER S. MCINNIS teaches history at St Francis Xavier University and is the author of *Harnessing Labour Confrontation: Shaping the Postwar Settlement in Canada, 1943–1950* (University of Toronto Press, 2002).

CULTURES OF CITIZENSHIP IN POST-WAR CANADA,
1940–1955

Recasting Canada's Post-war Decade

To date, the dominant historiographic account of Canada's post-war experience has viewed the years between 1945 and 1955 as characterized, for better or worse, by cultural quiescence, social conformity, and political consensus. The immediate post-war decade has received little specific attention from historians for two reasons. On the one hand, historians who have argued that the reconstruction process was, compared with the fractious aftermath of World War I, efficiently managed and that it occasioned little social disharmony have obviated the necessity of more penetrating analysis of an era which serves merely as a historical hyphen to link wartime to the expansionist 1950s.[1] On the other hand, Canadian historians most influenced by American trends have telescoped the whole post-war period until the 1960s into an investigation into what has come to be known colloquially as the "baby boom" era. As a result, meta-concepts such as mass culture, Americanization, anti-communism, and consumerist affluence have been deployed indiscriminately, rather than analytically, to describe the dominant leitmotif of several decades.

This periodization of the post-war era which has viewed the years from the end of World War II to the "radical turn" of the 1960s as a conformist and hegemonic continuum is one largely borrowed from American historiography. However, the importation of American historical paradigms has come under critical scrutiny from historians in Canada, Britain, France, and Germany. In Canada, Joy Parr has not only questioned the sudden arrival of consumerist prosperity, but in her study of the politics of female consumption, she has forcefully challenged the notion postulated by both Elaine Tyler May and Doug Owram that the Cold War provided the central imperative around which other cultural issues coalesced.[2] Robert Collins has recently confirmed that at the conclusion of the war in the United States, economic pundits such as Alvin Hansen shifted away from the static views of Keynesianism to an assertively growth-oriented economic perspective. As Collins argues, it was the reality of immediate post-war prosperity that allowed for a distinctively consumptionist ideology to take root among both big business and organized labour, who together embraced a commitment away from state planning to more corporatist reformism.[3] By contrast, as Nancy Christie has made clear for the Canadian context, the commitment to Keynesianism was driven by Depression-era ideology, and while the implementation of family allowances was intended to avert post-war economic collapse, it implied a producerist commitment to full employment, rather than the growth ideology of consumption that defined the American situation.[4] Similarly, Parr has stressed that Canadian consumption patterns were defined and, indeed, constrained by the slow return to prosperity in Canada, which occurred only in the mid-1950s.[5] The interpretation of the post-war Canadian experience as a unified continuum extending to the 1960s has also been challenged from a different perspective by Valerie Korinek in her study of *Chatelaine* magazine, in which she demonstrates that the image of "suburbia" was a feature of popular magazines only by the end of the 1950s. In a similar vein, the work of Shirley Tillotson on community organizations and leisure and that of Ruth Frager and Carmela Patrias on the development of human rights organizations argue for a bifurcation of the period, in which the late 1940s stand as an era of considerable change.[6]

In several respects, the Canadian pattern of economic change more closely resembles that of Germany, Britain, and France, which despite the injection of substantial American investment with the Marshall Plan in the late 1940s, did not experience an economic takeoff until after 1955. What this revisionist historiography reveals is that the years between approximately 1943 and 1955 form a distinct period and that what we designate the "fifties," the era of mass consumption, prosperity, faith in technology and expertise, growth of suburban culture, and an emulation of American lifestyles, is more characteristic of the years 1955–68. British cultural historians such as Frank Mort, Peter Bailey, and Nick Hayes question assumptions that historians have made about the imposition of American modernity upon British society in this period, and they show that Americanization and "modernization" were a very contested terrain, one constrained and limited by British domestic concerns.[7] The periodization struck by these British cultural historians is reinforced by the new economic and political historians in Britain. For example, Noel Whiteside, in her study of state regulation of employment, argues that there was very little real affluence in Britain until the late 1950s largely because of the high degree of irresolution between state, industry, and labour.[8] Revisionist political historians such as Daniel Ritschel, Ina Zweiniger-Bargielowska, Stephen Brooke, Harriet Jones, and James D. Marlow have shown a continuity in perspective within both the Conservative and Labour parties in Britain until 1958, when the Labour Party finally accepted the notion of a mixed economy and Keynesianism and abandoned its Depression-era commitment to socialist planning and nationalization.[9]

German historians such as Robert Moeller have recently called for the jettisoning of chronologies established around political regimes, and they have overtly drawn a distinction between the post-war reconstructionist era and the fifties based upon their studies of family policies, youth cultures, and patterns of leisure and consumption.[10] Axel Schildt and Arnold Sywottek identify 1955 as the pivotal end of the reconstruction period because it was only subsequently that older sensibilities and preoccupations revolving around productivity shifted to an ethos of consumption and leisure. What historians have identified as an era of "modernity," one bound up with "lifestyle," American values, a pluralism of identities, and the participation in public life through consumption, most notably by women, cannot be truly said to have arrived until the late 1950s. Not only can Americanization not be used as a descriptive category until the end of the fifties in Germany, as Heide Fehrenbach and Uta Poiger have argued, but the very notion of "modernist consumption" was irrelevant to the German experience until the rise of a standard of living among both the middle and working classes, coupled with the implementation of generous old-age provisions, removed the constraints of a traditionalist aesthetic.[11]

The new French historiography has also repositioned the chronology of reconstruction and the emergence of fifties prosperity by calling into question the swiftness of modernization that has so dominated earlier historical writing. Indeed, as Victoria de Grazia has argued concerning post-war European "modernity," societies such as West Germany and France lacked a significant "middle level" of consumption prior to the 1950s, and consequently, older hierarchies of taste and expenditure survived because of low wages. Even with the arrival of more consumer choices, older patterns of consumption, such as personal-service retail stores, existed alongside mass consumerist shopping centres and department stores.[12] Like Nicholas Hewitt, who has exposed the European emphasis upon a radical cultural rebirth as mere mythmaking,[13] Kristin Ross, in her studies of automation and consumption in France, has identified 1958 as the crucial turning point in the achievement of "high" modernism, where a privatized and depoliticized middle class, whose identity was oriented around private and family life rather than work, achieved cultural and political dominance.[14] Similarly, Susan Weiner's study of French women's magazines demonstrates that it was not until the early 1960s that *Mademoiselle* launched a conscious appeal to female teenagers as a consumer group in their own right.[15]

This volume takes its cue from this new international historiography, which has insisted that the immediate post-war years be treated as an era with its own cultural dynamic distinct from the "fifties." We have designated it as an "interregnum" because new historical writing has demonstrated that the decade functioned as a complex mediator between older institutional patterns and values and the supposed "modernity" of the later 1950s; this concept allows historians to discern both the elements of continuity and the often subtle new departures that frequently underlay seemingly traditional practices. On the other hand, we do not wish to stress the reconstruction period as a radical departure towards what was often called a "brave new world"[16] of social security, prosperity, mass democracy, and a new world of leisure, thus accepting at face value the rhetoric of wartime propaganda boosterism, much of which was intended to raise morale and paper over social tensions during a time of conflict. Indeed, this wartime consensual view of citizenship has all too often informed historical writing about this era. Historians of high politics have adopted what we term the "rhetoric of consensus" as a reality and, in turn, have suggested that social and cultural life likewise evinced the same consensual values. Here the approach of E.H.H. Green provides a useful conceptual framework by which to consider the problem of consensus which circumvents the likewise problematical dichotomy so dominant in recent Canadian historiography in which a supposedly hegemonic consensus is subverted by a variety of marginal and subordinate social groups.[17] As Green has observed concerning the British Conservative interpretation of the post-war welfare state, "the historical politics of the idea of consensus have as much, if not more, importance to historians than the actual existence of such a shared approach."[18] Although revisionist historians of wartime reconstruction have elucidated widespread support for the Mackenzie King Liberals' concept of social security planning and have demonstrated that among both right and left the prospect of an expansionist state unleashed a high level of public idealism and buoyancy, the wartime experience must be juxtaposed against the fact that, aside from family allowances, the actual expansion of welfare initiatives into universal health care and old-age pensions occurred only after 1955.[19] The absence of any real policy-making by the King government following the termination of World War II not only should lead historians to question the depth of this supposed wartime consensus around the notion of an interventionist state, but it also suggests the need to examine critically the rupture thesis, which contends that the immediate aftermath of war formed a crucial watershed that immediately catapulted Canadian society onto the high road to modernity. What Nick Hayes has written of British cultural life in the late 1940s can with equal effect be applied to Canada: "In periods of great social and economic upheaval it is perhaps continuity rather than change which requires our attention."[20]

Far from creating either political consensus or cultural hegemony, World War II in Canada, coupled with the millennialist expectations engendered by the Liberal propaganda regarding social security, unleashed a widely shared perception of the process of reconstruction as a positive moment characterized by a sense of limitless possibilities in the post-war world. Because the aftermath of war was so regarded as a social and cultural "ground zero" – to borrow a concept from German historiography – but one now touted by the producers of public ideologies as being defined by democratic and active citizenship, the promise of social transformation fostered a plurality in debate and, indeed, a fracturing of ideological perspectives as many groups competed to ensure that their post-war vision would prevail as the dominant one. Thus the historiographical conundrum of consensus: because each group sought to manipulate the public scene and was engaged in its own peculiar search for coherence, historians who have studied particular institutions or ideological groups have concluded that their focus of study was the dominant and consensual one.

Faced with this historical convention, which identifies the years between 1945 and the late 1950s as a period characterized by a high degree of public consensus, the authors of this volume have set a twofold task. First, the essays seek to deconstruct and hold up to critical scrutiny the very concept of consensus. Second, by overtly combining several analyses of political, social, and cultural themes, the volume strives to uncover the intersection of public ideologies in order to better disaggregate aspects of tradition and modernity that were in constant negotiation and tension throughout these years. Thus, while this era may at first glance appear monolithic because a shared language regarding democracy, mass citizenship, security, education, individualism, and domesticity was utilized by a variety of groups which crossed political, class, and ethnic lines, it would be wrong-headed to conclude that the era was monolithic or hegemonic. What the essays in this volume accentuate is the multiplicity of meanings that were given to concepts such as democracy and liberal nationalism, and that these were always contingent upon the outlook and agenda of those who deployed these concepts as rhetorical strategies. To take one example, the term "democracy" was susceptible to very different meanings. The cultural elites explored in the essay by Leonard Kuffert spoke about democratic participation in citizens' forums as a continuation of grass-roots localism, but they saw it as a means to promote the development of institutions to protect an educated elite against the inroads of the masses. When the students at the Université de Montréal studied by Karine Hébert considered the question of democratic activity, they were referring to a new definition of working-class mass citizenship, whereas the conservative critics of the interventionist state analyzed by Nancy Christie employed the concept of democracy to flay mass culture and the non-middle-class nature of political and cultural life. In the account of parent education offered by Denyse Baillargeon, the notion of the inner-directed democratic citizen became the means by which the individual was psychologized by experts. In the study of youth culture by Michael Gauvreau, democratic citizenship was synonymous with the traditional commitment of men to work and be family breadwinners, whereas by the end of our period, it implied access to leisure and lifestyles oriented to consumption.

By thus deconstructing the most common "keywords" of the post-war decade, this volume reinforces the interpretation of this era as one of fractious debate, ideological pluralism, cultural complexity, and disjunctures in social change. Following the lead of Jessica Weiss, the authors in this volume seek to demonstrate the way in which subtle innovations often occurred within traditionalist frameworks.[21] Thus under the supposed conformity of post-war domesticity, as Denyse Baillargeon has demonstrated, lay a more dynamic set of cultural practices. Even cultural conservatism was not monolithic, for out of the chrysalis of a reactionary backlash against the Liberal welfare state, there emerged surprisingly modern notions of individuality and citizenship. It is these cultural tensions and disjunctures – the subterranean layering below the placid surface of the post-war rhetoric of consensus – which forms the subject matter of *Cultures of Citizenship in Post-war Canada*. Rather than viewing this era through the nostalgic eyes of the baby boomers as the dark age preceding the radicalism of the 1960s or as an era of cultural conformity, economic prosperity, and the dominance of middle-class values, the contributors to this volume identify it as a period in which the proponents of several ideologies competed for space in the public realm and attempted to build new social and cultural coalitions.[22]

The major contribution of the essays by Leonard Kuffert and Nancy Christie, which open this volume, is to provide a new prism through which post-war reconstruction can be understood. As Kuffert demonstrates, government manipulation of the public perception of planning as accomplishing a wholesale reform of Canadian society in fulfillment of the ideal of a new democratic citizenship resulted in the enlistment of a wide range of social groups who actively participated in public discussions on the future contours of Canadian social life. By studying the contribution of an array of cultural critics, Kuffert has revised the standard view of reconstruction as one defined by state-directed military re-establishment and Keynesian-inspired economic recovery. Reconstruction, he argues, was emphatically a cultural process, and its boundaries lay far outside the purview of the state. This wartime promotion by Canadian cultural critics of an idea of "active citizenship" closely paralleled similar efforts undertaken in Britain to elucidate a new vision of national identity based upon citizen participation.[23] As Kuffert argues, the frenetic pace of wartime discussion revolving around the question of reconstruction paradoxically created a space in which traditional cultural elites could seize upon the new rhetoric of democratic citizenship in order to promote their own vision of "middlebrow" culture in response to their fears that the same wartime evocation of democracy might lend too much authority to the levelling imperatives of modern mass culture. More broadly, in tracing the development of Citizens' Forums and the adult education movement in this period, Kuffert shows that the cultural coalitions which formed the foundation for the Massey Commission of the early 1950s were in place during the latter stages of World War II. Where other historians have taken at face value the fact that popular culture was the defining leitmotif of post-war society, Kuffert demonstrates that what historians have defined as natural categories – namely, "high" versus "pop" culture[24] – were in fact a dichotomy assiduously constructed by wartime intellectuals.

Just as Kuffert suggests that the debate over mass culture is neither defined by the problem of Americanization nor should be read in the context of Cold War politics,[25] so Nancy Christie argues that the reorientation in conservative thought and the evisceration of a "moderate centre" that traditionally defined social and political thought was occasioned by a backlash against the perceived radical expansion of the welfare state. Although Canada emerged from the war with one of the most limited welfare states in the Western world,[26] the precipitous erosion of a broader wartime commitment to welfare planning was symptomatic of a more widespread cultural shift. While in Germany and France, wartime devastation legitimated a strong commitment to pronatalism, which in turn forged a political consensus oriented to the expansion of family welfare policies,[27] in Canada the implementation of family allowances in 1944 and immediate identification with older struggles over nationalism and ethnic identity triggered a wholesale rejection of the state and an evocation of the private family as the source of civic values for the individual. Despite the fact that many of the opponents of family allowances were supporters of the Conservative premier of Ontario, George Drew, the most vociferous critics of the modern state, such as Harold Innis and Arthur Lower, were adamantly opposed to the far right's embracing of old empire-oriented nationalism. By disaggregating the complexity of the conservative world view, Christie shows that the pervasive belief that the post-war was radically different from the past – a notion that currently informs much of the historiography of the post-war – was a vision created by the very conservatives who sought to impose their own criteria for a consensual society.[28] The implication of Christie's essay is a cautionary one: not only that historians should avoid conflating conservative thought with political Conservatism, but that conservatism was far from hegemonic and was itself riven with fragmentation and dissent. What this analysis also reveals is that within this conservative backlash there existed many elements of modern liberalism, such as an intense commitment to individual freedom and civil liberties. The definition of post-war society idealized by these social critics was not a retreat to traditionalism, but like that of Kuffert's cultural activists, contained the seeds of modern sensibilities which have come to be identified with the culture of the fifties: fears of totalitarianism, angst concerning the survival of individuals within constraining bureaucracies and the conformity of mass culture, a new accentuation of the role of the humanities in culture, and the reification of civic participation or voluntaristic citizenship, as against the passivity engendered by a state-dominated polity.[29]

The essays in this volume by Peter McInnis and Penny Bryden specifically address the issue of political consensus; the first studies the interplay between organized labour, business, and the state; and the second examines in detail the transition from a conflictual model of federal-provincial relations in the immediate post-war period to the emergence of a loosely ideological working relationship around the issue of health care in the mid-1950s. In keeping with the international revisionist perspective, which questions the extent of political cooperation that flowed out of the wartime experience, McInnis shows that the commitment to a consensual model of labour relations did not extend below the level of the labour elite itself and that the pole around which these groups cohered was the specific issue of full employment. But as he suggests, the Canadian version of post-war consensus was circumscribed insofar as the federal government's view of full employment was a specifically Keynesian one, whereas labour's support for full employment flowed from labour concerns about productivity, which fitted with the traditional preoccupations of the labour leadership in high-wage sectors of the economy. One of the significant contributions of McInnis's work is that he does not assume that, because the major labour centrals in Canada were affiliates of American labour organizations, Canadian union policies merely replicated the ideological dynamic of organized labour south of the border. Rather, he presents a much more nuanced rendering that gives due attention to the impact of our own domestic experience that adhered to a productivist ideology which contrasted sharply with American labour's allegiance to a consumptionist model, which since the Depression had advocated high wages for the purposes of stimulating working-class consumption.[30] Where organized labour in the United States displayed weaknesses similar to those of its Canadian counterpart, it decisively shifted from the idea of state planning to a more corporatist vision of the private welfare state achieved through collective bargaining.[31] This emerging state-business-labour consensus therefore excluded large sectors of the Canadian workforce, including women, agricultural workers, and unskilled workers.[32]

In many respects, the post-war Canadian labour experience paralleled that of Britain, where there was general agreement between government elites and the labour leadership on the issue of full employment, although it should be stated that in the British context the labour movement had greater influence over the articulation of social security measures. Britain, despite Keynes's active courting of organized labour during the war, categorically rejected demand-management economics and favoured government intervention for the purposes of controlling, rather than expanding, consumption. As Martin Francis has argued, in the post-war period there occurred a reassertion of masculinist values which was linked to a general demand for jobs for husbands rather than for married women, despite severe labour shortages after 1947. This in turn was coupled with a renewed emphasis upon productivity and less stress on expanding family-oriented welfare policies such as family allowances.[33] Moreover, the Labour Party remained wedded to its Depression-era socialist platform, which elevated public ownership as the key to a planned economy. As a result, the model of cooperation between a Labour government and organized labour in Britain was a fairly superficial and tenuous one – indeed, its very existence has recently been called into question by some historians[34] – and only by 1951, with a "quality of life" emphasis in the Labour platform, was there any true evidence of movement in the direction of accepting the Keynesian-Beveridgean mixed economy.[35] Paradoxically, the imbrication of British society in a consumptionist ethos was stimulated not by the left but by the political right, because the Conservative Party, seeking to return to power after 1945, courted the female electorate by creating an ideal of "modern" pluralist citizenship founded upon women as consumers in a society able to provide an endless spectrum of choices.[36] According to this revisionist historiographical paradigm, the left in both Britain and Canada emerges as strangely traditionalist and anti-modernist in its attitudes.

The emphasis upon the right as a catalyst for modernization, as identified by Zweiniger-Bargielowska, Harriet Jones, and Daniel Ritschel, is taken up in the essay by Penny Bryden, in which she elaborates an emerging consensus between the federal government and the Ontario provincial government over the question of welfare measures. As Bryden shows, much of the inflamed rhetoric that characterized the immediate post-war period was a function of a personality conflict between Prime Minister Mackenzie King and Premier George Drew. Drew's desire to appear in the role of statesman and to place Ontario at the forefront of policy initiatives within the larger dominion created a new context in which the Ontario government supplied the impetus that drove the federal Liberals under King towards an explicit commitment to welfare policies, particularly in the field of national health care, which they otherwise would not have made. This confrontation explains the conundrum identified elsewhere by Christie: that despite King's adamant resistance to government growth,[37] he found himself locked into a dynamic of federal-provincial diplomacy in which Drew cleverly forced his hand. Bryden's perspective mirrors the new and more nuanced British historiography on the question of the post-war consensus. By focusing upon the Ontario government responses to the Liberal government's post-war Green Book, she critically assesses easy conclusions that Canada's post-war social security state derived solely from the left-centre of the Liberal Party.[38] The traditional interpretation of the post-war consensus, largely inspired by the work of Paul Addison, accepted that there was a true ideological convergence between the right and the left in Britain over the question of Beveridge's blueprint for social security.[39] While it did indeed appear that politicians such as Churchill and Attlee were in principle committed to a radical new departure in welfare provisioning and new definitions of social citizenship, recent historians have demonstrated that there was no "middle ground," for as we have previously stated, not only was the Labour Party opposed to the ideal of the mixed economy as posited by Keynes and Beveridge, but there was an intense hostility within the Conservative Party and from Churchill himself to even the most modest aspects of new welfare entitlements. In her study of voting patterns between Labour and the Conservatives, Harriet Jones has argued that the ideological bias of both political parties remained unchanged by the rhetoric of wartime consensus and that if any consensus did emerge, it functioned at the level of language and was at best pragmatic, superficial, and contingent.[40] If we take the contributions of McInnis and Bryden together, it appears that this trend was replicated in Canada, where there was an ideological continuum beneath the rhetoric of radical change and modernization, but with the caveat that Canadian Conservatives, for pragmatic reasons – and probably, in Drew's case, driven by the threat posed by the popularity of the CCF – constructed a platform that centred on health insurance.

If a pragmatic consensus prevailed at the level of political and labour elites over the notion of state intervention to ensure full employment and a certain degree of social security, the terrain of social discourse was a much more contested one where new cultural departures overlapped or competed with survivals from the Depression era. The essays by Karine Hébert and Michael Gauvreau, both of which focus on the ideological construction of youth in the aftermath of World War II, address the tensions between the metaphor of youth as representing the past – or tradition – and the future – or social change. By examining the reports and debates of the Canadian Youth Commission, one of the many initiatives undertaken under the umbrella of post-war reconstruction, Gauvreau identifies the central preoccupation of those business leaders, youth workers, church leaders, and government officials as ensuring that post-war male youth thoroughly integrated the values of productivity and personal responsibility which would lead to proper family formation. In emphasizing the continuity in values surrounding work and saving rather than consumption, Gauvreau, like McInnis, debates interpretations that have seen World War II as forming a radical disjuncture with the past, arguing that the Depression continued to be of more importance than the war experience itself in determining public debates on youth prior to 1955. However, Gauvreau argues not only that the middle-class discourse on youth differed little from the perspective advanced by organized labour on these issues, but that it did not represent a mere evocation of tradition because the Canadian Youth Commission's emphasis upon voluntary civic participation, which emphasized the private, rather than the public or state, aspects of citizenship,[41] marked a more modern sensibility.

The view that modernization was a much more piecemeal process throughout this period is also articulated in Karine Hébert's discussion of Quebec university students. Her analysis serves as a methodological reminder to historians that different sites of cultural production could lead to the elaboration of dissimilar notions of citizenship, and it shows the incorporation of more modern values at a varying pace and following a different logic according to the institutional framework or ethnic cultural context in these notions were debated. As Hébert illustrates, McGill students pursued an idea of society and nation that maintained explicit references to the past and to history, whereas at the French-speaking Université de Montréal, students formulated a concept of citizenship that revolved around the present and future-oriented aspects of democratic values. Moreover, she demonstrates the way in which a language difference functioned as the conduit for a class bifurcation within concepts of civic participation. For example, at McGill the university students drew upon American middle-class college culture, while at the Université de Montréal, middle-class students borrowed from French and European working-class cultures. More significantly, in the immediate post-war years, the culture of francophone university students was thoroughly permeated by French currents of intellectual modernity that posited a sharp rupture between past, present, and future,[42] an outlook that legitimated a more radical social critique among the students at the Université de Montréal.

In this way, Hébert offers a counterpoint to concepts of modernization that currently prevail among Quebec historians, in which post-war Quebec is simply integrated into a framework of "North American" economic and cultural values.[43] By demonstrating the continuing importance of European concepts of modernism among a socially and politically significant group of middle-class professionals,[44] Hébert's essay demonstrates the need for a more critical scrutiny of conventional historical categories such as "Americanization." Another significant aspect of her contribution to this volume lies is her implicit challenge to notions that Quebec's cultural distinctiveness must be sought in "traditional" institutions such as the Catholic Church.[45] Hébert argues that it is in the very way in which Quebec elites formulated a concept of modernity that the core of French-speaking Quebec's divergence from English Canada lies. The essays by Hébert and Gauvreau not only disaggregate the post-war era by distinguishing what is modern and what is traditional, but they affirm that these concepts continued to oscillate until the mid-1950s, when a clearly modern view of the teenager emerged. As Gauvreau argues, modernity in this context represented a break with preoccupations with male work and centred around a concept of leisure identified with femaleness.[46]

This ongoing tension between tradition and modernism, popular democracy and control by experts, private civic values and public state citizenship, individual self-fulfillment and communitarian obligations, and the polarities between masculine and feminine identities, which form the central themes of this volume, are more specifically addressed in the contribution of Denyse Baillargeon, which analyzes a significant strand of post-war discourse on domesticity. Read alongside Christie's essay, Baillargeon's contribution questions interpretive frameworks which argue that a single hegemonic "normalized" ideal was asserted in this period.[47] Recently, historians in Britain and Germany have questioned whether culture was actually normalized or reconstructed after World War II, for the former concept implies simply a return to the past. The editors of *Moments of Modernity* have, for example, recommended the use of the word "restoration" because it combines notions of both traditionalism and modernity, and it is a concept that looks to the future and not just to the past.[48] In a similar vein, both Elizabeth Heinemann and Robert Moeller have seen the upsurge in state interest in public policy-making in the sphere of family welfare in Germany as not simply a "flight into domesticity" or a retreat into a reclusive, depoliticized private sphere; they argue that while the family continued to be a matter of public policy in the post-war period, as it had under the Nazi regime, the debates about the family served as a critique of older models of male authority and became an important site for shifting concepts of citizenship away from the authoritarian state to a liberal-democratic social pluralism.[49] As John Murphy and Nicholas Brown have illustrated for Australia[50] and Christie and Baillargeon argue in this volume, there existed several, often competing discourses on the family that functioned as rhetorical devices serving the strategic needs and objectives of the particular social groups that articulated them. On the surface, the conservative critics of the state examined by Christie appear to have been merely reasserting the older breadwinner ideal, but the context in which this ideal was being promulgated was decisively new, because for the first time what had formerly been conceived as a seamless, organic whole between family, church, community, and state was now sundered and seen to be a source of conflict and social rupture. Thus, as Christie and Baillargeon make clear, the family was posited as a moral basis of public citizenship that displayed certain affinities with an older philosophical idealism which was being reaffirmed by certain social critics in this period.[51] But its novel feature lay in the fact that it was regarded as irrevocably severed from the terrain of the "political," and more importantly, the family was characterized as the crucible for the development of the "modern" self-directed citizen. The family in the post-war era thus possessed a liminal function: it displayed tendencies towards privatization and individualism, but at the same time, it cohered around a notion of civic participation which was offset against the wartime emphasis upon state-directed citizenship, and thus the rhetoric of family frequently served as a critique of bureaucratic control and totalitarianism in church and state.

In Quebec, as Baillargeon asserts, the family in this period was also seen as the quintessential seedbed of individualized sociability, but where Christie's analysis shows how the language of family was used to shore up the authority of older cultural elites, Baillargeon demonstrates the way in which the family became the primary vehicle for advancing the claims of a new group of experts, child psychologists. In a nuanced discussion of the work of the École des Parents, Baillargeon revises the conventional historiographic dichotomy between imposition and subversion by showing that mothers who wrote letters to *Le Devoir* shared many of the values of child rearing proffered by the experts, which accentuated women's maternal functions and responsibilities in the formation of a new generation of citizens for a liberal democratic society,[52] but that they selectively appropriated the language of expertise in order to undermine what they saw as the primary imposition to be resisted: the unwarranted intrusion into the family by the Catholic Church in the form of an elite celibate clergy. Baillargeon thus offers a much more complex rendering of the relationship between tradition and modernity and imposition and subversion, and she effectively portrays how many ordinary people were able to construct their own discourse of domesticity, which did not simply replicate or reject the prescriptions of the new "modern" expert.

Baillargeon's essay, however, raises the question of the extent to which the tension between the modern and the traditional in post-war public discourses and private experience was also articulated around a notion of male domesticity and the reconstruction of male authority in the family.[53] The essays by Christie and Baillargeon clearly demonstrate that there was a multiplicity of views on how individual identities should be fostered. However, Christie and Baillargeon explore one variant of individualism that still implied a definite context for sociability in terms of the larger whole, namely, the family, and thus avoided a completely privatized, "modern" definition of identity calibrated purely upon an individualized, self-sufficient escapist search for personal pleasure through material consumption.[54] Therefore the post-war era was not one characterized by conformity to a single prescribed idealized family pattern, but one in which ordinary citizens enjoyed considerable flexibility in interpreting social codes. While it might be argued that both men and women participated in an ideology of citizen-as-consumer, differing levels of identification with the domestic space may have conferred a significant gender inflection on consumer practices. While both men and women participated in this ideology of citizen-as-consumer, male consumption, unlike that of women, was totally severed from the domestic space. Indeed, as Frank Mort has recently concluded, post-war culture spawned a multiplicity of male identities[55] – and by extension, female identities – an opening to a plurality of lifestyle choice, rather than a constriction towards conformity. As the papers by Christie and Baillargeon so clearly emphasize, beneath the post-war rhetoric of domestic nostalgia, traditionalism, and conformity, the family emerged as a crucial site of social innovation and cultural transition.

The central characteristic of the post-war interregnum in Canada – the years that lie between approximately 1943 and 1955 – was one of intense cultural and social negotiation, of a constant shifting of axes between the elements of tradition and modernity. Much of the historiography has viewed World War II as forming a decisive watershed that irrevocably ushered in a flood tide of Americanization, mass culture, depersonalization, mass consumption and economic prosperity. However, the essays in this book postulate that the process of modernization, as viewed by historians of the 1950s, was much more piecemeal and contested. This volume has interrogated the conventional picture of the post-war era as a monolithic period of cultural stasis broken only by the radical innovations of the 1960s. The contributors to this volume have reassessed this chronology not only by disaggregating the immediate post-war decade but by paying close attention to the rhetorical strategies employed by a variety of social groups and political organizations. They have penetrated beneath this illusion of wholeness constructed by various social groups, who employed the language of consensus, democracy, domesticity, and mass culture, to reveal that there was no one dominant social ideal but, rather, a multiplicity of voices competing to assert their own version of post-war planning. However, each of these groups, be they university students, middle-class reformers, trade union leaders, parents, psychologists, or conservative critics of the modern state and mass society, posited its own consensual ideal of citizenship in a reconstructed Canada. The post-war interregnum can thus best be described as a period in search of an elusive modernity. The producers of public ideologies analyzed in this volume at once embraced some of the central tenets of what we would call modernity: the sense of a world of unlimited possibilities, a belief in participatory democracy, a commitment to expert knowledge, the expansion of social security, a vision of active citizenship anchored in quality of life in the private sphere, and an extolling of the virtues of the inner-directed personality. Despite the language of rupture with the past, in which these ideas embodied an idealized present and future, the overwhelming preoccupation with asserting human agency within a framework of modern civic citizenship beyond the purview of the political state belied an anxiety over the question of how to loose the culture from the constraints of the past without abandoning social coherence. It is this ambiguity that constitutes the paradigm of Canada's reconstruction culture, which endured until 1955.

NOTES

1 See Robert Bothwell, Ian Drummond, and John English, *Canada since 1945: Power, Politics, and Provincialism* (Toronto: University of Toronto Press, 1989); Peter Neary, "Introduction," in Peter Neary and J.L. Granatstein, eds., *The Veteran's Charter and Post–World War II Canada* (Montreal and Kingston: McGill-Queen's University Press, 1998); Doug Owram, *Born at the Right Time: A History of the Baby Boom Generation* (Toronto: University of Toronto Press, 1996); Mona Gleason, *Normalizing the Ideal: Psychology, Schooling, and the Family in Postwar Canada* (Toronto: University of Toronto Press, 1999); Mary Louise Adams, *The Trouble with Normal: Postwar Youth and the Making of Heterosexuality* (Toronto: University of Toronto Press, 1997); Annalee Golz, "Family Matters: The Canadian Family and the State in the Postwar Period," *Left History* 1 (fall 1993): 9–49.

2 Doug Owram, "Canadian Domesticity in the Postwar Era," in Neary and Granatstein, *The Veterans Charter*, 205–23; Elaine Tyler May, *Homeward Bound: American Families in the Cold War* (New York: Basic Books, 1988). For the overarching application of the Cold War metaphor to Canadian politics and society, see Reg Whitaker and Gary Marcuse, *Cold War Canada: The Making of a National Insecurity State, 1945–1957* (Toronto: University of Toronto Press, 1994). For the critique, see Joy Parr, *Domestic Goods: The Material, the Moral, and the Economic in the Postwar Years* (Toronto: University of Toronto Press, 1999); Parr, "Household Choices as Politics and Pleasure in 1950s Canada," *International Labour and Working-Class History*, 55 (spring 1999): 113–15.

3 Robert M. Collins, *More: The Politics of Economic Growth in Postwar America* (New York & Oxford: Oxford University Press, 2000). Collins concludes (23–46) that growth economics came to end under Eisenhower with the onset of inflation, and he thus has also changed the chronology of the post-war era. Similarly, Lizabeth Cohen has argued that while the United States experienced prosperity, market structures remained informed by more traditionalist economic values until the late 1950s. See Cohen, "From Town Center to Shopping Center: The Reconfiguration of Community Marketplaces in Postwar America," *American Historical Review* 101 (Oct. 1996): 1050–81.

4 Nancy Christie, *Engendering the State: Family, Work, and Welfare in Canada* (Toronto: University of Toronto Press, 2000), 249–309.

5 Parr, "Household Choices," 114–15.

6 Valerie J. Korinek, *Roughing It in the Suburbs: Reading Chatelaine Magazine in the Fifties and Sixties* (Toronto: University of Toronto Press, 2000); Shirley Tillotson, *The Public at Play: Gender and the Politics of*

Recreation in Post-War Ontario (Toronto: University of Toronto Press, 2000); Ruth Frager and Carmela Patrias, "'This Is Our Country, These Are Our Rights': Minorities and the Origins of Ontario's Human Rights Campaigns" (unpublished paper). We thank Professors Frager and Patrias for sharing their new research with us.

7 Frank Mort, "The Commercial Domain: Advertising and the Cultural Management of Demand," and Peter Bailey, "Jazz at the Spirella: Coming of Age in Coventry in the 1950s," in Becky Conekin, Frank Mort, and Chris Waters, eds., *Moments of Modernity: Reconstructing Britain, 1945–1964* (London and New York: Rivers Oram Press, 1999). See also Nick Hayes, "Making Homes by Machine: Images, Ideas and Myths in the Diffusion of Non-Traditional Housing in Britain, 1942–54," *20th Century British History* 10 (1999).

8 Noel Whiteside, "Towards a Modern Labour Market? State Policy and the Transformation of Employment," in Conekin et al., *Moments of Modernity*.

9 Daniel Ritschel, "The Strange Triumph of Liberal England: A Whiggish Narrative of Twentieth-Century History" (unpublished paper, 2001). We thank Professor Ritschel for drawing our attention to Ina Zweiniger-Bargielowska, *Austerity in Britain: Rationing, Controls, and Consumption, 1939–1955* (Oxford: Oxford University Press, 2000); Stephen Brooke, *Labour's War: The Labour Party during the Second World War* (Oxford: Oxford University Press, 1992); Stephen Brooke, "Problems of 'Socialist Planning': Evan Durbin and the Labour Government of 1945," *Historical Journal*, 34 (1991): 687–702; Harriet Jones, "New Conservatism? The Industrial Charter, Modernity, and the Reconstruction of British Conservatism after the War," in Conekin et al., *Moments of Modernity*; and James D. Marlow, *Questioning the Postwar Consensus Thesis: Towards an Alternative Account* (Aldershot: Athenaeum Press, 1996).

10 Robert Moeller, "Introduction: Writing the History of West Germany," in Moeller, ed., *West Germany under Construction: Politics, Society and Culture in the Adenauer Era* (Ann Arbor: University of Michigan Press, 1997), 8–9.

11 Axel Schildt and Arnold Sywottek, "'Reconstruction' and 'Modernization': West German Social History during the 1950s," in Moeller, *West Germany under Construction*, 413–43; Erica Carter, *How German Is She? Postwar West German Reconstruction and the Consuming Woman* (Ann Arbor: University of Michigan Press, 1997); Heide Fehrenbach and Uta G. Poiger, *Transactions, Transgressions, Transformations: American Culture in Western Europe and Japan* (New York & Oxford: Berghahn Books, 2000), xiii, xxvi; Arnold Sywottek, "Americanization of Everyday Life? Early Trends in Consumer and Leisure-Time Behavior," in Michael

Ermarth, ed., *America and the Shaping of German Society, 1945–1955* (Providence and Oxford: Berg, 1993), 132–52.

12 Victoria de Grazia, "Changing Consumption Regimes in Europe, 1930–1970: Comparative Perspectives on the Distribution Problem," in Susan Strasser, Charles McGovern, and Matthias Judt, eds., *Getting and Spending: European and American Consumer Societies in the Twentieth Century* (Cambridge: Cambridge University Press, 1998), 59–83.

13 Nicholas Hewitt, "Introduction: Popular Culture and Mass Culture," *Contemporary European History* 8 (Nov. 1999), 351.

14 Kristin Ross, *Fast Cars, Clean Bodies: Decolonization and the Reordering of French Culture* (Cambridge, Mass.: MIT Press, 1995), 6, 11–12, 107. For the conflictual, rather than consensual, nature of French society and culture in the early 1950s, see Richard Vinen, *Bourgeois Politics in France, 1945–1951* (Cambridge: Cambridge University Press, 1995).

15 Susan Weiner, "Two Modernities: from *Elle* to *Mademoiselle*: Women's Magazines in Postwar France," *Contemporary European History*, 8 (Nov. 1999): 395.

16 For the use of this language in a number of Western countries during the reconstruction period, see Jose Harris, "Enterprise and the Welfare State: A Comparative Perspective," in Michael Katz and Chrstoph Sachsse, eds., *The Mixed Economy of Social Welfare: Public/Private Relations in England, Germany and the United States, the 1870s to the 1930s* (Baden-Baden: Nomos Verlagsgesellschaft, 1996), 47. For the identification in Canada of the concept of the "brave new world" with Mackenzie King's reconstruction plans, see University of Toronto Archives, Harold Innis Papers, B72–0003/05, G.V. Ferguson to Innis, 8 Feb. 1943.

17 On the dichotomy of consensus and subversion as the hitherto defining paradigm of post-war Canadian society, see Alvin Finkel, "Competing Master Narratives on Post-War Canada," *Acadiensis* 30 (2000): 188–204. On the notion of hegemony and subversion in this period, see Gleason, *Normalizing the Ideal*; Adams, *The Trouble with Normal*; Parr, *Domestic Goods*; Ian McKay, *The Quest of the Folk: Antimodernism and Cultural Selection in Twentieth-Century Nova Scotia* (Montreal and Kingston: McGill-Queen's University Press, 1994); Franca Iacovetta, "Parents, Daughters, and Family Court Intrusions into Working-Class Life," in Iacovetta and Wendy Mitchinson, eds., *On the Case: Explorations in Social History* (Toronto: University of Toronto Press, 1998), 312–37.

18 E.H.H. Green, "Thatcherism: An Historical Perspective," *Transactions of the Royal Historical Society*, 6th series, 9 (1998): 42.

19 Christie, *Engendering the State*; James Struthers, *The Limits of Affluence: Welfare in Ontario, 1920–1970* (Toronto: University of Toronto Press, 1994); P.E. Bryden, *Planners and Politicians: Liberal Politics and Social*

Policy, 1957–1968 (Montreal and Kingston: McGill-Queen's University Press, 1997).

20 Hayes, "Making Homes by Machine," 307.

21 Jessica Weiss, *To Have and to Hold: Marriage, the Baby Boom, and Social Change* (Chicago & London: University of Chicago Press, 2000), 7–12; Arthur Marwick, *The Sixties: Cultural Revolution in Britain, France, Italy, and the United States, ca. 1958–ca. 1974* (Oxford: Oxford University Press, 1998); Joanne Meyerowitz, ed., *Not June Cleaver: Women and Gender in Postwar America, 1945–1960* (Philadelphia: Temple University Press, 1994); Joel Foreman, ed., *The Other Fifties: Interrogating Mid-Century American Icons* (Urbana and Chicago: University of Illinois Press, 1997); Nicholas Brown, *Governing Prosperity: Social Change and Social Analysis in Australia in the 1950s* (Cambridge: Cambridge University Press, 1995).

22 On the formation of new coalitions out of seemingly conservative elements, see the analysis by Frager and Patrias, "'This Is Our Country, these Are Our Rights.'"

23 On this theme, see the essays in Richard Weight and Abigail Beach, eds., *The Right to Belong: Citizenship and National Identity in Britain, 1930–1960* (London: I.B. Tauris, 1998).

24 In this respect, the views of the elitist cultural critics analyzed by Kuffert resembled those of the Marxist intellectuals of the Frankfurt School and post-war British Marxists, whose negative views of mass culture had an enormous influence on post-war American intellectual life. See Martin Jay, *The Dialectical Imagination: A History of the Frankfurt School and the Institute of Social Research, 1923–1950* (Boston and Toronto: Little, Brown, 1973), 216–18; Dennis Dworkin, *Cultural Marxism in Postwar Britain: History, the New Left, and the Origins of Cultural Studies* (Durham and London: Duke University Press, 1997), 80; Meredith Veldman, *Fantasy, the Bomb, and the Greening of Britain: Romantic Protest 1945–1980* (Cambridge: Cambridge University Press, 1994), in which Veldman places J.R.R. Tolkien, C.S. Lewis, and E.P. Thompson on a continuum of idealizations of organic community against technocracy and mass culture.

25 In recent years, American historians have also questioned the conventional equation of the Cold War mentality with the whole of post-war culture. See Stephen J. Whitfield, *The Culture of the Cold War* (Baltimore and London: Johns Hopkins University Press, 1991), 12; Richard Fried, *Nightmare in Red: The McCarthy Era in Perspective* (New York and Oxford: Oxford University Press, 1990), 556, which sees the erosion of New Deal liberalism as originating in wartime rather than under the impact of the Cold War; Robert Latham, *The Liberal Moment* (New York: Columbia University Press, 1997); Brett Gary, *The Nervous*

Liberals: Propaganda Anxieties from World War I to the Cold War (New York: Columbia University Press, 1999); Alan Brinkley, "The Late New Deal and the Idea of the State," in Brinkley, *Liberalism and Its Discontents* (Cambridge: Harvard University Press, 1998), 37–62.

26 For this interpretation, see Harris, "Enterprise and the Welfare State," 45.

27 For Germany, see Elizabeth J. Heinemann, *What Difference Does a Husband Make? Women and Marital Status in Postwar Germany* (Berkeley: University of California Press, 1999); and for France, Claire Duchen, *Women's Rights and Women's Lives in France, 1944–1968* (London and New York: Routledge, 1994), 126.

28 On the issue of historical disjuncture as a constructed view, see Moeller, "Introduction," in *West Germany under Construction*. For the American context, see Richard H. Pells, *The Liberal Mind in a Conservative Age: American Intellectuals in the 1940s and 1950s* (New York: Harper & Row, 1985), viii, 51.

29 For similar interpretations, see Brown, *Governing Prosperity*; on the issue of voluntaristic citizenship, see Sonya O. Rose, "Sex, Citizenship and the Nation in World War II Britain," *American Historical Review* 103 (Oct. 1998): 1168. By contrast, in France technocratic planning was seen as the embodiment of new French citizenship. See Gabrielle Hecht, "Peasants, Engineers, and Atomic Cathedrals: Narrating Modernization in Postwar Provincial France," *French Historical Studies* 20 (summer 1997): 381.

30 On the issue of the consumptionist ideology of American workers, see Meg Jacobs, "Democracy's Third Estate: New Deal Politics and the Construction of a Consuming Public," *Journal of International Labor and Working-Class History* 55 (spring 1999): 29, 37, 47. Jacobs argues that consumption was not simply a middle-class model, and so she questions the paradigm of imposition/subversion. See also William Graebner, *The Age of Doubt: American Thought and Culture in the 1940s* (Boston: Twayne Publishers, 1991), 10; Charles McGovern, "Consumption and Citizenship in the United States," in Strasser et al., *Getting and Spending*, 37–58; Lizabeth Cohen, "The New Deal State and the Making of Citizen Consumers," in Strasser et al., *Getting and Spending*, 111–25; Lawrence B. Glickman, *A Living Wage: American Workers and the Making of a Consumer Society* (Ithaca and London: Cornell University Press, 1997).

31 Collins, *More: The Politics of Economic Growth in Postwar America*, 23. For a similar argument as applied to the Canadian experience, see Laurel Sefton MacDowell, *'Remember Kirkland Lake': The History and Effects of the Kirkland Lake Gold Miners' Strike, 1941–42* (Toronto: University of Toronto Press, 1983); Irving Abella, *Nationalism, Communism and Canadian Labour: The CIO, the Communist Party and the*

Canadian Congress of Labour, 1935–1956 (Toronto: University of Toronto Press, 1973).

32 On the exclusion of women workers from social security benefits by the labour leadership, see Ann Porter, "Women and Income Security in the Postwar Period: The Case of Unemployment Insurance, 1945–1962," *Labour/Le Travail* 31 (spring 1993): 111–44.

33 Martin Francis, *Ideas and Policies under Labour, 1945–1951: Building a New Britain* (Manchester and New York: Manchester University Press, 1997), 212–16, 228. See also Nick Tiratsu and Jim Tomlinson, *Industrial Efficiency and State Intervention: Labour, 1939–1951* (London and New York: Routledge, 1993).

34 Noel Whiteside, "Towards a Modern Labour Market? State Policy and the Transformation of Employment," in Conekin et al., *Moments of Modernity*, 79. For similar arguments regarding France and Italy, see Chris Howell, *Regulating Labor: The State and Industrial Relations in Postwar France* (Princeton: Princeton University Press, 1992); Peter Lange, George Ross, and Maurizio Vannicelli, eds., *Unions, Change and Crisis: French and Italian Union Strategy and the Political Economy, 1945–1980* (London: Allen & Unwin, 1982). Like Whiteside, these authors argue that the lack of commitment to Keynesian corporatism and state-building led to a later takeoff for labour radicalism in the 1950s.

35 Richard Toye, "Keynes, the Labour Movement and 'How to Pay for the War,'" *20th Century British History* 10 (1999): 256–73; Brooke, *Labour's War*, 329–30; Chris Wrigley, "Trade Unions, the Government and the Economy," in Katz and Sachsse, *The Mixed Economy of Social Welfare*, 59–62. There is some debate over when the reconstruction period and wartime ideology ended. Where Francis focuses on 1951, Jim Tomlinson cites 1955 as the decisive year in which the wartime rhetoric of full employment switched to a new emphasis upon consumption and the rising standard of living. See Francis, *Ideas and Policies under Labour*, 228; Jim Tomlinson, "Inventing 'Decline': The Falling Behind of the British Economy in the Postwar Years," *Economic History Review* 49 (Nov. 1996): 733.

36 In this respect, the British Conservative link between a consumptionist ethos and the politics of female citizenship paralleled the efforts of German conservative politicians to stimulate economic recovery by constructing an ideology of the "social market economy". See Ritschel, "The Strange Triumph of Liberal England"; Carter, *How German Is She?* 47.

37 Christie, *Engendering the State*, especially "Reconstructing Families: Family Allowances and the Politics of Postwar Abundance."

38 For this interpretation, see Doug Owram, *The Government Generation: Canadian Intellectuals and the State, 1900–1945* (Toronto: University of Toronto Press, 1986); Raymond B. Blake, "Mackenzie King and the

Genesis of Family Allowances in Canada, 1939–44," in J.L. Granatstein and Peter Neary, eds., *The Good Fight: Canadians and World War II* (Toronto: Copp Clark, 1995).

39 Paul Addison, *The Road to 1945: British Politics and the Second World War* (London: Cape, 1975).

40 Harriet Jones, "New Conservatism? The Industrial Charter, Modernity, and the Reconstruction of British Conservatism after the War," in Conekin et al., *Moments of Modernity*, 181–7; see also Marlow, *Questioning the Postwar Consensus Thesis*, 172; Green, "Thatcherism: An Historical Perspective," 22; Harriet Jones and Michael Kandiah, eds., *The Myth of Consensus: New Views on British History, 1945–1964* (London: Macmillan, 1996). For an identification of conservative thought with welfare initiatives, see Daniel Ritschel, *The Politics of Planning: The Debate on Economic Planning in Britain in the 1930s* (Oxford: Oxford University Press, 1997). On Beveridge as a conservative thinker, see Harris, "Enterprise and the Welfare State," and "Society and State in Twentieth-Century Britain," in F.M.L. Thompson, ed., *The Cambridge Social History of Britain, 1750–1950*, Vol. 3, *Social Agencies and Institutions* (Cambridge: Cambridge University Press, 1990); and Susan Pedersen, *Family, Dependence, and the Origins of the Welfare State in Britain and France, 1914–1945* (Cambridge: Cambridge University Press, 1993).

41 Gauvreau's argument underscores that of Tillotson, *The Public at Play*, and Mariana Valverde, "Building Anti-Delinquent Communities: Morality, Gender, and Generation in the City," in Joy Parr, ed., *A Diversity of Women: Ontario, 1945–1980* (Toronto: University of Toronto Press, 1995), 19–45. While Valverde is correct in identifying anxiety as a principal feature of youth discourse, Gauvreau believes that it was motivated by a fear of economic depression, rather than a moral panic surrounding juvenile delinquency.

42 For this aspect of wartime and post-war French thinking regarding the relationship of the future and the present to the past, see Jon Cowans, "Visions of the Postwar: The Politics of Memory and Expectation in 1940s France," *History and Memory* 10 (fall 1998): 68–101.

43 See, for example, the synthetic works by P.-A. Linteau et al., *Histoire du Québec contemporain: Le Québec depuis 1930* (Montréal: Boréal, 1989); John Dickinson and Brian Young, *Quebec: A Socio-Economic History* (Toronto: Copp Clark, 1994).

44 While historians of Quebec have generally acknowledged the important presence of "traditionalist" European ideas in the francophone cultural landscape before 1939, study of the impact of "modernist" French ideologies on Quebec after 1945 is only beginning to emerge. On aspects of the cultural transmission of French conservative thinking before World War II, see Catherine Pomeyrols, *Les intellectuels québécois: formation et*

engagements, 1919–1939 (Paris et Montréal: L'Harmattan, 1996). On post-war Quebec, see Simon Lapointe, *L'influence de la gauche catholique française sur l'idéologie de la CTCC-CSN de 1948 à 1964*, Études et documents, no 8 (Montréal, Regroupement des chercheurs-chercheures en histoire des travailleurs et travailleures du Québec, 1996); Michael Gauvreau, "From Rechristianization to Contestation: Catholic Values and Quebec Society, 1930–1970," *Church History: Studies in Christianity and Culture* 69 (Dec. 2000): 803–33.

45 For a reassertion of this view, see Ronald Rudin, "Revisionism and the Search for a 'Normal' Society: A Critique of Recent Quebec Historical Writing," *Canadian Historical Review* 73 (March 1992): 30–62.

46 For a similar argument for the German context that emphasizes the shift to a female-centred youth culture in the late 1950s, see Uta G. Poiger, "Rock n'Roll, Female Sexuality, and the Cold War Battle over German Identities," in Moeller, *West Germany under Construction*, 373–410. Likewise in France, Susan Weiner has posited a close link between a new mass-media definition of young womanhood, typified by the highly sexualized *enfant terrible* and the decline of the older cultural construction of the *jeune fille* oriented to marriage and family. See Weiner, *Enfants Terribles: Youth and Femininity in the Mass Media in France, 1945–1968* (Baltimore and London: Johns Hopkins University Press, 2000). In the Australian context, Esther Faye has noted that in the post-war period, there was a gradual tendency by experts to "feminise" how adolescence was conceived. See Faye, "Growing Up 'Australian' in the 1950s: The Dream of Social Science," *Australian Social Studies* 111 (1998): 357. For the emphasis in the 1950s on fears of teenage female sexuality, see Iacovetta, "Parents, Daughters and Family Court Intrusions into Working-Class Life."

47 Gleason, *Normalizing the Ideal*; Owram, *Born at the Right Time*, 3–30. A recent biography of the American feminist Betty Friedan has demonstrated that her critique of the domestic nuclear family was in fact not a description of social reality, but that it articulated, for middle-class women, post-war fears that affluence bred conformity. See Daniel Horowitz, *Betty Friedan and the Making of the Feminine Mystique* (Amherst: University of Massachusetts Press, 1998), 197, 207–8.

48 Conekin, Mort, and Waters, "Introduction," in *Moments of Modernity*, 3–4.

49 Heinemann, *What Difference Does a Husband Make?* xii, 12, 110; Robert Moeller, "Reconstructing the Family in Reconstruction Germany: Women and Social Policy in the Republic, 1949–1955," in Moeller, *West Germany Under Construction*, 109–33.

50 John Murphy, "Shaping the Cold War Family: Politics, Domesticity and Policy Interventions in the 1950s," *Australian Historical Studies*, 26 (Oct. 1995): 544–67; Brown, *Governing Prosperity*, 155.

51 In the British context, Jose Harris has noted the reinvigoration of Edwardian notions of voluntaristic citizenship in the immediate post-war period. See Harris, "Political Thought and Social Policy: The Public and Private Spheres," in Michael B. Katz and Christoph Sachsse, eds., *The Mixed Economy of Social Welfare: Public/Private Relations in England, Germany and the United States, the 1870s to the 1930s* (Baden-Baden: Nomos Verlagsgesellschaft, 1996), 52.

52 Like Baillargeon, Ruth Feldstein has observed, in the American context, the close convergence between post-war liberal definitions of citizenship and psychological views that placed a heavy priority on the role of mothers in child rearing. See Feldstein, *Motherhood in Black and White: Race and Sex in American Liberalism, 1930–1965* (Ithaca and London: Cornell University Press, 2000).

53 On the concept of post-war male domesticity, see Robert Rutherdale, "Fatherhood, Masculinity, and the Good Life during Canada's Baby Boom, 1945–1965," *Journal of Family History* 24 (July 1999): 351–73; Weiss, *To Have and to Hold*, 83–113. A significant strand of liberal Catholic discourse in Quebec regarding the reaffirmation of post-war fatherhood is analyzed by Michael Gauvreau in *Catholicism Betrayed: Elites, Popular Religion, and the Cultural Origins of the Quiet Revolution, 1931–1971* (Montreal and Kingston: McGill-Queen's University Press, forthcoming).

54 Leonore Davidoff, Megan Dolittle, Janet Fink, and Katherine Holden, *The Family Story: Blood, Contract and Intimacy, 1830–1960* (London and New York: Longman, 1999), 88–9. After the mid-twentieth century, individualistic notions of citizenship become a trope for both men and women, but by contrast, in the nineteenth century, male citizenship may have been expressed in terms of individual identity, but female citizenship was encased within the boundaries of marriage and thus defined by male citizenship rights. See Nancy Cott, *Public Vows: A History of Marriage and the Nation* (Cambridge: Harvard University Press, 2000); Christie, *Engendering the State*.

55 Frank Mort, *Cultures of Consumption: Masculinities and Social Space in Late Twentieth-Century Britain* (London and New York: Routledge, 1996), 3, 10, 205–6; see also Lynn Spigel, *Make Room for TV: Television and the Family Ideal in Postwar America* (Chicago and London: University of Chicago Press, 1992).

LEONARD KUFFERT

"Stabbing our spirits broad awake"
Reconstructing Canadian Culture, 1940–1948

A few historians of English Canada have identified, within the first half of the twentieth century, the seeds of what became a more effervescent cultural nationalism during the second.[1] Though emerging from World War II meant economic and social changes that are now well-documented, we have less frequently explored the war's significance as a staging ground for cultural activism or criticism. Neither do we often portray the years immediately following wartime as more than an awkward period in which the restoration of material well-being trumped other considerations.[2] In 1943, though millions were involved in the war effort overseas and on the home front, it seemed plain to one observer that the "favorite indoor sport for thousands of Canadians, including government officials and professional politicians, university professors, welfare workers and just plain everyday citizens, is post-war planning."[3] "Reconstruction" was the term most commonly used to refer to preparations for peacetime. Politicians exploited it to evoke images of a grateful nation repaying its debts, and businesses to market their products as re-engineered for a new era. The excitement over reconstruction also allowed cultural critics, an outspoken lot often in academe, the media, the arts, or educational organizations, to promote their own brand of rehabilitation. They did not aim to reinvent Canada's cultural life by outlawing the indolent habits of the typical consumer of mass culture, but to enshrine rather traditional tastes as part of any new post-war order. *Saturday Night* editor B.K. Sandwell acknowledged the vogue of foresight as early as 1941 and warned, "If we are to get and keep this new world of which we hear, we must be mentally well-nourished and mentally tough."[4] Despite the prominent place the democratic ideal held during and after the war, critics wanted to reserve decisions about what constituted nourishing fare to themselves. Taste was too important to grant a free hand to a public mesmerized by mass entertainments.[5]

Officially, "reconstruction" was about easing the economic transition to peacetime, and the mandates of Canada's two federally appointed committees on reconstruction reflected that definition.[6] Yet by so publicly preparing during wartime for the domestic and external problems of peacetime, these official bodies privileged planning and encouraged the production of reassuring, if somewhat illusory, visions of post-war democratic harmony. This essay uses the term "culture of reconstruction" to denote the attitudes and aspirations that leapt up around plans for peacetime; it discusses how cultural critics grafted their vision of a reconstructed nation – where citizens would be more at home with the classics than with comic books – onto the enthusiasm for more tangible things to come. Almost indistinguishable from the war effort, the culture of reconstruction engendered an atmosphere in which those not fighting overseas could be confident that life would be better when bombers were finally transformed into lounge chairs.[7] Wedded to some powerful assumptions about the sorts of culture the public would likely embrace – namely, formulaic and mass-distributed – they hoped that the attention focused upon reconstruction as a national ideal would allow beleaguered strains of "folk" and "high" culture to blossom, making the anticipated increase in post-war leisure time an edifying experience. Despite a desire to democratize access to the arts, experts on culture saw their role as parallel to that of the experts/planners who were busy during and after the war "reconstructing" the more mundane elements of Canadian life. In this important sense, they were not populist like the Ontario recreation officials whom Shirley Tillotson has recently profiled,[8] who took their cues from the public's recreational preferences. Rather than heralding or participating in a process of political radicalization that played out over the next generation, critics and activists worked to preserve the sorts of cultural activities that, intentionally or not, reinforced traditional social hierarchies. For many of the supporters of this project, the act of encouraging the less "popular" arts was not elitism, for they did not advocate *complete* control by "experts around a table."[9] To do so would have been disastrous in the context of wartime, where adopting "egregiousness as a deliberate policy"[10] could only be interpreted as antithetical to war aims. Rather, they viewed their own efforts to act as facilitators and promoters of discussion groups, galleries, community centres, and government support for the arts and humanities as cultural democracy in action because these efforts safeguarded alternatives to an increasingly commercialized leisure sphere.

The range of strategies for cultural rehabilitation – strategies that existed for the most part concurrently – should be considered both critical contributions to and appropriations of the larger propaganda-driven culture of reconstruction. Indeed, some observers believed that such a culture would not flourish until the public could be goaded beyond what University of Toronto psychologist Carl Bernhardt called an "it isn't for me to do" attitude towards reconstruction.[11] Perhaps the most well-known of these strategies, *Citizens' Forum*, was a national public affairs radio series conceived around neighbourhood discussion groups. Its creators expected democratic encounters over post-war issues to promote an awareness of the individual's role in the community and a sensitivity to tradition that would guide behaviour despite the rapid transition from war to peace. It also functioned to familiarize the public with government initiatives and to counsel patience during a period of upheaval. While it serves here as a central case study, the program was not an isolated example. Other plans to remake Canadians' post-war leisure time drew upon some of the same assumptions about the malleability of tastes and acknowledged the power of mass media, especially radio, to forge consensus. These wartime and early post-war efforts at cultural outreach also represent some of the earliest episodes during which a cultural elite acknowledged 'middlebrow' culture[12] as a positive means of maintaining their authority. Examining such changes can help us understand, even though the dream of Shakespeare in every village could not be made real, how some long-standing cultural prejudices responded to – or withstood – the wartime environment.

During World War I, both Canada and Britain inaugurated post-war preparation programs early, but these suffered until late in the war from under-promotion.[13] When war returned in 1939, the overall tendency was to reckon in terms of victory – a defiant reaction against the "sense of disillusion, in fact almost of defeatism, that was bequeathed to us by the last war and its aftermath."[14] Some government programs associated with rehabilitation and reconstruction, such as technical or university education offered to veterans, are familiar signposts in historical writing on post-war life because such opportunities have influenced the entire nation's course since 1945.[15] "Official reconstruction" may not have generated the scale and scope of changes that social planner Leonard Marsh's 1943 report on social security envisioned, but it nonetheless helped to erect and reinforce a framework of expectation in which Marsh and others could more easily propose their remedies.[16] A year into the war, expatriate academic Julia Grace Wales commented that mere criticism of the social order would not transform passive citizens into active ones, and she advocated a program to combat the "profound distrust of all institutions."[17] Historian Sonya Rose has argued that by continuously urging the public to cooperate actively with the war effort and to suppress the differences that would normally divide society during World War II, Britain and its institutions defined passivity and hedonistic behaviour as antithetical to citizenship. In Canada, wartime afforded authorities, both political and cultural, an ideal opportunity to, in Rose's terms, "manipulate patriotic sentiment" and "focus public attention on who 'we' are and what it is that 'we' stand for."[18] Wartime also afforded an opportunity to cultivate public confidence in the variety of experts who would manage the adjustment to, as the University of New Brunswick's J.R. Petrie called them, the new "social, economic, and political folkways" emerging from the war. On the cultural front, Petrie believed that universities, especially the humanities, were essential to maintaining a "civilized" perspective during such a transition, noting: "It is perhaps a pardonable prejudice to maintain that sanity will be provided by the universities, where at least an attempt is made to assess values and reach conclusions by methods that lie beyond the political hustings and market places of *popular prejudices*."[19] The comforting prospect of post-war renewal competently executed formed the basis of a culture of reconstruction that denied authority to a mass public, but required its participation in "normalizing" active citizenship.

While critics acknowledged that the details of reconstruction needed to be handled expertly, widespread and comforting knowledge of broader post-war national aims could only benefit the project. Efforts to assure Canadians that competent people were at work on the issue began to bear fruit almost immediately, and references to the post-war as a topic of public interest in Canada date from the earliest phases of the conflict. In January 1940 one observer remarked that "it is now becoming popular to think about the time of peace."[20] "Win the peace," an international motto entrenched in Canadian pamphlet literature by 1941, reminded the public that victory in battle was not enough.[21] Despite his own reserved attitude, even B.K. Sandwell capitulated in the summer of 1942, devoting a regular section in *Saturday Night* to post-war issues.[22] Judging from the volume of publications, officials and opinion leaders in the United States also did their best to make Americans reconstruction-minded.[23] Thanks to government publicity, by mid-war Canadians possessed a healthy awareness of the idea of reconstruction, often using it as a pretext for expressing their views on subjects only tangentially related to the post-war era and occasionally exploiting it for gain. In 1943 the Association of Canadian Advertisers brought out a monthly publication designed to keep members up on the most salient reconstruction issues, recognizing a natural fit between reconstruction's message of service through preparation and the promotion of products such as insurance and home heating.[24] Columnist Mary Lowrey Ross satirized, and simultaneously emphasized, a crucial feature of the culture of reconstruction – the warning to participate or suffer the consequences – "Don't be jittery, don't be dawdle-y. / Better to leap than be shoved in bodily. / Here's to the future and all who contrive it. / And the Post-war world. Let's hope we survive it."[25] "Planning" became almost synonymous with "winning the peace" and functioned within the culture of reconstruction as an implicit belief that existing flaws could be designed away. "It has almost become an adage," one observer remarked, "that after the war the 'old grey World won't be what it used to be.'"[26] Drawing up an appropriate national "blueprint" (a metaphor that recurred often) appeared to be a job especially suited to experts authorized to act in the public interest.[27] Planning was, of course, appealing as an individual strategy, and advertisers invited consumers to manufacture their own security, another theme that remained useful beyond the immediate post-war period.[28]

Regardless of its commercial currency, the wartime compulsion to think deeply about the civilization that Canadians and their allies wished to build did not always create unabashed post-war planners. Planning a "new order" seemed to be a post-war goal that remained laden with some pre-war baggage. Conservative commentators strove to identify regimentation, so useful to the military and so necessary for the efficient distribution of scarce resources in wartime, as unnatural and anti-democratic outside the context of war – "a form of *escapism* which would entrust the whole organization of society to a number of worthy but fallible individuals who happen to constitute the state."[29] Yet a public able to easily recall the destitution of the 1930s warmed to plans for social security during the war. Liberal and social democratic commentators were well disposed, or at least ambivalent, towards planning.[30] Some on the left even declared that "the social lessons which progressively minded people have been teaching this long while seem to have been more thoroughly absorbed than they realize and the problems of the next years are more likely to be those of working out the implications of principles already accepted, rather than of framing new blueprints."[31] Leonard Marsh warned that confusion was guaranteed "if we toss the words 'democracy' and 'national planning' around as if they were magic wands, or sticks of dynamite, according to taste."[32] Yet it was precisely because of these varying connotations that planning held a prominent place in the culture of reconstruction.

Planners could be villains or visionaries, depending upon one's conception of how instrumental the state should be in bringing about what educator E.A. Corbett called the "far-off divine event towards which the whole creation moves."[33] Though a considerable gap existed between working to shape post-war society and letting it unfold as it might, and both courses of action could be interpreted as founded upon democratic principles, planning for the post-war emerged as policy.

What methods could be employed to raise awareness of citizens' potential to shape not only their own material futures but the culture that would emerge after the war? Meeting in 1942, the Canadian Association for Adult Education (CAAE) attributed the "failures of 1919" to a "lack of realistic preparatory planning and to the failure to guide public opinion to a critical examination of the social processes by which these popular aspirations for a better world might be fulfilled." Yet the association's members feared "producing disillusionment and despair by pursuing a policy of offering facile promises of unrealizable immediate goals."[34] Though it appeared somewhat anti-democratic to suggest that wartime decisions or important post-war plans should be made unilaterally by experts, even staunch opponents of state planning distrusted popular opinion. As Queen's economist John L. McDougall complained, the great majority of the people could not bring themselves to make the effort required in a democracy: "the people whose lives will be most deeply affected by it will not read the reports of the discussion in the newspaper, brief though they are. They will turn instead to 'Little Orphan Annie,' or will skip the paper altogether that night in order to see 'Tarzan' at the movies."[35]

Reconstruction thus allowed commentators to position themselves as authorities capable of restoring a civilization lost to the ravages of modern life (of which war was a symptom) and its attendant mass culture. On his radio program devoted to cultural criticism, playwright John Coulter championed "sanity and dignity."[36] Declaring, "Social inertia is henceforth a crime," he prefaced a pamphlet version of his and Healey Willan's opera *Transit through Fire* with a prediction that if adults did not get involved in a thorough reconstruction effort, then "[e]very means will be used to help the next generation forget the fearful lessons of the recent past and set their feet once more on the good old beaten paths. If they should do that they will, in John Ruskin's phrase, without doubt be everlastingly damned."[37] The opera's libretto pointed to modern life as complex, disheartening, and disorienting. The protagonists, an idealistic young couple waylaid by the economic and spiritual stagnation of the 1930s, found hope in the reconstruction credo of avoiding old mistakes. The hero, armed with an MA, mocked a monotonous and materialist world when he sang: "Only by spilling lagoons of blood / could again be stirred / the genius and generosity / of living democracy."[38] The purchase of a new order – a transaction presumably just underway in 1942 – saddened Coulter, but represented an opportunity for those he considered worthy examples of humanity to take on leadership roles.

In venerating participation in a reconstructed democratic, Christian community and disparaging the homogeneity of a new continental or world order, *Transit through Fire* prefigured sculptor Elizabeth Wyn Wood's later call to "put our aesthetic resources forward"[39] as a means of national improvement. Putting aesthetic resources forward also involved moving out from under the shadows of both the "Old country" and Canada's continental neighbour.[40] John Coulter's vivid assessment of this need for a national cultural reconstruction by experts in the field embodied the belief that the arts were "the sensitive antennae of the community," and it recognized that this belief was not "shared by any but a pitifully small minority of the people of Canada, or of anywhere else." He contrasted the "big majority of people everywhere" with the noble but "unpractical and impossible minority" long denigrated as "at best the procurers of leisure relaxations, the cultural pastimes and graces which flower in times of peace."[41]

Expanding this minority became integral to critics' and activists' employment of the culture of reconstruction, for such expansion stood to augment their authority as arbiters of culture. Circumventing the popular will and granting a benighted public access to expert guidance demanded a more effective medium than even the most plain-spoken of the wartime pamphlets, which the University of Toronto's A.S.P. Woodhouse complained were virtually unknown.[42] Other activists cited traditional "democratic" institutions, along with new media, as likely conduits for inculcating an appetite for minority culture. Even though some identified these new media with enemy propaganda and mass conditioning, they represented an opportunity to turn "the one-way traffic of the mass-conditioning process into the two-way traffic of a sturdy democracy."[43] Columnist John Baldwin declared that "the problem [of reconstruction] and its tentative solutions should be set out in churches, in farm and labour organizations, in Home and School groups, among undergraduates, and opened for discussion. By radio, by movies, by circulating exhibitions, a two-way stream of information, comment, and interest would be generated which would be invaluable."[44] Father M.M. Coady of St Francis Xavier University reiterated that Canadians must be "mobilized for continuous enlightenment."[45]

One organization had, years before the war, placed itself at the centre of such a mobilizing effort. The Canadian Association for Adult

Education was seven years old in 1942. Its members had committed early in its career to freeing the public from "government oppression, materialism, from bad taste in living, in music, drama, recreation, and most of all from the utter drabness of human life," and to discussion forums as a vehicle for learning.[46] During the later 1930s, director E.A. Corbett kept a close watch on educational broadcasting, the better foreign examples of which, such as *Columbia School of the Air*, seemed rare and frequently replaced by commercially successful substitutes.[47] A few small-scale forum broadcasts tested these waters just before the war,[48] and in 1939 the CAAE hired Manitoba and McGill graduate Neil Morrison to organize, even *evangelize*, forum programs.[49] The war ensured that the organizations – the Canadian Broadcasting Corporation (CBC), the CAAE, and the Canadian Federation of Agriculture – cooperating in 1941 to produce the first nationwide discussion group program, *Farm Forum*, used "rhetoric charged with connotations of social action; even traditional voluntary association leaders used terms such as 'postwar planning' and 'social reconstruction' to describe their general aims."[50] Morrison planned a national affairs forum program early in 1941, but it took time to overcome CBC general manager Gladstone Murray's reluctance to stir up controversy for the corporation.[51]

Ultimately, close ties between the CAAE and the CBC, embodied in Murray's successor and association member J.S. Thomson, meant that a national forum could go forward. Democracy remained the watchword, but CAAE executive member Watson Thomson (no relation to J.S.) declared that "the best thinking on post-war reconstruction problems should be presented to the minds of the masses of the people concerned, in the kind of way that would make for vital change to those who are in the majority." The association's members were to ask "questions as to the kind of society that the people of Canada really want or think they want. *But we must have implied answers to these questions ourselves.*"[52] By mid-December 1942 J.S. Thomson was trying to combine the appeal and reach of radio with the comfortable reinforcement of the local discussion group, acknowledging the need to make planning techniques "instruments of the achievement of a creative democratic society."[53] While setting out the proposed program's structure in early 1943, members of the Inquiry Committee on the Post-war World started casting about for an auspicious name. An early working title had been "The Inquiry," and perhaps inspired by H.G. Wells's 1933 work *The Shape of Things to Come*, the group settled on "Of Things to Come: An Inquiry into the Post-war World."[54] The emphasis here was on distributing the results of learned inquiry and on reinforcing the notion that planners could creatively *represent* the popular interest.

Keen to strike a balance between gravity and broadcasting topics that would be relevant to the average Canadian, the program's organizers brought in writer Morley Callaghan as "Counsel for the People" during the first broadcasts in spring 1943, done without organizing local listening groups. In light of the topics presented in this "spring series," it seems that the broadcasts were intended to introduce abstract themes nonetheless accessible to both the casual listener and the committed reconstructionist.[55] Early audience response indicated that the program had been well received,[56] but Corbett worried that the public might not take the next step on its own. He wrote to a friend, "The average man is full of a naive faith that officials are planning a new world and that as soon as hostilities cease these officials ... will pop up with blue-prints and all will be well."[57] Still, listeners wrote urging the CBC/CAAE to organize listening groups. Comparing *Of Things to Come* to the fare customarily identified with commercial sponsorship, one correspondent praised "Mr. Callaghan's" program highly and complained, "We get too little of such programs and much too much soap [advertising]. I will admit there is a lot of good soap ... but soap will not remove that scale from the human brain."[58] The spring series succeeded in situating the program in opposition to commercial programming and convinced the CAAE that listening groups could succeed.

In mid-1943 J.S. Thomson, returning to his post as president of the University of Saskatchewan, compared reconstruction to the "intellectual and spiritual quickening" in ancient Greek civilization, the Judeo-Christian tradition, and the Renaissance. Plans to recivilize the post-war world, he contended, resembled these precedents in that "the new spirit is first the possession of a few, almost a secret doctrine, but it spreads abroad and like leaven hidden in the meal, it works until the whole lump is charged with a new life."[59] As Thomson explained it, using the relatively new technology of radio as a means to spur a "moral and intellectual revolution" would challenge "a culture that is very widely spread by modern technology, by the movies, by the radio, by cheap books, by music, dancing," on its own ground. Critics were not after a revolution but, rather, a shoring up of conventional cultural hierarchies. Thomson described the promise of radio outreach rather dramatically, declaring that "the whole question of artistic standards in music, in dancing, in literature, in pictures, in radio programmes, and in the religious life of the Churches is related to this venture we have in mind."[60] Thanks to provincial organizers, and in spite of some controversy about which political parties might reap the benefits of post-war planning,[61] *Citizens' Forum* debuted with listening groups attached in the fall of 1943. George Grant, later a central figure criticizing the strong American cultural presence in Canada, became national secretary, collaborating on the reading material and tending the central administration of the group network.[62]

The notion of "activity" was another important component of the culture of reconstruction, calling upon individuals to justify democracy by responding to the challenge of modern citizenship. It was also an important principle behind *Citizens' Forum*. The challenge, as Corbett perceived it, lay in resisting the impulse to become part of the mass. He wrote that apathy could be disparaged by showing Canadians that "they can't escape responsibility by refusing to take a hand in correcting the evils they deplore" and that the job of those committed to a meaningful reconstruction was to "to present as vigorously as possible the need for active citizenship."[63] But two conflicting conceptions of democratic virtue were at work, and the program tried to satisfy both of them. Seemingly oblivious to the distinction between passivity/mass culture and activity/elite-led reform that the show's organizers wanted Canadians to embrace, columnist Violet Anderson wrote of *Citizens' Forum*: "How significant for our time – that Canadians should hunger so to become active citizens, participating in the solution of problems vital to their country! How democratic that it should be wide open to anyone wishing to participate, and to participate by the democratic method of discussion!"[64] Though he fully supported discussion as an important step in the process of drawing the public into contact with some of the issues with which post-war planners were dealing, George Grant found little to recommend such an attachment to populist ideals about democracy. For him, *Citizens' Forum* discussions were too contrived, too neatly packaged as a digest of moderate reform sentiment. Early in the first season, Grant told a trusted friend within the CAAE that the program needed to embrace more than "middle of the way" or "mediocre" opinions, or else its group structure would accomplish little beyond its own survival. It needed to awaken from an anodyne, supposedly democratic "dullness."[65]

Grant's prescription would prove difficult to fill, and his warning would prove somewhat prophetic. *Citizens' Forum* did not intend to pander to mass tastes or to prescribe rigid courses of action. From its inception, it incorporated a panel format similar to that of the middle-brow American program *Invitation to Learning*, quizzes, and study materials that were less "dry" and more "eye-catching" than wartime pamphlets.[66] This compromise between the high-flown rhetoric of an engineered post-war order and the pervasive presence of mainstream radio clearly supported a liberal-democratic system which appreciated popular input but scorned the mob mentality that brought to mind Nazi "conditioning." By the end of the first successful season, CBC program supervisor Ernest Bushnell praised *Citizens' Forum*'s at least partially fulfilled potential to engage a "wide, continuous" audience comprised of "the best and most responsive type of listener."[67] Listening and joining a forum made active citizenship a *consumable* thing. The forum member could flatter himself to think that he was participating in the process of reconstruction alongside the experts. Although it tried to entertain while it educated, the program's tone remained too lofty for some and may have tempered enthusiasm for reconstruction among groups otherwise eager to educate themselves and advise post-war planners.[68] The officer-organizer of an armed forces listening group noted that the "broadcasts tended to lull the gunners into an advanced state of somnolescence, shared by myself. It was only *after* the broadcast was over and when the gunners were able to express themselves that the true spirit of discussion and free speech shone through."[69] *Citizens' Forum* organizers seemed less concerned with Grant's objections to the program's mediocrity. To them, the armed forces group's self-expression was an indispensable attribute of the active citizen, the very purpose of forums in communities where spectating had come to replace the almost lost art of social and cultural engagement. Within their own neighbourhoods, forum participants were to seek an informed consensus, rather than awaiting answers from on high, and the panel segment of the program served as a model of civilized debate.

Helping the public realize its role in shaping post-war society meant drawing a wide audience, and the program's organizers could not achieve this goal. Just as it aimed at recreating a community of communities, so *Citizens' Forum* encountered some of the forces that divided the larger society. While the war was still on, each *Citizens' Forum* episode reached about 500,000 listeners, and distribution of the study outlines accompanying both *Farm Forum* and *Citizens' Forum* was over a million a year.[70] Given the recommended forum size of ten to twelve, probably about twelve to fifteen thousand people were full-fledged members of the over 1,200 local forums organized during the first full season. Even at its height, membership did not comprise much of the population, but tended to overrepresent community leaders – clergy, teachers, merchants, and professionals – who were themselves eager to be seen at the forefront of cultural and social endeavours.[71] Despite the program's appeals to democratic fundamentals, the impression persisted that it somehow shortchanged the majority, perhaps through a dependence on existing community structures in which the likes of clergy, teachers, merchants, and professionals retained a great deal of power to mobilize others even outside the context of war. At the local level, even the modern means of radio was not enough to alter social hierarchies based on education and committed to continuity. At the national level, the language used in the on-air discussions was rather ambitious and again reflected the abilities of educated elites, or at least the aspirations of the larger audience hoping to be seen as active citizens. The Lieutenant leading the aforementioned armed forces group asked, "is it necessary for the learned Joes, including Callaghan, to latch [sic] out with such phrases as 'economic bourbons,' 'Pan-Germanic,' and 'financial oligarchy[?]'"[72] George Grant sensed a clear division in the *Citizens' Forum* membership when he reported on the state of the project at the end of 1943–44, the program's first season: "We have in fact drawn a line. People above that line have become part of the *Citizens' Forum*, people below the line, the *Citizens' Forum* has not gone down to reach ... Among the middle class, the Forums have done a good job. Reading the reports and sitting in with the various Forums, one gets the sense that many people are studying citizenship for the first time."[73]

As long as the war and visions of its aftermath could sustain interest in a new and ostensibly democratic order, *Citizens' Forum* could define participation in such projects as active citizenship. Yet as the war ended in 1945, the middle-class composition of *Citizens' Forum*'s core membership – and the middlebrow tone adopted to build that membership – became more apparent. Radio maintained its potential to affect listeners, but many listeners no longer faced circumstances where support for reconstruction could be presented as having crucial post-war implications. N.A.M. MacKenzie predicted in 1944 that "conditions and attitudes which have made it possible for us to do what we have done during the war will tend to change or disappear and will be replaced by other conditions and attitudes."[74] Without the atmosphere of urgency that characterized wartime and preparations for the post-war period, *Citizens' Forum* became a public affairs program much like any other, and its experts found themselves the targets of Wayne and Shuster's good-natured ribbing.[75] The program failed, as historians of the adult education movement have noted, to develop the momentum necessary for continued local action, and it failed to reach the listener through "emotion and delight."[76] Though it employed a flattering middlebrow approach over a medium extremely suited to persuasion, it could not overcome the lure of individual gratification. Canadians in the early post-war period wanted to resume "the unfinished business of personal living."[77] Becoming less earnest and more popular in tone was not part of the program's post-war agenda, because *entertaining* the audience was not part of its wartime mandate.

Reconstruction-era critics of mass culture recognized the ability of governments at all levels to create a cultural infrastructure through which seeds of 'civilization' could be planted. Before the war ended, two more efforts arose with the object of enhancing the position of what could be considered "high" or "folk" culture, and they would continue their work in the years following the war. The first, a movement to create a network of community centres, encouraged participation in cultural and recreational pursuits as preferable to more passive forms of leisure. The second, an alliance of groups, made a case for the arts as the basis of civilization by presenting their plans for a national cultural ministry to the House of Commons Special Committee on Reconstruction and Re-establishment. Their plans for the post-war cultural order assumed a basic equality among people, but not among those activities that people might choose to undertake.

The idea of establishing a physical locale for cultural redemption in Canada developed before World War II, with the most prominent interwar argument for establishing a place where community members could gather to participate in creative leisure-time pursuits coming in 1925 from publisher Lorne Pierce. In *The Beloved Community* he outlined a community council system and predicted that rural areas, especially when organized through rural schools, would provide fertile ground. Presumably more patient than the city dweller, the farmer would respond to such a straightforward scheme simply because "[h]e detests sham; and the brightest candidate for odium, the individual marked for the speediest excursion to limbo and emptiness, is that citizen who would substitute swank and camouflage for the real thing."[78] Though Pierce would have to wait almost twenty years to see his ideas taken up, many wartime supporters of small-scale, participatory community arts and recreation programs nonetheless believed that local access to worthwhile pastimes would help Canadians rediscover authenticity. Much of the support directed towards establishing facilities for community cultural outreach came from people who were themselves artists and musicians, members of organizations such as Toronto's Arts and Letters Club or the CAAE, and who recognized that community-centre projects would be organized locally but draw upon the resources of such larger organizations.[79] Perhaps one of the more outspoken of these supporters, critic and teacher Barker Fairley, decried the fact that there was in Canada no "obvious place for artist to hang his hat," and he denounced those who would see the proliferation of community centres as a wasteful surrender to bohemianism. "It's not out of the way to think of spending two or three dollars a year per person for this, after we've spent perhaps $50 per year to get him a formal schooling, and a hundred times that to train him to fight, is it?"[80] In some cases, the movement's promoters portrayed citizenship and cultural uplift as their twin aims.[81]

Though some community councils and community centres existed prior to the war, early in wartime much of the responsibility for instilling "democratic" values and an appreciation for the arts still rested with the schools.[82] New schools, however, were larger and tended to be built in urban settings, circumstances that could be – if vigorous community organizations chose to seize the opportunity – conducive to community revitalization through improved leisure.[83] The key to planning a satisfactory post-war physical environment was planning cultural and recreational spaces that encouraged a sense of being connected to one's neighbourhood or town, rather than tethered to a larger, bureaucratized reconstruction scheme or, worse yet, entrapped by the debilitating rhythms of mass culture. Though suburbs grew rapidly in the post-war period, it was difficult to determine before 1945 whether sprawl or the rebirth of existing neighbourhoods would result after the war. Worried observers noted that the average Canadian's post-war surroundings would need to be both a product of and a haven from modern pressures, which included more leisure. As one pamphlet pleaded: "Children are not made to take root in unyielding pavement, bleak tenements or impersonal suburban dwellings. Space and neighborliness for individual expression and community development will become more than ever necessary as applied science brings increasing leisure hours from the field, factory, office and transport."[84] Urban planning's role in community development came to garner more attention, especially in the context of an acute housing shortage, an issue to which *Citizens' Forum* devoted an early show in 1943.[85] One urbanist urged cities to plan, but avoid planning ugly, utilitarian housing tracts for the masses, for such monotonous surroundings would only contribute to the corruption of youth.[86]

The tension between 'winning the peace' through planning and preserving apparently unstructured (i.e., non-commercial) leisuretime existence remained central to this discourse. F. Cyril James, principal of McGill University and chair of Parliament's Dominion Advisory Committee on Reconstruction, speaking to a gathering of Canadian architects, argued, "If community planning is to satisfy the souls of men, as well as the dreams of aesthetes," traditional and, above all, *personal* avenues of learning from one's community "must recover for us the reality of home influences in moulding character, and of church and school in shaping the further development of human life."[87] Social worker and academic Stuart Jaffary commented in 1943 on the importance of guided recreation to the larger sphere of social services. "How eagerly this new arrival is to be welcomed and nurtured," he declared, "after our past decades of vacuous movies and the insidious passivity of 'spectating,' whether to the radio, sports, or politics!"[88]

By 1944 the community-centre ideal, although part of the support for a broader renewal of long-neglected urban areas, shouldered hopes for more than the prevention of juvenile delinquency. A leadership disposed towards traditional "high" and "folk" cultural forms boded well for the "development of personality" through "a more democratic distribution" of opportunities to encounter original, professionally produced works. This attitude would survive the war. Anthropologist Marius Barbeau denounced the commercialization of handicrafts, claiming that those arts should be practised in leisure time and learned through apprenticeship or in a self-expressive environment such as the community centre.[89] Purveyors of "culture" did not want artists to keep to themselves but to practise their art in public, where the people could come to understand that the artist was not just creating for him or herself. Such a community connection would ensure that traditional conceptions of beauty would not be sacrificed to an uncompromising modernism – the sort supposed to fester in the garret of the lonely artist. As Blodwen Davies put it, the post-war abundance of creative energy could prove destructive "if turned inward into abnormal channels."[90]

Existing facilities showed their age and were often ill-designed for the purposes they had come to serve. The success of well-subscribed itinerant events such as the Dominion Drama Festival convinced one Maritime drama supporter that "definite physical plans for artistic development are absolutely necessary to make us more closely knit and culturally lifted, if this present struggle for democratic privileges is to be worth fighting through."[91] Yet deciding how to make real these physical plans was not to be democratic in the sense that it solicited and incorporated popular input. Architects became involved early in suggesting model sites and producing floor plans scalable to a community's size.[92] Amid the discussion of how to accommodate drama, art, sport, and other community events under one roof, the most comprehensive statement of purpose for a network of community centres came from musician Marcus Adeney. Expressing his reverence for Lorne Pierce as an unheeded visionary, Adeney recalled his hometown of Paris, Ontario, during the 1910s, where "church organ and choir allowed for self-expression," and visiting lecturers were rare. "We reflected all that we had seen and known," he admitted, adding that the coming of the movies affected the town's cultural and recreational facilities, which were still well used but inadequate. To tip this balance in favour of locally produced plays, crafts, and sport required the leadership of professionals.

Another of Adeney's confessions emphasized the extent to which hopes for post-war cultural revitalization via the community centre rested with an elite. He reasoned that post-war integration with other organizations such as the YMCA, churches, or the CAAE would be necessary in many communities, so the organization of community centres would hardly be a grassroots effort. Given this kind of integration, the community centre would be the site of a brokered anti-modernism, for the members of such groups in wartime Canada could not look to contemporary mass culture for examples of what they wished to accomplish. Foremost in his conception of the community-centre movement's tasks was its attention to and exploitation of "the deep impulse of every man toward a rounded life experience. Nothing is too rare and precious, no art too high-brow, no sport too simple or craft too humble, for the interests we must cater to."[93] The community centre Adeney envisioned was to be a "socially active" place, "with programmes and resources always a little ahead of the average citizen's wishes and requirements." Citizens should be allowed access to a range of arts and activities, but only those that developed taste, appreciation, and skill should be endorsed. Amateur theatre, evening courses in art and handicrafts, folk dance, and sports programs in which community members themselves participated – rather than spectating – already topped the agenda in towns that had organized their own centres,[94] but Adeney and others wanted these activities to become the staples of a larger, publicly funded network. He recommended against the business community's involvement in financing community centres, not necessarily because business people would find a way to turn a profit from their association with such a noble cause, but because "business cannot take a long term view. Its agents must follow and not lead public opinion."[95] The notion that a commercial presence would have a debilitating influence on community centres originated in the assumption that profit-seeking firms would favour the most popular activities, leaving the more difficult, more esoteric ones to wither.

Inclined towards the public sector as its chief potential benefactor and towards voluntary associations such as the CAAE for supporters, the community-centre movement could play yet another strong card. Though not of long standing, a tradition of war memorialization allowed community-centre boosters to tout their project as sacred to the memory of World War II's fallen, whose numbers were still mounting in 1945. Perhaps because rituals of remembrance had been established by the later 1930s, it seemed that, unlike the period following World War I,[96] less acrimony existed during World War II over the question of ornamental versus utilitarian forms of commemoration. Marcus Adeney cited an opinion poll showing that 90 per cent of Canadians polled favoured "useful" war memorials, and he fused the "arts and crafts, community planning, growth of mind and body for every citizen," with a sentiment he knew would gather support. He concluded that the obvious memorial was the active, organic community centre. "[W]e can draw no distinction," Adeney wrote, "between the useful and the monumental. Indeed, a Community Centre, designed by one equal to his task, would be the most splendid of cenotaphs."[97]

After the war ended, community-centre boosters continued to present their plans, and these embodied the same sense of mission that the movement's core supporters shared during wartime. Occasionally, optimism ran rather high and included a scheme to convert (presumably deserted) movie theatres into community meeting places.[98] The belief persisted that Canadians needed immediate instruction in matters of culture, so dissolute were popular tendencies assumed to be. "Many today do not know how to spend their leisure time constructively. They are attracted to the nearest or most advertised activity," Martyn Estall reported dryly in 1946.[99] Railing against the conception that recreation and physical education were synonymous, David Murray nonetheless saw both those fields suffering at the hands of decidedly more passive pursuits.[100] In proposing that they be funded extensively by local, provincial, and federal governments, CAAE director Corbett produced a fascinating catalogue of hopes for community centres in 1947, noting, "Community Centres in which our people can spend their leisure time pleasantly and profitably are widely accepted as an appropriate form of living war memorial."[101] As well as serving as living war memorials, community centres were to be the locus, he insisted, where the "comradeship, unity and devotion to a common purpose which characterized our life during the war can be maintained and developed in peace." Echoing Estall's assessment of popular tendencies, Corbett called for the promotion of "worthwhile recreation" in the same way as commercial entertainments (which he called "special interests") were promoted. Though reasonably certain that mass culture could be blamed for North Americans' decline into sloth and delinquency,[102] he did not want to replace other forms of leisure but to expose the public to new ones, trusting, as Marcus Adeney had, that people would "develop taste, appreciation and skill, according to their experience and contacts."[103] The tastes and skills to be developed would of course reflect those of the cultural experts driving the movement.

As potential exhibition and teaching spaces, a network of community centres played an important role in the presentation that a united front of arts groups, dominated by representatives from the visual arts, made in late June 1944 to the House of Commons Special Committee on Reconstruction and Re-establishment. This presentation has drawn some scholarly attention as an important moment in the history of Canadian cultural policy.[104] The arts groups declared that cultural

matters deserved the same consideration that the government was
giving the social programs which, for many Canadians, defined post-
war reconstruction. This was an ultimatum to the state, asking that it
encourage cultural forms that were not commercially motivated. War
had not brought about a sudden sense that certain arts were important
repositories of civilization, but it presented an opportunity to relate the
age-old theme of cultural decay to the neglect of both great works and
new talent. Reflecting during the war's early days upon artistic trea-
sures and their value, Morley Callaghan noted that scientific and technical advances brought on by war were glad tidings, but that war's toll
was considerable in human terms, "for the spirit needs beautiful and
spiritual things to feed on, and not many of those things are
around."[105] As chair of the group taking its cultural reconstruction
plan to Ottawa, Elizabeth Wyn Wood noted the wartime collaboration
between "[a]rtists and others of vision" and drew upon immediate
wartime concerns to justify an unprecedented expansion in state
funding for culture. "A nation's culture is an essential asset on its home
front, before the world and before history," Wyn Wood wrote, "[a]nd
by culture I do not mean literacy and gentility. I mean active, progressive, and creative achievement."[106] Asking Parliament to underwrite
the task of bringing culture to the streets and hamlets of Canada still
meant that "artists and others of vision" would continue to define
what constituted achievement. These visionaries would, like members
of Parliament, represent the public in choosing the works, perfor-
mances, and skills worthy of passing on.

An early draft of the "Artists' Brief" listed a "capacity for intelligent
and cultured living" as one of the goals of reconstruction.[107] Similar in
structure to many of the briefs that the Royal Commission on National
Development in the Arts, Letters and Sciences (Massey Commission)
would receive about five years later, the "Artists' Brief" stands out not
only because it prefigured such submissions but because its signatories
believed the nation's cultural development might best be served by peti-
tioning a committee with no pretensions to the title of "cultural
agency." This approach alone testified loudly to reconstruction's currency. If we examine the brief's proposals, however, it is clear the
sixteen arts groups believed that their audience of parliamentarians
would be more interested in the nation's "bottom line" than in cultural
prospects for the post-war. Accordingly, they emphasized the economic
and social benefits of investing in culture and the creative forces instrumental in such fundamental sectors of the economy as construction,
manufacturing, and broadcasting.[108] The brief called upon the government to model Canada's cultural infrastructure upon European examples rather than American ones. Notable among these models was pre-

war France, a place where "[e]very original thinker, from dressmaker to building engineer ... found, not only opportunity, but promotion through public interest." Sweden and Denmark also received laurels for their integration of design and the manufacture of everyday objects – objects that were not only functional and modern but, perhaps more importantly, "original." The final example, intended to be the most stirring, was Britain's generous support of music and the arts – some of the measures undertaken during wartime – under the slogan: "The best for the most."[109] Columnist Blodwen Davies encouraged cosmopolitanism, reporting that without the "New Canadians" who played an instrumental role in galvanizing an artists' gathering at the Art Gallery of Toronto in February 1944, the brief itself might not have been presented. The contributing groups organized as the Arts Reconstruction Committee, which became the Canadian Arts Council in late 1945 and consequently told the federal government it had "no reasonable excuse" for delaying an arts overhaul.[110]

"Overhauling" the arts would, critics hoped, catapult Canada into a different status among nations. David Lewis may have best captured the nervously optimistic tone of some early post-war cultural self-assessments when he asserted, "Canada must *crusade* its dawning artistic prominence."[111] This "crusade" was to form part of what A.J.M. Smith dubbed the "new role to be played by Canada in world affairs which the war and the ending have brought home to everyone." Of course, this role became primarily a diplomatic and ultimately even a military one, but many wanted post-war global links to involve John Coulter's "cultural pastimes and graces which flower in times of peace." Smith saw some encouraging evidence that "Canadian literature which formerly aimed to be 'national' is now, here and there at least, taking on a cosmopolitan maturity."[112] Although Barker Fairley believed Canadian artists were "not sufficiently interested in humanity to develop a great human art,"[113] he did not rule out the careful cultivation of such an interest. While Montreal would not turn into Paris overnight, commentators believed that participating in a worldwide literature, visual arts, and educational interchange would help Canadians recognize what animated the world's cultural metropolises. One important facet of such participation was membership in the United Nations Educational, Scientific, and Cultural Organization (UNESCO), for cultural reconstructionists a post-war opportunity not to be missed.[114] Part of the anxiety surrounding Canada's post-war cultural ties and prospects exhibited itself through a sense of marginality and a fear of being left behind for a backwater by other industrialized nations. Academic and broadcaster Arthur Phelps warned more than a year after the war ended that Canada sat perched "on the edge of world culture" and must "learn how to rise into it or die."[115] Embarrassment seemed like a fate still worse than death. Samuel Roddan complained of Canada's "internal self-perpetuating resistance toward honest, imaginative writing" as a handicap placing the nation behind others with lower educational and literacy standards.[116]

Relative rates of literacy did not change the fact that the "best" elements of culture remained scarce in Canada, and the allied groups proposed that the state undertake a "distribution of opportunity" to bring "all hands … into the service of the state, for the welfare of the people, in peace as they are in war." This was hardly a vision of a nationalized culture. Still, the brief went on to recommend that the state help initiate "a way of thought among the Canadian people [that] would create a vast enlivening movement." This would require a governmental body for the supervision of culture and all its branches, including crafts and the "everyday aesthetic values pertaining to the consumer." In the artists' plan, community centres would play an important role as concrete expressions of national purpose and local gathering places for citizens seeking self-improvement.[117] One report on the brief made it plain that the sort of activities befitting the post-war community centre would be those requiring mental effort and careful attention. "Some day there will be a Community Centre at Mud Corners," wrote one observer. "It will be a spot where nearby folk will gather to hear good music and to see good pictures and shows. A spot where children and grown-ups will learn to make pottery, to act in plays, to blow saxophones and trumpets, to paint, to sing. It will be a spot for baseball games and picnics and concerts and discussions." Though this was a rather inclusive list of activities, no elaborate treatise on what defined "good" pictures and shows accompanied it. In choosing what went on in the post-war community centre and how culture was to be promoted, educators, experts, and critics would be involved in the process of exposing the public to challenging works, just as they had been involved in choosing topics and sitting on panels for *Citizens' Forum*. Making, acting, blowing, painting, and singing were all therapeutic, participatory pastimes – suitable antidotes to the commercial films and radio, which had only produced "cultural hunger."[118]

The man who filed that report on the artists' presentation, Walter Herbert, was director of an agency called the Canadian Committee and responsible for a program supplying educational material on Canada to American and British officers stationed in Canada. He had been weighing the pros and cons of a national cultural ministry since earlier in the war.[119] Herbert lobbied for the sort of government involvement in cultural affairs that the artists' groups did in 1944, citing "colossal" indifference, which "must be undermined and dissipated; because our nation cannot achieve the spiritual maturity which will eventually make us great if our cultural life continues cramped and runted."[120] He was not, however, convinced that the establishment of an advanced state cultural apparatus would be simple,[121] and in this way he appreciated the complexity of cultural promotion in advance of the Massey Commission's monumental effort to study the problem of establishing and paying for a cultural infrastructure. By October 1945 Herbert had become head of a new organization, the Canada Foundation, which was to function as a cultural clearing house, generating publicity for Canadian artists, writers, and musicians until a ministry of cultural affairs could be set up. Without the lump sum of $10 million that the artists' alliance had requested as seed money for community centres, Herbert's organization set out to secure private funds for its work and to find champions for its cause, an effort that was not always appreciated.[122] Herbert even wrote to Mrs John Bracken in an attempt to persuade her husband, the Conservative party leader, to listen to an upcoming CBC broadcast of a Willan-Coulter opera – and perhaps be drawn into the culture battle. "If you could induce Mr. Bracken to relax for three hours to listen with you," Herbert pleaded, "I think it would be good for his restless soul."[123] In the decade or so that followed, Herbert and his small staff served as advocates for the restless souls practising the fine arts and preserving Canadian variations upon them. Typical of the work the organization undertook during the early post-war period was an index of cultural publications, a project that continued into the mid-1960s.[124] Arising out of the reconstruction-era concern with the nation's cultural diet and government hesitancy to endow a ministry of culture, the Canada Foundation functioned as a kind of privately funded prototype of the Canada Council, which would not begin to operate until 1957.

Dire as their diagnoses were, critics inspired by the ferment of reconstruction remained optimistic about a market for their remedies: programs at community centres, broadcasts providing an introduction to great musical and literary works, and discussion circles tackling a new issue each week. These became ways of intervening *on the behalf* of an audience whose untended habits of cultural consumption could otherwise prove destructive. *Citizens' Forum*, an invitation to planning for the post-war that employed the modern means of radio and mass mailings but featured a town-meeting style, billed itself as a bastion of democracy. At best, Canadians remained ambivalent towards efforts to structure their cultural lives. Ever mindful of its potential to co-opt and thereby transform the growing "middle" of the population, the CAAE's immediate post-war priorities included "to awaken people to

the possibilities and dangers of modern life, to help them with knowledge and leadership."[125] Only the most sanguine supporters of a new
order forecast that the public could be remade and went as far as
assuming what the public wanted: "The common man today ... wants
opportunities for self-improvement, control of his environment, and
fruitful leisure. ... He does not want a world half slave and half free,
no matter what delectable form the bondage may take."[126] This
oblique reference to the absolute control ascribed to communism
ignored the formidable sameness of the discourse surrounding what an
elite considered the problem of cultural decline. The province of Manitoba's inquiry into adult education, which included economist-histo-
rian Harold Innis and documentary filmmaker John Grierson,
appeared to be alone in drawing attention to the near monopoly that
well-meaning joiners had over the direction of cultural affairs in
Canada and in urging a separation between education and state
propaganda.[127]

The liberal-democratic approach to cultural reconstruction was one
of education and consensus reached within an informed, critical population. Cyril James cautioned the audience for a radio performance of
Faust in 1943, "we shall not, upon the morrow of victory, enter into a
brave new world. If we are to attain the ideals for which we are fighting, everyone of us must continue during the post-war period to work
with an energy and determination comparable to that which has been
displayed during the last two years."[128] James's audience could likely
be counted on to follow his advice, for they were also likely too well
educated and too prominent in their respective towns to escape serving
in the sort of arts or educational association that carried a reflexive critique of mass culture into peacetime. Although the culture of reconstruction owed its initial power to the fact that there was a war from
which to emerge, the will to exploit it did not evaporate at war's end.
Even advertisers, who knew a good angle when they saw one, longed
to extend the powerful theme of the common task into the post-war
period.[129] Neither did the arrival of peace – and a new, "cold" war –
diminish commentators' calls for active citizens, for a world with
atomic weapons loomed as a more complex, precarious place.[130] In
contrast, popular attention to the ideal of rebuilding Canada as a
nation of debating societies and critical audiences would prove, like the
culture of reconstruction itself, "illusory and short-lived."[131] When the
burden of war lifted, elite support for deliberate measures to preserve
lofty standards of citizenship and culture remained strong. During
wartime the culture of reconstruction made possible a level of integration between voluntary cultural and educational associations which in
turn allowed "civilization" and the conditions necessary for its perpet-

uation to continue to be presented to the public, even after the war, as imperatives that defined the nation's identity and were essential to democracy. The most visible part of this transformation's legacy, taken up before the decade was out, was the Massey Commission. In the intervening years, cultural activists testified to the need to situate Canada – especially English Canada – within a cosmopolitan cultural orbit, a task that also involved pulling it away from the commercial culture they saw as so distressingly dominant on the North American continent.

Publisher C.J. Eustace complained that it was "too much to hope that the ideals which are to mould the world of the future will come from the new middle-class," for neither a "spiritual community" among the cultural elite nor a corps of political idealists was sufficient to keep the marketplace from prevailing.[132] Entrepreneurs who treated culture as a business remained the villains, dispensing chaos where guidance was needed. Literacy looked like a modern handicap when well-subscribed modes of mass culture such as the pulp novel and the comic book could be unproblematically identified with a "lowering of the cultural tone of the nation."[133] Arthur Phelps condemned the opportunists in radio whose slavish recourse to popularity ratings only "nourishes the calculated appeal to the presumed soft emotions and flaccid minds of the audience." Yet he was "sure that there exists a public wistful for better programmes in the name of entertainment than it is now getting." Phelps wanted radio to be a "nutrient medium in the interests of public cultivation," and he praised the CBC's drama series *Stage 46* as successful "in the tradition of Dickens and Galsworthy and Shaw, stabbing our spirits broad awake."[134] The "tradition" he so valued grappled with big questions in war or in peace. Broaching complex topics – on the radio, for instance – seemed an opportune way to draw in the middle class and fight the "spiritual loneliness abroad in the world today."[135]

For those convinced that Canadians could become a cultivated people if exposed to the right sort of influences, a precipitous return to normalcy after the war would not do. The dream of a post-war common culture drawing upon local or regional traditions and 'civilized' activities seemed almost attainable in a wartime environment that helped cast the preservation of such traditions and the pursuit of such activities as indistinguishable from "active local citizenship of a positive constructive sort."[136] Employing modern means of communication such as radio to absorb and refashion the rhetoric of reconstruction, the elite critique of modern life and mass culture endorsed local, participatory cultural alternatives under the banner of democracy. Still, rather than turning the direction of such initiatives over to the public, cultural critics considered the stakes high enough to model what they considered desirable behaviours. With its localized group structure and emphasis on participation, *Citizens' Forum* was the most prominent example of a will to counter the influence of mass culture by making virtuous citizenship more accessible. In the process they expressed their own understanding of democracy. Community-centre proposals relied upon the perceived need to escape the passivity and uniformity of modern life. Though these efforts burned brightly for a short time, within two or three years it was clear that post-war patterns of living and consumption, including the consumption of culture, favoured the mass society. For ordinary Canadians, getting on with work, family, and personal security concerns remained a form of reconstruction with more resonance than plans for drama classes. For the extraordinary Canadians who envisioned wholesale changes to the way that the society would operate after the war, their attempts to harness the culture of reconstruction institutionalized the critique of mass culture by privileging antidotes to it – community centres, radio forums, active citizenship – and by exploring the possibility of using the considerable resources of the national broadcaster and the state to promote examples of "authentic" or worthwhile entertainments. Though they did not succeed in cultivating a general vigilance towards some of the very diversions that buoyed spirits on the home front or towards the compelling promises of modern life, this vocal elite drafted its own set of blueprints for post-war cultural development against which English-Canadian culture would be measured into the next decade and beyond.

NOTES

I would like to thank the editors of this volume and the other contributors for their valuable questions and comments on this essay, which is an adaptation and a re-thinking of a chapter in my forthcoming book, *A Great Duty: Responses to Modern Life and Mass Culture in Canada, 1939–1967* (Montreal: McGill-Queen's University Press).

1 Paul Litt, *The Muses, the Masses, and the Massey Commission* (Toronto: University of Toronto Press, 1992); Maria Tippett, *Making Culture: English-Canadian Institutions and the Arts before the Massey Commission* (Toronto: University of Toronto Press, 1990); Mary Vipond, "The Nationalist Network: English Canada's Intellectuals and Artists in the 1920s," *Canadian Review of Studies in Nationalism* 5 (spring 1980): 32–52; Ramsay Cook, "Cultural Nationalism in Canada: An Historical Perspective," in Janice L. Murray, ed., *Canadian Cultural Nationalism:*

The Fourth Lester B. Pearson Conference on the Canada-U.S. Relationship (New York: New York University Press, 1977), 15–44. See also Vipond's "National Consciousness in English-Speaking Canada in the 1920's: Seven Studies" (PhD diss., University of Toronto, 1974).

2 Peter Neary and J.L. Granatstein, eds., *The Veteran's Charter and Post–World War II Canada* (Montreal and Kingston: McGill-Queen's University Press, 1998); Greg Donaghy, ed., *Uncertain Horizons: Canadians and Their World in 1945* (Ottawa: Canadian Committee for the History of the Second World War, 1997). Two recent exceptions are Nancy Christie, *Engendering the State: Family, Work, and Welfare in Canada* (Toronto: University of Toronto Press, 2000), and Shirley Tillotson, *The Public at Play: Gender and the Politics of Recreation in Postwar Ontario* (Toronto: University of Toronto Press, 2000).

3 Leonard L. Knott, "Post-War Preview," *Montreal Standard* (magazine section), 30 Oct. 1943.

4 "Begin Now?" *Saturday Night* (SN), 27 Dec. 1941, 3.

5 On critical consensus, see T.J. Jackson Lears, "A Matter of Taste: Corporate Cultural Hegemony in a Mass-Consumption Society," in Lary May, ed., *Recasting America: Culture and Politics in the Age of the Cold War* (Chicago: University of Chicago Press, 1989), 38–57.

6 Charged with advising and overseeing plans for the transition from war back to peace were, respectively, the Dominion Advisory Committee on Reconstruction, under McGill University principal F.C. James, and the House of Commons Special Committee on Reconstruction and Re-establishment, chaired by James Gray Turgeon, MP. The Advisory Committee advocated the creation of a Department of Reconstruction. When that department was formed in 1944 under C.D. Howe, the Advisory Committee ceased to function.

7 John B. Collins, "'Design in Industry' Exhibition, National Gallery of Canada, 1946: Turning Bombers into Lounge Chairs," *Material History Bulletin* 27 (spring 1988).

8 Tillotson, *The Public at Play*, 44–5.

9 "You and Me and Reconstruction," CBC Discussion Club, 28 Aug. 1942, National Archives of Canada (NA), CAVA/AVCA, 1984–0164, reference copy at 1982–0043/63.

10 Lister Sinclair, "Art in the Community," typescript, [1944, NA, Lister Shedden Sinclair Papers, MG 31, D44, vol. 32.

11 "You and Me and Reconstruction," 28 Aug. 1942.

12 Here middlebrow culture is associated with "voluntary education" carried on via affordable reprints of literary classics, cultural programming on the radio, or participatory events in community facilities. See Joan Shelly Rubin, *The Making of Middlebrow Culture* (Chapel Hill: University of North Carolina Press, 1992), xi–xii.

13 Desmond Morton and Glenn Wright, *Winning the Second Battle:
    Canadian Veterans and the Return to Civilian Life, 1915–1930* (Toronto:
    University of Toronto Press, 1987), 98–9, 106; Craig Brown and Ramsay
    Cook, *Canada 1896–1921: A Nation Transformed* (Toronto: McClelland
    and Stewart, 1974) especially Chapter 15: "O Brave New World ...";
    Barry Ferguson, *Remaking Liberalism: The Intellectual Legacy of Adam
    Shortt, O.D. Skelton, W.C. Clark, and W.A. Mackintosh, 1890–1925*
    (Montreal and Kingston: McGill-Queen's University Press, 1993), chapter
    9; Maria Tippett's *Art at the Service of War: Canada, Art, and the Great
    War* (Toronto: University of Toronto Press, 1984). On Britain, see Paul
    Johnson, *Land Fit for Heroes: The Planning of British Reconstruction,
    1916–1919* (Chicago and London: University of Chicago Press, 1968),
    1–9; and Kenneth O. Morgan, *Consensus and Disunity: The Lloyd
    George Coalition Government, 1918–1922* (Oxford: Clarendon, 1979),
    especially chapter 4.
14 Albert C. Wakeman, "New Year Thoughts on the War – and After," SN,
    6 Jan. 1940, 7.
15 Robert Bothwell, Ian Drummond, and John English, *Canada since 1945:
    Power, Politics and Provincialism*, rev. ed. (Toronto: University of
    Toronto Press, 1989), 82, 109–11; Doug Owram, *Born at the Right
    Time: A History of the Baby Boom Generation* (Toronto: University of
    Toronto Press, 1996), 24–5.
16 Other wartime remedies appearing in a flurry in 1943, close on the heels
    of Britain's Beveridge Report of December 1942, were Harry Cassidy's
    Social Security and Reconstruction in Canada, Marsh's *Social Security for
    Canada*, and Charlotte Whitton's *The Dawn of an Ampler Life*.
    Whitton's work "was both a direct attack on Marsh's proposals and an
    alternative vision of Canada's social welfare future." See Brigitte Kitchen,
    "The Marsh Report Revisited," *Journal of Canadian Studies* 21 (summer
    1986): 38–40.
17 Julia Grace Wales, "Pro, Not Anti: A Principle of Integration," *New Age*
    2 (8 Aug. 1940): 9–10.
18 Sonya O. Rose, "Sex, Citizenship and the Nation in World War II
    Britain," *American Historical Review* 103 (Oct. 1998): 1148, 1159–62.
19 J. Richards Petrie, "The Universities and the War," *Brunswickan* 60 (8
    Nov. 1940): 3, 6; italics added. The belief that the university should be
    the site of rational research into social problems hardly emerged during
    World War II. For examples of similar confidence in the university during
    the early part of the 1920s, see Ferguson, *Remaking Liberalism*, 211. See
    also Paul Axelrod, *Making a Middle Class: Student Life in English
    Canada during the Thirties* (Montreal and Kingston: McGill-Queen's
    University Press, 1990), 12–15.
20 Wakeman, "New Year Thoughts on the War – and After," 7; W.D. Black,

"Industrial Development in Canada to Meet the War Emergency," broadcast on CBC, 13 Nov. 1940, NA, Clarence Decatur Howe Papers, MG 27 III B20, vol. 140, series 89, Articles, Speeches, Books; G.W. Brown to A.R.M. Lower, 31 July 1940, Queen's University Archives, A.R.M. Lower Papers, Correspondence re: "Social Sciences in Post-war World," box 13, B 142.

21 Claris Silcox, *The War and Religion* (Toronto: Macmillan, 1941), 10; Young Men's Christian Associations of Canada, National Council, *We Discuss Canada* (Toronto: Ryerson, 1942), 57; Bruce Hutchison, "Win the Peace NOW!" *Maclean's,* 15 April 1943, 18, 44–6.

22 Editorial notice, "'After the War,'" SN, 15 Aug. 1942, 3. See also "Thinking about Canada," SN, 2 May 1942, 3.

23 Some of the most prominent books produced on reconstruction themes in the United States were George B. Galloway, *Post-war Planning in the United States* (New York: Twentieth Century Fund, 1942); Fawn M. Brodie, *Peace Aims and Post-war Planning* (Boston: World Peace Foundation, 1942), and Brodie, *Peace Aims and Post-war Reconstruction* (Princeton: American Committee for International Studies, 1941); Office of War Information, *Toward New Horizons: The World beyond the War* (Washington: Government Printing Office, 1942). For a more comprehensive listing of reconstruction publications from the United States, Canada, and Britain up to 1943, see Ralph Flenley, *Post-war Problems – A Reading List* (Toronto: Canadian Institute of International Affairs, 1943).

24 Association of Canadian Advertisers, *Continuing Study of Trends in Post-war Planning.* Among the numerous advertising campaigns making use of the idea of reconstruction were "Two Shoulders to the Same Wheel" (1941); "Canadian Nickel: Serving Today ... Preparing for Tomorrow" (1943); "Post-war Planner" (1943); "What's Coming is ... PLENTY!" (1943); "Think Big ..." (1944); "Postwarithmetic" (1944); and "The Challenge" (1945). The International Order Daughters of the Empire recognized discussion of the post-war as an opportunity to nominate the dominion for a greater role within the empire at war's end. See "Canada's Future Possibilities in Post-war Reconstruction as Suggested by an Englishwoman," *Echoes* 161 (Christmas 1940): 8; Velyien E. Henderson, comp., "Reconstruction: Resolutions of National Empire Study Committee," *Echoes* 166 (spring 1942): 24, 167; (summer 1942): 9, 45.

25 Mary Lowrey Ross, "A Reverent Ode to the Great Modern Goddess Panacea," SN, 29 Jan. 1944, 29.

26 John P. Kidd, "Planning the Community," *Food for Thought* 6 (Nov. 1945): 24.

27 "The Men Who Are Planning the World of Tomorrow" (1945); "'Caught Short' through Lack of Planning" (1945).

28 "Post-war Planner" (1943); "Are You a Post-war Planner?" (1945);
    "Young Man with a Plan" (1948)
29 Stanley McConnell, "The Menace of Collectivism," SN, 19 Sep. 1942),
    34; my italics. Illustrators producing editorial cartoons for *Saturday
    Night*'s business section, "Gold & Dross," imported or emulated the
    work of conservative British cartoonist David Low, ridiculing planning.
    Examples are "Better Get Ready to Turn Those Theories into Blueprints,
    Mister," SN, 18 Sep. 1943, 33; "Not So Nice for Him to Come Home
    to," SN, 18 March 1944, 33. Such material carried on well into peacetime
    in the pages of SN. A sampling: P.M. Richards, "Free Enterprise Must
    Plan Now," SN, 30 Jan. 1943, 34; Stanley McConnell, "The State: In
    Theory, Practice, Prospect," SN, 11 Nov. 1944, 20; C. Monte Roberts,
    "*Saturday Night* Presents Its Own Dictionary for Socialists," SN, 28 April
    1945, 41; Wilfrid Eggleston, "Do Most Canadians Really Want More
    Government Intervention?" SN, 12 April 1947, 8.
30 Bruce Hutchison, "Where Now, Canada?" *Maclean's*, 1 July 1942, 7, 38,
    50-1; "Planning Our Civilization," *Canadian Forum* (hereafter CF) 20
    (July 1940): 100-1; Fergus Glenn, "Anatomy of the Little Man," CF 25
    (Aug. 1945): 109-11; F.R. Scott, "Social Planning and the War," CF 20
    (Aug. 1940): 138-9.
31 "A New Approach," CF 21 (Sep. 1941): 166. "Planning Post-war
    Canada" began its run as a regular section in CF in April 1943.
32 L.C. Marsh, "Is National Planning a Threat to Democracy?" (prepared
    for *Citizens' Forum*, 3 Dec. 1947), UBC Archives, Leonard C. Marsh
    Papers, box 6, Broadcasts.
33 E.A. Corbett, "Director's Report" (1946), 7, NA, Records of the Wartime
    Information Board, RG 36/31, vol. 14, file 8-20-1, Canadian Association
    for Adult Education.
34 CAAE, "Report of the Proceedings of a Special Programme Committee of
    the Canadian Association for Adult Education," 27-31 Dec. 1942: 4,
    Archives of Ontario (AO), CAAE Papers, series B-I, box 3, *Citizens'
    Forum*, administrative, 1943-60.
35 John L. McDougall, *The Foundations of National Well-Being – Post-war*
    (Kingston, 1944), 10.
36 John Coulter, "Books and Shows," talk no. 7, first series, broadcast 28
    July 1942: 6, McMaster University Archives, John Coulter Papers, box
    36, f. 1.
37 *Transit through Fire*, words by John Coulter and music by Healey Willan
    (Toronto: Macmillan, 1942), 1.
38 Ibid., 6.
39 Ibid., 8; Elizabeth Wyn Wood, "A National Program for the Arts in
    Canada," *Canadian Art* 1 (Feb.-March 1944): 93-4.
40 "Canadian Criticism," SN, 27 Nov. 1943, 3.

41 John Coulter, "Books and Shows," talk no. 7, second series, broadcast 5 January 1943, 2–3,McMaster University Archives, John Coulter Papers, box 36, f. 2.

42 A.S.P. Woodhouse et al., "Remaining Material," *University of Toronto Quarterly*, 11 (April and July 1942): 347.

43 Watson Thomson, "Adult Education and the Crisis of Democracy," *Public Affairs* 6 (winter 1943): 133–4. Thanks to Nancy Christie for this reference.

44 John Baldwin, "Approach to Reconstruction," SN, 24 Oct. 1942, 28.

45 Father M.M. Coady, "Blueprinting Post-War Canada," *Culture* 4 (1943): 161–71.

46 Quotation from E.A. Corbett, "Adult Education," typescript (1938), 5, NA, R.A. Sim Papers, vol. 11, file 11; see number 6 in the CAAE's "Live and Learn" series: John Macdonald, *The Corner Stone of Democracy: The Discussion Group* (Toronto: Ryerson, 1939).

47 Frank Chamberlain, "The School of the Air," SN, 20 Sep. 1941, 16.

48 E.A Corbett, "Education by Radio," CF 18 (March 1939): 374–7. In Nova Scotia and Ontario, some educational organizations and extension departments had integrated listening groups with short broadcast series during the winter of 1938–39, including the Workers' Educational Association (WEA) program *Labour Forum* in Ontario. See David P. Armstrong, "Corbett's House: The Origins of the Canadian Association for Adult Education and Its Development during the Directorship of E.A. Corbett, 1936–1951" (MA thesis, University of Toronto, 1968), 110–12; "W.E.A. Radio Forum," *Adult Learning* 4 (Nov. 1939): 23–4. Michael Welton, "An Authentic Instrument of the Democratic Process: The Intellectual Origins of the Canadian Citizens' Forum," *Studies in the Education of Adults* 18 (April 1986): 35–49; Ronald L. Faris, "Adult Education for Social Action or Enlightenment? An Assessment of the Development of the Canadian Association for Adult Education and its Radio Forums from 1935–1952" (PhD diss., University of Toronto, 1971), chapters 2–5; Gordon Selman, *Adult Education in Canada: Historical Essays* (Toronto: Thompson Educational Publishing, 1995); Gerald Friesen, "Adult Education and Union Education: Aspects of English-Canadian Cultural History in the 20th Century," *Labour/Le Travail* 34 (fall 1994): 163–88.

49 Neil M. Morrison, "Community Problems," broadcast on CKUA and CFCN, 20 Nov. 1939. NA, Neil M. Morrison Papers, vol. 28; Armstrong, "Corbett's House," 112.

50 Ron Faris, *The Passionate Educators: Voluntary Associations and the Struggle for Control of Adult Educational Broadcasting in Canada, 1919–52* (Toronto: Peter Martin Associates, 1975), 99, 153. The show's regional predecessors, *Inquiry into Co-operation, Community Clinic,* and

Canadian Farm Problems, met with some success in organizing listening groups early in wartime. See John Nicol, Albert Shea, and G.J.P Simmins, *Canada's Farm Radio Forum* (Paris: UNESCO, 1954), 40–6; Marc Raboy, *Missed Opportunities: The Story of Canada's Broadcasting Policy* (Montreal and Kingston: McGill-Queen's University Press, 1990), 75.

51 Philippe J. Baillargeon, "The CBC and the Cold War Mentality, 1946–1952" (MA thesis, Carleton University, 1987), 18–24.

52 CAAE Council meeting, Toronto, 16 Nov. 1942. NA, CBC *Citizens' Forum*, vol. 1, file 2; italics added.

53 "Report of the Proceedings of a Special Programme Committee of the Canadian Association for Adult Education," 27–31 December 1942, 15, 28, NA, CBC *Citizens' Forum*, vol. 1, file 3.

54 Morley Callaghan to Watson Thomson, 5 Feb. 1943, and Inch to Hugh Morrison, 11 Feb. 1943, NA, CBC, vol. 187, file 11–18–5, part 4.

55 Topics included "The Last Peace and the Next One," "Are Wartime Controls Here to Stay?" and "Social Security – Housing." See "List of Participants in 'Of Things to Come'" spring series 1943, NA, CBC *Citizens' Forum*, vol. 1, file 9.

56 Responses to spring series, "OTTC", 1943; NA, CBC, vol. 186, file 11–18–5, part 1. Kathleen Strange, "Report No. 2," 8 March 1943, NA, Canadian Authors Association Papers, vol. 1, Manitoba.

57 E.A. Corbett to John Grierson, 22 April 1943, NA, Records of the Wartime Information Board, vol. 14, file 8–20–1.

58 H. McDonald, Crossfield, Alberta, to CBC, NA, CBC, vol. 186, file 11–18–5, part 1.

59 James S. Thomson, "The New Phase of Adult Education," address delivered at the Macdonald College Conference, 10 Sep. 1943: 12, NA, CBC *Citizens' Forum*, vol. 1, file 8.

60 Ibid., 14–19.

61 For a detailed description of the Liberal government's objections to the program's early format and some of its panelists, see Baillargeon, "The CBC and the Cold War Mentality," 28–32; Faris, *The Passionate Educators*, 104–8. See also "The Job Ahead," *Canadian Business* 17 (Jan. 1944): 17–18; and "Radio News and C.C.F.," *Ottawa Citizen*, 28 Feb. 1944, 3.

62 Grant's involvement in the project is best covered in William Christian's *George Grant: A Biography* (Toronto: University of Toronto Press, 1993), 96–102.

63 E.A Corbett to Col. G.G.D. Kilpatrick, 18 Jan. 1944. NA, CBC, vol. 187, file 11–18–5, part 3. Kilpatrick was director of education for the Department of National Defence (Army).

64 Violet Anderson, "*Citizens' Forum*s Breed Democracy in Canada," SN, 20 May 1944, 16.

65 George Grant to Harry Avison, 18 January 1944, 3, AO, CAAE Papers, series B-I, box 3.

66 "Report of the Proceedings of a Special Programme Committee of the Canadian Association for Adult Education," 30, in Huntington Cairns, Allen Tate, and Mark Van Doren, *Invitation to Learning* (New York: Random House, 1941).

67 "Memorandum from the General Supervisor of Programmes to the Board of Governors," 8 May 1944, cited in Faris, "Adult Education for Social Action or Enlightenment?" 293.

68 [Martyn Estall], "The War Has Changed Things," [1945], 2, 5, AO, CAAE Papers, series B-I, Box 3.

69 "Comments about 'Of Things to Come' from former McGill student, now Lieutenant in the Artillery." [1944], NA, CBC *Citizens' Forum*, vol. 1, file 10.

70 "Submission by the Canadian Council of Education for Citizenship." 16 Nov. 1945, NA, Wartime Information Board, vol. 14, file 8–20–3. Rev. F.W.L. Brailey estimated the number of organized listening groups at 1,450 "among civilians" during the first season; see F.W.L. Brailey, "Citizens' Forum in the Churches" [1944], 1, AO, CAAE Papers, series B-I, box 3, Citizen's Forum, administrative, 1943–60.

71 One report listed as members of a British Columbia group a doctor, a principal, a minister, a priest, a postmaster, a rancher, merchants, clerks, and housewives. An Ituna, Saskatchewan, group included three teachers, two druggists, a municipal secretary, an implement dealer, and two housewives. See Anderson, "*Citizens' Forum*s Breed Democracy in Canada," 16–17.

72 "Comments about 'Of Things to Come' from former McGill student, now Lieutenant in the Artillery," [1944]; Manitoba Citizens' Forum, "Survey Report," April 1946, AO, CAAE Papers, series B-I, box 3, Citizen's Forum, administrative, 1943–60.

73 George Grant, "*Citizens' Forum* – So Far," *Food for Thought* 4 (Nov. 1943): 20; "Report to the Executive of the C.A.A.E. on the Progress of Citizens' Forum," (1944), 2, AO, CAAE Papers, series B-I, box 3.

74 N.A.M. MacKenzie, "Canada and the Post War World," address before the Vancouver Canadian Club, 15 Sept. 1944, 3–4, University of British Columbia Archives, N.A.M. MacKenzie Papers, box 97, folder 1.

75 Wayne and Shuster's R.C.A. Victor Show, "Story of the CBC," CBC Trans-Canada Network, 24 October 1946, NA, Frank Shuster Papers, vol. 2.

76 J.R. Kidd, "Foreword," in Isabel Wilson, *Citizens' Forum: "Canada's National Platform"* (Toronto: Ontario Institute for Studies in Education, 1980); Faris, "Adult Education for Social Action or Enlightenment?" 336. William Brewer, "The Three Stages," *Reading* 1 (Feb. 1946): 32.

77 R.T. McKenzie, "Report on Citizens' Forum 1946–47," NA, CBC *Citizens'*

Forum, MG 28, I 400, vol. I, file 58, National Secretary's Report, 1946–47; Morley Callaghan, "Youth Suffer War's Aftermath," *New World*, Aug. 1945, 29–30.

78 Lorne Pierce, *The Beloved Community* (Toronto: Ryerson Press, 1925), 20.

79 Marcus Adeney, "Community Organization," CF 25 (Oct. 1945): 159, 162.

80 Barker Fairley, "Art – Canadians, for the Use of," *Canadian Affairs* 1 (1944): 7, 18.

81 "Early Lesson in Citizenship," *New World*, June 1945, 30.

82 "You and Me and Reconstruction," CBC *Discussion Club*, broadcast 28 Aug. 1942, NA, CAVA/AVCA, 1984–0164, ref copy at 1982–0043/63.

83 The "lighted schoolhouse" was an important element of the community centre movement. See Canadian Youth Commission, *Youth Challenges the Educators* (Toronto: Ryerson, 1946)

84 *Letter from Home! From a Soldier of 1914–19 to A Soldier of 1939–194?* (1943), University of Saskatchewan Archives, pamphlet LX-23.

85 "Of Things to Come," n.d. [1943], "Housing," broadcast from Halifax, NA, Morley Callaghan Papers, MG 30, D365, vol. 35, Transcripts.

86 Dr. E.G. Faludi, "Housing Is Science," SN, 15 Aug. 1942, 8.

87 F. Cyril James, "Stained Glass," address before the Royal Architectural Institute of Canada, 20 Feb. 1943, 5, McGill University Archives, F. Cyril James Papers, MG 1017, Addresses and Other Papers, 1943.

88 S.K. Jaffary, "The Social Services," in C.A. Ashley, ed., *Reconstruction in Canada* (Toronto: University of Toronto Press, 1943), 111.

89 Marius Barbeau, "Are the Real Folk Arts and Crafts Dying Out?" *Canadian Art* 5 (winter 1948): 128–33.

90 Blodwen Davies, "Quickening of the Arts in Canada," CF 26 (May 1946): 34, 36.

91 George E. Buckley to Reconstruction Committee, 20 June 1944, NA, RG 14, 1987–88/146 (39), Reconstruction, W-4. Buckley was president of the Theatre Guild of Saint John, NB.

92 Eric R. Arthur, "Town Planning and Tomorrow," *Food for Thought* 3 (April 1943): 6–7; Campbell Merrett, "Planning with the People," *Canadian Art* 3 (Oct.-Nov. 1945): 18–21.

93 Marcus Adeney, "Community Centres in Canada," *Journal of the Royal Architectural Institute of Canada* 22 (Feb. 1945): 22. The power of an anti-modern perspective in a postmodern society (capitalist modernity plus globalization, cybernetics, and fragmentation of traditional systems of meaning) is well discussed in Ian McKay's essay on the packaging of history in mid-twentieth-century Nova Scotia. See McKay, "History and the Tourist Gaze: The Politics of Commemoration in Nova Scotia, 1935–1964," *Acadiensis* 22 (spring 1993): 102–38.

94 Richard E. Crouch, "A Community Art Centre in Action," *Canadian Art* 2 (Oct.-Nov. 1944): 22–8; Paul Duval, "Arthur Lismer, Canadian Artist, Led World in Art Education," *SN,* 13 Oct. 1945, 24–5.

95 Adeney, "Community Centres in Canada," 23.

96 See especially chapter 7 of Jonathan Vance's *Death So Noble: Memory, Meaning and the First World War* (Vancouver: University of British Columbia Press, 1997). Vance notes on 204–5 that the impulses to build purely "aesthetic" or utilitarian monuments each had vocal support, a difference of opinions that could, in some cases, be overcome. On one aspect of the aesthetic style of monument, see Maria Tippett's aforementioned *Art at the Service of War.*

97 Adeney, "Community Centres in Canada," 23. See also Fred Lasserre and Gordon Lunan, "Community Centres," *Canadian Affairs* 2 (1945): 3–5; Fairley, "Art – Canadians, for the Use of." A detailed bibliography of reconstruction-era material on community centres in Canada, the United States, and Britain is James Dahir, comp., *Community Centers as Living War Memorials: A Selected Bibliography with Interpretive Comments* (New York: Russell Sage Foundation, 1946). See also George Mosse, *Fallen Soldiers: Reshaping the Memory of the World Wars* (Oxford: Oxford University Press, 1990). On commemoration generally, see John E. Bodnar, *Remaking America: Public Memory, Commemoration, and Patriotism in the Twentieth Century* (Princeton: Princeton University Press, 1992); Michael Kammen, *Mystic Chords of Memory: The Transformation of American Culture* (New York: Knopf, 1991).

98 R.A. Morton, "Culture in the Little Places," *New Trail* 4 (Jan. 1946): 18–20; Herman Voaden, "A National Arts Board," (1946), NA, H.R.C. Avison Papers, MG 30, D 102, vol. 6, file 30, CAAE, 1946; A.J. Arnold, "Movie Houses Destined to Be Club Centres," *SN,* 26 Jan. 1946, 16–17; Loosley, "Solving Community Problems," *Food for Thought* 10 (Dec. 1949): 17–21.

99 Martyn Estall, "Proposals for Government Action," (1946), NA, H.R.C. Avison Papers, MG 30, D 102, vol. 5, file 28, CAAE, 1946; "What about Our Cultural Resources?" *Citizens' Forum* Bulletin no. 10 (15 Jan. 1946), NA, Canada Foundation, MG 28 1179, vol. 25, file 4b, CBC, 1942–51.

100 David Murray, "Planned Recreation in Canada," *CF* 26 (July 1946): 84–5.

101 E.A. Corbett, "Proposals for Government Action to Assist Community Centres and Leisure-Time Programs in Canada," (1947), 7–8, NA, Records of the Wartime Information Board, RG 36/31, vol. 14, file 8–20–1, CAAE; Lawren Harris et al., "Community Art Centres," *Canadian Art* 2 (Dec. 1944–Jan. 1945): 62–3, 77, 85; Anthony Walsh, "Rehabilitation through Art and Handicrafts," *Canadian Art* 2

(summer 1945): 3–5, 38; Murray G. Ross, "The Community Centre Movement," *Food for Thought* 6 (Jan. 1946): 10–17; Canadian Youth Commission, *Youth & Recreation: New Plans for New Times* (Toronto: Ryerson, 1946); [H.R.C. Avison], "Memorandum re: Proposed Action by National Organizations in Recreation, Adult Education and the Arts towards a Federal Government Program on Community Centres and Community Leisure-Time Programs," (1946), NA, H.R.C. Avison Papers, MG 30, D 102, vol. 6, file 30, CAAE, 1946; Lionel Scott, "A Community Centre Plan that Works," *Food for Thought* 7 (April 1947): 9–13.

102 Corbett, "Proposals for Government Action to Assist Community Centres," 1–2, 7–8. On recapturing the fraternity that Canadian soldiers "knew overseas," see the issue on "Community Centres," *Canadian Affairs* 2 (1945): 2. On links between "popular" culture and delinquency a few years later, see James Gilbert, *A Cycle of Outrage: America's Reaction to the Juvenile Delinquent in the 1950s* (New York: Oxford University Press, 1986).

103 Adeney, "Community Centres," 21.

104 Paul Litt and Maria Tippett both cite the 1944 brief as a prominent wartime declaration of cultural activism. See Litt, *The Muses, the Masses and the Massey Commission*, 23–4; Tippett, *Making Culture*, 171–2.

105 Morley Callaghan, "If Civilization Must Be Saved," *SN*, 16 Dec. 1939, 6.

106 Elizabeth Wyn Wood, "A National Program for the Arts in Canada," *Canadian Art* 1 (Feb.-March 1944): 93–4.

107 The draft document was entitled "Suggestions for Increased Government Support of the Arts in Canada," (1944), NA, Canada Foundation, MG 28, 1179, vol. 20, file 3b, Arts and Letters Club, Toronto, 1944–66.

108 [Associated Arts Groups], "Brief Concerning the Cultural Aspects of Canadian Reconstruction," NA, RG 14, 1987–88/146 (39), Reconstruction, W-2; "Canadians Ask Cultural Freedom," *Canadian Author and Bookman* 20 (Dec. 1944): 10; reprinted from *Free World* (1944, issue unknown).

109 "Brief Concerning the Cultural Aspects of Canadian Reconstruction," 3.

110 Blodwen Davies, "Quickening of the Arts in Canada," *CF* 26 (May 1946): 34.

111 David Earl Lewis, "A Timid Renaissance," *Culture* 7 (1946): 48–53.

112 A.J.M. Smith, "Canadian Renaissance," *Canadian Author and Bookman* 22 (June 1946): 32; Blodwen Davies, "The Significance of UNESCO," *CF* 26 (Aug. 1946): 107–9; C.F. Fraser, "Canada and UNESCO," address at the National Conference of the Canadian Associa-

tion for Adult Education, Toronto, 26–29 May 1947, reprinted in *The Job Ahead in Adult Education* (Toronto: CAAE, 1947), 24–8; Coulter, "Books and Shows," talk no. 7, second series, 3.

113 Barker Fairley, "What Is Wrong with Canadian Art?" *Canadian Art* 6 (autumn 1948): 29.

114 Walter B. Herbert, "Some Thoughts on Canada's Cultural Situation," address before the Canadian Institute on Public Affairs, Geneva Park, Lake Couchiching, 16 Aug. 1947, NA, Canada Foundation, MG 28, 1179, vol. 2, file 5, articles concerning Canada Foundation.

115 A.L. Phelps, "Culture and Radio," address before the Royal Canadian Institute of Science, 1946, reprinted in *Canadian Author and Bookman* 22 (Dec. 1946): 49.

116 Samuel Roddan, "Writing in Canada," CF 26 No. 308 (Sept. 1946): 137.

117 "Brief Concerning the Cultural Aspects of Canadian Reconstruction," 4–5.

118 Walter B. Herbert, "An Acorn of Culture Is Planted on the Hill," *Ottawa Journal*, 29 June 1944, 4.

119 According to Herbert, £10,000 was made available in 1942 by a Michael Huxley for what became the Canadian Committee; see Herbert to Thomas A. Stone, 21 Oct. 1942, NA, Walter B. Herbert Papers, MG 30, D 205, vol. 1, Correspondence, 1942–44.

120 Walter B. Herbert, "A Ministry of Fine Arts: A Contrary View," [1944], 4, ibid., Addresses, Articles, and Lectures.

121 Walter B. Herbert to Paul Martin, 20 May 1944, NA, Canada Foundation, MG 28, 1179, vol. 20, file 3b, Arts and Letters Club, Toronto, 1944–66.

122 Arthur L. Neal, "Is Culture Business's Business?" *Canadian Business* 19 (Feb. 1946): 26–7, 104–5.

123 Herbert to Mrs John Bracken, 17 April 1946, NA, Canada Foundation, MG 28, 1179, vol. 25, file 4b, CBC, 1942–51.

124 "Project. Publication of a *Canadian Cultural Index,*" ibid., vol. 33, file 3, Cultural Index, 1947–48.

125 CAAE, "Building Community Programmes: Report of CAAE National Conference, Kingston, 20–24 May 1946," (1946), 4, NA, H.R.C. Avison Papers, MG 30, D 102, vol. 5, file 28, CAAE, 1946; "What Makes a Good Citizen?" SN, 20 Sept. 1947, 19.

126 F.M. Salter, "On the Other Hand," *New Trail* 4 (April 1946): 79.

127 Manitoba, *Report of the Manitoba Royal Commission on Adult Education* (Winnipeg: King's Printer, 1947), 10–11; Jack Sword, Manitoba Royal Commission on Adult Education, to S.D. Clark, 16 October 1945, University of Toronto Archives, S.D. Clark Papers, 1990–027, vol. 1. Thanks to Nancy Christie for this reference.

128 F. Cyril James, address during the radio intermission of Gounod's *Faust*, CBC, 30 Jan. 1943, McGill University Archives, F. Cyril James Papers, MG 1017, Addresses and Other Papers, 1943.

129 "Our Sleeves Are Now Rolled Up for Peace," *SN*, 26 Jan. 1946, 11.

130 Lister Sinclair, "Epitaph on a War of Liberation," CBC Trans-Canada network, broadcast 6 Jan. 1946, Concordia Centre for Broadcasting Studies, CBC Drama Collection, script M002571.

131 Faris, *The Passionate Educators*, 153.

132 C.J. Eustace, "Our New Middle-Class," *SN*, 20 Sept. 1947, 32.

133 Murray, "Planned Recreation in Canada," 84–5.

134 A.L. Phelps, "Culture and Radio," address before the Royal Canadian Institute of Science, 1946; reprinted in *Canadian Author and Bookman* 22 (Dec. 1946): 49.

135 Howard Y. McClusky, "The Job Ahead in Adult Education," address at the National Conference of the Canadian Association for Adult Education, Toronto, 26–29 May 1947; reprinted in *The Job Ahead in Adult Education* (Toronto: CAAE, 1947), 24.

136 John Grierson, "Education and the New Order," address at the closing banquet of the CAAE annual convention, Winnipeg, 31 May 1941, 11, McGill University Archives, John Grierson Collection, MG 2067, container 4, file 110.

NANCY CHRISTIE

"Look out for Leviathan"[1]

The Search for a Conservative Modernist Consensus

It is the turn away from the old ideas and non-arrival of a new and accepted philosophy of society which explains our era. Something is striving to be born.

Arthur Lower, 1945[2]

In January 1956 W.O. Fennell delivered a speech to a round-table session sponsored by the Workers' Education Association of the University of Toronto entitled "Soviet Materialism versus American Materialism." Fennell diagnosed what he believed to be the central problems of modern society. The relentless search for economic prosperity, combined with the growth of scientific rationalism in both government and business, had, in his estimation, eroded spiritual values that he identified as the essence of individual self-identity and true democracy. So dominant did he consider the convergence of materialism and social engineering that "even in the intimate realms of pesonal relations" were human values and desires externally dictated by the laws of the marketplace.[3]

Although Fennell's address was given at the session on "The Cold War and History," it cannot simply be read as a response to the threat of Marxism or as a critique of American mass culture, like that offered by the Massey Commission.[4] Rather, the genesis of this critique of post-war Canadian society lay in the political and cultural dynamics of the war and its immediate aftermath, when a group of university educators and church leaders, self-proclaimed traditional elites and makers of public opinion, declared their opposition to the modern social security state and its corollary: policy-making by a minority of technocratic experts. Thus in his 1945 analysis of recent social trends,

written for the Canadian Youth Commission, Arthur Lower, professor
of history at United College, University of Manitoba, and an influential lay member of the United Church Commission on the Church,
Nation and World Order, spoke of the weakening of an individualist
ethos. The principal symptoms of this, Lower discerned, were the
decay of a middle-class Protestantism as a result of the incursions of
"lower-class" emotional revivalist sects; the increasing materialism of
Canadian life, wherein work and material success defined one's character; and the diminishing of hierarchical notions of both society and
family as a result of the rights-based language of welfare liberalism.[5]
What was under debate was not simply what Robert Warren of the
Institute of Advanced Study at Princeton University described to
Harold Innis as the dialectic between "the state" and "free enterprise."[6] Certainly, historians of high politics have defined the parameters of post-war reconstruction in Canada around this axis.[7] However,
when viewed from the perspective of contemporary commentators
who considered the impact of modern social security planning, the
implications were much more decisive and far-reaching. Church
leaders such as C.E. Silcox and Gordon Sisco and university educators
such as Harold Innis, Norman McKenzie, S.D. Clark, and the young
Northrop Frye, all of whom were later associated with the Massey
Commisson, maintained that the spectre of state growth had negative
implications for the role of church and university in society, for traditional hierarchies both in terms of the role of educated elites and in
terms of the status of the male breadwinner within the family, for the
relationship between economic and spiritual or humanistic values, and
for the pre-eminence of individual liberty and human agency within
Canadian society.

What was under debate was the very definition of liberal democracy.
Was it to be a mass democracy ruled by the vagaries of majority rule
and the propaganda of political polls and lobby groups, or was it to be
a democratic state in which the university and the church mediated
policy-making and where voters respected the pronouncements of a
selfless educated "intelligentsia" (a word first commonly used in
Canada in this period)? Was Canada to be a nation whose values were
formulated by secular, scientistic experts, or were its values to be
shaped in the traditional bosom of church and family? In short, these
critics of modern trends were searching for a new intellectual synthesis
that could rationally challenge the threat of statism, so that their cultural authority and the set of values it represented might be preserved
during a period of fractious transition. These questions about the function of religion and the church vis-à-vis the state, the way to preserve
and heighten the freedom of individuals and human values in an

increasingly bureaucratic society, and how best to define democracy in a world of mass politics and mass culture formed some of the major cultural and social fault lines of the post-war discussion about the state.

For the most part, the social analyses of these older elites were merely reactive in so far as conservative post-war commentators believed that the creation of a modern welfare state by expert planners represented an abrupt and complete rejection of the Canadian past, for they commented frequently that the end of the war marked the end of the "old culture," wherein traditional verities were replaced by unrest and uncertainty. But the social diagnosis offered by these church and university leaders was not simply a retreat into a reflexive traditionalism or a timorous nostalgia, for in presenting an individualist counterpoint to the centralized welfare state, they were elaborating a quintessentially modern view of citizenship in which the locus of identity and values rested with the individual. No longer was the ideal of good citizenship founded upon one's participation in the public sphere; now it revolved principally around one's personal conduct within the private sphere of the family. Nationalism was not expressed in terms of race, language, or other group loyalties; rather, it was defined in largely psychological terms, as akin to one's personal search for identity. According to Arthur Lower, then, national problems could be defused and solved only through the creation of a collective "esprit de corps" which resulted from individual citizens "finding themselves."[8] The consensus that reached its apogee with the Massey Commission in 1951 is best labelled a conservative modernism. It is only through this definition that we can make sense of what appear to be conflicting imperatives in the thought of Lower, who at the conclusion of World War II both condemned the shedding of old values and at the same time called for a loosening of the shackles of the past so that Canadian society could experience a new renaissance.[9] In the end, for these conservative modernists, the decade between 1943 and 1953 was not one of consensus and stability, as historians have portrayed it, but one characterized by liminality, anxiety, and a constant striving for an undefinable and unknowable utopia.[10]

The publication of the Marsh Report in 1943 was the primary catalyst undergirding the reorientation in the thought of both the United Church of Canada and university educators. In March of 1943 Leonard Marsh released his *Report on Social Security for Canada*, which synthesized for Canadian conditions the social security blueprint outlined by Sir William Beveridge in England for a comprehensive state welfare scheme aimed at protecting an individual from the "cradle to the grave."[11] What was noteworthy about the creation of this now-famous report from the perspective of the United Church leadership is that it included no members of any of the mainline Protestant churches. Where previously the promoters of social Christianity within the United Church had assumed that the interests and outlook of the church and government were similar and that the church in fact functioned as the primary mediator between the individual and the state, the glaring absence of any church leaders who could speak to the issue of the preservation of spiritual values within the post-war world engendered a new pessimism among church leaders about the prospective authority both of the institutional church and of ethical values within post-war reconstruction.

The United Church quickly set about articulating its own program of reconstruction as a rejoinder to this supposed "secularization of the social services"[12] by the Mackenzie King government. In the very month that the Marsh Report was released, the church unveiled its own panel of experts, namely, the Commission on the Church, Nation and World Order (CNWO). While its secretary, Gordon Sisco, made a show of inviting high profile figures such as the Queen's political economist W.A. Mackintosh and Leonard Marsh himself onto the commission, as well as former members of the left-leaning Fellowship for a Christian Social Order, such as Eugene Forsey, the chief agenda of the CNWO was to thwart the growth of the progressive reformist wing of the church and thus undermine the very concept of a "full-orbed Christianity" which had traditionally seen the consonance between the ideals of church and state. Indeed, according to Sisco, any interconnection between religious and economic views must be interpreted as a dangerous left-wing extremism.[13] To this end, the commission accorded prominence to the views of businessmen such as William H. Birks and right-wing accountants such as Hugh Wolfenden, and to clerics and laymen such as the Reverend Harvey Forster and Arthur Lower, who eschewed the central tenets of social Christianity because it tended to enhance collaboration with political economists, labour unions, and social reform organizations, which would "compromise our [Christian] idealism to the level of those who have a secular outlook."[14]

The very terms of the commission were intended to marginalize the advice of older advocates of Christian social reform such as the Reverend J.R. Mutchmor, who continued to advocate close ties with organized labour on such issues as family allowances, or that of active church laymen such as N.J. McLean of Canada Packers or H.M. Tory of Carleton College, who both believed that the United Church should draw up its own program regarding welfare reform in order that it could continue to influence public opinion outside church quarters.[15] From the point of view of Gordon Sisco, the church's realm was distinct from that of the policy-making imperatives of government experts, but what he defined as the church's contribution to reconstruction was a far cry from the broader social and cultural implications of social Christianity as it had been defined prior to World War II. According to Sisco and like-minded anti-progressives within the United Church, the church could speak only within the terms of "its own distinctive revelation,"[16] by which they meant a decidedly more privatized religion, where the Gospels provided guidance only in terms of personal conduct. Having redefined the church's social role in such constricted terms, Sisco accordingly eschewed any references in the final report of the commission which might propose any political or economic solutions, preferring merely to enunciated specific "spiritual needs" and a strong assertion of "moral law."[17]

In the view of United Church leaders, the church in modern society was a beleaguered institution in a world of "secularism and materialism,"[18] and consequently they firmly rejected any dialogue with other institutions, but especially the state. Where in earlier decades religious leaders such as C.E. Silcox and Hugh Dobson had conceived of society as "an organic whole" defined broadly by a religious outlook, they now defined the state and society as "an economic machine,"[19] a repository of purely secular values whose goals were consciously antagonistic to the church. As Silcox announced his CBC International radio address in the 1950s: "We believe that the churches must be free to be the conscience and soul of the nation; when they are bound to the government they become the echo of the politicians and the nation is in grave danger of losing both its conscience and its soul."[20] For unlike the pre-war advocates of social Christianity, who optimistically believed that the values of the church suffused the wider society, postwar conservative Protestants maintained that the churches were, with the growth of state planning, in the "bondage of paganism."[21] Their solution was to define a culture of separate spheres in which the church could remain supreme as a function of its autonomy from the state.

The preoccupation that Protestant leaders evinced about the issue of secular values in the wake of the publication of the Marsh Report and the increasing bifurcation that they elucidated between church and state was not entirely a symptom of the exclusion of church leaders from the social security planning process. Even university political economists such as Harold Innis who had been courted by Leonard Marsh[22] found themselves traversing a similar intellectual terrain. Like the pre-war Protestant church leaders, Innis had been nourished in a cultural environment that interpreted society and culture in organic terms, whereby religion was seen as the basis of all social thought and action. From this perspective, the study of political economy, sociology, and anthropology were sciences that naturally furthered, rather than impeded, the search for human values. In this context, Innis envisioned the social sciences as the "handmaidens" of the humanities. In his ideal society, institutions such as the university, government, and the church remained in equipoise because they were similarly animated by common Christian ideals.[23] The exigencies of wartime government centralization, together with the apparent wholesale co-optation of university political economists into the federal bureaucracy, was seen by Innis as a betrayal of this creed. Indeed, it was the supposed eradication of this organic view of culture perpetrated by the Liberals' emulation of technocratic policy-making that induced the Dalhousie political scientist R.A. MacKay to argue that the church must retreat from economic issues to focus upon policy options from "a moral, humanitarian, and probably religious basis." Similarly, Lower championed a much narrower compass for church authority, stating that the United Church could speak only to "the Church constituency" and thus treat only "the fundamental religious convictions."[24] It was the growth of state apparatus in wartime, therefore, which impelled Lower to reject the organic synthesis between religion and reform, and which precipitated his retreat towards private religion and a definition of individualism in terms of control from within, rather than reformation through external controls.[25]

Innis and his colleagues, such as the McMaster political economist Humphrey Michell and E.J. Urwick, the former head of the Department of Political Economy at the University of Toronto, all railed against the increased centralization of government. However, the focal point of their attack was the blatant incursion of government into the universities, which so overtly transformed the social sciences into appendages of the state and thus wrested them from their moorings in their traditional nexus of history and values.[26] Certainly, much of Innis's complaining that the social sciences were becoming overly presentist in their bias was due to his fear that their function in terms of government policy-making might detract from the intellectual authority of his own historicist approach. Likewise, his fear that the social sciences were becoming divorced from the humanities may have had roots in his annoyance that federal conscription policies had severely diminished student numbers in the humanities disciplines. Despite his personal animus against the syphoning off of his teaching staff to Ottawa, Innis and his colleagues saw in centralized planning by technocrats a dangerous tendency to rule by a minority. In his famous diatribe against modern policy-making, "Political Economy and the Modern State," Innis argued that once the social sciences became mere tools of government, the nature of the discipline was irrevocably transformed, so that students were taught methods but were not taught to think. Moreover, once social scientific practice became untethered from a broader system of values, not only was individualism undermined, but the wider public would remain uneducated and unthinking, thus leading to a "tyranny of opinion" wielded by a group of intellectually and spiritually sterile bureaucrats and pollsters.[27] As a result of wartime planning, Innis became active in the adult education and municipal reform movements, which he saw as necessary prophylactics against totalitarian government; for in his view, only in smaller communities would voluntary citizenship and a spirit of civic obligation reinforce human values, individual freedom, and a thoughtful democracy.[28] And just as conservative United Church leaders reacted to the modern state by calling for a retreat to private religion, so conservative social scientists such as Innis and R.A. MacKay preached the segregation of their disciplines from state control. And although both conservative social scientists and church leaders were engaged in a common mission to restore human or spiritual values against the incursions of what they now defined as a secular state, theirs was not a mere quest for traditionalism; for in the process of resisting state centralization, they abandoned their older commitment to social organicism in positing a conflictual relationship between church, university, and the state. And in their effort to resurrect a system of values, these thinkers unwittingly stood in the vanguard of a cultural modernism by centring a concept of post-war social analysis around the figure of the individual personality.[29]

The introduction of family allowance legislation by the Mackenzie King Liberals in 1944 elicited an immediate storm of protest, not least because it was a cynical political move, but one which, because of its widespread appeal to anti-poverty constituencies, pronatalist groups, and champions of child protection, as well as exponents of full employment and Keynesian fiscal management, was difficult to combat.[30] Even Alberta premier Ernest Manning confided to Charlotte Whitton, one of the most vociferous opponents of the legislation, that family allowances were a bad issue upon which to fight centralization of government.[31] The opponents of a government-funded system of family allowances fought its implementation either by arguing that it would not relieve family poverty or that it would fail to enhance purchasing power because it would result in heavier taxation for middle-class purchasers, depending respectively on their political allegiance to either the left or the right.[32]

However, the most politically explosive and effective attack revolved around the population question. The United Church minister C.E. Silcox, an ally of both Charlotte Whitton and Ontario premier George Drew, emerged as the leader of the campaign against family allowances on the basis that they would dramatically increase the population of Quebec. Prior to the war, Silcox had, as the head of the Social Service Council of Canada, been a consistent exponent of greater ties between church and government and had even been favourable to a policy of family allowances. In a 1941 article entitled "Why Anti-Semites Hate Christ: A Study in Hitleresque Pathology," he called for greater government control of the economic structure for in his view, "All modern philanthropy, social service and even social security rest ultimately upon the validity of this faith in the graciousness of God."[33] Confidently believing that the Protestant denominations would remain at the fulcrum of the democratic process because of their vast cultural authority, he confidently advocated a coalition with Roman Catholic and Jewish religious groups in the early years of the war. A series of skirmishes during the war heightened tensions between Protestantism and Roman Catholicsm. Nevertheless, Silcox remained commited to the ideal of Catholic-Protestant cooperation on social problems, even in the wake of the conscription crisis. This spirit of cooperation was, however, irrevocably shattered and replaced by an attitude of irreconcilable difference with the implementation of family allowance legislation. Because family allowances defined welfare entitlements in terms of the number of children within a family, rabid and even lukewarm Protestants protested that King had been the dupe of a conspiracy organized by the Roman Catholic hierarchy and that the primary intent of the legislation was to promote population growth in Quebec.[34] In the wake of the introduction of family allowances, a concerted backlash ensued among what the McMaster political economist W. Burton Hurd called "Imperialistic-Anglo-Orange" Ontarians, those politically linked to the extreme Toryism of George Drew, who shrilly condemned government subsidies for "propagating the species in isolationist-Catholic-French-Canada."[35]

While it is not surprising to hear virulent Drewites such as C.E. Silcox and Charlotte Whitton fulminating about how family allowances were encouraging Quebec women to become "breeding machines"[36] and how they were a mere political gambit to siphon off federal funds to Quebec,[37] what is particularly significant is that the population debate precipitated by King's family allowance legislation impelled many Liberals and traditionally anti-Drewite Conservatives towards an increasingly antithetical positiion vis-à-vis the Roman Catholic Church and Quebec. Carl Berger has argued that the conscription crisis contributed to the increasing tendency to view French and English Canada as two solitudes.[38] The implementation of a government system of family allowances in 1944, in turn, transformed wartime anti-Catholic and anti-French-Canadian attitudes into new battle lines between the sacred and the secular, in which anti-Catholicism became absorbed into a broader critique of the modern state. Once government-funded family allowances became a reality, the established rhetoric that had previously surrounded the spectre of centralized government was sharpened into a strident and comprehensive attack on Catholicism, which now became overtly identified with totalitarianism and secularization. For those, such as Harold Innis, Arthur Lower, and C.E. Silcox, who had redefined the relations between church and state in terms of a retreat into privatized religion, the ostensible new union of the state and the Roman Catholic Church was interpreted as a decided threat to Protestant authority. Thus Lower identified the primary antithesis of Canadian life as that between Protestant individualism and Catholic statism, or what he privately called Catholic "fascist authoritarianism."[39] Protestants such as Harold Innis, whose anti-Catholicism had remained latent even in the wake of the conscription crisis, had by 1944–45 shifted inexorably towards the Silcox-Drew position of identifying Catholicism – what Silcox termed "totalitarian sacerdotalism"[40] – as the principal symbol of the expansion of an oppressive state bureaucracy and a metaphor for the erosion of individualism and democracy in Canadian life.[41]

The dominant aspect of post-war social analysis was the emphasis that church leaders and university educators placed upon the theme of family and domesticity. There is no doubt that the rhetoric about the family took many forms immediately after the war and that part of the immense focus upon home was the result of an intense yearning for stability after decades of depression and war, as Doug Owram has hypothesized.[42] However, if a vague search for stability and normalcy was the primary impetus behind the turn to domesticity, why did family values not become the fulcrum of social analysis among church reformers following World War I? While it is true that war greatly disrupted traditional family patterns, in so far as there was an escalation in the rates of family desertion and divorce, Owram's explanation is far too general to account for the dramatic and persistent theme of the family in the discourse of post-war elites.

Indeed, the rhetoric about the family was not simply "romantic" and nostalgic; rather, it was very specific in its aim. According to conservative analysts, the "totalitarian" social security state had given priority to economic definitions of security at the expense of traditional spiritual values, and more troubling still, post-war welfarism defined social citizenship in terms of social rights and thus underscored the obligation of the individual to the state at the expense of one's traditional obligations to family and community. The central dynamic of post-war social commentary, therefore, was the juxtaposition between the family and the state. Accordingly, critics of the modern state articulated their societal ideal as one in which all cultural values were built outwards from the domestic unit, where the emphasis upon character and the spiritual life would enhance the tendency towards voluntarism, inner directedness as opposed to conformity, and where the homogenizing attributes of the private family or a Christian "way of life" functioned as a consensualism founded upon the integrated individual "personality" and a panacea that would remedy the "troubled and tempestuous" interracial and interclass strife which was being fostered by state welfarism. Thus the family was both the "key to democracy" and the precondition of the "integration of society."[43] According to this strain of post-war analysis, the prescription for common values and ideological accord – and as Lower so often stated, the very basis of a renewed nationalism[44] – lay not with political and economic citizenship but with private "cultural" values, in that quintessential watchword of the post-war era, the Canadian "way of life."[45]

When Silcox condemned the King Liberals for erecting welfare programs that substituted "social security for salvation, economics for philosophy, sociology for theology," his remedy was to jettison social Christian reformism in favour of emulating home life as the means to definitively safeguard his notion of individual spiritual citizenship from the secularizing tendencies of modern statism.[46] Likewise, Hugh Dobson blamed Beveridge's blueprint for post-war planning for "this shift of the family associations from the home to the community, from the cradle to the grave," which resulted in the destruction of "the binding ties of the family."[47] What Silcox and Dobson were actually criticizing was that, in their estimation, the federal government had drastically reformulated the primary function of the family from one defined by spiritual and affectional ties to one defined by economic values. They argued that the welfare package proposed by Leonard Marsh had redefined the notion of family security wholly in terms of state economic support, and with its overweening emphasis upon economic prosperity, it had seemingly redefined the Canadian social landscape in terms of materialistic values. Thus Gwyneth Howell, an old-style social reformer and the assistant director of the Montreal Council of Social Agencies, critized Marsh's social security report because it placed a priority on physical welfare rather than on the emotional, moral, and spiritual stability of family life.[48] Similarly, Silcox tried to circumvent the social vision of the economic experts by proclaiming that economic security could never truly stabilize family life, for the essence of family unity rested upon firmer foundations, namely, the "imperatives of moral responsibility."[49]

It was this reformulation of family and society in terms of economic security rather than spiritual stability which esssentially provoked the overwhelming backlash against the state by United Church clergymen. It was this government transgression to which clergymen alluded when they argued that the "acids of modernity" had begun to corrode the family, for they believed that the preservation of Christian values, and thus ultimately the public authority of Protestantism, rested upon the reinforcement of that intimate connection between marriage, family, and evangelicalism that had been traditionally viewed as the inviolable terrain of church governance.[50] According to Silcox, it was the invasion of the family by state authorities through education, family allowances, and civil marriages that was the primary catalyst for "modern secularization,"[51] for by asserting that "all problems are essentially economic," the state was allowing materialism and hedonism to penetrate into the home"[52] through state welfare protection from the cradle to the grave. If the moral and spiritual determinants of society were to continue to reign supreme over the merely economic and political, it was incumbent that the church more forcefully promote "the rights of personality and the family as against the absolute value of the state."[53]

The immediate post-war preoccupation with redefining the family as a haven for individual self-worth and the development of character-building and conduct was not simply a response to fears raised by divorce, delinquency, and the pursuit of sexual pleasure by working-class youth;[54] rather, Protestant clergymen and university commentators stressed the private realm of the family and its role in building spirituality and character because it was a powerful counterweight to the rights-based, econocentric vision of society promoted by the modern social security state. When Arthur Lower, like other opponents of the state, excoriated the modern tendency towards hedonism and the new paganism of sex indulgence, he was not merely referring to "delinquency"; rather, he took aim at the encouragement of large families by the new family allowance legislation as part of his general critique of the excessive turn to materialism by government handouts.[55] Likewise, Lower inveighed against any form of social insurance, because it covered up a deeper selfish materialism "with fine phrases" such as "a high standard of living." Where some Protestant laymen such as Gregory Vlastos saw in the promise of material wealth through state management of employment and welfare a solvent that might smooth out social conflict between the classes and resolve the French-English antagonism, Lower recoiled from any nationalist "renaissance" that might tend to uphold collectivism, by which he meant state control of Canadian spiritual values.[56] Thus Lower roundly castigated the Keynesian notion of full employment, a generally innocuous policy that effectively won widespread support among Canadians and even conservative businessmen, because, in his view, it focused the mind too much upon the notion of prosperity at the expense of "fundamental religious convictions."[57] Likewise, Harold Innis made circuitous connections between Keynesian economic policies, the increase in hedonism, the neglect of cultural factors in Canadian life, and the diminution of the humanities within scholarly precincts.[58]

Where in Australia the figure of the consumer was central to a wider post-war project to reclaim citizenship from the terrain of state planning because it was associated with individual identity, women, and private spaces,[59] in Canada the opposite obtained. Here, because a state-funded system of family allowances was celebrated by the King Liberals as the chief means by which to ensure post-war employment, the rhetoric of post-war abundance was ineluctably associated with a statist vision of economic citizenship. Conservative critics thus objected to debates surrounding the standard of living issue, not because they rejected the notion of an adequate living wage or were necessarily anti-labour, but because they associated prosperity with government control and thus moral laxity. Arthur Lower, for example, made no telling distinction between state welfare funding to families, the excesses of materialism, the secularization of Canadian culture, the growing trend towards divorce, and faith in gadgets, for all evinced a much more troubling declension into amoral selfishness.[60] Lower and his colleagues took aim at the goal of government policies, namely, prosperity itself, rather than the means by which full employment was brought about. In other words, Canadian post-war opponents of managerial reform failed to distinguish between economic recovery by the state and that brought about as a result of the normal workings of the marketplace. In this case, their critique of state welfarism was but a touchstone for a broader condemnation of materialism, and as a result, the remedy they offered was both extremist and antediluvian.

In his submission to the United Church Commission on the Church, Nation and World Order, E.W. White forcefully criticized technocratic government planning, for in emulating the scientific outlook as well as removing the fear of poverty, the modern social security state had ushered in "a moral degradation ... that was as great as the prosperity that produced it. It was checked by adversity."[61] Significantly, White's diagnosis of the pathology of post-war materialism was not singular but one repeated by a range of United Church clergy and laymen. No better benchmark of the conflation between social conservatism, anti-statism, and neo-orthodoxy can be offered than the lucubrations of Arthur Lower on the issue of the declension of liberalism before the utopian excesses of state-funded materialism, written in 1943 in the wake of the Marsh Report:

It is proper to envisage the goal at which we aim but again I question whether it is the business of the Christian Church to depict that goal in the colours of worldly well-being. It seems to me that one of the chief functions of the Church is to remind mankind *that no easy solutions may be expected, that a facile materialism is no answer to life's problems.* Surely all history cries aloud against perfectionist hopes. Our creed is founded upon a Man of Sorrows and I suspect that in the future as in the past man will be born to trouble as the sparks fly upward. History states rather clearly that man's lot is tragic – and therefore noble – not easy. It seems to me the Church does itself much harm by standing for easy and materialistic solutions, as if Heaven were just around the corner. I would rather see it take courage to proclaim the essentially tragic character of life and further encourage to assert that *unless there were this tragic character in our lives we would not amount to very much and not be the first of creatures.*[62]

Lower has been often characterized by his defenders as an advanced liberal because of his advocacy of civil liberties during World War II.[63] However, a close analysis of his social views during the post-war era reveals a more conservative wellspring for his definition of individual freedom. As historians have observed, the reification of the individual was a particular feature of post-war culture and was symbolized by the rediscovery of biography and the history of ideas in historical writing and by the predominance of psychological analysis and psychiatry following the war, to cite just a few examples, while the term "personality," by which one meant the fully socialized or integrated individual, was a watchword of the 1950s.[64] Indeed, other important keywords such as "freedom," "democracy," "morality," and "nationalism" became once again intimately connected with the ideal of the singular individual. What must be stressed, however, is that the notion of individualism was itself a very contested term, especially in the decade immediately following World War II, when a conservative consensus was still in the making and when a firm notion of voluntary citizenship connected to the private realm of the family was still an important cultural territory being carved out of older concepts of communitarian liberalism, which had seen the liberation of the human personality in terms of one's participation in the civic polity. Where early twentieth-century New Liberal social thinkers had envisioned a natural consonance between the individual and the wider society, in which the notion of society itself incorporated within its boundaries a concept of the state,[65] post-war liberals' concept of the individual conscience took on rigour only when it was tethered to this anti-statist and anti-secularist perspective. But by so doing, Lower and other post-war conservatives helped to redefine the modern, privatized individual whereby the "conscience of the sincere individual"[66] operated outside the gaze of the state.

In some respects it might be argued that Lower and his conservative colleagues were clear anti-modernists because they wished to turn the tide away from new pathways of social citizenship established by the modern state. It is true that post-war social conservatives hoped to reorient concepts of identity and nationalism back to their moorings in the voluntaristic community and away from the coercive state. Hence Lower constantly employed the term "community" rather than "citizenship" when describing the new post-war nationalism, for he wished to underscore the relationship between values and voluntarism which he hoped would become a counterweight to the technocratic statism, in which individual free will was eradicated by government paternalism. In a similar vein, C.E. Silcox reflected in "The Future of Patriotism" that "the very concept of the welfare state tends to shift responsibility away from the individual to the impersonal society."[67] In addition, the new emphasis that state welfarism placed upon one's right to a higher standard of living, Silcox believed, would only result in greater conflict between classes, races, and nations, who must now fight to maintain "their alleged rights."[68] Lower also feared a new definition of state patriotism, for it invited lobby groups representing pluralist social groups to directly influence government and thus circumvent the church's traditional role as the primary mediator between the individual and the state. As a corrective to these tactics of a new mass democracy and the consequent loss of "values," Lower advocated a notion of psychological nationalism that highlighted an inner-directed (Christian) and individualized concept of collective identity, one that was ideally formed within the private realm of the family. Therefore the post-war definition of the socialized individual was not one in which his or her identity was enriched through participation in a wider civic sphere, as liberal thinkers had traditionally maintained, for in the view of Lower and Silcox, the civic public was no longer independent. Rather, it had been absorbed into the polity via the modern culture of rights implied by the new politics of mass democracy.

In this regard, Lower even rejected recommendations by colleagues for a form of business corporatism as a counterweight to state planning, for not only did corporatism emulate economic values, but it would also enlist the "action by interest groups" that Lower identified with rights-based or "intense individualism."[69] Believing that the principles of social cohesion must be located outside the larger entities of race, religion, and "interested political sentiments," post-war conservative thinkers postulated an ideal of the inner-directed, selfless, dutiful individualism, which was nourished wholly outside long-held notions of what constituted the public. In post-war Canada, conservatives placed voluntarist organizations in their definition of the public, which also included governmental institutions, thus leaving the family as the truly private space. According to this outlook, the modern individual was largely defined in terms of an inner-directedness closely identified with Christian values and notions of moral conduct; thus it was believed that these attributes could be nourished only within the private sphere of the home. By thus highlighting the family as a haven for Christian, individual, and democratic values, Canadian post-war conservatives were attempting to formulate a concept of citizenship and social consensus that obviated the need for state intrusion and the pluralism of modern mass democracy, and in so doing, they were overturning older communitarian definitions of individualism. As a reaction against the modern state-defined vision of welfare rights, post-war conservatives were instrumental in refuting older organic notions of the social and national, and though they did so through a decidedly conservative lens, their ideal of the privatized family, voluntary citizenship, and the inner-directed personality placed them in the slipstream of a modernist current.

At the centre of Lower's animus against the modern state was the fact that it promoted the notion of individual *rights*, which flew in the face of his desire to conceive of social consensus in terms of an individual's duties and obligations. To combat this "excess individualism," he recommended marriage and a stable married life, where obligations between kith and kin could be reinforced.[70] What Lower, C.E. Silcox, and Hugh Wolfenden meant when they fulminated about the the modern state denigrating individualism was, in actual fact, a plea for a return to an era of self-help and individual responsibility. Reacting against the new form of social citizenship incorporated in the Marsh Report, the accountant Wolfenden informed Gordon Sisco in 1943 that "too much of our modern economic thinking is predicated on the assumption that every man has a whole set of inalienable 'rights.'"[71] In a similar vein, Lower criticized the ordinary "petty bourgeoisie, the lower middle classes," whose desire for immediate material gratification through purchasing a house, refrigerator, and "nice radio" had compelled them to be duped by the materialistic hopes held out by the placebo of government-engineered prosperity. As a remedy to this modern emphasis upon wish-fulfillment, especially the desire for security, Lower recommended a return to the stern drive of puritanism, which, he argued, was embodied in the figure of the duty-bound, hard-working pioneer, the immigrant, and the farmer.[72] The only prophylactic against the incursions of modern rights-based citizenship was the development of a "religious sense of mutual responsibility,"[73] and the primary site for the development of this socially integrative force of obligation and interdependence was not government-planned prosperity but the home. All the attributes of citizenship, social planning, individual responsibility, and productivity were believed to emanate principally from the private sphere. The traditional vision of the interdependent family economy was resurrected in wartime but its social context was quite novel, for now it functioned as a counterweight to the impersonal nature of state planning and its consumptionist politics. Thus Frank Fidler wrote in 1943 that "children who help to plan the family economies required in every home today are learning to participate actively in a realistic form of social planning. Even the six-year-old who purchases *saving* stamps with his pocket money, instead of buying candies with it, learns the satisfaction of a partnership in national effort as well as in his family's responsibilities."[74]

When Lower and his colleagues averred the irresponsibility engendered in the individual by the welfare state, what they were actually criticizing was the fact that government-funded social security was undermining the responsibility of the male breadwinner to work and support his dependents. As W.J. Gallagher noted in his article "The Christian Family Faces the Post-War World," both modern industry and the "new morality" had undermined the traditional family, but the most potent usurper of the family's function had been the state, whose concept of welfare rights had undermined the male incentive to earn. Hence Gallagher remarked, "Modern individualism has undermined its old patriarchal authority."[75] In turn, conservative thinkers linked the espousing of welfare rights with other societal rights. They included the notion of women's rights as well as the new youth culture of "radio stars, pin-up girls, bathing beauties, comedians, leaders of jazz-bands and any one who can command an enormous income" within their general condemnation of what they termed "selfish" or "hedonistic" individualism, because all of these tended to enshrine a "false egalitarian philosophy."[76] Thus in the same breath C.E. Silcox criticized modern anthropology because of its rebellion against "older hierarchies" of race and culture and women who worked outside the home.[77] In reaction to these new egalitarian trends, he called for a new

Christian theology that rested upon "the transference to the world of the concept of the father."[78]

In drawing a direct parallel between a masculine godhead and the upholding of the status of the male breadwinner in the home, post-war Protestants were positing a view of the family in which economic incentives were intertwined with, and thus diluted, spiritual values as a way to offset the supposed materialism fostered by welfare citizenship. In post-war conservative rhetoric, the image of the "paternalistic" state, which supposedly undermined ethics, was juxtaposed against the "paternalistic" family, where faith was safeguarded against material things through the figure of the "changeless Father." In the post-war period Protestant conservatives argued for the remasculinization of the family because they identified male governance with things of the spirit, whereby hierarchical authority was believed to be passed from the heavenly Father to the temporal breadwinner.[79] And because of the modern demand for women's right to work outside the home, femaleness was identified with egalitarianism, materialistic consumerism, and selfish individualism. In order to counteract this new ideal of the democractic family, opponents of the modern state argued against King's politics of consumer abundance, supporting instead the traditional producer ideology of the home where women indirectly served the state by imbuing their children with a strong work ethic and by fostering virtues of thrift through a model of responsible female consumption and household budgeting.[80]

In terms of post-war social analysis, the reintegration of the father into the family was not necessarily part of the process of modernization, as some have argued; nor did the symbol of fatherhood contribute to a democratization of the family, by which historians have usually meant the increasing egalitarianism of family relations.[81] Conservative commentators shared with exponents of the democratic family the idea of the private individual imbued with Christian values, far removed from the public sphere of contentious, politicized group loyalties, and the view that social consensus grew outward from the family. Yet they employed the rhetoric of the family to foster a very particular brand of individualism, one that was wedded to a vision of a hierarchical, masculinized family of affectional obligations and duties, as opposed to an idea of individual freedom based on abstract and externally imposed rights. In short, the ideal of the normal family was a decidedly contested terrain in the post-war era in Canada, as was the interpretation of democracy to which it was connected.

If the unified family was, according to opponents of the modern state, to be the wellspring of social consensus and a new individualized nationalism, its hierarchical nature was no longer simply assumed but was forcefully promoted in the post-war era to provide a counterpoint to the new mass democracy of thoughtless individualism run rampant. Here again, the modern state was the touchstone for a more pervasive social criticism. In his 1944 article "Family Allowances and the Population Question," Silcox once again returned to his favourite theme of the modern state, which he believed had created a "social revolution." He described the domino effect of family allowances: not only did this legislation create a "false egalitarianism" by stressing quantity of children over quality, but its universalist nature had broken down class hierarchies by giving the "rank and file" the same rights as the educated elites. More disturbing still, it had given new authority to modern mass politics and thus had eradicated those strict boundaries between the natural leaders and the governed. Believing that democracy should founded upon a public opinion created by an educated elite devoted to uplifting the common man, Silcox was now faced with the reality of opinion polls, which resulted in policy-making as the culmination of the emotional desires of the unthinking masses.[82] He railed against family allowances for their "pious vestment of concern for the common man," and for his part, he continued to attempt to instruct the working classes by pointing out to skilled workers how family allowances would seduce them into uncontrolled spending.[83] Interpreting the creation of the modern social security state as the outcome of the materialistic outlook of working-class men, Silcox stridently proclaimed in 1945: "I am tired of the apotheosis of the common man, his idiotic boasting, his demand for his rights, his insistence that the world owes him a living, his shirking from responsibility, his fierce envy of anyone who seems to have anything more than he has. I am tired of the demand for a socialization of everything with its apparent disregard for individuality."[84]

Silcox was, of course, not alone in his suspicions that the state was destroying true democracy. The Anglican Church likewise saw in the expansion of state welfare the roots of a false egalitarianism that extolled the productivity of the less competent,[85] while Harold Innis and his colleagues in the adult education movement criticized the introduction of government wartime films to the local citizens' forums. The government, they claimed, had exploited "mass emotion" through the "mass conditioning" of wartime propaganda. They in turn denigrated mass democracy by claiming that in undermining the "integrated personality," which combined emotions and intellect, government leaders were merely exploiting the realm of individual desires, a tendency that would lead ineluctably to the totalitarian state.[86] Even more tellingly, Jack Pickersgill drew direct links between Mackenzie King's personal lack of intellectualism and his short-sighted social security measures, which Pickersgill pictured as the "quintessence of the popular."[87]

What post-war commentators feared most was that by carefully manipulating mass opinion, the modern state was creating a system of direct democracy whereby the educated voice of traditional elites were being bypassed. This view was particularly common among United Church leaders, whose only remedy to this dangerous form of egalitarian rule by the masses was to assert that democracy must be rooted in an "essentially Christian" system of values.[88] The repugnance they felt against the mass politics of the King Liberals had wider implications for the way in which clergymen and laymen conceived of Protestantism. They saw a direct parallel between mass democracy, the unthinking voter, and evangelistic religion. Hence Silcox eschewed the power of emotional evangelicalism, once seen as an important taproot of the United Church, what he disdainfully termed "religious caterwauling," for he and many others increasingly interpreted this as a form of religious practice for the lower orders, who sought immediate gratification with therapeutic notions of redemption.[89] Similarly, the young Northrop Frye, who later became a prominent voice behind the United Church submission to the Massey Commission, expressed his disdain for popular religious sentiments, seeing religious conversion as a sham, akin to an adolescent descent into the "rabble of confused and chaotic feelings," far removed from his conception of the true "consolidation of spirit," which he increasingly identified with the high culture of art and music.[90]

There was perhaps no greater articulation of the equation between mass evangelicalism and the dangers of mass democracy than a series of studies that were undertaken about the rise of Social Credit in Alberta. Of particular note were the investigations of the philosopher John Irving. In his book *The Social Credit Movement in Alberta*, Irving saw the political movement as a direct outcome of its evangelical complexion. Not only did he describe the emotional religious fervour that sustained Social Credit as redolent of a "collective behaviour of psychosis," but more tellingly, he saw "mass evangelism" as a distinctly class-based movement because of its appeal to railway workers, poor farmers, clerks, the urban poor, and "generally uneducated people." While, on the surface, Irving set out to describe the collective behaviour of democracy, he in fact drew direct comparisons with the vacant emotionalism that had given rise to fascism and Nazism during World War II.[91] Arthur Lower evinced a similarly disparaging attitude to modern evangelical sects, describing their religion as "a highly emotional, simple religion, of sentiment and salvation," which appealed specifically to "people whose educational and economic status is low."[92]

Lower – and to a lesser extent, Innis – made little distinction between mass evangelism, mass democracy, and mass culture, for they were all symptomatic of a degenerative tendency that reduced culture to pandering to the lowest common denominator.[93] Hence Lower's diatribes against the philistinism and sentimentalization of Canadian culture, the "soap opera" style of evangelicalism, and market-driven tastes symbolized by the "salesman priest" were concepts that were entirely interchangeable, for they all emanated from a lack of stewardship from intellectual elites. "Everyman," commented Lower in 1958, "has had little taste and he has worshipped the god Equality under his other titles of Sameness and Conformity. Consequently he has invariably taken what the mass producers have given him."[94] As Lower concluded, this "chewing gum" culture was the direct outcome of the general trend towards secularization in all facets of Canadian life, but his vision of a renewed "Protestant, liberal humanism" was one defined wholly by middle-class parishioners, just as his ideal of a consensual liberal democracy was one founded upon a notion of a classless, individual nationalism.[95] In a similar vein, Gordon Sisco and the organizers of the Commission on the Church, Nation and World Order posited a post-war incarnation of the United Church founded upon "our middle class liberal Protestantism."[96] If the church was to set cultural standards, these values must be hived off from the plebeian "savages of the modern age," who preferred popular culture – movies, magazines, and rock and roll – to the more refined and spiritual aspects of the theatre, museum, and the literary spiritualism of the church.[97]

If post-war leaders within the United Church saw a distinct bifurcation between the church and the state, between the sacred and the secular, they likewise envisioned a clear division between highbrow and lowbrow culture, a perspective enshrined both in their Commission of Culture report, *The Church and the Secular World*, and in the Massey Commission itself. If the "deep moral undertones of society" were to be resurrected out of the false egalitarianism engendered by the modern welfare state, this must be effected by a return to an Arnoldian vision of culture, in which an educated elite set universal standards through a system of cultural noblesse oblige[98] – hence the overwhelming emphasis placed by post-war conservatives on the importance of education to Canadian society.[99] As Arthur Lower admonished J.S. Ewart, if Canada was to be "civilized," there was an urgent need to "capture our intelligentsia for nationalism," for if a "common will" was to be forged in Canada, the masses must be adequately trained by a cadre of the intellectual elect.

In a 1949 article written to celebrate twenty-five years of the reform journal *Social Welfare*, Mackenzie King extolled the virtues of private organizations and the development of individual duties rather than rights. Although he elucidated the growth of the centralized welfare state from the Depression onwards, his concept of the "public will" had been decidedly reinvented in terms of decentralized and private values. Similarly, prominent architects of wartime welfare planning such as Harry Cassidy and Brooke Claxton centred their analysis of democracy upon the the private sphere, which they saw as a more creative force, rather than upon the public terrain of government. And as Claxton informed the Massey Commission, "The future of the nation depends upon things of the spirit as well as material progress."[100] I have argued elsewhere that King and his expert advisers had deployed welfare entitlements as a means to uphold traditional values,[101] and hence it might be argued that little had changed between King's views of 1945 and those set forth in 1949. What was new was the emphasis placed upon terms such as "community," "voluntarism," "individualism," and the "spiritual realm" of the government, emphases that had formed the centrepiece of the post-war conservative critique of the modern state.

Although I would hesitate to postulate that the barrage of attacks brought to bear by conservative social analysts against the modern state and its consequences for traditional institutions and beliefs was a causal factor behind the shift in the attitude of political clites, I would argue that by 1949 the statements by King, Cassidy, and Claxton reflected a more pronounced galvanizing of Canadian culture around a much more conservative axis. As Lower confided to M.J. Coldwell in 1942, "Liberalism, like all parties, has been passing across the stage to the right and is now conservative."[102] But the social diagnosis offered by Lower, Innis, and the conservative wing of the United Church did not establish a "middle way" like that in Britain, where the ideal of a mixed economy anchored both the Labour and the Conservative parties. For as Lower himself admitted in 1950, the "difficult centre position of liberalism has disappeared."[103] Although Lower's own ideal of a cultural and political consensus was John A. Macdonald's Tory-Liberal fusion of 1854, the post-war conservative turn that this essay has analyzed established an outlook that could form few bridges to other constituencies. This conservative modernist *Weltanschauung* was one that contributed to the fracturing of ideologies, for it was an outlook that had eschewed older organic sensibilities in favour of a series of antitheses. Thus post-war conservatives envisioned an inherent conflict between the spiritual and the secular whereby the church "stands over-against the world"[104] of the wider culture; they pitted church against state; they reinterpreted individualism in terms of the inner-directed spiritual conscience as against externally defined values of materialism and state propaganda; they conceived of citizenship around the notion of obligations rather than rights; and they adumbrated a sharp division between high and low culture and between mass democracy and that led by educated elites. Seen from this perspective, the better-known antithesis between French and English Canada, which formed the centrepiece of Lower's historical analysis, was but a small part of a much broader critique of the modern state. If the post-war search for a conservative synthesis outlined a society in conflict despite their belief that they were establishing a ideological basis for social integration, theirs was not simply a "fundamental conservativism" or a form of anti-modernism, for thinkers such as Innis and Lower eschewed nostalgia, which they associated with the rearguard nationalism of Abbé Lionel Groulx and George Drew.[105]

While it is not necessary to take at face value the self-assessments of these opponents of the welfare-planning mentality, it is important to point out that in positing a consistent response against one form of modernism, they actually contributed to carving out other modern perspectives. Most importantly, by tying ideas of nationalism, social progress, and religious practice to the private sphere of the family rather than the state, and by redefining citizenship and social integration in terms of personal behaviour rather than older group loyalties of class, race, and religion, post-war conservatives contributed to that quintessentially modern notion that ideological debate occurs in the nexus of private culture, rather than at the level of high politics, because social values are believed to be the product of personal behaviour and social analysis the stuff of the individual conscience. In this way, the post-war critique of modern state planning yielded a new "conservative modernist" outlook. It is significant, therefore, that what had begun as a crisis of political policy-making had, as a result of the new conservative telos, become a crisis of culture in 1950. And its remedy lay in the creation of a "way of life" – what Lower termed the new nationalism – which conservatives conceived of as a psychological state of mind developed through the spirit acting on the inner conscience.

NOTES

1 C.E. Silcox, "Look Out for Leviathan," *Saturday Night,* 30 Sept. 1944.
2 Queen's University Archives (QUA), Arthur Lower Papers, Vol. 1, Lower to Murray G. Ross, 20 April 1945.

3 W.O. Fennell, "Soviet Materialism vs American Materialism," *Canadian Journal of Theology* 2 (Jan. 1956): 95–6.

4 For the orthodox interpretation, which sees the Cold War as the matrix of post-war conservatism, see Elaine Tyler May, *Homeward Bound: American Families in the Cold War Era* (New York: Basic Books, 1988). In *The Muses, the Masses, and the Massey Commission* (Toronto: University of Toronto Press, 1992), Paul Litt interprets the Massey Commission largely as a nationalist response to American mass culture. Moreover, he argues that by recommending federal funding for universities, it marks a continuation of state expansion. I dissent from this view, arguing that the Massey Commission's intellectual roots were much earlier and that the vast majority of its members were critics of the centralized state.

5 QUA, Lower Papers, vol. 1, Lower to Murray G. Ross, 20 April 1945.

6 University of Toronto Archives (UTA), Harold Innis Papers, B72–0025, box 6, Robert Warren to Innis, 21 April 1944.

7 Jack Granatstein, *The Politics of Survival: The Conservative Party of Canada, 1939–1945* (Toronto: University of Toronto Press, 1967), 134; Robert Bothwell, *C.D. Howe: A Biography* (Toronto: McLelland and Stewart, 1979), 180–2; Doug Owram, *The Government Generation: Canadian Intellectuals and the State, 1900–1945* (Toronto: University of Toronto Press, 1986).

8 QUA, Arthur Lower Papers, vol. 1, Lower to N.A.M. MacKenzie, president, University of British Columbia, 18 June 1946. MacKenzie was one of the vice-chairs of the Massey Commission. Lower's psychological phrase later became the watchword of the Symons Report, *To Know Ourselves* (1967).

9 Ibid.

10 Carl Berger has captured the post-war era as a combination of continuity and change in his chapter entitled "Reorientation and Tradition," in *The Writing of Canadian History: Aspects of English-Canadian Historical Writing, 1900–1970* (Toronto: Oxford University Press, 1976). For the consensus view of the post-war period, see Robert Bothwell, Ian Drummond, and John English, *Canada since 1945: Power, Politics, and Provincialism* (Toronto: University of Toronto Press, 1981); Doug Owram, *Born at the Right Time: A History of the Baby Boom Generation* (Toronto: University of Toronto Press, 1996). For an analysis of this perspective, see Alvin Finkel, "Competing Master Narratives on Post-War Canadian History," *Acadiensis* 30 (2000): 188–204. For the view that mainstream culture was hegemonic in this period, see Mary Louise Adams, *The Trouble with Normal: Postwar Youth and the Making of Heterosexuality* (Toronto: University of Toronto Press, 1997); Mona Gleason, *Normalizing the Ideal: Psychology, Schooling and the Family in Postwar Canada* (Toronto: University of Toronto Press, 1999).

11 For a discussion of the Marsh Report, see Nancy Christie, *Engendering the State: Family, Work, and Welfare in Canada* (Toronto: University of Toronto Press, 2000), 276–82.

12 United Church Archives (UCA), Commission on Christian Marriage and the Christian Home, 1:1, Hugh Dobson, "Suggested Revision of the Terms of Reference; ibid., C.E. Silcox Papers, 6:85, "Protestantism and Roman Catholicism Their Similarities and Differences," The Importance of the Church for the World Today Series, Lecture II, Yonge Street United, Feb. 1955.

13 UCA, Commission on the Church, Nation and World Order (CNWO), 1:7, Sisco to Hugh H. Wolfenden, 4 March 1943. Wolfenden was a close associate with Charlotte Whitton and an American with close ties to big business and its corporatist ideals.

14 Ibid., 1:9, Gordon Sisco to Principal R.C. Wallace, 4 Jan. 1944.

15 Ibid., N.J. McLean to Gordon Sisco, 11 Jan. 1944; H.M. Tory to Dr H.W. Avison, 13 Jan. 1944.

16 Ibid., 1:7, Sisco to William H. Birks, 8 Feb. 1943; ibid., Sisco to Mrs Mel Staples, 22 June 1943; ibid., E.W. White, St Marys, Ontario, to Sisco, 18 Feb. 1943; ibid., Rev. Harvey Forster to Sisco, 20 Feb. 1943; ibid, 1:1, Professor R.A. McKay, Dalhousie University, to J.R. Mutchmor, 2 Feb. 1943, in which he argued against the presence of political and economic experts on the commission.

17 Ibid., 1:1, Minutes, 1 April 1943.

18 UCA, Commission on Christian Marriage and the Christian Home," *Report*, 1946, 106; E. Gilmour Smith, "The Christian Home," *United Church Observer*, 1 July 1945, 9.

19 UCA, Silcox Papers, 13:16, "Private Enterprise and Ownership of Control," in *Private and Public Enterprise* (Church of England pamphlet, no. 113, 10 April 1944), 5.

20 Ibid., 11:7, "Canadian Christians and Czecho-Slovakia," CBC International Service, n.d.; ibid., 6:80, "The Church-State Conflict in Eastern Europe," CBC International Service, 1951, 4; ibid., 6:85, "Protestantism and Roman Catholicism, Their Similarities and Differences."

21 "Religious Education in the Schools," *United Church Observer*, 1 Aug. 1944, 10.

22 UTA, Innis Papers, box 3, Leonard Marsh to Innis, 8 Aug. 1942.

23 For a discussion of the impact of Innis's religious thought upon his definition of the social sciences, see Michael Gauvreau, "Baptist Religion and the Social Science of Harold Innis," *Canadian Historical Review* 76 (June 1995): 162–75. Because of his Baptist roots, Innis had always feared government expansion and its impact upon individual freedom, but his critique of the state was heightened by the rapid centralization of government in wartime.

24 UCA, CNWO, 1:1, Minutes, 1 April, 1943; ibid., 1:7, R.A. McKay to J.R. Mutchmor, 2 Feb. 1943. See also *Church, Nation and World Order: A Report of the Commission on Church, Nation and World Order* (1944).

25 QUA, Lower Papers, vol. 1, Dr F.D. McKenty to Lower, 13 March 1946. I argue that Lower envisoned religion as prior to both individualism and nationalism. As he commented in 1944, "true liberalism, which comes close to true Christianity, must rank above nationalism." See QUA, Lower Papers, box 1, Lower to editor, *The Native Son*, 18 March 1944. For a different interpretation, see Berger, *The Writing of Canadian History*, 135.

26 UTA, Innis Papers, box 3, Humphrey Michell to Innis, 4 April 1944; ibid., box 6, E.J. Urwick to Innis, 3 April 1944. On the defence of ethics in sociology, see Nancy J. Christie, "'Pioneering for a Civilized World': Griffith Taylor and the Ecology of Geography," in Richard Jarrell and Roy McLeod, eds., *Dominions Apart: Comparative Studies in the History of Science in Canada and Australia* (Toronto: Scientia Press, 1995); Nancy Christie and Michael Gauvreau, *A Full-Orbed Christianity: The Protestant Churches and Social Welfare in Canada 1900–1940* (Montreal and Kingston: McGill-Queen's University Press, 1996).

27 Harold Innis, "Political Economy in the Modern State," *Proceedings of the American Philosophical Association* 87 (1944): 334–5.

28 UTA, Innis Papers, box 11, Innis to Professor Arthur H. Cole, 1 June 1941; ibid., S.D. Clark Papers, 1990–027, box 1, Jack Sword, Manitoba Royal Commission on Adult Education to Clark, 16 Oct. 1945. The commission was particularly exercized about the impact of state propaganda upon community education. See also QUA, Lower Papers, box 14, Lower, "What Is Democracy?" 7 Nov. 1950; UCA, Silcox Papers, Premier George Drew to Silcox, 6 Nov. 1945.

29 For the paramountcy of the "individualized subject" in post-war social analysis in Australia, see Nicholas Brown, *Governing Prosperity: Social Change and Social Analysis in Australia in the 1950s* (Cambridge: Cambridge University Press, 1995), 9–11.

30 For a longer discussion of the Liberal government's goal of using family allowances to shore up traditional liberal precepts such as individual choice, the free market, and the work ethic of the male breadwinner, see Christie, *Engendering the State*, chapter 7, "Reconstructing Families: Family Allowances and the Politics of Postwar Abundance." See also James Struthers, "Family Allowances, Old Age Security, and the Construction of Entitlement in the Canadian Welfare State, 1943–1951," in Peter Neary and J.L. Granatstein, eds., *The Veteran's Charter and Post-World War II Canada* (Montreal and Kingston: McGill-Queen's University Press, 1998), 179–204.

31 National Archives of Canada (NA), Charlotte Whitton Papers, MG 30,

E256, vol. 4, file correspondence March 1945, Manning to Whitton, 10
March 1945.

32 UCA, Silcox Papers, ll:5, "Independence, Interdependence and Dependence"; ibid., "Silcox Says Family Grant Plan Precipitate and Indefensi-
ble," undated newspaper clipping; Silcox, "Are Family Allowances
Unconstitutional?" *Saturday Night*, 7 Oct. 1944, 13.

33 UCA, Silcox Papers, 13:1, "Why Anti-Semites Hate Christ: A Study in
Hitleresque Pathology," *Churchman*, 1 Jan. 1941, 13; Silcox, "In Search
of a Formula: An Attempt at Social Reconstruction in Canada," *United
Church Observer*, 15 Jan. 1941, 9; Silcox, "Monetary Policy and Recon-
struction," *Food for Thought*, 11:9, May 1942, 11. Indeed, in the 1930s
Silcox had criticized the Roman Catholic Church because of its opposi-
tion to the increasing centralization of government. See UCA, Silcox
Papers, 8:19, "The Church, Community and State," 25 Sept., 1935; ibid.,
5:13, "The Intergroup Situation in Canada: A Protestant Viewpoint," 28
Aug. 1935, 5.

34 See, for example, NA, George Drew Papers, vol. 20, passim.

35 University of British Columbia Library, Department of Special Collections, Leonard Marsh Papers, W. Burton Hurd to Marsh, 17 March
1943.

36 UCA, Silcox Papers, vol. 1, Silcox to Mary Scott, president of Women's
School of Citizenship, 30 Jan. 1945. By campaigning on the issue of birth
control, Silcox hoped to enlist women's groups to the Drew position. See
also Silcox, "On Large Families and Allowances," *Ottawa Citizen*, 1 Feb.
1945.

37 NA, Whitton Papers, vol. 4, Whitton to Senator A.C. Hardy, Brockville,
29 June 1945.

38 Berger, *The Writing of Canadian History*, 181. In the United States the
congruence between anti-Catholicism and secularization had been precipitated by debates surrounding religion in the schools. See Martin E.
Marty, *Modern American Religion*, Vol. 3, *Under God, Indivisible,
1941–60* (Chicago and London, University of Chicago Press, 1990),
140–3.

39 Arthur Lower, "The French Origins of English Civil Liberty," *Culture* 9
(1948): 19–20; UCA, CNWO, 1:7, Lower to Gordon Sisco, 16 Feb. 1943;
QUA, Lower Papers, vol. 2, Lower to Dean Nelson, 15 Feb. 1956. As a
result of the threat of communism, Lower was able to envision some
spirit of reconciliation between Protestantism and liberals within the
Catholic Church, but he still referred to the Roman Catholic hierarchy as
an "absolute monarchy." See ibid., Lower to B.K. Sandwell, 8 Aug. 1951;
Lower to Miss Freda F. Waldon, 9 Jan. 1951. Watson Kirkconnell who
recommended a continued rapprochement between Protestant and
Catholic to fight communism in 1945, remained a minority voice until

the 1950s. See UCA, Inter-Church Committee on Protestant-Roman Catholic Relations Papers, vol. 1, Kirkconnell to B.K. Sandwell, 10 Nov. 1945.

40 UCA, Silcox Papers, 11:5, Bishop of Quebec to Silcox, 17 Nov. 1941. Prior to King's family allowance policies, Anglican leaders had seen the challenges of Roman Catholicism as a means to preserve the vitality of Protestantism.

41 UTA, Innis Papers, box 26, "The University and the Modern Crisis," 14 May 1945, convocation addresss, McMaster University, 8.

42 Doug Owram, "Canadian Domesticity in the Postwar Era," in Neary and Granatstein, *The Veteran's Charter*, 205–23. Owram is, however, quite right in linking the Canadian post-war discourse on family with domestic events rather than the Cold War.

43 UCA, Silcox Papers, 9:39, "The Menace of Modernity to Christian Life"; Frank Fidler, "War Strikes at Our Homes," *United Church Observer*, 15 April 1943, 6; Hugh Dobson, "The Family in the Present Unstable World," *United Church Observer*, 1 May 1946, 11; UCA, Silcox Papers, 5:36, "The Foundations of Morale," Couchiching Chapel address, 23 Aug. 1942, 6. See Arthur Lower, "Two Nations or Two Nationalities," *Culture* 4 (1943): 481, for the view that a new kind of nationalism must be founded on the "common norms and conduct" which flowed from privatized religion, for only through the religious emphasis upon individualism could the deep-seated inter-group and interracial antitheses of Canadian life be circumvented. See also QUA, Lower Papers, vol. 2, F.D. McKentry to Lower, 13 March 1946; Lower, "No Class in Canada?" *Saturday Night*, 12 July 1952.

44 Lower's model of nationalism was strongly individualistic and psychological, and was thereby intended to overcome limited identities of race, class, religion, and province. On the non-group bias of post-war thinking in Australia see Brown, *Governing Prosperity*, 140.

45 For a discussion of how the concept of "a way of life" entered the post-war discourse on youth, see Michael Gauvreau, "The Protracted Birth of the Canadian 'Teenager,'" in this volume.

46 UCA, Silcox Papers, 6:78, "The Priority of Religion in Modern Life," CBC radio address, 9 Dec. 1951; ibid., 5:15, "Living Dangerously," CBC radio pulpit, 27 March 1937.

47 Hugh Dobson, "Attention to Divorce," *United Church Observer*, 15 Aug. 1945, 10. The phrase "from the cradle to the grave" was a direct reference to the Beveridge Report in Britain. Dobson linked increasing divorce rates with these new state powers on the presumption that state economic protection obviated the need for a male breadwinner.

48 NA, Whitton Papers, vol. 4, "Corr. Dec.–July 1944," Howell to Whitton, 10 July 1944.

49 UCA, Silcox Papers, 9:28, "The Interest of the Christian Churches in Marriage and the Home," 2–3; ibid., 9:29, "Toward a Philosophy of Christian Marriage," 22 Jan. 1946, 2; Manson Doyle, "Evangelism – a Home Responsibility," *United Church Observer*, 15 March 1945, 5. For a longer discussion of the ostensible secularization of family life, see Nancy Christie, "Sacred Sex: The United Church and the Privatization of the Family in Post-War Canada," in Nancy Christie, ed., *Households of Faith: Family, Gender and Community in Canada, 1760–1969* (Montreal and Kingston: McGill-Queen's University Press, 2002).

50 UCA, Silcox Papers, "Possibilities and Limitations of Social Planning in a Dynamic World," address to the Central Council of Social Agencies, Winnipeg, 21 Oct. 1935.

51 Ibid., 9:28, "The Interest of the Christian Churches in Marriage and the Home," 3; ibid., 5:38, "On What Basis Can Protestants and Catholics Collaborate on the Peace Front?" 7 June 1943, 3; ibid., 5:5, "Sources and Psychology of Intergroup Prejudices as Illustrated by the Relations of Protestants and Catholics," 11 July 1934, 2; Silcox, "Drew, Duplessis and Dominion-Provincial Relations," *Globe and Mail*, 11 Aug. 1947, 5.

52 UCA, Silcox Papers, "The Menace of Modernity to Christian Life," 1946, 1.

53 Ibid., 9:19, "Canadian Churches and Postwar Reconstruction," *Religion and Life*, 1943, 3; ibid., 6:52, "Which Way Canada," n.d., 4.

54 For this line of interpretation, see, for example, Annalee Golz, "Family Matters – The Canadian Family and the State in Postwar Canada," *Left History*, 1 (fall, 1993); Mariana Valverde, "Building Anti-Delinquent Communities: Morality, Gender, and Generation in a City," in Joy Parr, ed., *A Diversity of Women: Ontario 1945–1980* (Toronto: University of Toronto Press, 1995); Franca Iacovetta, "Parents, Daughters, and Family Court Intrusions into Working-Class Life," in Iacovetta and Wendy Mitchinson, eds., *On the Case: Explorations in Social History* (Toronto: University of Toronto Press, 1998); Adams, *The Trouble with Normal*.

55 UCA, CNWO, 1:1, "Silcox Memorandum," 11 Oct. 1943, in which he states his agreement with Lower on the issue of hedonism and the state.

56 See QUA, Lower Papers, vol. 2, Gregory Vlastos to Lower, 22 Nov. 1945; ibid., Lower to Vlastos, 28 Jan. 1946; ibid., vol. 1, Clive S. Thomas to Lower, 2 Feb. 1945. Lower even rejected economic interpretations of French- and English-Canadian cultural differences and thus criticized Enid Charles, "Trends in Canadian Family Size," which stressed economic factors. See ibid., Lower to Enid Charles, Dominion Bureau of Statistics, 28 Feb. 1945.

57 UCA, CNWO, Minutes, 1 April 1943.

58 UTA, Innis Papers, box 11, Innis to Professor Arthur H. Cole, 20 Jan. 1950; ibid., Innis to John Marshall, Rockefeller Foundation, 27 Sept.

1947; ibid., box 5, Innis to Rt Hon. Angus L. Macdonald, premier of Nova Scotia, 12 Jan. 1946. See also B.S. Keirstead and S.D. Clark, "The Social Sciences," in Royal Commission on National Development in the Arts, Letters and Sciences, *Studies* (Ottawa: King's Printer, 1951).

59 See, for example, Brown, *Governing Prosperity*, 119. Joy Parr offers a similar interpretation in *Domestic Goods: The Material, the Moral, and the Economic in the Postwar Years* (Toronto: University of Toronto Press, 1999).

60 UCA, CNWO, Lower to Gordon Sisco, 25 March 1943.

61 Ibid., 1:10, E.W. White, "Comment on 5th Draft of the Basic Memorandum," 7.

62 Ibid., 1:10, Arthur Lower, "Memo, re the Basic Memorandum," 9 Aug. 1943.

63 Ramsay Cook, "Canadian Freedom in Wartime 1939–1945," in W.H. Heick and Roger Graham, eds., *His Own Man: Essays in Honour of Arthur Reginald Marsden Lower* (Montreal and London: McGill-Queen's University Press, 1974).

64 On this point, see Berger, *The Writing of Canadian History*, 160; Brown, *Governing Prosperity*, 193; Gleason, *Normalizing the Ideal*.

65 For a discussion of the tenets of New Liberalism, see Christie and Gauvreau, *A Full-Orbed Christianity*, 151–5.

66 UCA, CNWO, 2:15, Lower, "Comments and Suggestions on the Ninth Draft," 2.

67 UCA, Silcox Papers, 9:58, "The Future of Patriotism," *Saturday Night*, 15 Sept. 1949, 6.

68 UCA, Silcox Papers, 13:7, *The War and Religion* (Macmillan War Pamphlets, n.d), 28.

69 QUA, Lower Papers, box 1, Lower to M.J. Coldwell, 23 Sept. 1942.

70 Ibid., vol. 1, Lower to Sisco, 29 April 1944.

71 UCA, CNWO, 1:8, 2 Sept. 1943. See also *Church, Nation, and World Order*, 11–13.

72 QUA, Lower Papers, box 14, "Canada & a Free Society or Liberalism, Its Nature and Prospects," n.d.

73 UCA, Silcox Papers, 13:7, "The War and Religion."

74 Frank Fidler, "War Strikes at Our Homes," *United Church Observer*, 15 April 1943.

75 W.J. Gallagher, "The Christian Family Face the Post-War World," *United Church Observer*, 1 May 1945.

76 C.E. Silcox, "Family Allowances and the Population Question," *Saturday Night*, 23 Oct. 1944, 4; UCA, Silcox Papers, 9:39, "The Menace of Modernity to Christian Life," 1946, 2.

77 UCA, Silcox Papers, 9:39, "The Menace of Modernity to Christian Life," 1946, 12.

78 Ibid., 9:28, "The Interest of the Christian Churches in Marriage and the
    Home," 2. See also "The Home Faces Whole Life."
79 "The Home Faces Whole Life."
80 See UCA, Silcox Papers, 9:39, "The Menace of Modernity to Christian
    Life," 1946, 12; UCA, CNWO, 1:10, "Memorandum re Aplication of the
    Christian Charter in the Economic Field," which opposed day nurseries;
    Lillian D. Millar, "Is Economic Education of Women a Way to More
    Stable Economy?" *Saturday Night*, 13 Sept. 1947; Lois Wilson, "What Is
    the Next Step of Women as Citizens," *United Church Observer*, 1 May
    1943. For an opposing view, see UCA, CNWO, 1:9, Mary A. Endicott to
    Sisco, 11 March 1944; Jean Shilton, "The Mother Is the Home," *United
    Church Observer*, 1 May 1953.
81 On the conception of the democratic family, see C.W. Topping, "The
    Egalitarian Family," *Canadian Journal of Economics and Political
    Science* 8 (1942); Mona Gleason, "Psychology and the Construction of
    the 'Normal' Family in Postwar Canada, 1945–60," *Canadian Historical
    Review* 78 (Sept. 1997): 442–77; Jessica Weiss, *To Have and to Hold:
    Marriage, the Baby Boom and Social Change* (Chicago: University of
    Chicago Press, 2000).
82 Silcox, "Family Allowances and the Population Question," 4.
83 Silcox, "Are Family Allowances Unconstitutional?" *Saturday Night*, 7
    Oct. 1944, 13; UCA, CNWO, 1:8, Silcox to G. Mason, 28 Oct. 1943.
84 UCA, Silcox Papers, 5:42, "The Consecration of Power and Intelligence,"
    Fellowship, Sept.–Oct. 1945, 2.
85 "Private Enterprise and Social Ownership or Control," in *Private and
    Public Enterprise* (Church of England Bulletin, no. 113, 10 April 1944).
86 Watson Thomson, director, Adult Education of Manitoba, "Adult Educa-
    tion and the Crisis of Democracy," *Public Affairs*, spring 1943, 135–6. In
    the same volume, see Wilfrid Sanders, director, Canadian Institute, "How
    Good Is the Canadian Gallop Poll?" See also QUA, Lower Papers, box 1,
    Arthur Maheux to Lower, 15 Aug. 1944.
87 QUA, Lower Papers, box 1, Jack Pickersgill to Lower, 1945, n.d.
88 UCA, CNWO, 1:1, Minutes, 4 March 1943.
89 UCA, Silcox Papers, 5:32, "Religious Liberty," University College
    lecture, 18 Feb. 1942; ibid., 6:79, "Religion – Bane or Blessing," 16 Dec.
    1951.
90 See Northrop Frye to Helen Kemp, 19 Jan. 1934, Frye to Kemp, 24 July
    1935, quoted in Robert D. Denham, ed., *The Correspondence of
    Northrop Frye and Helen Kemp, 1932–1939* (Toronto: University of
    Toronto Press, 1996).
91 John A. Irving, *The Social Credit Movement in Alberta* (Toronto: Univer-
    sity of Toronto Press, 1959), ix, 260–1, 265; University of Toronto,
    Thomas Fisher Rare Book Library, MS collection 132, John Irving Papers,

box 8, "Field Notes on the Calgary Prophetic Bible Institute Church";
"Questionnaire on Evangelical and Fundamental Sects."

92 A.R.M. Lower, "Religion and Religious Institutions in Canada," in
George W. Brown, ed., *Canada* (Los Angeles: University of California
Press, 1950), 12; QUA, Lower Papers, vol. 1, Lower to S.D. Clark, 15
July 1944, in which he links Social Credit with "high-pressure reli-
gion."

93 See Berger, *The Writing of Canadian History*, 189.

94 A.R.M. Lower, "The Gods Canadians Worship," *Mclean's Magazine*, 25
Oct. 1958; Lower, "The Social Sciences in Canada," *Culture* 3 (1942):
433–4. Sentimentalism was often used as a codeword either for emotional religion or for secularization. See, for example, R.C. Chalmers,
Report of the Board of Evangelism and Social Service (1950), 3.

95 Lower, "Religion and Religious Institutions in Canada."

96 UCA, CNWO, 1:7, Sisco to Lower, 20 Feb. 1943. This rejection of social
Christianity, certain forms of evangelicalism, and the lack of interest
demonstrated in working-class Canadians was criticized. See, for example,
UCA, Commission on Christian Marriage and the Christian Home, 1:1,
Minutes, 23 Jan. 1946. Donald Creighton was also quick to distance
himself from the emotionalism of his Methodist roots, which in post-war
Canada would be associated with a lack of culture and intellect. See UTA,
S.D. Clark Papers, vol. 1, Creighton to S.D. Clark, 11 Nov. 1944.

97 UCA, Silcox Papers, 9:28, "The Interest of the Christian Churches in
Marriage and the Home," *Home and School Review*, 4.

98 Ibid.

99 See, for example, Eugene Forsey to his mother, 21 Jan. 1940, in J.E. Hodgetts, *The Sound of One Voice: Eugene Forsey and His Letters to the
Press* (Toronto: University of Toronto Press, 2000); Editor, "The Purpose
of the Journal," *Canadian Journal of Theology*, 1:1, 1955, 1; UTA, Innis
Papers, box 15, "The Crisis in Public Opinion," 1–2; ibid., box 6, Innis
to Frank Knight, 21 May 1952; Hilda Neatby, "The Challenge of Educa-
tion to the Christian Church," *Canadian Journal of Theology* 1 (1955);
Northrop Frye, "The Freshman and His Religion," in Alvin Lee and Jean
O'Grady, eds., *Northrop Frye on Religion*, Vol. 4 (Toronto: University of
Toronto Press, 2000), 242. For a discussion of the critique of popular
culture from the political left, see Paul R. Gorman, *Left Intellectuals and
Popular Culture in Twentieth-Century America* (Chapel Hill and London:
University of North Carolina Press, 1996).

100 W.L.M. King, "Welfare and the Modern State," *Canadian Welfare* 24
(15 Jan. 1949); Harry Cassidy, "The Dilemma of the Chests," *Canadian
Welfare* 24 (1 Sept. 1949); Litt, *The Muses, the Masses, and the Massey
Commission*, 12. On the reciprocity between voluntary organizations
and the state, see Royal Commission on National Development in the

Arts, Letters and Sciences, *Report* (Ottawa: King's Printer, 1951), 19–22.
101 See Christie, *Engendering the State*.
102 QUA, Lower Papers, vol. 1, Lower to M.J. Coldwell, 23 Sept. 1942.
103 Ibid., Lower to Glen Shortcliffe, 1 Aug. 1950.
104 United Church, *The Church and the Secular World* (1950), vii.
105 QUA, Lower Papers, vol. 1, Lower to Harry K. Hutton, 13 Feb. 1952; ibid., Lower to C.G. Power, 25 Nov. 1944; UTA, Innis Papers, box 11, Innis to Gerald Graham, 12 Nov. 1948.

PETER S. MCINNIS

Teamwork for Harmony

Labour-Management Production Committees and the Post-war Settlement in Canada

In October 1942 Prime Minister Mackenzie King addressed a convention of the American Federation of Labor in Toronto, and he called for the formal establishment of labour-management committees "in every industry in our country."[1] His remarks signalled the start of one of the most successful and long-lived cooperative experiments in Canadian industrial relations: the labour-management production committees (LMPCs). Designed to encourage teamwork and harmony among competing interests in the workplace, these committees were to counter the critical wartime problems of worker absenteeism and low industrial productivity. They were also to function as conduits for the exchange of productivity information between workers and management in a way that did not usurp collective bargaining procedures.[2] To this end, a plethora of guidebooks, films, posters, and other propaganda extolled the virtues of labour-management cooperation schemes. Supported by both the Trades and Labour Congress (TLC) and its rival, the Canadian Congress of Labour (CCL), as well as by the Canadian Manufacturers' Association and the Canadian Chamber of Commerce, LMPCs rapidly expanded, so that by the war's end, hundreds of committees existed in many large- and medium-sized industrial settings.[3] As well, many individual unions, including the United Automobile Workers, the United Steelworkers, and the United Electrical Workers, lobbied government officials for the inclusion of such forms of cooperation.[4]

World War II brought about massive state intervention on a scale thought unimaginable during the years of the Depression. Now Ottawa held the reins of a "command economy" and, with it, had considerable leeway for implementing a wide range of programs for social engineering. Given this mandate, the government acted to meet these industrial challenges through the sweeping powers sanctioned under the War Measures Act and the Defence of Canada Regulations. F.R. Scott considered these powers equivalent to a "second constitution," and Ramsay Cook has judged them to be the "most serious restrictions upon the civil liberties of Canadians since Confederation."[5] All three departments of Labour, Finance, and Munitions and Supply were actively engaged in designing programs for the nation at war. Among the most pressing of the issues facing these officials was that of assimilating organized labour into the larger national war effort. The concept, evoked time and again, was productivity; with sufficient productivity, Canada could make a vital contribution to defeating world fascism, while the alternative of industrial stagnation could serve only to exacerbate the crisis. In the lexicon of wartime rhetoric, productivity and patriotism were drawn as equal equations. It was true that ample room for improvement existed in worker productivity, since Canada had entered the war trailing the Depression-era legacy of underused human and physical resources. The results were twofold: the dominion government acted constantly to devise schemes to retain the support of business and labour, and officials within the Department of Labour exercised considerable latitude to experiment within this hypertrophic bureaucracy.[6] New ideas were welcome, as the increasing volume of war-related mediations and conciliation tribunals overwhelmed existing industrial relations machinery.

In the broader context of the frenetic war years, the modest plans to establish labour-management production committees drew scant attention or comment. The overall cause justified such innovation, since the war was to be won at any cost. On one level, asking Canadian workers and managers to pull together was both common sense and the patriotic duty of citizens facing a national emergency. Where patriotism itself would not suffice, LMPCs offered a concrete response to workers' demands for stability in industrial settings that were undergoing rapid transformation. At the outbreak of the war, the Canadian government could confidently draw on the productivity of more than 400,000 unemployed men and women. Yet by 1943, not only was this labour reserve exhausted, but the state found it necessary to develop mechanisms to guarantee "maximum production and harmonious relations."[7] The terms "teamwork," "harmony," and "cooperation" proliferate throughout government literature, as if officials hoped these invocations themselves could invoke such a reality. With an industrial relations system overburdened by adversarial confrontation and chafed in the binds of autocratic orders-in-council, LMPCs offered the soothing balm of consent.

For many engaged in industrial work, LMPCs provided routine access to the boardrooms of management, a bonus that not even compulsory collective bargaining had ensured.[8] This program came at a time when collective agreements were beginning to assume their modern form as a complex list of rights and responsibilities minutely enumerating the actions of labour and management.[9] Formal and informal mechanisms for labour-management cooperation allowed for the negotiation of issues not specifically encompassed in contract language. As such, LMPCs were an important adjunct to the achievement of compulsory collective bargaining. In the two decades following the war, the number of committees rose as their mandates were broadened to include issues such as health and safety and the quality of working life. Eventually, LMPCs served as springboards to full collective bargaining activities in settings where traditional recruitment methods had failed.

Analysis of labour-management production committees may offer an opportunity to learn how the routine of industrial relations functioned, in the words of historian David Brody, to mediate the polarity between "sources of stability" (traditionally pragmatic trade union leadership) and "sources for change" (a militant rank and file)."[10] This study addresses the issue of industrial legality, with reference to the familiar dichotomy of consent and coercion. But whereas we know how organized labour found itself increasingly entangled in a web of legal and procedural encumbrances, we learn little of the role that consent played in the shaping of the post-war milieu. How, then, did cooperation, in the mundane routine of workplace interactions, serve to cement the bonds of labour-management interactions in the next four decades?"[11] By tracing the history of this cooperative venture, we may discover how collective-bargaining procedures were successfully inculcated into the workplace; we may understand the gender assumptions by which trade union jobs were allocated; and, more broadly, we may learn how LMPCs helped to consolidate a new era of routine state intervention under the rubric of cooperation. As a result, union members were locked into a model of behaviour premised upon productivity bargaining and material consumption that formed the basis for the post-war compromise in Canada.[12]

Existing studies of LMPCs have been restricted to technical articles on labour-management cooperation as they relate to the specialized fields of industrial relations or business administration.[13] Generally, these analyses adopt an uncritical assessment of workplace cooperation modelled on liberal pluralist paradigms that promote rules of conduct and administrative processes to achieve industrial democracy and social stability. These rules are premised on the assumption that labour and capital share a basic equality of economic power and that the

fundamental dialectic of class conflict can be assuaged by the achievement of "a state of antagonistic cooperation."[14] Surveys of Canadian
labour history have also tended to neglect this topic in favour of
accounts of overt conflict and intra-union political rivalry.[15] But if we
are to understand the complexities of the post-war compromise, we
must situate the role of consensual programs within the broader
context of this social history. Although historians now concede that the
achievement of the fundamental rights of collective bargaining during
World War II was neither "labour's Magna Carta" nor an insidious
conspiracy leading to present-day dilemmas confronting working
Canadians, we still do not know how the "hard" issues of wages or job
control melded with the "soft" advances in workplace cooperation.[16]
Indeed, the history of Canada's immediate post-war era, as it pertains
to LMPCs, is one of complex negotiations between employers, unions,
and the state at a time when the shape of both wartime and post-war
industrial relations was subject to ongoing renegotiation.

Labour-management production committees, as they functioned in
the Canadian context, were not examples of the overarching tripartism
found in European corporatist structures in countries such as Sweden
or Austria. Canadian unions did not possess the economic and political leverage to assure such a redistribution of workplace control, just
as they lacked the strongly unified central organizations requisite for
such tripartism.[17] Instead, LMPCs emerged from the desire for corporatist consensus-building seen in the American Wagner Act of the New
Deal era and the post–World War II epoch.[18] These committees were
concerned with the "achievement of peaceful and integrative bargaining with a high recognition of a mutuality of interest."[19] In 1945 Paul
Martin, then parliamentary assistant to the minister of labour,
described this corporatist cooperation as part of a new "democratic
citizenship" for the post-war era, one where unionized labour would
gain entitlement to substantive economic benefits if it conducted itself
as a mature and responsible junior partner.[20]

During the war, the first such cooperative ventures were in the burgeoning aircraft industry, as Canada struggled to fulfill its obligations
under the British Commonwealth Air Training Plan. It is not surprising that LMPCs demonstrated their potential in the aircraft industry.
This sector, which at the start of the war employed fewer than 2,000
people, grew exponentially until it numbered more than 120,000
employees, most of them newcomers to aircraft production. The Aircraft Industrial Relations Committee, formed in December 1941, pre-
dated the official government adoption of LMPCs by several years and
was characteristic of the move towards cooperative rationalization of
heavy industry. Because of the severe shortage of skilled labour, some

contractors hoped that the LMPCs would smooth relations on the busy shop floors. They reasoned that new workers to the aviation industry, especially women (who by 1943 constituted 25 per cent of the labour force), might be satisfied with committee representation instead of a trade union.[21] Other aircraft manufacturers feared any compromise of their managerial prerogatives and remained intransigent, despite frequent requests by their workers for such committees.[22]

In 1943 there was a massive two-week strike by 21,000 aircraft workers employed in Montreal at Canadair, Fairchild Aircraft, and Noorduyn Aviation.[23] Spearheaded by the militant Lodge 712 of the International Association of Machinists and by the Montreal Metal Trades Council, this vital sector of war production remained a trouble spot for federal authorities. Other attempts at joint labour-management production committees in basic steel, shipbuilding, and munitions met with mixed success. Taken together, these initiatives were all part of the general experimenting propelled by relentless pressure for wartime industrial productivity. LMPCs were concentrated in the construction, transportation, mining, and heavy manufacturing areas, particularly the aircraft, iron-steel, and coal-mining sectors where there was tremendous wartime expansion.[24] Production committees became widespread later in the year after an interdepartmental committee met and proposed a national plan.

In January 1944 Ottawa decided to boost the development of LMPCs and, by Order-in-Council PC 162, it established the Industrial Production Cooperation Board (IPCB). This body was to act as an intermediary to facilitate the resolution of conflicts at the point of production. Because of the opposition of both business and unions towards government interference with established contractual procedures, the IPCB's mandate noted gingerly that it would concern itself exclusively with "problems of production and should leave problems relating to wages, working conditions and similar matters to the appropriate collective bargaining procedure."[25] The federal government moved to institute labour-management committees so as to ensure a harmonious balance in the workplace. It based its cooperative program on the British National Joint Advisory Council and, after 1941, the American War Production Board.[26] The original impetus for a formal cooperative structure stemmed, not from the Department of Labour, but from its rival "superministry," the Department of Munitions and Supply, and it was this department that most directly shouldered the mandate for war production.[27] By the war's end, almost four hundred functioning LMPCs covered nearly 300,000 workers, and between 1943 and 1945, more than a thousand committees were created. As a percentage of the industrial labour force, these figures show a higher rate of compliance than in Britain or the United States.[28]

The establishment of the IPCB was but one initiative among many with organized labour in the years since 1939. Most efforts proved unsuccessful, as unionists questioned whether the true motivation of the federal government was to foster corporatism or something less functional. Although Canadian trade union officials were consulted in many state-sponsored initiatives, ranging from the National Selective Service and the National War Labour Board to the Unemployment Insurance Commission, the experience usually proved frustrating for labour because real influence was retained by the country's traditional power-brokers in the corporate sector.[29] All civilian industrial workers were subject to strict governmental controls issued through a complex series of orders-in-council regulating wages and closely monitoring transfers between jobs. Workers saw their opportunities to take advantage of high pay and better jobs mired in bureaucratic red tape. The *Canadian Forum* chastised government actions as ineffective and anti-union, noting that "emergency powers have been given to the government to deal with emergencies, not in order that they should put democracy and democratic procedure into cold storage for the duration of the war."[30]

In the spring of 1945 C.D. Howe, minister of reconstruction and supply, joined with his colleague Humphrey Mitchell, minister of labour, in issuing a statement that both celebrated the vital role workplace cooperation had played in shaping Canada's contributions during World War II and articulated the government's plans for peace: "The experience of war industries has justified our experiment in Joint Labour-Management Production Committees. These Committees have promoted industrial cooperation by creating a better understanding and mutual confidence between management and labour ... Since maximum production and harmonious relations between labour and management will be essential to the successful solution of the problems which we shall have to face, we hope that these Joint Production Committees will continue to function in the reconstruction and post-war periods ... Government, labour and management will look to these Committees for advice on many problems."[31] Howe and Mitchell were not alone in their concern for improved labour-management relations in post-war Canada, however. This issue, given the attention the labour problem received both in government documents and in the popular press, was of critical national significance.

After the war, the federal government continued to promote LMPCs as a tool for redressing economic uncertainty in the immediate reconstruction period. The numbers of committees and overall worker percentages continued to climb, though as war contracts began to dwindle, government enthusiasm for LMPCs was questioned.[32] The advisory committee of the IPCB did not meet for several months, and the CCL executive wrote to federal officials to complain that the IPCB budget was insufficient for its mandate.[33] Change came quickly, however, with the upsurge in union militancy and strike activity in the immediate post-war era. For trade unions, numerically strong but still weak politically, much was at stake, including their very survival in a hostile and often reactionary climate. As a statement of sheer economic power, the strike wave was an important and necessary gesture.[34] Commenting before a federal committee in the midst of the tumult, Pat Conroy, secretary-treasurer of the Canadian Congress of Labour, glibly noted that "the lid had, figuratively, been put on wages for a period of nearly six years, and it was inevitable that, unless the pressure was eased, the lid would blow off."[35]

The ensuing explosion surpassed all predictions, as strikes disrupted numerous industrial sectors between 1946 and 1947. Woodworkers on Vancouver Island struck for better wages and conditions; automotive workers protested long-festering issues of job security in southern Ontario; coal miners in Alberta and Nova Scotia stopped production, as did steelworkers at the country's primary producers. Miserable conditions in Quebec's textile industries resulted in bitterness and violence on the picket line. These events were compounded by significant disputes in the electrical and rubber industries. Members of the United Packinghouse Workers of America held their first-ever national strike against Canada's meat-packing industry, one of the most notorious anti-union sectors.[36] This post-war strike wave was an indication that rank-and-file unionists in their tens of thousands were determined not only to consolidate their wartime gains but also to situate themselves better in the era of reconstruction. These events built on precedents of an earlier strike wave in 1943.[37] They were also a stark reminder that, despite planning and cooperative efforts, the essential rights of free association and collective bargaining would have to be secured through economic struggle, as neither the state nor private businesses were willing to concede anything for which labour was not prepared to strike. Again, government action made clear its intention to use coercion to quell industrial disputes. Plans for the post-war period may have continued apace, but state-sanctioned violence and repression always waited offstage.

The strike wave, however, compelled the state to encourage consensual, rather than coercive, measures in the workplace. Suddenly, official support for the LMPC idea was gaining, not losing, momentum, and consequently, the program was extended.[38] Under the National Emergency Transitional Powers Act, the federal government retained the power to extend such measures until May 1947. Specifically, LMPCs were to be promoted through a new agency, functioning under the Department of Labour's Industrial Relations Branch, known as the Labour-Management Cooperation Service. Government intervention had to be applied, with due circumspection for the political liabilities. Canadians were tired of wartime controls, tired of sacrificing for the common good of the nation and the Commonwealth. Unless LMPCs could be adjusted to coincide with the shifting public mood towards consumerism, the project was unlikely to survive in the post-war era.

The mood for experimentation, induced by wartime pressures for industrial productivity, continued to hold sway among the ranks of the federal civil service. Whatever future faced the country as it emerged from a costly and protracted war would depend on an aptitude for rapid conversion to peacetime production. In Ottawa not only had the absolute number of bureaucrats expanded considerably, but the war itself had greatly enhanced the prestige of a group long considered drab minions toiling in obscurity. In an address before the Canadian Political Science Association, John Deutsch, an economist with the Bank of Canada who had served during the war as special assistant to the Department of External Affairs, commented that the government had, of necessity, become "a highly centralized machine" capable of much innovation and experimentation.[39] This view was shared by Leonard Marsh, a man renowned for progressive reform. In retrospect, Marsh recalled, "the war, whatever it was in death and destruction, was a vortex in terms of social ideas and political ferment."[40]

In this spirit of ferment, the government turned to the continuing problems of industrial strife and planned to fashion a permanent mechanism to further labour-management cooperation. Part of the task was to reaffirm the concept of cooperation with business leaders. In a series of articles appearing in *Industrial Canada* and *Canadian Business*, the respective publications of the Canadian Manufacturers' Association and the Canadian Chamber of Commerce, LMPCs were touted as part of the solution to post-war uncertainty. Observers noted that such committees coincided with the move in many larger unions, such as the United Steelworkers, towards centralizing of negotiation procedures and industry-wide pattern bargaining.[41] The propaganda zeroed in on key post-war issues, stating that labour-management committees must "seek to shift the emphasis from production for victory to production geared to the needs of the post-war competitive era, in terms of wage levels, and job security ... The employed worker's profit is his job security as well as money in his pay envelope ... One big task for labour-management cooperation is to cut workers in on the profits of peacetime production and to let them know they are being cut in, show them that profitable operation means expansion and more jobs [and] job security."[42]

Along with the pleas for post-war productivity, an important message was included that any Canadian worker who had survived the Depression could not fail to grasp. Accompanying these articles were numerous photographs of labour and management representatives sitting across boardroom tables discussing the future in an atmosphere of mutual respect. For unionists accustomed to the unrelenting management hostility of the 1930s and much of the war years, this potential for recognition must have seemed enticing. The new arrangement was to leave intact the adversarial process of collective bargaining, where labour and management could often agree only to disagree, and combine it with LMPCs, where the two sides would discover points of harmony.

The appearance of wartime LMPCs was part of a matrix of government directives involving war freezes, wartime conciliation machinery, and the tacit, if sporadic, acceptance of no-strike policies. An IPCB publication, *Teamwork in Industry*, pressed home the need for labour and management to further their efforts at joint consultation while noting that the rationale for this cooperation might have changed. Earlier, the task had been to defend Canada from fascism; now, in the transition to a peacetime economy, it was to remain economically competitive with other nations. During the war, lucrative government cost-plus contracts (which guaranteed manufacturers a minimum profit) offered few incentives for industrial efficiency. Then, the goal was to produce at any cost; later, in the reconstruction era, the issue would be to satisfy a domestic market hungry for consumer products. Business writers were careful not to pose the matter in a context threatening to organized labour. They argued that continued cooperation would not usurp established collective bargaining rights but, instead, improve efficiency in the workplace. Branch offices with fieldworkers were instructed to visit shops and factories regularly in their assigned territories to push the idea.[43]

The IPCB actively solicited correspondence from businesses, particularly factory personnel managers, on the efficacy of LMPCs. Many of these comments would be incorporated in future brochures and booklets published by the government. Most accounts explained how labour-management committees had "intangible benefits" as they encouraged improved relations between employers and unionized workers in breaking down the "invisible wall" that separated the two. The rhetoric is instructive, since LMPCs were touted as encouraging "operational efficiency," instilling "common sense" on the shop floor, and providing an avenue for the "flow of ideas" or the "frank and open discussions" necessary to ensure corporate profitability in the uncertain post-war era.[44] Joint labour-management cooperation was pitched not only as a matter of common interest (some committees were given the moniker "mutual interest boards") but also as an appeal to the assumed rationality incumbent in mature industrial relations policies. The hope was that from these reforms would emerge a working environment where each side knew the rules and was prepared to abide by established procedures. In this respect, LMPCs served to entrench a functioning model of industrial democracy on a micro-level that, in turn, helped to build confidence in the larger macro-level strategies under development for post-war industrial legality.

The concept of industrial democracy was in need of all the support it could garner. Throughout the war, organized labour had continually pursued the issue of fair procedures to ensure that its members were represented before employers and government boards. In many instances, these efforts had met with frustration. Unions continued to participate in government-directed procedures not only because they were the law but also because there was little else to replace this process. To some extent, LMPCs provided just the sort of quietly effective mechanism for workplace cooperation that many business executives and union officials desired. The Industrial Production Cooperation Board frequently reminded LMPC participants to carry out shop-level policies that immediately responded to any instances of workers' participation, however slight. The central focus of this approach was transmitted through company "suggestion plans."

Suggestion plans, by which workers contributed advice on matters from workplace safety to production efficiency, had long been a feature of many corporate policies. Collective bargaining offered an imperfect apparatus of grievance resolution, and many unionists came to resent the "obey now – grieve later" policies that relegated their complaints to a process that seemed as mystifying as it did interminable. LMPCs offered a contrast to the standard grievance route in both style and substance, since they were intended to function in a more congenial atmosphere and their benefits could be instantly gratifying and financially lucrative. Workers who suggested cost-saving tips or new production methods were to be rewarded with cash bonuses that ranged from $2–25 for minor improvements to $750 for major ideas.[45] Many companies developed elaborate formulas for calculating these bonus rewards. Government brochures instructed employers to make sure that their suggestion plans provided for the "continuous publicity" of each program. All participants were to receive personal letters of commendation (regardless of the utility of the proffered advice), while beneficiaries garnered prominent notice in company newsletters or on posters for factory bulletin boards. Since some proposals might be construed as "suggesting fellow workers out of their jobs," employee anonymity could be ensured. Factory managers were also encouraged to keep the daily functioning of LMPCs "personal and friendly" so as to foster a mutually productive mood of cooperation. In instances where union stewards shunned management enticements, LMPCs could streamline the grievance procedure, bypassing stewards on "non-contractual" issues where the line separating informal correctives from official process blurred.

Union business agents also considered that the habit of filing suggestion plans was useful, since each successful program reinforced the procedures of participatory cooperation with rank-and-file members. A new spirit of cooperation would prevail and would carry over to all aspects of the job. Suggesting how an employer could, for example, save time by more efficiently transferring supplies arriving at the loading dock melded smoothly with the orderly filing of grievance claims dealing with broader contractual matters. In both instances, workers were told to stand aside and trust in the functioning of due process – to fill out the proper forms and leave the matter to others. Such boundaries on worker activity served to define expected roles for all concerned.

This definition was an important principle if the extended structure of industry legality was to take hold on the shop floor. Prominent American industrial relations experts of this era, including economists Clark Kerr, John Dunlop, and Sumner Slichter, spoke of a reassertion of communitarian solutions and a role for public opinion in labour-management conflicts, with the eventual goal of displacing conflict with cooperation.[46] In these instances, many issues of wages and working conditions proved intractable, and production committees may have functioned as a necessary release. One government pamphlet enumerating the benefits of joint consultation succinctly noted just such a prescript when it stated that "joint consultation provides a safety valve."[47] At a time when the Canadian state regulated job opportunities through the National Selective Service, froze wage rates under the National War Labour Board, refereed workplace conflicts with the Industrial Disputes Inquiry Commission, and rationed food under the Wartime Prices and Trade Board, such a safety valve had obvious practicality.

On the shop floor, the war years had done much to erode the standing and prestige of foremen. Government-imposed controls on job mobility, combined with relentless pressures for industrial production, meant that few companies wished to lose skilled personnel. Workers knew that the power of foremen in this situation was diminished, and foremen themselves were increasingly alienated from corporate decision-making.[48] Cooperative programs were adapted to reverse this state of affairs. An IPCB publication, *The Foreman and the* LMPC, discussed strategies for enhancing the status of foremen "caught in the crossfire of labour-management differences." Foremen would be active in various LMPC subcommittees, while they attempted to appear neutral in votes or decision-making. Other booklets suggested training projects to be known as "management forums"; they were intended to train prospective foremen or subforemen in the art of workplace cooperation by emphasizing that "we're all human beings rather than labour and management." In a move to alter workplace semantics, employers were encouraged to substitute the phrase "team leaders" for "foremen," as the latter was judged to be too hierarchical.[49] While examples of subtle coercion may have concerned union representatives, their official support for workplace cooperation remained unshaken. Organized labour appeared willing to accommodate such transgressions in return for the promise of economic prosperity.

Despite constant assurances that these committees would in no way encroach on collective bargaining procedures, one employer triumphantly noted how, through the medium of LMPCs, workers had come to appreciate the necessity of increased hours and productivity, for which they "volunteered" to contribute an additional four-hour shift above their regular schedule.[50] In another case, an IPCB booklet entitled *A Stitch in Time* presented the examples taken from LMPCs functioning in the Brantford and Simcoe, Ontario, plants of the Kitchen Overall & Shirt Company. Here LMPCs discussions were used in the application of new, continuous, production-line machinery. In addition, productivity had been greatly enhanced by the reorganization of employees, based not on individual piece-work but on group structures. Here LMPCs, with their emphasis on cooperation and harmony, had proved invaluable. Initially, management was concerned that plans might be construed as a "speed-up," but it discovered that consultation via LMPCs resulted in general employee acceptance; in the words of one plant manager, the resulting production system was "partially of their own creation."[51]

Throughout the latter stages of the war, the Industrial Production Cooperation Board published its monthly newsletter, *Teamwork for Victory*. In appearance, the newsletter was a crudely mimeographed report, typewritten on legal-sized paper, which adhered to the common format of most war-era "news bulletins" and conveyed the impression that it held timely, unsifted accounts taken from the factories and workshops of the nation. Compared with slick governmental publications, *Teamwork for Victory* resembled a club newsletter. Whether understated by design or by default, this publication represented one tool for broadcasting the idea of industrial cooperation. The National

Figure 1: NA, C 142803

Film Board was enlisted to produce films with titles such as *Workers at War* (1943), *Coal Face – Canada* (1943), *Smoke and Steel* (1944), and *Work and Wages* (1945) and to distribute similar films from Britain, all in an effort to exhort workers to new levels of patriotism through industrial production. Film footage culled from the British shorts *Partners in Production* (1944), *Democracy at Work* (1944), or *The New Pattern* (1945) was combined with Canadian-produced "discussion prefaces and trailers" under the overall title *The Joint Labour-Management Production Committee* (1945).[52]

In another approach, a series of posters and pay-packet inserts commissioned under the general theme "Produce for Prosperity" was devised to publicize the importance of continuing the spirit of cooperation that had won the war, since "the security of Canada's industries no less than the workers' jobs depends on cooperation."[53] The first poster issued in the series portrayed a horse-drawn cart in which was piled a cornucopia of goods intended both for export and for domestic consumption. Holding the reins to the vehicle of Canada's future were two male figures, dressed respectively in a business suit and overalls, depicting labour and management working together in harmony (see figure 1). The post-war industrial world would be one of unbridled aspirations and, in terms of employee composition, an implied return to the status quo.

Women may have found their way into the workplace in record numbers during the wartime crisis, but from now on their roles would return to those of wife, mother, and creator of the idealized post-war household. Elaine Tyler May suggests that the tendency towards highly organized and bureaucratized blue-collar jobs led to an image of the home as a "warm hearth" of freedom and individuality.[54] Poster 9 in the series made the connection even more explicit. Arranged around the central figure of a dollar sign that was coloured bright red in the original were images of household necessities (a dress, a kitchen pot, a shoe, and a new house in which to place them), while presented diagonally were the objects of desire (a radio, a refrigerator, an automobile). The caption "Everything we need – everything we want – depends on greater production" frames these pictures. In both sets of images the appeal was to be transmitted to the male breadwinner as well as his spouse. The grouping "everything we need" includes kitchen utensils and a dress, while "everything we want" makes reference to durable goods – even to a full-length fur coat, the epitome for many women of conspicuous consumption. Moreover, the image of a house was that of a suburban single-family dwelling, the type most likely to appeal to the aspirations of the upwardly mobile and those with a steady, secure income (see figure 2).[55] Thus the intended post-war social formation was revealed: the home would remain the locus for consumption and leisure of material wealth, which was secured by male breadwinners whose unions had signed wage contracts premised on a strategy attuned to the national drive for industrial productivity. With the timely application of state assistance, labour and management could now move to accommodate each another.

A further poster in the series demonstrated the "before" and "after" situations. It depicted columns of stylized tanks rolling off wartime military assembly lines with the caption "then it was QUANTITY," contrasted with an image of a single domestic automobile and the phrase "now it's QUALITY" (see figure 3). Text accompanying the poster clarified what was at issue: "You have a personal stake in the quality of the goods you help produce. A growing demand for the goods or services of your firm means steady employment, greater opportunity for

Figure 2: NA, C 142804

advancement, and the possibility of increased pay for you."[56] The connection between labour-management cooperation and job security, future promotion, and higher wages would prove a powerful incentive for many Canadian workers terrified of returning to the despair of the Depression or afraid of losing the precious gains secured during the war years. For organized labour, the stability of the post-war family was to be anchored to a base of workplace standards that would provide the required financial and social security for the happiness and prosperity of the nation.

Just as the prosecution of World War II had dominated most activities of the state and civil society, the debate about the future of the nation in the post-war era engaged a diverse group of participants. By 1943–4 Canadians may have expressed cautious optimism as to the eventual outcome of the war, but many citizens viewed the task of post-war reconversion with consternation. Loath to repeat the events that had followed the Armistice in 1918, many now looked to the state for

Figure 3: NA, C 142802

direction and planning.[57] It was, after all, an obvious solution. Had not the dominion government amassed unprecedented powers during the war years, and were not its citizens led to believe that these powers were generally successful in coordinating the nation's activities? If the "command economy" had served this role since 1939, could it not suffice for the aftermath? As Robert Campbell observes in a study of post-war political economy, the experience of the war had "legitimized the idea of economic planning and an increased role for the state in the economy." This trend manifested itself both in broad strategies, such as the question of Keynesian macroeconomic policy, and in specific actions to stimulate domestic output and boost employment.[58]

The emphasis would change after the Allied victories in the European and Pacific theatres. The constant cajoling of workers to use industrial production to win the war was transformed in the post-war years to focus on global competitiveness, a trend in keeping with the emphasis on international exports articulated in the 1945 White Paper on Employment and Income (see figure 4).[59] LMPC pamphlets with

Figure 4: NA, C 142805

such wartime titles as *Victory in the Making* and *Back the Attack* were rephrased to become *Partners in Production*, *Industrial Democracy at Work*, or *Working Together in a Democratic Society*. The implication was that, contrary to the cynical rhetoric of World War I propaganda of a "war for democracy," military conflict this time had ushered in a new phase of cooperation to the post-war industrial workplace. For now the war was over, and victory held the promise of unimagined prosperity – but only if Canadians were prepared to join in and "win the peace."

Full employment, made necessary to satisfy a modern war machine, was fast becoming something from which many employers sought to withdraw their commitment. The extension of formal mechanisms for labour-management cooperation offered the hope of maintaining high productivity, despite the "inevitable" layoffs that were to accompany the cessation of hostilities. The initial economic indicators for the immediate post-war period were not at all positive, as experts were divided over what the future would bring. In their annual state-of-the-economy forecasts, the country's major chartered banks warned that although organized labour posed a threat to the nation's stability, the problem lay not with unions themselves but with their "maladministration." This threat could be overcome if labour and management worked together to "unselfishly distribute their earnings."[60]

Not all economic predictions for the post-war period suggested a recession; indeed, several polls identified a pent-up desire among Canadians to purchase the consumer goods they had so long been denied by wartime restrictions. Generally high wages and a long workweek meant that the money for these goods was in ready supply. Trade publications in the manufacturing sector confidently spoke of a high potential demand for durable goods. Maclean-Hunter, the nation's largest publisher of specialized trade magazines, established a Post-War Research Department to survey Canadian citizens and industrialists about their plans, going so far as to determine that exactly 762,568 new cars would be needed for "V+2," the two years immediately following victory. Another survey, of 1,526 housewives found strong markets not only for "big ticket" domestic appliances such as washing machines, refrigerators, and electric stoves but also for radios, vacuum cleaners, and other consumer items. Consequently, manufacturers predicted 47 per cent more spending than in the pre-war years on office and plant infrastructure.[61] Although circumspect business forecasters cautioned investors to remain wary of declines from the wartime peak figures, many, including the minister of reconstruction and supply, C.D. Howe, suggested the possibility of substantial expansion if the domestic labour front could be eased into the reconstruction phase without undue disruption.[62] The dominion government had closely monitored the variables affecting organized labour in the immediate post-war period. There was every possibility this latent demand would be translated into demands for increased wages for trade union members. Ottawa's goals for "the maintenance of a high and stable level of employment and income" were plausible, given that federally funded wartime industrial expansion combined with continued post-war consumption had positioned the economy for rapid growth.[63]

Gary Cross, one of the few historians who has assessed the culture of mass consumption in the immediate post-war era, writes that "a consumerist consensus emerged after 1945. It had been built upon mass production, balanced with high wages, and buttressed by Keynesian macro-economic management and manipulated needs creation."[64] Male workers in heavy industries were offered the option of maintaining their longer week and the opportunity for abundant overtime hours or accepting a sharp reduction of hours if the workweek was more evenly distributed among others, including women restricted to part-time jobs. LMPCs may have played a role in establishing that further benefits take the form of increased wages rather than a shorter work week. If LMPCs were intended to assuage workplace conflict, they were not felt to be the vehicle for redressing the standard hours of work. Economist Juliet Schor notes how the desire for consumer goods led in turn to personal debt, and how that debt forged ever stronger chains of dependence to the job and the dictates of employers.[65] She argues that "workers want what they get" and that the ideological pressures associated with a society that creates material desire leads people to look for ways to accommodate those urges.[66] For many workers this meant acquiescence and cooperation, rather than struggle and resistance through vehicles such as an LMPC.

The post-war role for LMPCs was outlined in the federal government's brief to the 1945–46 Dominion-Provincial Conference on Reconstruction. Contained in the federal "Green Book" were comprehensive proposals for labour legislation as part of a broadly cast approach to national health and welfare.[67] LMPCs were presented as an important adjunct to existing collective bargaining machinery. Ottawa expressed the wish that these committees would now be accepted as "permanent democratic institutions," part of the post-war "positive" state, and allowed to function through the delegation of provincial authority to federal administration.[68] Throughout the conference, the central issues surrounding provincial autonomy under the BNA Act remained major hurdles, but LMPCs were viewed by civil servants as a non-controversial way for federal officials to retain a role in the field of industrial relations.[69] At a time when hopes for a unified industrial relations system administered from Ottawa were rapidly dissolving, the prospect of extending LMPCs past the wartime crisis may have seemed one of the few avenues open to federal officials.

Other aspects of the post-war world were also subject to renegotiation. Historians Ruth Roach Pierson and Gail Cuthbert Brandt have suggested that World War II and the reconstruction period posed an ideological challenge to accepted definitions of marital and familial relationships, just as they modified social constructions of gender and sexuality.[70] As had been seen in previous wars, gender boundaries were first extended and then retracted during the war and its immediate aftermath. Serious concern was expressed about the state of the post-war family and its adjustment in the reconstruction period.[71] Many Canadians, men and women trade unionists among them, wished to move away from the overt patriotism or civic-mindedness of the war years and retreat to the private realm of the family. Although some working women said they would fight to retain these higher-paid jobs after the war, the sentimental image of the "home and family" as a bastion from society's troubles continued to have widespread appeal both during the war and after.[72] The Produce for Prosperity poster series emphasizing working men's responsibilities to provide economic sustenance for their wives and families found constant emphasis, and it did so in a manner that was often uniquely Canadian in perspective.[73] Part of the country's opportunity for national renewal would come from a more holistic redefinition of economic security.

Although the trade union movement would continue to lobby for broad legislative reforms, the focus shifted to comparatively narrow and specific measures likely to be secured through contractual negotiations and greater cooperation. To a large extent, organized labour withdrew from the challenge to reformulate the gender dynamics of the workplace in a way that would address the inequalities that chronically afflicted female wage earners. The priority for post-war jobs continued to privilege unionized male wage earners. Women were informed they could best benefit from these specific contractual reforms, and the modestly expanding welfare state, indirectly as spouses of these men, rather than as paid workers outside the home.[74] The grudging acceptance by male unionists of family allowances (in lieu of a minimum industrial wage) was made more palatable with the promise of financial benefits to be secured through close cooperation with government and employers. Organized labour in Canada consented to this arrangement and continued its support for LMPCs.

The gender assumptions of labour-management cooperation are revealed in case studies published by the IPCB. In industrial settings employing large numbers of women workers, such as the textile/clothing sectors, government literature encouraged the use of LMPCs, not in the "masculine" sense of problem-solving devices to resolve non-contractual issues, but as "feminine" committees promoting recreational or social clubs outside the workplace. An issue of *Teamwork in Industry*, that proclaimed, "LMPCs Help Women Adjust to Industry" detailed how labour -management cooperation had proved useful in "acclimatizing" women to their post-war job opportunities.[75] Examples drawn from the St Thomas, Ontario, plant of the Monarch Knitting Company, organized as Local 777, Textile Workers Union of America (CCL-CIO), described how LMPCs mainly took the form of recreational subcommittees that helped in boosting morale and maintaining high productivity. LMPC subcommittees sponsored contests for regular job attendance and "good housekeeping" that offered cash rewards for compliance. Compared with LMPC literature intended for male-dominated workplaces, the contrast in subject and in editorial tone is notable. Women were assumed to be most interested in social interactions, while men focused on health and safety or production efficiency.[76] In another Monarch plant located in southwestern

Ontario, LMPCs functioned not only as social outlets but in helping to resolve long-standing matters related to factory working conditions, a balance attributable perhaps to the equal numbers of male and female employees.[77]

For the most part, women accepted these ongoing social and political renegotiations. Many trade unionists realized that militancy itself would no more suffice following the second World War than it had after the first. Throughout the mid-1940s, unions associated with the Canadian Congress of Labour continued to search for solutions by way of negotiation rather than confrontation. The reason stemmed not only from wartime regulations that remained in effect during the reconstruction phase but also from efforts that unions had made to obtain expertise in industrial relations. As part of the move away from voluntarism, labour sought to bolster semi-permanent structures such as LMPCs. Similarly, federal officials understood the value of continuing programs that fostered cooperation. It was no coincidence that the 1947 decision to reaffirm LMPCs under the Labour-Management Cooperation Service coincided with a national strike wave.[78]

In 1946 the CCL, under its National Wage Coordinating Committee, fronted a nationally coordinated minimum wage campaign as part of an aggressive push to entrench union security and a so-called prosperity wage.[79] The congress was supported in this initiative by its major component unions such as the United Automobile Workers and the United Steelworkers. The latter had formed a National Advisory Committee to aid in the process. These large-scale campaigns made demands on union leadership for informed negotiating. In turn, these placed a premium on the timely collection and analysis of wage and price data. They also emphasized to ambitious local union officials that the way forward was to be conversant with the increasingly economistic and legalistic procedures now applied to contract negotiations. The message was clear: labour must learn the new language of industrial relations in order to bargain from a position of strength in its dealings with government and business representatives. If the union movement could not build upon the foundations of wartime tripartite cooperation, then it stood to lose heavily in the post-war period.

Addressing the House of Commons Industrial Relations Committee in 1946, the CCL recounted its efforts to establish a series of industrial councils. "These industrial councils would be, in effect, boards of management in their respective industries and would have the right to discuss all matters relative to maintaining peace in each industry. In short, the jurisdiction of each council would be all-embracing, and take in production, wages, practices, and anything and everything that would have to do with the welfare of the industry and in developing and maintaining good relationships."[80] Candidates under serious consideration for such an experiment were to be the steel and automotive industries, but other sectors were under consideration as well. While the prospects of such a corporatist structure may have appeared excessively ambitious, the CCL suggested a modest proposal to sustain momentum for the concept. In a letter to a union organizer hoping to build a base in British Columbia's fruit-packing industry, Pat Conroy recommended the establishment of LMPCs as an interim step along the path to a labour-management "board of governors for industry."[81] If labour could demonstrate effective cooperation through LMPCs, then perhaps these more ambitious concepts would follow.

The ongoing discussions and experiments with industrial relations blended into the larger debates surrounding the future of the Canadian welfare state. The war had provided the opportunity to establish long overdue policies such as unemployment insurance, and the prospect of peace offered hope that more comprehensive welfare measures would be introduced. In Britain, plans for a cradle-to-grave state, outlined in the influential Beveridge Report of 1942, led some Canadians to hope that this model might set the tone for reforms in Canada.[82] The Dominion Advisory Committee on Reconstruction (James Committee) and its Subcommittee on the Post-War Problems of Women were kept busy throughout 1942–43 with representations from various groups concerned with the post-war state.[83] Another significant part of this reformist milieu was the Marsh Report of 1943, with its pessimistic economic forecast for the immediate post-war era. That the efforts of both the James Committee and Leonard Marsh were largely shunted aside in favour of political expediency and a more conventional view of the Canadian state does not detract from what historian Doug Owram refers to as a "bureaucratic enthusiasm for reconstruction."[84] Trade unions appearing before the House of Commons Special Committee on Reconstruction and Re-establishment in support of many of the recommendations for an expanded welfare state emphasized the relationship between the achievement of collective bargaining and a broader post-war vision of social security for Canada.

Labour's participation in the limited tripartism of wartime boards acknowledged the temporary power of these government institutions, which functioned as a "parastate" to mediate between society's dominant institutions.[85] Canadian-style tripartism often served to maintain wage differentials in the post-war years. A select and privileged stratum of unionists, those most securely situated within the ranks of organized labour, found themselves best able to negotiate with management and the state on the basis of a confined equality. LMPCs, and all that they stood for, functioned alongside the new rules of law that became entrenched in the workplace following World War II.[86] These developments in the field of industrial relations were part of a broader debate as to the future of the Canadian welfare state. But as with the failure of the 1945-46 Dominion-Provincial Conference on Reconstruction to achieve constitutional solutions for the post-war period, including a unified national labour code, the promise of this moment faded, and Canada was left to ponder what, for many, were diminished expectations.

The willingness of unions to consent to a structure of workplace cooperation in the immediate post-war era may have spurred the development of a "split-level" economy that privileged only the strongest trade unions with high wages and favourable working conditions at the expense of their less well-positioned confederates.[87] Beyond the goal of mere legal recognition, participating unions sought inclusion in the emerging regulatory regime. But not all unions were welcome. Cold War politics served to narrow greatly the range of dialogue on progressive social reform. In the post-war atmosphere of hostile name-calling, violence, and dirty tricks, official support for expanded welfare provisions and equality for wage-earning women were easily conflated with intrusive state-planning regimes of nations situated on the wrong side of the Iron Curtain. In what was a startling example for the domestic use of a foreign threat, any evocation of Stalinist intrigue forced closure on vital domestic issues of social policy. Canada's communist labour movement, now exposed to withering attacks from its many opponents, retreated from the public sphere, leaving the debate on the future of industrial relations to those groups that were prepared to adopt more conciliatory positions in their transactions with government and management representatives. In return for purging Canada's labour movement of its "disreputable" communist-led organizations, those unions that remained were rewarded for their cooperation with an entree as legitimate interests into the new regulatory state. This tacit precondition was achieved by the end of the 1940s, as both the CCL and the TLC engaged in rancorous internal battles.[88] Those labour leaders remaining in the fold were now deemed eligible to participate on various tripartite boards, commissions, and advisory panels. Union cooperation with management brought a concurrent linkage with the state.

Following the war and the initial transition phase to a peacetime economy, government officials redirected LMPCs to health and safety issues. While improved productivity remained a key element of the program, the focus during the 1950s was to link industrial production with job security. Throughout the 1950s, interest in labour-management cooperation continued to gain momentum. Between the fiscal years of

1950 and 1955, the number of LMPCs grew from 684 to1,029, covering 260,000 and 310,000 workers respectively.[89] Small industrial plants started to account for a large number of new committees. At the level of union locals, this increase resulted in bridges that eventually led to co-management schemes between labour and business. Not all of these developments were positive. The federal Labour-Management Cooperation Service sponsored its bulletin *Teamwork in Industry*, as well as commissioning films and radio projects intended to broaden the appeal of this concept. At times, these tactics degenerated to the level where a mawkish cartoon character, known as Tommy Teamwork, was enlisted to remind production workers of the importance of cooperation and the commonality of interests they shared with their employers and the state.[90]

In his 1954 Labour Day message, the federal minister of labour, Milton F. Gregg, emphasized the heuristic value of LMPCs for trade unions, observing that "labour, over the years, has gained a heightened appreciation of the responsibilities of management and of the interests of industry and the community ... there is evidence that in a relatively short space of time labour has come to the fore as a full partner with management in the industrial life of our country."[91] If by full partnership the minister meant that Canadian unions had learned to acquiesce in matters of managerial prerogative and, instead, take the proffered reward of monetary gain, then cooperation had indeed achieved its goal. A LMPC poster issued at this time confirmed the linkages of union productivity bargaining in return for secure employment achieved through cooperation, not confrontation. The poster bears an image of a manager and a worker standing together looking skyward above their factory to see the invocation "More Teamwork, More Production, More Sales, More Jobs."

By the early 1960s, the idea of labour-management consultation had spread into many areas of state and parastate institutions, notably hospitals. In 1964 almost three hundred LMPCs acted as "dual capacity" committees, serving the traditional role of stimulating greater productivity as well as taking on the capacity to negotiate terms hitherto restricted to collective agreements.[92] Through institutions such as the National Productivity Council (1961–63) and the Economic Council of Canada (1963–92), organized labour sought out new liaisons with business and the state. The Industrial Production Cooperation Board (subsequently renamed the Labour-Management Cooperation Service) was formally terminated, along with a general reorganization of the Department of Labour, in 1965–66. At the time, there were 1,957 active LMPCs on record, with the participation of more than 584,000 workers.[93] The monthly publication *Teamwork in Industry* continues as *Worklife*.[94] By the 1960s, organized labour had become accustomed to a pattern of annual wage increases and cost-of-living allowances linked to productivity bargaining. In some cases, the structures of LMPCs were subsumed into the complex language of collective bargaining agreements between employers and the major unions, as, for example, in the health and safety provisions included in contracts with the United Steelworkers. Echoes of LMPCs resonate in recent experiments with Quality Circles, Quality of Working Life (QWL), and Total Quality Management (TQM), initiatives launched by many provincial governments and corporations eager to increase employee productivity, reduce payrolls, and still retain a semblance of workplace "harmony."[95]

In the late 1970s, cooperation had reached the point where the executives of the Canadian Labour Congress routinely consulted with the C.D. Howe Institute and sat across the conference table with the Business Council on National Issues as joint members in the Canadian Labour Market and Productivity Centre. Whatever potential might have developed from this high-level move to diminish the adversarial nature of collective bargaining, it failed to garner approval from many militant rank-and-filers, who questioned the value of such initiatives at a time when fundamental rights of free association were under attack from both employers and the state. However, these initiatives in support of corporatism did meet with the approval of a quiescent majority who were anxious to substitute cooperation for confrontation. The long-term consequences of such ersatz corporatism eventually surfaced. In one telling example, the province of Nova Scotia (through the Institute of Public Affairs at Dalhousie University) supported a Joint Labour-Management Study Committee from the early 1960s until 1979, when unions left the body in the fallout of the infamous "Michelin Bill."[96] The corporatist process continues in the form of a bipartite consultative body known as the Canadian Labour Market Productivity Centre (with the curiously familiar sounding acronym of CLMPC).[97] Was this body the result of the complex negotiation of power that has formed part of the complicated equation of consent and coercion since the years of World War II and the immediate post-war period?

The arrival of a "professional" stratum of labour officials shifted the focus of decision making away from the shop stewards and their rank-and-file constituency. Industrial legality stifled spontaneous self-activity, replacing it with complex, routinized collective bargaining procedures, activities that posed no serious threat to capital's essential property rights. LMPCs and their materialist focus on productivity and consumption blended smoothly with the post-war prospects

for a select and privileged cohort of predominately male trade unionists in Canada's resource, transportation, and manufacturing sectors.
In the immediate post-war era, Canadian trade unions were presented
with a choice that many found congenial. In return for the promise
of unprecedented wealth and stability, workers were counselled by
management and the state, as well as by their union and political
leaders, to consider only their paycheques – and what these could
purchase. Teamwork and harmony served to reinforce an active but
rigidly circumscribed sphere for labour's actions. Contentious issues
of workplace control or class solidarity were shunted aside in the
rush to consumerism.[98] Recent efforts by the nation's largest unions
to resurrect a class-conscious "social unionism," sensitive to the
changing nature of both the workplace and Canada's workers, have
failed to deliver on the promise that this new approach differs sub-
stantively from traditional "business unionism."[99] The choice made
from the mid-1940s onward, to step onto the escalator of regular and
predictable material gain, still guides the intent of current union
strategy.

   In the years following World War II, labour-management production
committees presented a model of a shared community of interests
premised on the mutuality of productivity and consumption. For
Canadians emerging triumphant from another global conflict, with
collective memories of wartime sacrifices and privations, this post-war
"social contract" proved highly seductive. Aspects of the hegemonic
notions of the post-war settlement continue in the limited institutional
forms and practices of the state and labour. It was not the first instance,
or the last, where organized labour championed reforms it would live
to regret in later years. The decisions made during World War II and
the immediate post-war era simultaneously opened up opportunities
for progressive change and led to complacency. For labour, such complacency has resulted in political atrophy that has left it ill-equipped to
confront a resurgence of employers' reactionary incursions within
today's "global" economy.

NOTES

This essay has been reprinted with permission from the *Canadian Historical
Review* 77 (1996): 317–52.

1 W.L. Mackenzie King, *Canada and the Fight for Freedom* (Toronto:
   Macmillan 1944), 200–6.
2 While government-sponsored materials made it clear that wages or basic

working conditions were not in the purview of LMPCs, the line delineating these activities was often unclear.

3　See *Saturday Night*, 27 June 1942, 6–7; Canadian Manufacturers' Association, *The War and After* (Toronto: CMA, 1944), 12; H.A. Logan, *Trade Unions in Canada: Their Development and Functioning* (Toronto: Macmillan, 1948), 521–8. This concept was also supported by the independent railway brotherhoods and the Confederation of Catholic Workers of Canada (CTCC). The Canadian Congress of Labour was especially fervent in its calls for federal action. See, for example, editorials in the CCL's monthly magazine, the *Canadian Unionist* 16 (April 1942): 257; 16 (Sept. 1942): 79.

4　LMPCs were not new, for a similar concept of "production councils" had originated with unions associated with the Labour Progressive Party (Communist Party of Canada) to promote the Allied war effort. See, for example, pamphlets of the United Electrical Workers, including *We Produce for the Second Front and Victory* (Toronto: Eveready Printers, 1942). The politically left Canadian leadership of the United Automobile Workers (District Council 26) advocated this form of cooperation in early 1942; see Charlotte A.B. Yates, *From Plant to Politics: The Autoworkers Union in Postwar Canada* (Philadelphia: Temple University Press, 1993), 37–40.

5　F.R. Scott, "The Constitution and the War," *Canadian Forum* 19 (Nov. 1939): 243–4; Ramsay Cook, cited in Reg Whitaker, "Official Repression of Communism during World War II," *Labour/Le Travail* 17 (spring 1986): 135–66

6　Both the Department of Labour and the Department of Munitions and Supply (DMS) experienced tremendous growth. In less than five years, Labour multiplied from under 250 personnel to a wartime peak of 3,100. Starting with 1,000 staff in 1939, DMS witnessed a fourfold expansion by 1942. See *Labour Gazette* (LG), Nov. 1943, Sept. 1950; *Annual Reports of the Department of Labour*, 1943–48. Overall, appointments to the civil service increased tenfold between 1938 and 1943. See J.E. Hodgetts et al., *The Biography of an Institution: The Civil Service Commission of Canada, 1908–1967* (Montreal: McGill-Queen's University Press, 1972), 185–206.

7　See also "Manpower," *Maclean's*, 1 Sept. 1942, 5–7.

8　The wartime rules and procedures for compulsory collective bargaining culminated with Order-in-Council PC 1003, "The Wartime Labour Relations Regulations" (17 Feb. 1944). For details, see John A. Willes, *Contemporary Canadian Labour Relations* (Toronto: McGraw-Hill Ryerson, 1984), 75–9.

9　For examples of the way that contractual language rapidly assumed a formidable complexity, see Peter Warrian, "'Labour Is Not a Commodity':

A Study of the Rights of Labour in the Canadian Postwar Economy, 1944–48" (PhD dissertation, University of Waterloo, 1986).

10 David Brody, *Steelworkers in America: The Nonunion Era* (Cambridge, Mass.: Harvard University Press, 1960)

11 An assessment of the Canadian situation is offered in H.C. Pentland, "The Canadian Industrial Relations System: Some Formative Factors," *Labour/Le Travailleur* 4 (1979): 9–23. Revisionist accounts of an American perspective, taken from the "critical legal studies" school, include Karl E. Klare, "Judicial Deradicalization of the Wagner Act and the Origins of Modern Legal Consciousness, 1937–1947," *Minnesota Law Review* 62 (1978): 265–339; James B. Atleson, *Values and Assumptions in American Labor Law* (Amherst: University of Massachusetts Press, 1983); Christopher L. Tomlins, *The State and the Unions: Labor Relations Law and the Organized Labor Movement in America, 1880–1960* (Cambridge: Cambridge University Press, 1985). The best synthesis of this literature is Nelson Lichtenstein and Howell John Harris, eds., *Industrial Democracy in America: The Ambiguous Promise* (Cambridge: Cambridge University Press, 1993). For Canada, see David W.T. Matheson, "The Canadian Working Class and Industrial Legality, 1939–1949" (MA thesis, Queen's University, 1989).

12 The phrase "post-war compromise" describes the peace treaty brokered by the state between labour and capital that established the rudimentary framework for industrial peace following the end of World War II. See Claus Offe, *Contradictions of the Welfare State* (Cambridge, Mass.: MIT Press, 1982), 147–61

13 Among the studies dealing specifically with Canada are H.A. Logan, *State Intervention and Assistance in Collective Bargaining: The Canadian Experience, 1943–1954* (Toronto: University of Toronto Press, 1956); W. Donald Wood, *The Current Status of Labour-Management Cooperation in Canada* (Kingston: Industrial Relations Centre, Queen's University, 1964); K.G. Waldie, "The Evolution of Labour-Government Consultation on Economic Policy," in W. Craig Riddell, ed., *Labour-Management Cooperation in Canada* (Toronto: University of Toronto Press, 1986), 151–201; Leslie M. Darby, *Labour Management Cooperation: A Study of Labour -Management Committees in Canada* (Kingston: Industrial Relations Centre, Queen's University, 1986); John C. Anderson and Morley Gunderson, eds., *Union-Management Relations in Canada* (Don Mills, Ont.: Addison-Wesley, 1982), 308–42.

14 For a definition of liberal pluralism in this context, see Katherine Van Wezel-Stone, "The Post-War Paradigm in American Labor Law," *Yale Law Journal* 90 (June 1981): 1509–80. The term "antagonistic cooperation" is found in E. Wright Bakke, *Mutual Survival: The Goal of Unions and Management* (New Haven, Conn.: Yale Labor and Management Center, 1946).

15 For example, Stuart M. Jamieson, *Times of Trouble: Labour Unrest and Industrial Conflict in Canada, 1900–1966* (Ottawa: Supply and Services Canada, 1968); Irving M. Abella, *Nationalism, Communism, and Canadian Labour* (Toronto: University of Toronto Press, 1973); Desmond Morton, *Working People*, 3rd ed. (Toronto: Summerhill Press. 1990); Craig Heron, *The Canadian Labour Movement* (Toronto: Lorimer, 1989); Bryan D. Palmer, *Working-Class Experience: Rethinking the History of Canadian Labour, 1800–1991* (Toronto: McClelland & Stewart, 1992). Revisionist industrial relations monographs have also avoided this topic; see Gerard Hebert, Hem C. Jain, and Noah M. Meltz, eds., *The State of the Art in Industrial Relations* (Kingston: Industrial Relations Centre, Queen's University, 1988); Bob Russell, *Back to Work? Labour, State, and Industrial Relations in Canada* (Scarborough, Ont.: Nelson, 1990); Larry Haiven, Stephen McBride, and John Shields, eds., *Regulating Labour: The State, Neo-Conservativism and Industrial Relations* (Toronto: Garamond, 1990).

16 See Michael Earle and Ian McKay, "Introduction: Industrial Legality in Nova Scotia," in Michael Earle, ed., *Workers and the State in Twentieth Century Nova Scotia* (Fredericton: Acadiensis Press, 1989), 9–23; Daniel Drache and Harry Glasbeek, *The Changing Workplace: Reshaping Canada's Industrial Relations System* (Toronto: Lorimer, 1992), 9–31

17 The European model of tripartism involves the allocation of a permanent place for organized labour on administrative bodies alongside state and corporate representatives; it also provides substantive procedures for long-range planning, instead of defaulting into a highly adversarial approach within a traditional market economy. For a discussion of these themes, see Leo Panitch, "The Tripartite Experience," in Keith Banting, ed., *The State and Economic Interests* (Toronto: University of Toronto Press, 1985), 37–119.

18 See Nelson Lichtenstein, *Labor's War at Home: The CIO in World War II* (Cambridge: Cambridge University Press, 1982), 26–43.

19 Matthew A. Kelly, *Labor and Industrial Relations* (Baltimore: Johns Hopkins University Press, 1987), 48–9

20 Paul Martin, "Labour's Post-War World," *Behind the Headlines* 5, 1 (1945): 24–5

21 *Financial Post*, Jan. 1944, 15–19; annual aircraft production in Canada expanded from 31 planes in 1939 to 4,133 in 1943. The industry employed 15,802 workers in 1939, a number that rose to 122,765 in 1943.

22 See, for example, "Labour and Management Must Get Together," *The Effort* (IAM Lodge 719, Fort William, Ont.), Oct. 1942, 1–2; De Havilland Aircraft Worker (UAW Local 112, Malton, Ont.), 18 June 1943, 3.

23 For further details of the aircraft sector, see Valerie Endicott, "'Woman's
    Place [Was] Everywhere': A Study of Women Who Worked in Aircraft
    Production in Toronto during the Second World War" (MA thesis, Univer-
    sity of Toronto, 1991). On the Montreal aircraft strike, see *The History
    of the Labour Movement in Quebec* (Montreal: Black Rose Books,
    1987), 136–7; Jamieson, *Times of Trouble*, 287.
24 National Archives of Canada (NA), Records of the Canadian Labour
    Congress (CLC Records), MG 28, I 103, vol. 223, Minutes of the IPCB
    Advisory Committee; Department of Labour, Annual Report of the
    Deputy Minister, 1944, 43–4; LG, March 1943, 304. See also Norman S.
    Duce, "Plant Level Labour Management Cooperation in Canada" (MBA
    thesis, Queen's University, 1965).
25 *LG*, Feb. 1944, 144.
26 See James E. Cronin, *The Politics of State Expansion: War, State and
    Society in Twentieth-Century Britain* (London: Routledge, 1991),
    138–45; Dorothea de Schweinitz, *Labor and Management in Common
    Enterprise* (Cambridge: Harvard University Press, 1949); LG, May
    1945, 595. In Britain the Trades Union Congress co-sponsored "joint
    works production committees" intended to revive the "Dunkirk spirit"
    of mutuality and self-sacrifice. All three allied nations exchanged
    details of their respective efforts at joint labour-management
    cooperation.
27 The term "superministry" is drawn from John Smart, "Administrative
    Outline," *Records of the Department of Labour*, General Inventory
    Series (Ottawa: National Archives of Canada, 1988), 25–6. During the
    war, the department had seven main branches and nearly two dozen
    boards, commissions, and specialized divisions. The Department of
    Munitions and Supply, directed by the imperious C.D. Howe, retained
    far-reaching authority over all aspects of Canada's war effort. Drawing
    on the expertise of economists, DMS was a strong advocate of conserva-
    tive, fiscally responsible policies that made few compromises to labour
    interests. See John de N. Kennedy, *A History of the Department of Muni-
    tions and Supply: Canada in the Second World War* (Ottawa: King's
    Printer, 1950), 354–66.
28 LG, Oct. 1945, 1415. In the United States a total of 5,300 committees
    was established, with 3,800 active at one time, involving more than eight
    million workers. The British participation figures approximate those of
    the Americans; see Carol Reigelman, *British Joint Production Machinery*
    (Montreal: International Labour Office, 1994). See also de Schweinitz,
    Labor and Management in a Common Enterprise, 1–27; Carol Reigel-
    man, *Labor-Management Cooperation in United States War Production*
    (Montreal: International Labour Office, 1948); G.D.H. Cole, *The Case
    for Industrial Partnership* (London: Macmillan, 1957).

29 Robert Bothwell and William Kilbourn, *C.D. Howe: A Biography* (Toronto: McClelland & Stewart, 1979), 156–96

30 G.M.A. Grube, "Labour Law by Order in Council," *Canadian Forum* 21 (Nov. 1941): 237–40.

31 Canada, Industrial Division, Wartime Information Board (WIB), *Partners in Production: A Report on Labour-Management Production Committees in Canadian Industry* (Ottawa, 1945), 2–3. This statement, issued as a supplement to the 1945 White Paper on Employment and Income,was reiterated in WIB, *Postwar Planning Information – 4B* (Ottawa: King's Printer,1945), 22–3.

32 At a three-day conference of the Industrial Production Co-operation Board, LMPCs were declared "essential to the successful solution of the problems of peace." See LG, Jan. 1945, 2; Feb. 1945, 126–7.

33 NA, CLC Records, RG 28, I 103, vol. 145. IPCB, *Quarterly Report*, March 1946

34 For details, see Donald Kerr and Derek W. Holdsworth, eds., *Historical Atlas of Canada*, vol. 3 (Toronto: University of Toronto Press, 1990), plate 62; Wayne Roberts and John Bullen, "A Heritage of Hope and Struggle: Workers, Unions, and Politics in Canada, 1930–1982," in Michael S. Cross and Gregory S. Kealey, eds., *Modern Canada: 1930–1980s* (Toronto: McClelland & Stewart, 1984), 105–40.

35 NA, Records of the Department of Labour (DL Records), RG 27, B 6, vol. 896, CCL National Wage Coordinating Committee submission, 1 Aug. 1946

36 For commentary and statistical analysis of these strikes, see Gregory S. Kealey and Douglas Cruikshank, "Strikes in Canada, 1891–1950," *Labour/Le Travail* 20 (fall 1987): 85–145; Jamieson, *Times of Trouble*, 295–305; Morton, *Working People*, 175–200. For details of the packing-house strikes, see Alton W.J. Craig, "The Consequences of Provincial Jurisdiction for the Process of Company-wide Collective Bargaining in Canada" (PhD dissertation, Cornell University, 1964); Bryan Mahn and Ralph Schaffner, "The Packinghouse Workers in Kitchener," in J.T. Copp, ed., *Industrial Unionism in Kitchener* (Elora, Ont.: Cumnock Press, 1976).

37 A strike of 13,000 steelworkers in January 1943 caused severe production shortages. See Laurel Sefton MacDowell, "The 1943 Steel Strike against Wartime Wage Controls," *Labour/Le Travailleur* 10 (autumn 1982): 65–85.

38 Department of Labour, Information Division, 2 Feb. 1946; G.R. Blake, "Employee Participation with Management in Business Administration," Quarterly Review of Commerce 13 (1947–48): 226–7.

39 J.J. Deutsch, "Some Thoughts on the Public Service," *Canadian Journal of Economics and Political Science* 23 (Feb. 1957): 83–9.

40 Leonard Marsh, "Introduction," in Michael Bliss, ed., *The Report on Social Security for Canada, 1943* (1943; Toronto: University of Toronto Press, 1975), xiii.

41 H. Carl Goldenberg, "Labour-Management Cooperation," *Canadian Business*, Feb. 1945, 27–9, 72.

42 Arthur McArthur, "Peacetime Functions of Labour-Management Committees," ibid., Nov. 1945, 36–8, 118.

43 The Advisory Committee included representatives drawn from the all three major labour congresses (TLC, CCL, CTCC), the railway brotherhoods, and the Canadian Manufacturers' Association, as well as employers' associations for the railway, construction, and pulp and paper industries. Branch offices were situated in various industrial or production centres, including Toronto, Hamilton, London, St Catharines, Windsor, Montreal, Trois-Rivières, Vancouver, Winnipeg, Amherst, Glace Bay, and Fredericton.

44 See, for example, Department of Labour, *Common Sense in Labour Relations* (Ottawa: King's Printer, 1945); *Partners in Production* 2 (1949): 8–9, 12–19. See also de Schweinitz, *Labor and Management in a Common Enterprise*, 78–9, 142.

45 Allen May, "Letting Labour into the Front Office," *Liberty*, 28 Feb. 1944, 10. During the latter stages of the war, the aircraft manufacturers alone paid out an estimated $38,000 in suggestion awards.

46 A representative work of Harvard economist Sumner H. Slichter is *The Challenge of Industrial Relations: Trade Unions, Management and the Public Interest* (Ithaca: Cornell University Press, 1947). See also Clark Kerr and E. Wright Bakke, eds., *Unions, Management, and the Public* (New York: Harcourt, Brace, 1948). John T. Dunlop, who would eventually become U.S. secretary of labor, authored one of the major works in this field, *Industrial Relations Systems* (New York: Holt, 1958). Clark Kerr, another key figure in industrial relations, later assumed the presidency of the University of California. During World War II all three served on the staff of the influential National War Labor Board.

47 Department of Labour, IPCB, *Labour-Management Cooperation through Joint Consultation* (1949), 18–19; *Handbook on Suggestion Plans* (1946). Workers with non-contractual grievances were told to do as an NFB film (produced for the IPCB) suggested, "Take It Up with the LMPC."

48 In the United States, employers were alarmed about a nascent union, the Foreman's Association of America, fearing it would spread across the continent. See Lichtenstein, *Labor's War at Home*, 118–20; Steve Jefferys, *Management and Managed: Fifty Years of Crisis at Chrysler* (Cambridge: Cambridge University Press, 1986), 93–100; David Brody, *Workers in Industrial America: Essays on the 20th Century Struggle* (Oxford: Oxford University Press, 1980),180–211.

49 NA, DL Records, RG 27, B 6, vol. 8, IPCB, *The Foreman and the LMPC*,
    Information Bulletin 1, 21 Oct. 1946; *Pattern for Production* (1948), 6–8.
    The use of terminology replacing "workers" with "associates" and pro-
    duction teams is currently a widespread practice in contemporary indus-
    trial settings. For example, see David Robertson, James Rinehart, Christo-
    pher Huxley, and the CAW Research Group on CAMI, "Team Concept and
    Kaizen Japanese Production Management in a Unionized Canadian Auto
    Plant," *Studies in Political Economy* 39 (autumn 1992): 77–107; Bryan D.
    Palmer, *Capitalism Comes to the Backcountry: The Goodyear Invasion of
    Napanee* (Toronto: Between the Lines, 1994), 136–9.

50 IPCB, *Handbook on Suggestion Plans* (1946), 6–7. In this case, Pacific
    Mills, Limited (Vancouver) increased production to meet a rush export
    order for paper containers.

51 IPCB, *A Stitch in Time* (1948). The Brantford and Simcoe plants had been
    organized since 1917 under the United Garment Workers of America
    (AFL-TLC). See also *The Story of Five LMPCs* (1949).

52 For a listing of these wartime films, see Donald W. Bidd, ed., *The NFB
    Film Guide: The Productions of the National Film Board of Canada,
    1939–1989* (Montreal: NFB, 1991).

53 *Teamwork in Industry*, Sept. 1945, 4. Workers were also encouraged to
    make their own home-made posters to add credibility to the campaign.
    See also Marc H. Choko, *Canadian War Posters: 1914–1918, 1939–1945*
    (Ottawa: Éditions du Meridien, 1994).

54 Elaine Tyler May, *Homeward Bound: American Families in the Cold War
    Era* (New York: Basic Books, 1988), 58–91. See also Stephanie Coontz,
    The Way We Never Were: American Families and the Nostalgia Trap
    (New York: Basic Books, 1992), 92–121; Joanne Meyerowitz, ed., *Not
    June Cleaver: Women and Gender in Postwar America, 1945–1960*
    (Philadelphia: Temple University Press, 1994).

55 The post-war push for women to return to the household is addressed in
    Veronica Strong-Boag, "Home Dreams: Women and the Suburban Exper-
    iment in Canada, 1945–60," *Canadian Historical Review* 72 (Dec.
    1991): 471–504; Doug Owram, "Home and Family at Mid-Century"
    (paper presented to the Canadian Historical Association, 1992). On the
    subject of government-sponsored domesticity, see Margaret Hobbs and
    Ruth Roach Pierson, "'A Kitchen That Wastes No Steps': Gender, Class
    and the Home Improvement Plan, 1936–1940," *Histoire sociale/Social
    History* 31 (May 1988): 9–37.

56 Department of Labour, Industrial Relations Branch, Poster 7 (1946).
    Other posters dealt with workplace health and safety in the (apparently)
    all-male world of the post-war factory. In this context, the image of a
    workman tripping over shop debris with the caption "Good Housekeeping
    Is Important to Safety" held a particular irony.

57 Representative of this literature is Wartime Information Board, *Canadian Affairs* I, 18 (Oct.1944); Leonard Marsh and O.J. Firestone, "Will There Be Jobs?"; Department of Labour, *Dismiss – But What of a Job?* (Ottawa: King's Printer, 1945). See also Canadian Broadcasting Corporation, *The Soldier's Return* (Toronto: CBC 1945), 1–48.

58 Robert M. Campbell, *Grand Illusions: The Politics of the Keynesian Experience in Canada,1945–1975* (Peterborough: Broadview Press, 1987), 25; Mabel F. Timlin, *Keynesian Economics* (Toronto: University of Toronto Press, 1942)

59 For details on Canada's export market orientation, see Paul Phillips and Stephen Watson, "From Mobilization to Continentalism: The Canadian Economy in the Post-Depression Period," in Cross and Kealey, *Modern Canada*, 20–45; Glen Williams, *Not For Export: Towards a Political Economy of Canada's Arrested Development* (Toronto: McClelland & Stewart, 1983).

60 *Saturday Night*, 16 Dec. 1944, 48. Annual report by C.H. Carlisle, president, Dominion Bank. Similar positions were expressed by the Bank of Montreal, The Bank of Commerce, and the Bank of Nova Scotia. This viewpoint coincided with Ottawa's interpretation; see *Annual Report of the Bank of Canada* (1944), 11–15; (1946), 8–12.

61 Archives of Ontario, Pamphlet Collection, 13, *Wanted: 762,568 New Cars* (1945); 14, *The War and After* (1944); 15, *Canada's Market in Home Equipment* (1945); 16, *Jobs for Tomorrow* (1944). See also Association of Canadian Advertisers, *A.C.A. Continuing Study of Post-War Trends* (Montreal [monthly], 1943–45); and Joy Parr, "Shopping for a Good Stove: A Parable about Gender, Design, and the Market," in Joy Parr, ed., *A Diversity of Women: Ontario, 1945–1980* (Toronto: University of Toronto Press, 1995), 75–97

62 For details on C.D. Howe's post-war economic predictions see Campbell, *Grand Illusions*, 19–20; Bothwell and Kilbourn, *C.D. Howe*, 181–2.

63 Department of Reconstruction and Supply, Directorate of Economic Research, *Location and Effects of Wartime Industrial Expansion in Canada, 1939–1944* (Ottawa, 1945), 6–15; Ian Drummond, "Economic History and Canadian Economic Performance since the Second World War," in John Sargent, ed., *Postwar Macroeconomic Developments* (Ottawa: Supply and Services, 1986), 17–19

64 Gary Cross, *Time and Money: The Making of Consumer Culture* (London: Verso, 1993), 184.

65 Juliet B. Schor, *The Overworked American: The Unexpected Decline of Leisure* (New York: Basic Books, 1991), 60–6.

66 Ibid., 128–9.

67 See Alvin Finkel, "Paradise Postponed: A Re-examination of the Green

Book Proposals of 1945," *Journal of the Canadian Historical Association* 4 (1993): 120–42.

68 The inability of federal and provincial authorities to resolve conflicts relating to the delegation of authority under the BNA Act led to the eventual failure of the Dominion-Provincial Conference on Reconstruction. See NA, DL Records, RG 27, B 6, Deputy Minister's Files, vol. 8–7–8–9; *Canadian Affairs* 2, 13 (Aug. 1945), Boris Swerling, "Conference for Ten"; Doug Owram, *The Government Generation: Canadian Intellectuals and the State, 1900–1945* (Toronto: University of Toronto Press, 1986), 319–25; and Robert Bothwell, Ian Drummond, and John English, *Canada since 1945* (Toronto: University of Toronto Press, 1981), 91–8.

69 Dominion-Provincial Conference on Reconstruction, *Proposals of the Government of Canada* (Aug. 1945), 18–20; Health, Welfare and Labour, *Reference Book for the Dominion-Provincial Conference* (Aug. 1945), 63–112. See also LG, May 1945, 621; Maxwell Cohen, *The Dominion-Provincial Conference: Some Basic Issues* (Toronto: Ryerson Press, 1945), 16–17. On the issue of provincial autonomy, see James P. Bickerton, *Nova Scotia, Ottawa and the Politics of Regional Development* (Toronto: University of Toronto Press, 1990), 119–24.

70 See Ruth Roach Pierson, *They're Still Women after All: The Second World War and Canadian Womanhood* (Toronto: McClelland & Stewart, 1986); Gail Cuthbert Brandt, "'Pigeon-Holed and Forgotten': The Work of the Subcommittee on the Post-War Problems of Women," *Histoire sociale/Social History* 15 (March–May 1982): 239–59.

71 For example, see Charlotte Whitton, *The Dawn of Ampler Life* (Ottawa: Macmillan, 1943). See also Annalee Golz, "Family Matters: The 'Canadian Family' and the State in the Postwar Period," *Left History* 2 (fall 1993): 9–49; Owram, "Home and Family at Mid-Century"; Strong-Boag, "Home Dreams"; Margaret Higonnet et al., *Behind the Lines: Gender and the Two World Wars* (New Haven: Yale University Press, 1987); Barry Broadfoot, *The Veteran's Years: Coming Home from the War* (Vancouver: Douglas & McIntyre, 1985).

72 For an contemporary example of this debate see Agnes MacPhail and Helen MacGill, "Do Women Expect to Go Back to Kitchens after the War?" *Monetary Times*, Oct. 1943, 29–31, 103.

73 It must be noted that women wage-earners continued to increase numerically in the immediate post-war era, but structural barriers often maintained gender inequalities. For one case study of this issue, see Pamela Sugiman, *Labour's Dilemma: The Gender Politics of Autoworkers in Canada, 1937–1979* (Toronto: University of Toronto Press, 1994).

74 Jane Lewis, *Women in Britain since 1945: Women, Family, Work, and the State in the Post-War Years* (Oxford: Blackwell, 1992), 36–9, 92–4.

75 *Teamwork in Industry* 5 (Sept. 1948).

76 For example, compare the subject matter of the IPCB booklet, *Pattern for Production* (1948), which dealt with the case study of LMPCs at the Market Street plant of Massey-Harris in Brantford, Ontario. In this factory with an overwhelmingly male labour force of more than 1,100, LMPCs were assumed to deal with issues closely related to the workplace, not the home. An LMPC was later established at the Massey-Harris "M" Foundry (Brantford), one of the nation's largest.

77 H. Ross Rutherford, "Partnership at Monarch," *Plant Administration*, May 1948. At the plant in Dunnville, Ontario (southwest of Hamilton), the recently (1945) certified union, Local 736, TWUA (CCL-CIO) used LMPCs to address "long smoldering" issues of workplace ventilation, lighting, heating, and employee lockers and lunchrooms. This focus on shop-floor conditions mayhave been the result of a predominately male workforce. The article claimed that labour-management cooperation at Dunnville served as a model for Monarch's Ontario facilities in St Thomas and St Catharines. Kent Rowley, spokesperson for the rival UTWA (TLC-AFL), provided a detailed assessment of abysmal conditions in textiles industry to the 1943 National War Labour Board hearings. See NWLB, *Proceedings*, Report 5 (26 May), 400–14; "Developing Good Labour Relationships," *Canadian Unionist*, June 1947, 27–9.

78 W.R. Dymond, "Production Committees Can Bring Industrial Peace," *Saturday Night Magazine*, 15 June 1946. See also W.R. Dymond, "Union-Management Cooperation at the Toronto Factory of Lever Brothers Limited," *Canadian Journal of Economics and Political Science* 10 (Feb. 1947): 26–67.

79 "The Congress Wage-Policy," *Canadian Unionist*, March 1946, 51–2.

80 NA, DL Records, RG 27, B 6, vol. 896, CCL National Wage Coordinating Committee submission, 1 Aug. 1946. This trend to permanent state intervention was widespread across North America. In the United States, speaking before the 1945 Labour-Management Conference, Congress of Industrial Organizations (CIO) president Philip Murray embraced what amounted to a corporatist state, to be known as "The Industry Council Plan."

81 NA, CLC Records, MG 28, I 103, vol. 223, Pat Conroy to W.H. Sands (UPWA), Kelowna, BC, 17 July 1946.

82 For background on the Beveridge Report, see Paul Addison, *The Road to 1945: British Politics and the Second World War*, rev. ed. (London: Pimlico, 1994), 210–28.

83 The Dominion Advisory Committee on Reconstruction (also known as the James Committee, after its chairman, McGill president Cyril James) was established in 1941. Associated with the project was a study of postwar social programs, the *Report on Social Security for Canada*, prepared by social scientist Leonard Marsh.

84 Owram, *The Government Generation*, 287. See also Dennis Guest, *The Emergence of Social Security in Canada*, 2nd ed. (Vancouver: UBC Press, 1985), 104–41.

85 The term "parastate" as a description of state intervention during the World War I era is used in Alan Dawley, *Struggles for Justice: Social Responsibility and the Liberal State* (Cambridge, Mass.: Belknap-Harvard University Press, 1991), 196–203; see also Howell J. Harris, "The Snares of Liberalism? Politicians, Bureaucrats, and the Shaping of Federal Labour Relations Policy in the United States, ca. 1915–47," in Steven Tolliday and Jonathan Zeitlin, eds., *Shop-Floor Bargaining and the State* (Cambridge: Cambridge University Press, 1985), 148–91.

86 The federal government codified many of the reforms initially introduced in its wartime regulations with the Industrial Relations and Disputes Investigation Act (1948). Most provinces adopted aspects of the IRDIA for their labour codes.

87 On the stratification of trade unions, see Mike Davis, *Prisoners of the American Dream* (London: Verso, 1986); Kim Moody, *An Injury to All: The Decline of American Unionism* (London: Verso, 1988), 41–69; Robert Brenner and Mark Glick, "The Regulation Approach: Theory and History," *New Left Review* 188 (July–Aug. 1991): 45–119.

88 For details of the anti-communist battles, see Abella, *Nationalism, Communism, and Canadian Labour*, 44–53, 66–85, 168–87.

89 Department of Labour, *Report of the Deputy Minister* (1950), 29–31; (1955), 29–30; *Teamwork in Industry* 10 (Oct. 1953): 1–2.

90 In what became the focus of considerable worker derision, General Motors Corporation used a similar strategy in the 1980s for its automotive assembly plants with the characters of "Quality Cat" and "Howie Makem." See Ben Hamper, *Rivethead: Tales from the Assembly Line* (New York: Warner Books, 1991), 111–16.

91 *Teamwork in Industry* 11 (Sept. 1954): 4

92 Wood, *The Current Status of Labour-Management Cooperation in Canada*, 16; the author observes that "by 1964, almost 50 per cent of the total were committees covering fewer than 100 employees."

93 Department of Labour, *Report of the Deputy Minister* (1965), 8–9.

94 The mandate of *Worklife* appears to be both less specific and less ambitious than its IPCB forerunners. The National Film Board continued to deal with issues related to workplace cooperation, producing a filmstrip for Labour Canada, *Labour-Management in a Changing World* (1967).

95 For example, the Ontario QWL Centre (1978–88). See also Charlotte Gold, *Labour-Management Committees: Confrontation, Cooptation, or Cooperation?* (Ithaca: ILR Press, 1986); Jerome M. Rosow, *Teamwork: Joint Labor-Management Programs in America* (New York: Pergamon Press, 1986); Donald V. Nightingale, *Workplace Democracy* (Toronto:

University of Toronto Press, 1982); Norman Eiger, "Organizing for Quality of Working Life," *Labor Studies Journal* 3 (fall 1989): 3–13; Don Wells, *Empty Promises: Quality of Working Life Programs and the Labor Movement* (New York: Basic Books, 1987). For two views of Total Quality Management schemes, see Cathryn Klassen, "TQM – Improving Quality Means Improving Communication," *Canadian Business Review*, summer 1993, 15–8; Mike Parker and Jane Slaughter, "TQM: Lean Production Is Mean Production," *Canadian Dimension*, Jan.–Feb. 1994, 21–2.

96 The Michelin Bill was an amendment to the provincial Trade Union Act, stipulating one certification vote for three plants, despite wide geographic separation, which made unionization of the company operations in Nova Scotia virtually impossible. See Kell Antoft, "Harnessing Confrontation: A Review of the Nova Scotia Joint-Labour Management Study Committee, 1962–1979," in Robert Canteloup, ed., *Labour in Atlantic Canada* (Saint John: University of New Brunswick, 1981), 103–16; Bickerton, *Nova Scotia, Ottawa, and the Politics of Regional Development*, 283–5; Ian McKay, *The Craft Transformed: An Essay on the Carpenters of Halifax, 1885–1985* (Halifax: Holdfast Press, 1985), 129–38; Ken Clare, "Michelin: The Fortress That Didn't Fall," *New Maritimes*, July–Aug. 1986.

97 For a representative example of its work, see *Business-Labour Task Force on Adjustment: Report of the CLMPC Task Forces on the Labour Force Development Strategy* (Ottawa: CLMPC, 1990). See also Sarah Beth Wild, *The Future for Consultation in Canada: Views from Inside the CLMPC* (Kingston: Industrial Relations Centre, Queen's University, 1992); Anthony Giles, "The Canadian Labour Congress and Tripartism," *Relations industrielles/Industrial Relations* 37 (1982): 93–124.

98 For further discussion of this point, see Brody, *Workers in Industrial America*, 173–257; Lichtenstein, *Labor's War at Home*, 203–45; Michael Goldfield, *The Decline of Organized Labor in the United States* (Chicago: University of Chicago Press, 1987), esp. 180–230; Juliet Schor, *The Overworked American*, 60–6; Bruce Levine et al., *Who Built America? Working People and the Nation's Economy, Politics, Culture, and Society*, American Social History Project, vol. 2 (New York: Pantheon, 1992), 469–77.

99 For discussions on this point, see Palmer, *Working-Class Experience*, 370–7; Carla Lipsig-Mumme, "Unions Struggle with New Work Order," *Policy Options* 16 (Oct. 1995): 3–6.

P.E. BRYDEN

Beyond the Green Book

The Ontario Approach to Intergovernmental Relations, 1945–1955

Although the Dominion-Provincial Conference on Reconstruction in 1945–46 failed in spectacular fashion, producing neither an agreement on the issues nor an agreement to adjourn, the federal government proposals contained in the Green Book are nevertheless regarded as having provided the blueprint for the Canadian social security net that had developed by the end of the 1960s. But the eventual success of the 1945 proposals would surely not have been apparent to an observer a decade after the conference: with the establishment of unemployment assistance, pensions, and health insurance still yet to come, from the vantage point of 1955 the conference on reconstruction must have seemed as much of a failure then as it did when angry premiers left the meeting room early in the afternoon of 3 May 1946.

Yet the following decade of apparent inactivity on the issues raised in the Green Book was an important one for the Ontario delegation and its successors at Queen's Park. Widely regarded as having been at the root of the failure of the reconstruction conference, the Conservative Ontario government under George Drew had, in fact, been experimenting with a new approach to federal-provincial relations which would both end the acrimony that had characterized Ontario's relations with Ottawa and simultaneously achieve a more agreeable place for Ontario within the federation.[1] Always jealous of provincial autonomy and desirous of a broad reading of provincial powers conferred under the BNA Act, the Ontario government shifted its strategy in 1945 from actively confronting Ottawa's proposals to offering alternative, nationally viable proposals of its own. The experiment had not been particularly successful at first, but ten years of perfecting, combined with a change in leadership, left Ontario in the position of being able to articulate the national interest. By the time the Green Book came to be regarded as the "blueprint" for social security in Canada, the image had more truth than most commentators have recognized: it bore a lot of "blue" finger "prints" from the eager and ultimately successful massaging of ten years of Conservative governments in Ontario.

Drew's bailiwick was post-war planning. This was an area that he had already argued from the Opposition benches was in need of attention, and an issue that would distinguish him from his counterpart in Ottawa. The Port Hope Conference in September 1943 had already laid some of the foundations for the Conservative reconstruction plans: as an "unofficial meeting" of Conservatives, the "round table conference called ... to consider war and post-war problems" was not supposed to result in "binding" policies so much as "stir up some fresh interest throughout the country in the Party."[2] It did serve to announce that the Conservative Party was prepared to give thought to post-war planning. Drew developed some of the Port Hope ideas into his own twenty-two-point plan, which formed the basis of his election platform in 1943. In addition to providing vague but enumerated promises to cut school taxes, restructure and de-politicize Ontario Hydro, and develop a more coherent plan for social security in Ontario than currently existed, Drew also gave some indication among his twenty-two points of his intergovernmental strategy. The second of his points read as follows: "We will at all times work in effective cooperation with the Dominion Government and with all other governing bodies in Canada in all activities which will assist in the prosecution of the war to a successful conclusion, and in establishing a sound basis of social security, health insurance and protection in their old age for all our people. At the same time we will insist that the constitutional rights of the people of Ontario be preserved and that the Government of Ontario exercise full control of its own provincial affairs."[3] Drew was at once distinguishing himself from his federal counterparts in his desire to begin contemplating post-war policies immediately and emphasizing his intention to continue to protect provincial jurisdiction in the process.

The Liberals were swept out of office in August 1943, and the government was turned over to Drew's thirty-eight Conservative members, who were able to maintain the confidence of the legislature only with the support of the thirty-four elected members of the CCF. Nevertheless, Drew governed as if he enjoyed a majority and immediately set about preparing Ontario for life after the war. On the domestic front, that largely meant introducing the reforms contained in the twenty-two-point plan; in intergovernmental relations, it meant trying to convince a reluctant Mackenzie King of the need for a conference on reconstruction. What was quickly perceived as a leadership vacuum in Ottawa provided the premier with the opportunity to define himself as a truly national leader and to present his proposals as in the interests of more than just Ontarians but also of Canadians across the country.

Suspicious that any plans the federal government had for reconstructing Canada after wartime were being made in isolation, without consultation with the provinces over issues that involved shared jurisdiction, Drew pressed early and often for an intergovernmental meeting to address the issue. He urged Prime Minister King "that a Dominion-Provincial Conference be called at the earliest possible date to consider the broad question of post war planning and reconstruction."[4] King responded in his usual careful style: he proposed a conference but refused to set a date, and instead, he announced that material was being prepared for use by the conference and requested the assistance of the provinces in providing the financial data needed for the consolidation of the federal proposals.[5] This very cautious movement in the direction of intergovernmental discussion left ample opportunity for disagreement between the leaders in Ottawa and Toronto. Drew argued repeatedly for calling an early conference and just as frequently refused King's request for Ontario civil servants to report to Ottawa to assist in the preparation of the financial material. On the one hand, Drew wanted "to know more definitely what is proposed" before relinquishing a much-needed expert and, on the other, insisted that the conference should not be "so much a question of figures and facts as it is of working principles."[6] King's delaying tactics and public statements that Drew was to blame for the long pre-conference preparation period increasingly frustrated the Ontario premier. "It seems to me," he wrote to King, "that personal opinions regarding any of the individuals or the political complexion of the various Governments is a matter of no concern whatever. What is of consequence is that the Governments of this country get together as soon as possible."[7] But his arguments went unheeded in Ottawa for many months; King did not set a date for the Dominion-Provincial Conference on Reconstruction until the summer of 1945, a mere six weeks before the first ministers met in August.[8]

The dominion-provincial conference seemed destined to get off to a bad start in more ways that one. Not only had there been over a year of quarrelling between politicians and officials from Ottawa and Toronto, but the federal government had already shown enough of its hand to suggest to the provinces that its wartime expansion of power was unlikely to be discontinued. In announcing the introduction of a universal system of family allowances in the summer of 1944, the federal government had made known that it, not the provinces, would be the social security benefactor for the nation; moreover, the obvious long-term expense of such a program meant that "the federal government quickly gained the upper hand in its fiscal dealings with the provinces."[9] Drew was quick to question the motives in Ottawa in a speech on 9 August 1944 which suggested that Ontario was prepared to use every means possible to reject family allowances: "If the Ontario Government submitted to the arrogant usurpation of power in passing the baby bonus bill then we would be handing over the rights of the Province to a Government which has shown only too clearly that it submits to the will of Quebec."[10]

But an unconsidered rejection, even if that were possible, of a policy that was wildly popular with the public would do more harm than good. Drew settled in to assess the situation, which included discussions with cabinet on "the course we are to follow in regard to the constitutional rights of this province, [which are] inseparably tied in with the special privileges which have been extended to Quebec in almost every field," and discussions with the dean of conservative social policy in Canada, Charlotte Whitton. [11] As much as Drew might bemoan, both publicly and privately, the "steady trend toward a Quebec-dominated Canada," his real concerns were that Ontario's fiscal position was being "impaired" in the cause of a social program which with "more localized ... supervision [would be] more humane and ... carefully supervised."[12] There seemed little in Drew's power to avert the federal action, however, and instead, the battlefield for control of the post-war purse and the responsibility for post-war health and welfare shifted squarely to the meeting rooms of the Dominion-Provincial Conference on Reconstruction.

Well aware that Ottawa probably intended to hang on to the taxation fields it had moved into in 1942 for the purposes of mounting and financing an effective war, the Ontario government designed an opposition position that it hoped would be more effective than merely rejecting the federal reconstruction proposals out of hand. Having already established himself as a chief advocate for intergovernmental discussions, and working in part on behalf of all the other premiers, who were keen to begin the negotiations early, Drew was in a position to try to build some provincial consensus in opposition to Ottawa.[13] He gave serious thought to the advice of some of his provincial civil servants. Chester Walters of the Treasury Department urged both preparedness and alliances: "By being well briefed we can hope to uphold our own viewpoint at Ottawa and may reasonably expect to carry with us some of the stronger provinces such as Quebec and British Columbia. A pre-conference conference before the plenary session would be of advantage to all provinces and would save time later on; a more or less informal inter-provincial conference would also help."[14] There was no pre-conference conference, but there was plenty of informal discussion between the various premiers over the next several months.

The first step, however, was to establish an Ontario approach to reconstruction. When Mackenzie King announced that the federal government would be using the August meetings as an opportunity to table a number of proposals, Drew responded that "the Ontario government will do the same and I assume the Governments of the other provinces will do likewise."[15] The Ontario government was well prepared. The background studies prepared by the provincial Bureau of Statistics and Research made a number of points clear. First, provincial jurisdiction was sacrosanct, and the provincial government should remain free to legislate in any way it saw fit in areas that were clearly its constitutional responsibility. Second, the economic stability of Ontario had to be maintained at all costs. Within this framework, then, measures that would address the concerns of other provinces could be considered. Ontario's main goals as it prepared for the conference on reconstruction were thus fairly clear. The wartime system by which the federal government had moved into provincial tax fields in order to accumulate the capital necessary to finance the war effort had to be stopped; this would provide the opportunity for the provinces to cover the costs associated with post-war reconstruction. Provincial spending on such things as school and hospital construction, as well as on mother's allowances and old-age pensions, would serve to inject money into the economy and thereby jump-start economic recovery.[16] All was dependent, however, on the termination of the irksome Wartime Tax Rental Agreements, the system by which the federal government had moved into taxation areas traditionally under provincial jurisdiction as a "temporary" measure necessary to finance the war effort.

The Ontario position was one that held an enormous appeal for a large province, rich in both resources and corporate tax bases, but Drew's government was attempting to do more than merely outline an alternative to the anticipated federal position that would serve its purely provincialist goals. Instead, it was clear from the Ontario brief that it was designed to appeal to a much broader spectrum of the country. For example, despite acknowledging "a strong conviction in Ontario ... that when a provincial government got into financial

difficulties it should find its own solution by resorting to direct taxation or curtailing expenditure," the brief nevertheless proposed a
system of subsidies for have-not provinces.[17] The complaints about the
current fiscal situation were moderate, at least in contrast to the traditional Ontario strategy of detailing at length the costs of Confederation
that it bore, and the document was able to end on a much more positive note than was common: "We consider that Ontario now has a
splendid opportunity as the 'keystone' province to give leadership in
establishing subsidies on a sound basis and to improve Dominion-
Provincial and interprovincial relations generally."[18]

As the opening of the conference neared, there was "increasing hope
that the Dominion and nine Provinces may achieve through the preliminary talks ... a new and satisfactory working agreement in their
relations."[19] If so, it would not be easy, a fact made clear when, immediately after the prime minister's opening greeting to the conference
delegates, George Drew rose to object to the tabling of the federal proposals prior to an agreement on the general procedure to be followed.
He was joined in this opposition by the premiers of Quebec and New
Brunswick, although King confined his disgust with this grandstanding
to Drew and Maurice Duplessis.[20] After much debate, it was finally
agreed that the federal government would have the opportunity to
present its proposals for post-war reconstruction, an agreement with
little significance since the proposals had already been distributed to
members of the press.

The federal scheme, commonly referred to as the Green Book proposals, was, not surprisingly to the Ontario delegation, predicated on
the continuation of the wartime policy by which Ottawa collected all
direct and indirect taxes and returned to the provinces a premium to
compensate for this invasion of provincial jurisdiction. With this added
revenue, the federal government pledged to offer a social security
package that included unemployment insurance, disability allowances,
pensions, and a joint federal-provincial health insurance system. If
adopted, the policies would be "the instrument of completely changing
the emphasis of administration and legislation on social problems from
the provinces to the dominion."[21] The Green Book also promised a
system of equalization grants to assist provinces in which the standard
of living was considered to be below the national average.[22] As
planned, the first session of the conference was devoted primarily to an
airing of the federal proposals, very brief preliminary responses from
the provincial premiers, and the striking of various subcommittees of
the conference to give detailed consideration to the relevant issues.[23]
Despite newspaper reports that the conference adjourned on a high
note of conciliation, as a province that commanded a large and stable

tax base, Ontario stood to lose if its taxes were collected by the federal government and redistributed across the nation.[24] When the conference adjourned on 10 August 1945, Drew and his colleagues returned to Toronto to begin the task of preparing a detailed response.

Clearly, there were problems with the division of tax powers, for the two levels of government shared rights to the lucrative direct tax fields, but Ontario's answer was not to merely continue allowing Ottawa sole jurisdiction as the Green Book proposed. Instead, after careful study of the alternatives, the province advocated a fiscal structure whereby corporate and personal tax fields would be vacated by the provinces, but they would retain control over succession duties.[25] In addition, the provinces would take over complete control of the so-called nuisance taxes – gas, amusement, racetrack and taxes and the like. In response to the clear regional inequality, Ontario proposed a system of adjustment grants that would bring the poorer regions a level of income impossible to achieve simply through provincial taxation. The experience of the Depression had left little doubt in anyone's mind that new social welfare programs were necessary in order to combat the exigencies of old age, unemployment, and poor health, but all these fell under the constitutional authority of the provinces. Ontario's reconstruction plan anticipated a system of social security that would see Ottawa footing most of the bill and the provinces retaining administrative control, in line with Drew's thinking that such projects were best left to local authorities.[26]

If the first component of Ontario's new approach to intergovernmental relations was to draft an alternative set of solutions to national problems, the second component was to try to cultivate support for the plan. An alternative to the federal proposal for constitutional change and economic renewal was of little use without some assurances that it met not only the concerns of the Ontario delegation but also those being felt in other provincial capitals. Drew's public statements, ostensibly addressed to the Ontario voters but designed for broader consumption, made clear that the provincial government was preparing its counter-proposals with the best interests of the nation in mind. "I believe that a high measure of uniformity of [federal and provincial] legislation and simplification of tax collection is a vital necessity," he informed a Canadian Club audience. "Neither should anything I have said be interpreted as an objection to the pooling of our resources for the welfare of Canada as a whole. I believe that Ontario should take her full share in building the strength and security of every part of Canada." Make no mistake about it, Drew warned. Ontario's position was "not only in the interests of the people of Ontario but it is also in the best interests of the whole of Canada."[27]

Both Drew and the provincial treasurer, Leslie Frost, had informally approached some of the other provincial premiers to gain their support,[28] but perhaps the most important opportunity for developing these relationships occurred during the in-camera sessions of the coordinating committee and the meetings of the various subcommittees of the reconstruction conference. Although each province was required to make submissions elaborating its particular financial situation and the "effects of the Dominion proposals on the budgetary position of the provinces," Ontario's submission went considerably further in outlining alternative arrangements.[29] As a result, it became just as important to the background of the debate as the proposals outlined by the federal delegation.[30] Many of the premiers pressed to begin the discussions of the coordinating committee with the Ontario proposals; according to the Ontario officials, the earlier Economic Committee meetings had made it "apparent to all the provinces that the Dominion proposals of last August were not acceptable in any case from the point of view of being able to finance their own responsibilities, quite apart from any question as to the principle underlying the proposals."[31] But despite the suggestion from provinces well versed in the content of the Ontario document that it provide the starting point for discussion, Drew wanted to keep the initial debate focused on the Green Book. He believed that "by removing the discussion to the Ontario proposals [the federal government] would have avoided embarrassment and been in a position to place responsibility on the Ontario Government for a breakdown of the Conference if our proposals were not accepted. In fact Mr. King's subsequent course throughout the Conference went so far as to suggest the possibility that he was deliberately planning to wreck the Conference if he could once get the discussion on to the Ontario proposals."[32] Thus, on Drew's insistence, debate revolved around the federal proposals and, within that framework, focused on taxation arrangements.[33]

During the course of the in-camera meetings, the Ontario delegation was joined in its criticism of the Green Book by, at various times, each of the provinces except Prince Edward Island. It was becoming clear that, on some level, "the Provinces are unanimous in a strong opinion that the Dominion should vacate those fields of taxation which they entered during the war period [and] ... the Dominion should not go into any other fields of taxation heretofore occupied by the Provinces."[34] Agreement on this most fundamental opinion in Ontario was important to securing consensus on the components of the province's alternative proposals. It had made some effort to deal with the federal government in a new and less-confrontational manner by designing alternatives and seeking support for those alternatives from other provinces. The new approach seemed to be working, for Drew could declare that "our position is extremely strong," in large part because "Ontario has been acting on behalf of other provinces."[35] The Ontario plan clearly merited serious consideration, and certain elements of the plan were enthusiastically received: the British Columbia representatives called Ontario's "a well-proportioned scheme," and Nova Scotia's Angus L. Macdonald, who thought that "there are some germs of good things in what Drew has said," agreed that the provinces must have "certain definite fields of taxation" reserved for themselves.[36]

But as far as one participant was concerned, the only clear alliance that was developing was the one between Drew and Quebec's Maurice Duplessis. Although the federal "experts seem to think that Drew will have to yield his point of view" on the necessity of some provincial taxation autonomy, Prime Minister King remained convinced that he "will follow Duplessis in opposing the other provinces."[37] King was probably mildly paranoid about the alliance, but he did not underestimate the degree to which the premiers of Ontario and Quebec were of one mind. Although Drew was prepared to make some concessions to Ottawa, particularly in respect to the vacation of personal income and corporation taxes, when "Duplessis came out strongly against allowing the Dominion to have the succession duties ... Drew took a similar stand."[38] He argued "that the B.N.A. Act in spirit, if not on strict legal grounds, provided for exclusive provincial jurisdiction in the direct tax fields, and he argued that the cause of the breakdown of every federation in history had been the abandonment of provincial rights of direct taxation."[39] The most unlikely person to be convinced of the legitimacy of this position was the prime minister himself, who, when it became "quite apparent that neither Ontario nor Quebec will give up this field," could only comment privately that he did "not blame them."[40]

Under pressure from Drew that the closed meetings of the coordinating committee be replaced by open sessions to eliminate the possibility of views being misrepresented in the press, the full conference reconvened at the end of April 1946.[41] There could not have been much hope for success: neither of the architects of the two main proposals, Ontario and Ottawa, had been able to convince enough of the others of the utility of its position to ensure victory. Drew and Duplessis consistently backed each other up in their arguments against the principle of excessive centralization, although the Ontario premier accompanied his denunciations of the Green Book with solid counter-proposals. He also continued to hammer home the message that "our proposals are made in the belief that they should be equally acceptable in every part of Canada and are in no instance put forward with the thought of giving any special advantage to those who live in the Province of Ontario."[42] Nevertheless, leaks to the press had allowed for a certain sense to grow that Ontario was thwarting the efforts of the dominion-provincial conference; the opportunity to meet again, this time under public scrutiny, offered Drew the chance to clarify that not only was Ontario's opposition valid but that its alternatives were as well.[43] Thus the Ontario brief first outlined the promises that had been made when the Wartime Tax Rental Agreements had been entered into, specifically that it had been proposed, according to the federal finance minister, J.L. Ilsley, " as a temporary expedient for the duration of the war only." It then criticized both the principle of continuing to invade provincial taxation jurisdiction and the formulas used by the federal government to determine the compensation paid to the provinces for this privilege. After pointing to the Ontario proposals, which protected provincial fiscal autonomy while providing for an adjustment grant for poorer provinces, Drew concluded his statement to the conference by reiterating that "the Government of Ontario is not prepared to place itself in the position of legislative or economic dependence upon the Dominion Government."[44]

At this point, it was somewhat difficult to determine the degree of provincial support that Drew had been able to secure. On one level, his statement to the conference made occasional note of Ontario's attempts to address extra-provincial concerns: Drew emphasized the adjustment grant proposal, for example, and also noted "that the arguments we put forward are not directed toward the special advantage of Ontario, but that in our opinion they are arguments which apply with equal force to all the provinces."[45] Most of the other premiers seemed oblivious to these claims, however. Manitoba's Stuart Garson, while "commenting on Mr. Drew's statement that it was the provinces that were being asked to make concessions not the Dominion ... said Manitoba is not being asked to make concessions"; Saskatchewan's Tommy Douglas called Ontario's proposals a "holy horror."[46] Yet King seemed to think that Drew was amassing substantial support, not just from the usual sources such as Quebec, but also from Nova Scotia and perhaps other provinces.[47] But regardless of the shifting alliances among the provincial premiers, this particular group of politicians would prove unable to reach an agreement of any sort.

The Dominion-Provincial Conference on Reconstruction concluded on 3 May 1946 with vitriol and acrimony but without agreement. It was, according to one historian, "one of the most important [conferences] in Canadian history – not for what it accomplished, but for what it did not."[48] While the conference was clearly a failure at the time, a number of elements of a new Ontario approach to intergovernmental relations began to emerge. First, every policy initiative would have to be weighed in the context of a relatively conservative assessment of Ontario's financial capacity – an assessment which, in the case of the reconstruction conference, was based both on a fear of post-war economic collapse and a hugely curtailed tax base, thanks to the federal proposals. Second, federal invasion of provincial jurisdiction had to be limited, if not avoided entirely. Once these conditions had been met, Ontario then confronted Ottawa with a much more sophisticated strategy than had characterized bilateral negotiations in the pre-war period. Ontario politicians armed themselves with an alternative proposal to that being promoted by the federal government, one which both conformed to the internal criteria of the province and also purported to solve the same national problems that had usually been considered Ottawa's responsibility. By appealing to other provinces, both informally through personal contact and formally in the elements of the Ontario proposal, Drew and his colleagues attempted to enlist enough support to ensure that the Ontario scheme became the national policy. In the case of reconstruction, Ontario was less than successful, although the federal government could certainly not count the victory for itself. Furthermore, while the conference itself was over, the debate over the issues raised in the aftermath of World War II had hardly begun. The two key issues of fiscal arrangements and social policy would continue to be discussed over the next decade, and in the course of these discussions, Ontario would continue to utilize and perfect the strategies that it had first brought into play in the tension-filled environment of the reconstruction conference.[49]

The benefit of hindsight shows us that the reconstruction conference was truly over on that afternoon in early May 1946, but the participants had no such luxury. Before admitting failure, Drew and a number of other premiers devoted considerable energy over the next several months to resuming the conference and continuing the discussions within the forum of an official, multi-item conference. Drew's task was made all the more monumental by the perception that he himself had been at the root of the premature adjournment. Manitoba's premier, Stuart Garson, seemed to strike an appealing chord when he declared that "it is calamitous for Canada that the Ontario and Quebec governments could not have continued with those of the other seven provinces in the negotiation of a compromise of the small area of disagreement which still remains between the seven provinces and the Dominion."[50] The characterization of the evil Drew-Duplessis axis thwarting the efforts of the dominion-provincial conference was created at the beginning and, to a large extent, has remained in the historical literature.[51] None of this really seems to have been George Drew's intention, although he too often let his hatred for Mackenzie King dictate his behaviour. Paralleling his letter-writing activity of 1944 and 1945, Drew spent the summer and fall of 1946 attempting to convince the prime minister of the necessity of reconvening the conference; far from wanting the debate to end, he desired an agreement on an "overall plan for effective co-operation between governments which will provide a simple mechanism for handling those matters of common concern which are constantly demanding joint action."[52]

Furthermore, Drew was offended by his depiction "as the Big Bad Wolf of the Dominion-Provincial Conference." He emphasized to an audience in Winnipeg that the Ontario position had never wavered from "the assumption that the future strength of Canada and the welfare of all its people will depend upon the measure of co-ordina-tion and continuing co-operation which can be established between all governments in Canada."[53] Drew's right-hand man through all of this, his provincial treasurer, Leslie Frost, was also convinced that all efforts had been directed toward proposing alternatives to the federal Green Book that would address the various concerns of provincial governments across the country. In the aftermath of the spring 1946 conclusion of the conference, Frost laid out a number of things that the Ontario government would have to consider, acknowledging that "quite properly, in view of the Conference, [thus far] our approach has been calculated to assist our relations with other provinces." Most importantly, Frost urged Drew to consider the political and financial cost of rejecting the federal government's final offer, and in proposing ways around the impasse, he suggested that "we can discuss the matter with some of the provinces whose views are similar to our own."[54]

The fact that King never recalled the meeting on reconstruction did not seem to deter Drew. His opposition to the federal proposals, as contained in the Green Book or later in Ilsley's 1946 budget, never wavered, and his attempts to woo provincial allies to his cause only increased. Angus Macdonald of Nova Scotia continued to defend Drew's actions at the conference, arguing that "the rigid attitude of the Dominion people had as much, if not more to do with the unfortunate results."[55] By the fall of 1946 he was attempting to court Alberta premier Ernest Manning, hoping "to have the pleasure of a personal conversation with you" to discuss the situation. Manning responded positively to Drew's revised suggestion for an alternative formula for tax sharing between the federal and provincial governments, considering it one that "should be acceptable to all of the non-agreeing Provinces." In Alberta, he said, "we are ready and anxious to do anything we can to facilitate unanimity among the non-agreeing Provinces."[56] It was all just too late: Ilsley's budget had introduced the continuation of the of tax rental system, despite a failure to achieve agreement at the intergovernmental conference, and any agreement between those provinces in opposition was illusory since Ottawa made individual deals with each of them. But despite Ontario's somewhat sloppy efforts at the dominion-provincial conference of 1945–46, at cultivating provincial allies and despite its ultimate failure, there was the beginning of the articulation of a new approach to intergovernmental negotiations.

Instead of merely trying to assert a provincial rights agenda, as had been the tactic of several generations of Ontario premiers before him, Drew sought to offer an alternative to the Green Book proposals. While this alternative protected provincial taxation jurisdiction to a much greater degree than the federal position, it also included elements designed to address the specific concerns of other regions. The Ontario proposal recognized the need for equalization to redress regional imbalance, allowed federal occupancy of both income and corporate taxes, and included an expanded welfare system. It was not, then, a purely pro-Ontario position but, instead, a first step in the direction of a national plan for reconstruction. In the absence of a resumption of negotiations in conference, however, the only alternative left to Ontario was to pursue its counter-proposals through other means. For Drew, the problems involving federal-provincial relations clearly fell into two, hierarchical categories: the first, and most important from Drew's conservative vantage point, was the settling of the fiscal relationship between the two governments; the second, both in timing and importance, was the establishment of some means of providing social assistance to the population.

Finance Minister Ilsley's budget of June 1946 acknowledged the failure to reach an agreement with all provinces on tax-sharing and opened up the possibility that individual provinces could accept the federal offer of vacating the personal, corporate, and succession taxes in return for a lump-sum "rental" payment.[57] Essentially, this action ripped apart the implied "all or nothing" nature of the Green Book proposals and embarked Canadian public policy on an adventure in "ad-hocracy" or the achievement of change through "informal accommodations."[58] Ontario's delegates had made their position clear in regards to tax-sharing at the conference and, having failed to convince enough of the other provinces to support their position, they were unable to do anything other than watch events across the county unfold. Drew remained adamant that accepting the terms outlined in Ilsley's budget amounted to a rejection of the possibility of any future agreement on any of the other issues raised at the reconstruction conference. As he told Angus Macdonald, who was becoming something of a confidant to Drew, given his similar antipathy toward the prime minister, "the present uncertainty is leading us into the possibility of economic chaos." If the federal rental scheme was accepted, he argued, "then instead of having made it possible for agreement to be reached on social security and public investment measures, the very agreements the provinces are being asked to sign would preclude the possibility of agreement in those other fields along the lines originally suggested."[59]

Drew could not move beyond the failed tax negotiations and was powerless to dictate anything as, one by one, all the provinces except Quebec accepted the terms of the federal offer. His emotions fluctuated erratically as he watch the other provinces negotiate from the sidelines. At times, he seemed euphoric. First, it was because British Columbia's premier, John Hart, "expressed very strong disapproval of the [federal] proposals and left the impression that he would not accept them."[60] New Brunswick's decision to suspend fiscal negotiations with Ottawa because of the unsatisfactory nature of the federal offer led to increasing optimism that the strategy of negotiating with provinces individually would prove a failure. According to the "Capital Report," "the greatest satisfaction seems to be felt by those who rejected the Dominion's offer last May ... [who] don't seem to want other provinces to take it up, and they seem to be delighted now that Ottawa is making slow progress."[61] Nova Scotia's anticipated rejection of the tax rental agreements was particularly important to Drew, who was finding himself increasingly marginalized and allied in the public perception with Maurice Duplessis. When news of Nova Scotia's acceptance reached Drew, he felt betrayed. Returning from a gossip-filled jaunt to Ottawa, he had this to say to Macdonald:

King told Caucus the day before yesterday that Nova Scotia had now definitely decided to complete an agreement, and that as this left Quebec and Ontario on the opposite side, all members were encouraged to take issue on the subject of Dominion-Provincial relations and to attack Duplessis and myself with complete freedom in view of the fact that the decks were now clear to deal only with political enemies. I am not concerned with such an event from the personal point of view or from the political point of view. I am greatly concerned with what is happening from your own point of view. Anything I say is based upon a complete and unqualified confidence in your own good faith in this whole matter. Even to an extent, however, of which I was not aware earlier in the week tongues are wagging and the very high position you have occupied throughout all of Canada for your courageous stand on principle is being impaired by the suggestion that you have made a deal to assist the Dominion Government in their Halifax by-election ... The simple truth is, Angus, that I find it difficult how the public is likely to come to any other conclusion ... For these reasons, I do presume to urge you to reconsider your situation if the door is not yet closed.[62]

The more flexible attitude of Douglas Abbott as minister of finance, as well as revised federal tax proposals, meant that the door, unfortunately, was firmly closed: British Columbia did accept the offer, New Brunswick resumed negotiations and accepted a new offer, and Nova Scotia signed on with little concern for the public perception.[63] Ontario and Quebec were left alone in their refusal to accept the federal government's tax rental offer.

Drew had invested so much energy in first securing an agreement on Ontario's reconstruction proposals and then foiling the federal government's counter tax offer that he had little desire to pursue any of the social policies debated in 1945. In fact, he was growing weary of the constraints of provincial politics and pined for an opportunity to play a role in the national sphere. Conservative leader John Bracken's decision to resign in the summer of 1948 opened up new options for Drew, who won an easy victory in the leadership convention of October 1948. He was never able to crack the Liberal machine in Ottawa, however, and his eight years in the office of Leader of the Opposition were not particularly happy ones. The reputation he had earned for himself while premier of Ontario did not serve him well in his later career; as suspected, the Liberals did "use as a slogan 'the axis Drew-Duplessis' which [was] harmful in Quebec and elsewhere."[64] Moreover, Drew's strategy in negotiation never developed, and what had begun as an attempt to bring harmony to federal-provincial relations ended with him feeling wounded and betrayed but incapable of changing strategies. According to a long-time Drew supporter who became disillusioned, "Mr. Drew has never learned that a leader gains and holds power by making friends rather than enemies. He has a fatal facility for arousing antagonisms even within his own party. He has been superior and patrician ... he has indulged in personalities, called names and imputed motives."[65] But if the man and the technique had departed Ontario politics, the strategies remained in the figure of the new premier, Leslie Frost.

In part elected thanks to Ontario Conservative Party machinations and in part as a genuine nod to rural Ontario and a genial, mild-mannered representative, Frost was better prepared than anyone else to take on the task of federal-provincial relations.[66] Where Drew was combative and argumentative, Frost was low-key and, at least on the surface, agreeable. It was Frost who had leapfrogged around the country at various times during the reconstruction conference trying to lay the groundwork for trans-provincial agreement; it was his able and loyal department in the Provincial Treasury that had laid out Ontario's position on the tax agreements. Frost had been part of virtually all of the negotiations and understood Ontario's strategy as well as Drew, but he understood the need for a velvet touch far better than Drew. Under Frost's leadership, Ontario would continue to try to dictate the national agenda by offering solutions to the problems facing Canadians that not only secured Ontario's position within the federation but also offered appealing solutions to other regions.

The obsession with the tax rental agreements and with recalling the aborted dominion-provincial conference ended when Frost took office. This shift was partly due to the changes that had taken place in the Prime Minister's Office: Louis St. Laurent, who was regarded as having "made one of the most conciliatory speeches at the Dominion-Provincial Conference," had replaced King in the fall of 1948, and optimism over a new approach to intergovernmental relations was palpable. Officials in the Treasury Department argued that neither Ontario nor the country as a whole was adversely affected by Ontario's and Quebec's decision to remain outside the tax rental agreements, and that the ad hoc arrangements currently in place made possible the reopening of discussions on pensions and a health insurance program: "Why should the Dominion government make Ontario's and Quebec's signature on a tax pact the price of its co-operation on social security and employment measures?"[67] The federal strategy at the reconstruction conference had been to tie the unpleasant tax rental proposals to the much more popular social policy offers; the Ontario position, established in the provincial submission to the conference, had always been that this link was unnecessary. When the federal government moved to separate the two pieces of the Green Book, the intergovernmental relationship began to change in two important ways. First, the crisis that had loomed in May 1946 did not transpire, and Ontario could no longer be blamed for the breakdown of Canadian federalism. Second, if Ontario's position in terms of the separability of fiscal and social policy had been correct, perhaps so too was the provincial position on the shape of those social policies.

The social security measures raised at the reconstruction conference included, in increasing significance from the Ontario vantage point, unemployment assistance, pensions for the aged, and health insurance. The problem of the unemployed hardly garnered a moment's consideration at Queen's Park because Ottawa already had authority over insurance, granted in a 1941 constitutional amendment, and had claimed responsibility over assistance measures in the Green Book. The absence of the anticipated post-war recession allowed the Ontario officials and politicians to essentially ignore the plight of the thousands of Ontario residents who were either deemed "unemployable" or had come to the end of their unemployment insurance eligibility. Therefore Ontario did not have a plan for providing unemployment assistance, content to insist that it was entirely a federal responsibility.[68] Pensions, however, had long been an area in which changes were agreed to be necessary, and there is certainly evidence that Ontario developed a position which would provide the framework for a national approach to assistance for the aged. Neither level of government had put forward a particularly coherent solution to the problem of providing health care to the population, but in this area more than most, Ontario attempted to dictate the national agenda by being the first to design and sell a scheme to the rest of the country. In both pensions and health, it sought to pursue the strategies employed at the reconstruction conference – hopefully, this time through to a more satisfactory conclusion.

Under the 1927 Old Age Pensions Act, Canadians over the age of seventy were eligible for federal assistance if they met the requirements of poverty established under a means test. This pension was then financed through a 75 per cent/25 per cent sharing of costs between the federal and the provincial governments. The experience of Depression, however, had convinced most people that a means test was demeaning, and thus even at the time of the reconstruction conference, plans were underway to remove the most odious features of the 1927 act. Interestingly, the very fact that there was not only agreement on this subject but a considerable amount of work already done towards finding a viable alternative meant that Ontario was a little slow in advocating a provincially designed scheme that met its particular concerns within the context of a national program. At first, it remained content to merely express a desire to eliminate some of the overlap in jurisdiction, arguing that this made the machinery of payment more complex than necessary.[69] The problems were seen as affecting the administration of the program, not its shape, and could "readily be solved by direct approach and consideration."[70] A federal-provincial conference was called for December 1950 to discuss, in part, the question of old-age pensions, and it was there that the various positions became clear. For the most part, there was surprisingly little disagreement.

Ottawa offered to eliminate the means test entirely for those over seventy, providing a universal subsidy of $40 a month, and introduce assistance to people between the ages of sixty-five and sixty-nine who

could demonstrate need through a means test. Ontario's welfare minister, W.A. Goodfellow, while noting "that there was nothing essentially wrong with the present system of old age pensions," went on to
endorse the federal proposal for the universal pension but question the
advisability of offering anything at all to the younger age group.[71] The
other provinces were in general agreement with both Ottawa and
Ontario; unlike other intergovernmental meetings, this one indicated
no great divergence of opinion on fundamental principles. Even the
question of constitutional amendment, which arose because of the universal nature of the federal proposal and the need to implement a tax
increase to cover the costs involved, raised little opposition.[72] It would
appear that Ontario had shifted gears dramatically since attending the
reconstruction conference and was prepared to follow Ottawa's lead
on matters of concurrent jurisdiction.

In reality, however, Ontario's agreement with the terms of the federal
proposal on old-age security reflected a shared opinion, near universal
throughout the governments of the federation, on the nature of the
problem. The existing system was no longer viable, and the change to
a flat-rate pension for everyone over seventy was widely accepted as
both necessary and positive. The key points of agreement were that the
new system, without the means test, would be administratively simple
and that the pension of $40 a month was low enough that it would not
adversely affect the size of the labour force or the work of private
insurance and investment agencies. As Frost noted, in agreement with
a recent statement made by the federal finance minister, "it is contrary
to public policy that we in this important welfare matter should take
steps which would encourage the immobilizing of a large and useful
section of our labour force."[73] Having established that the provincial
and federal governments were essentially of one mind on this issue,
Ontario had no need to devise an alternative.

Under Frost's leadership, Ontario had used quiet diplomacy to ascer-
tain the position of the other participants in regards to the pension
issue. That there was a relative degree of unanimity should not cloud
the fact, however, that the province still endeavoured to flex its muscles
on the details of the program. In private conversations with both
George Davidson, federal deputy minister of welfare, and his minister,
Paul Martin, Frost offered Ontario's advice on how Ottawa could
produce a better national policy. While Ontario's interests are evident,
Frost had some useful insight into federal responsibilities. In planning
to leave the question of the means test for the sixty-five-to-sixty-nine
category up to the whims of the provinces, he thought the federal government was abdicating its responsibility to provide national leadership. As he explained it,

I quite recognize the difficulty of the Federal Government in establishing a standard which would fit evenly across a great country like Canada with its varying conditions, at the same time it is a matter which should be closely kept in hand by the Central Government because after all the Central Government contributes fifty per cent of the pensions. There are many extremely undesirable features of such a plan. It immediately places all of the ten provinces in competition against the others and it means that the whole matter becomes the subject of pressures from various sources, with the result that what may be done in Ontario is forced upon the other provinces, in many cases against their better judgment. The converse is also true. The governments of Alberta or Saskatchewan may decide upon a certain course and then the Government of Ontario may be pressured into accepting this although in actual fact the policies have in these western provinces might have little common to our conditions here. This is extremely unsound. For the protection of all, it seems to me to be better that the Federal Government and the provinces should agree upon a common plan.[74]

Even when the two levels of government were in agreement about the need for, and the shape of, a particular piece of social policy, the new Ontario strategy of attempting to dictate the shape of national policy can be seen. In the case of old-age security, it was only partially successful, but it was a strategy that would be employed triumphantly in the next major social policy issue on the intergovernmental relations agenda.[75]

The health policy proposals raised in embryonic form at the reconstruction conference were unlike either of the other two social policies. If Ontario wanted to keep responsibility for unemployment assistance firmly in the federal corner and was in agreement on old-age pensions but still offered input into making the program more "national" in scope, the province had very real ideas about health insurance, which were likely contrary to the conclusions being slowly reached in Ottawa. The best strategy, then, was to formulate a coherent plan that would address the concerns of all areas of the country and try to sell it before the federal thinking became too far advanced. Although by all accounts, Frost was a reluctant initiator of the debate on national health insurance, the fact that it had been raised ten years earlier at the dominion-provincial conference, meant that it was bound to resurface sometime.[76] If Ontario was to play anything like a determinative role, it would have to act quickly.

The first step was to ensure that health insurance was included on the agenda for discussion at the next federal-provincial meeting. At a time when most attention was directed to solving the continuing problems of unemployment assistance and the continuation of the tax rental agreements, Frost spoke in favour of shifting the debate to matters of health. He argued that "the study of health insurance would help to clarify the thinking of all in a field in which there unquestionably is a great deal of misunderstanding and confusion."[77] The premiers of Manitoba, Saskatchewan, and British Columbia quickly agreed with their colleague from Ontario, and in closed sessions with the prime minister, they succeeded in getting the discussion included on the agenda for the conference to be held in October.[78] After years of fretting that it was losing the initiative on intergovernmental issues, Ottawa was once again forced to accept the leadership of Ontario.[79]

In the intervening months between the preliminary, agenda-setting meetings and the formal federal-provincial conference, Ontario worked to establish its plan in regards to health insurance. Under the guidance of health policy expert Malcolm Taylor, the Ontario report on health contained a thorough study of the current political and economic environment, an analysis of hospital insurance programs in other provinces, and five different possibilities on the road to full hospital coverage. While the report was under preparation, the Ontario officials engaged in a series of discussions with their counterparts in other provincial capitals and in Ottawa. At the provincial level, a number of points of agreement were becoming clear, including the significance of federal involvement both through direct health assistance and through the existing fiscal arrangements, and the need for flexibility in meeting the needs of each province.[80] The federal government also watched events in Ontario with increasing curiosity and made preparations to counter a suspected proposal for an insurance program that "might not involve very large provincial expenditures and ... would permit commercial and voluntary plans to continue in the field."[81] The prime minister confidentially asked Frost for a memorandum detailing the provincial "suggestion that there might well be a government scheme which would provide free diagnoses and also assistance whenever an individual or family incurred heavy medical expenditures that might prove crippling if there were no public assistance toward discharging the liability."[82] But the contents of the Taylor report remained a closely guarded secret. Apparently, "Ottawa thought [Frost] was bluffing" when he put health services on the conference agenda at the April meetings, convinced that he was merely positioning himself for an election. But the continued talk from Ontario of the need for national health insurance indicated that "quite clearly he has something in mind, something which Ottawa has been unable to find out."[83]

The prime minister found out what Ontario intended to do at the end of September when Frost forwarded a draft of his intended conference remarks;[84] the other premiers remained in the dark until the opening of the conference itself at the beginning of October. According to one observer, there was "nothing very revolutionary" in the Frost proposals, although the "Federal reaction [was] positive."[85] According to one of the participants, however, the Frost statement, with its specific alternative proposals, had an almost electrifying effect on the conference ... Never before had there been such a specific health proposal from the largest province, with alternatives designed to elicit maximum support from the other provinces."[86] Ontario's scheme, which anticipated hospital insurance either through a series of steps or all at once, was based on a federal contribution of approximately 60 per cent of the cost and a provincial contribution raised through premiums and co-insurance. Without a proposal of its own, the federal government was not really in a position to be able to concur with Ontario's plan, and instead, the conference merely agreed to strike a committee to devote more study to the question of hospital insurance.[87]

When hospital insurance eventually came into being, it was under a plan that was not exactly as Ontario had suggested. The federal contribution was lower than proposed, the coverage was not as broad, and implementation was originally predicated on six provinces announcing their intention to join with Ottawa in operating the system. Nevertheless, in snatching the initiative from the federal government, and in proposing a scheme that was designed to appeal to as many of the other provinces as possible, Ontario was finally able to see its post-war strategies in intergovernmental negotiations succeed. It had been something of a long road. Similar strategies at the reconstruction conference had been a failure and had only succeeded in obsessing George Drew to the point of distraction. Leslie Frost was far better equipped to smooth intergovernmental relations, but his efforts at asserting a national position rather than expressing purely provincial opposition had met with mixed success: the Ontario position that Ottawa was solely responsible for the unemployed was studiously ignored for a full decade, and the Ontario suggestions in regards to old-age security were taken only as far as they were in complete accord with an already-established federal position. With health insurance, however, the early and well-researched arrival of a complete insurance design resulted in Frost being an unlikely initiator of a national social program. Over a decade of practice left Ontario in the position of being able to shape national policy from a provincial perspective, while at the same time shaking its reputation as the "Big Bad Wolf of Confederation."

NOTES

The research for this chapter was made possible thanks to the financial support of an SSHRCC general research grant and an SSHRCC strategic grant under the Federalism and Federations program.

1 See especially, Marc Gotleib, "George Drew and the Dominion-Provincial Conference on Reconstruction," *Canadian Historical Review* 66, (1985): 27–47; on Ontario's normally confrontational approach to Ottawa, see Christopher Armstrong, *The Politics of Federalism: Ontario's Relations with the Federal Government, 1867–1942* (Toronto: University of Toronto Press, 1981); Garth Stevenson, *Ex Uno Plures: Federal-Provincial Relations in Canada, 1867–1896* (Montreal and Toronto: McGill-Queen's University Press, 1993); Robert Vipond, *Liberty and Community: Canadian Federalism and the Failure of the Constitution* (Albany: State University of New York Press, 1991); John T. Saywell, *"Just Call Me Mitch": The Life of Mitchell F. Hepburn* (Toronto: University of Toronto Press, 1991), 375–82.

2 Archives of Ontario (AO), Hugh Latimer Papers, MU 4544, file: Correspondence, 1934–52. Cecil Frost to members of the executive of the Ontario Conservative Association, 8 Aug. 1943.

3 Private collection, Ontario Conservative Party Papers, "George Drew, Speaking over a Province-Wide Network, July 8th 1943."

4 AO, Department of Finance Papers; Dominion-Provincial Conferences, 1935–55, RG 6–41, box 3, file: Inter-provincial Conference, 1945, Drew to King, 6 Jan. 1944.

5 Ibid., A.D.P. Heeney to Drew, 28 Feb. 1944.

6 Ibid., Drew to King, 1 April 1944. On the issue of refusing to send a provincial official to Ottawa, see "Drew Record on Holding of Dominion-Provincial Meeting," *Toronto Daily Star*, 20 Jan. 1945; Provincial Treasurer Leslie Frost maintained that in a meeting with Alex Skelton, the secretary of the Cabinet Committee on Dominion-Provincial Relations, he was assured that "the Province of Ontario had supplied 98% of the information that was required, and he gave his own estimate at that time that only about 2% of the information was outstanding." Frost went on to suggest that "this is pretty full and complete cooperation, and I say Mr. King's excuse for calling off the conference [in the summer of 1944] was an excuse of a most flimsy nature." See *Debates of the Legislative Assembly of Ontario*, 20 March 1945.

7 AO, Department of Finance Papers, Dominion-Provincial Conferences, 1935–55, box 3, file: Inter-provincial Conference, 1945, Drew to King, 21 Aug. 1944.

8 National Archives of Canada (NA), George Drew Papers, MG 32, C3, reel C-9047, King to Drew, 21 June 1945.

9 James Struthers, "Family Allowances, Old Age Security, and the Con-
struction of Entitlement in the Canadian Welfare State, 1943–1951," in
Peter Neary and J.L. Granatstein, eds., *The Veterans Charter and
Post–World War II Canada* (Montreal and Kingston: McGill-Queen's
University Press, 1998), 185.

10 *Globe and Mail,* 10 Aug. 1944.

11 NA, Roland Michener Papers, MG 32, A4, volume 88, file: Drew, Hon.
George, n.d., 1941–47, Drew to Michener, 3 Aug. 1944; NA, Drew
Papers, reel M-9025, Transcript of telephone conversation between Drew
and Charlotte Whitton, 20 Feb. 1945.

12 AO, George Drew Papers, RG 3–18, box 5, letterbook 9, Drew to Hugh
C. Farthing, 21 Aug. 1944; AO, Department of Finance, Policy Division
Subject Files, RG 6–44, box UF 22, file: Dominion-Provincial Relations,
Ontario Bureau of Statistics and Research, "Facts Pertinent to Dominion-
Provincial Relations," 16 July 1945, 41; AO, Drew Papers, box 5, letter-
book 9, 1 Aug. to 11 Sept. 1944, Drew to John Diefenbaker, 24 Aug.
1944.

13 See, for example, AO, Department of Finance Papers; Dominion-Provincial Conferences, 1935–55, box 3, file: Inter-provincial Conference, 1945,
Tommy Douglas to Drew, 9 Feb. 1945, and Drew to provincial premiers,
21 Feb. 1945.

14 Ibid., C.S. Walters, "Memorandum re: Forthcoming Dominion-Provincial
Conference," 30 March 1944.

15 NA, Drew Papers, reel C-9047, Drew to King, 28 June 1945; ibid., J. H.
Chater (provincial statistician) to Drew, 4 July 1945.

16 AO, Department of Finance, Policy Division Subject Files, box UF 22, file:
Dominion-Provincial Relations. Ontario Bureau of Statistics and
Research, "Facts Pertinent to Dominion-Provincial Relations," 16 July
1945, 39–48.

17 Ibid., 44, 46.

18 Ibid., 48.

19 *Globe and Mail,* 4 Aug. 1945.

20 NA, William Lyon Mackenzie King Papers, Diary, 6 Aug. 1945. See also
Globe and Mail, 7 Aug. 1945.

21 NA, King Diary, 5 Aug. 1945.

22 Government of Canada, *Proceedings of the Dominion Provincial Conference on Reconstruction* (Ottawa: King's Printer, 1946).

23 NA, Drew Papers, reel C-9047. J.H. Chater, provincial statistician to
Drew, 4 July 1945.

24 *Globe and Mail,* 11 Aug. 1945.

25 Ontario commissioned the services of Harvard public administration professor Alvin Hansen to prepare a proposal on how to equitably divide
fiscal responsibility between the two levels of government, but his suggestions that Ottawa take complete control and provide each of the

provinces with a compensatory subvention was not well received in the provincial capital. See AO, RG 6–116, box 19, UC 19–20, Hansen to Frost, 17 Oct. 1945; ibid., J.H. Chater to Frost, 24 Oct. 1945; ibid., "Dr. Hansen's Formulae and an Alternative Proposal," n.d.

26 AO, Department of Finance Papers, Dominion-Provincial Conferences, 1935–55, vol. 7, file: From PMs "red book," vol. 2, "Summary of the Minutes of the Dominion-Provincial Economic Committee, 4–14 December 1945 and 8–17 January 1946," 1–6.

27 AO, Department of Finance Papers, RG 6–15, vol. 27, file: Prime Minister no. 18, Canadian Club, "Speech by Premier George A. Drew before the Canadian Club, Toronto, October 1, 1945."

28 See, for example, Drew's attempts to cultivate John Hart, who King believed had already noted "his intention to co-operate at the Conference," but whom Drew found receptive to the Ontario critique of the current fiscal arrangements. See King Diaries, 3 Aug. 1945, and AO, Department of Finance Papers, Dominion-Provincial Conferences, 1935–55, box 5, file: Dominion-Provincial Conference, British Columbia, 1945, Telephone conversation between Colonel George Drew and Premier Hart, 1:30 pm, 16 Nov. 1945. Frost had met with Maurice Duplessis prior to the August meetings and had paved the way for something of an alliance between Ontario and Quebec. See Roger Graham, *Old Man Ontario: Leslie M. Frost* (Toronto: University of Toronto Press, 1990), 110.

29 AO, Department of Finance Papers, Dominion-Provincial Conferences, 1935–55, vol. 7, file: From PMs "red book," vol. 2, "Summary of the Minutes of the Dominion-Provincial Economic Committee, 4–14 December 1945 and 8–17 January 1946," 1–6.

30 The federal government was equally aware of the importance of Ontario's proposals, and gave them considerable attention. See NA, Louis St. Laurent Papers, MG 26L, vol. 5, file: Minutes of the Economic Committee of the Federal-Provincial Conference – received while the minister in England, "Comment on the Ontario Submission by the Prime Minister of Canada," n.d., but after 8 Jan. 1946.

31 NA, Drew Papers, reel M9047, Memorandum "Re: Dominion-Provincial Conference, Ottawa, January 28th to February 1st, 1946," n.d.

32 Ibid.; see also, AO, Department of Finance Papers, Dominion-Provincial Conferences, 1935–55, vol. 7, file: From PMs "red book," vol. 2, "Statements by the Ontario Premier at Co-ordinating Committee Meeting January 28 to February 1, 1946," 1–2; King diaries, 29 Jan. 1946.

33 Brooke Claxton, newly appointed minister of national health and welfare, thought that perhaps this was a mistake. He reflected that the Green Book proposals were "so much greater than [the provinces] expected that some of the premiers were thrown for a loop ... and resented it." See NA, MG 32, B5, Brooke Claxton Papers, vol. 220,

Claxton memoirs, Vol. 3: 676; quoted in David Bercuson, *True Patriot: The Life of Brooke Claxton, 1898–1960* (Toronto: University of Toronto Press, 1993), 140. Subsequent opinion in Ottawa seemed to confirm this view: in a memo setting out the background to past dominion-provincial conferences, Gordon Robertson was informed that the reconstruction conference "appeared [to be] called by the Federal government in pursuance of aims defined by the Federal government ... The whole approach smacked of autocracy and clearly was a psychological error." See NA, MG 31, E87, Gordon Robertson Papers, vol. 29, file: conference of Federal-Provincial Governments, Dec. 1950 – Planning (1 of 2), n.d., 1946–50, Memo for R.G. Robertson, no author, 5 April 1950.

34 Public Archives of New Brunswick (PANB), John McNair Papers, RS 414, box C5, file: Correspondence relating to Dominion-Provincial Conference, 1946. "Points for Consideration by Dominion and Provinces," n.d. These were Nova Scotia's version of the "points" made at the coordinating committee of the conference, and while perhaps not a completely accurate view, they certainly resonated with Drew. "I am very glad to have this," he wrote, "as it summarizes extremely well points that were under discussion when we adjourned. I must say that there have been times when I wondered whether the Conference that some of the newspapers were talking about was really the Conference we were at." See Nova Scotia Archives and Records Management (NSARM), Angus L. Macdonald Papers, MG 2, vol. 899A, file: Dominion-Provincial Conference, Drew to Macdonald, 1 March 1946.

35 *Debates of the Legislative Assembly of Ontario*, 25 March 1936, 1127.

36 AO, Department of Finance Papers, Dominion-Provincial Conferences, 1935–55, vol. 7, file: From PMs "red book," vol. 2, "Statements by the Ontario Premier at Co-ordinating Committee Meeting January 28 to February 1, 1946"; NSARM, Macdonald Papers, vol. 903, file: Personal and confidential, Macdonald to Alex Johnson, 18 Jan. 1946; NA, King Diary, 31 Jan. 1946.

37 NA, King Diary, 23 Jan. 1946.

38 Ibid., 31 Jan. 1946.

39 AO, Department of Finance Papers, Dominion-Provincial Conferences, 1935–55, vol. 7, file: From PMs "red book," vol. 2, "Statements by the Ontario Premier at Co-ordinating Committee Meeting January 28 to February 1, 1946."

40 NA, King Diary, 31 Jan. 1946. In fact, King thought there were certain issues that the federal government "could not defend. The first was in not being prepared to state definitely we did not intend to go further. No mere intention, but to say definitely there were certain sources of taxation we would not take up in the next three years."

41 AO, Department of Finance Papers, Dominion-Provincial Conferences,

1935–55, box 3, file: Dominion-Provincial Conference, 1945 – original
letters, Drew to King, 16 April 1946.

42 *Debates of the Legislative Assembly of Ontario*, Throne Speech, 4 March
1946, 4.

43 On the press leaks, see Blair Fraser, "Confederation, 1946," *Maclean's*, 1
March 1946. Fraser identified some of the points in the Ontario proposal
but exaggerated the devolution of power that Ontario proposed. He was
probably right in noting that "no conceivable modification of [the
Ontario proposal] would be acceptable to Ottawa, or to at least seven of
the other eight provinces," although Drew still hoped to be able to per-
suade others.

44 NA, Drew Papers, vol. 428, reel M-047, file: Submission – Ontario,
"Provincial Conference, April 25, 1946, Ottawa."

45 Ibid., 14.

46 AO, Department of Finance Papers, Dominion-Provincial Conferences,
1935–55, vol. 7, file: From PMs "red book" notes on statements, "Notes
on Statements of Premiers at Co-ordinating Committee Meeting, April
25th and 26th."

47 NA, King Diary, 25, 26, 27 April 1946.

48 Bercuson, *True Patriot*, 140.

49 Determining exactly what were considered the key issues raised at the
reconstruction conference has proven difficult, since there are as many
different versions as there were participants. James Struthers, for
example, maintains that in the public perception, social policy issues were
seen to be the raison d'être of the meetings. See Struthers, *The Limits of
Affluence: Welfare in Ontario, 1920–1970* (Toronto: University of
Toronto Press, 1994), 125. Members of the Ontario legislative assembly,
perhaps blinded by the government's obsession with the tax agreements,
concluded that "that is what the conference is discussing – the taxes that
we as citizens of the Province of Ontario and the Dominion of Canada,
pay" A.A. Macleod, Labour-Progressive MLA for Bellwoods, 26 March
1946, in *Debates of the Legislative Assembly of Ontario* 1290.

50 AO, Department of Finance Papers, Policy Division Subject Files, box UF
22, file: 6 "S" Speeches: G.A. Drew, "Speech by Premier George Drew to
Progressive Conservative Business Men's Club, Tuesday, May 14, 1946."
The *Globe and Mail* (7 June 1946) accused Garson of "frequently ... fal-
sifying facts, misrepresenting the positions, not to say the motives, of
others," although the opinion of a paper so clearly supportive of the
Drew government must also be suspect. On the other hand, Garson's
antipathy toward Drew should have come as little surprise, since he was
consistently regarded as the premier most likely to side with the dominion government at the conference and, by autumn 1946, was preparing
to move into the federal cabinet himself (NA, King Diary, 22 Oct. 1946).

51 See Gotleib, "George Drew and the Dominion-Provincial Conference on Reconstruction," 27–52. In contrast, Alvin Finkel argues that the federal government wanted the conference to fail and therefore ought to bear the burden of blame ("Paradise Postponed: A Re-examination of the Green Book Proposals of 1945," *Journal of the Canadian Historical Association*, new series, 4 [1993]: 120–42). For an alternative view of the axis, see P.E. Bryden, "The Ontario-Quebec Axis: Post-War Strategies in Intergovernmental Negotiations," in Edgar-André Montigny and Lori Chambers, eds., *Ontario Since Confederation: A Reader* (Toronto: University of Toronto Press, 2000).

52 NA, Drew Papers, reel M-9047, Drew to King, 7 Sept. 1946; see also AO, Department of Finance Papers, Dominion-Provincial Conferences, 1935–55, box UJ 3–4, file: Dominion-Provincial Conference, Original letters to and from Mr King and Col. G.A. Drew, 1945, Drew to King, 7 Sept. 1946 and 2 Oct. 1946. Also see NA, Drew Papers, reel M-9018, Drew to Louis St. Laurent, 6 Nov. 1947.

53 AO, Department of Finance Papers, Policy Division Subject Files, box UF 22, file: 6 "S" Speeches: G.A. Drew, "Canada at the Crossroads," speech by Premier George Drew to Canadian Club, Winnipeg, 17 June 1946.

54 NA, Drew Papers, vol. 428, reel M-9047, Frost to Drew, 15 July 1946.

55 NSARM, Macdonald Papers, vol. 899A, file: 1, Macdonald to J.R. Stirrett, 11 June 1946.

56 AO, Department of Finance, Dominion-Provincial Conferences, 1935–55, box 6, file: Dominion-Provincial Conferences – Statistics and Tables, 1945–47, Drew to Manning, 18 Oct. 1946; ibid., file: Dominion-Provincial Conference Statistics and Tables of other countries re: Tax Systems. Manning to Drew, 23 Nov. 1946.

57 J. Harvey Perry, *A Fiscal History of Canada – The Postwar Years*, Canadian Tax Paper no. 85 (Canadian Tax Foundation, 1989), 40.

58 Richard Simeon and Ian Robinson, *State, Society and the Development of Canadian Federalism*, Royal Commission on the Economic Union and Development Prospects for Canada, volume 71 (Toronto: University of Toronto Press, 1990), 120.

59 NSARM, Macdonald Papers, vol. 899A, file: 1, Drew to Macdonald, 26 Oct. 1946.

60 Ibid.

61 PANB, McNair Papers, box C6, file: Correspondence Relating to Federal-Provincial Relations, 1946–49, Press release, 6 Jan. 1947, and "Capital Report" transcript, 12 Jan. 1947.

62 NSARM, Macdonald Papers, vol. 899A, file: 2, Drew to Macdonald, 9 May 1947.

63 PANB, McNair Papers, box C6, file: Correspondence Relating to Federal-Provincial Relations, 1946–49, Press statement, 25 Jan. 1947, and

Abbott to Angus Macdonald, 25 Jan. 1947; NSARM, Macdonald Papers, volume 899A, file: 2, Macdonald to Drew, 10 May 1947.

64 NA, Donald Fleming Papers, MG 32 B39, vol. 35, file: Correspondence, Nov.–Dec. 1948, A.R. Gobeil to John Bracken, 14 Sept. 1948.

65 Ibid., file: 1948 Election, National Convention (2). George Little to J.M. Macdonnell, 10 Aug. 1948.

66 AO, Clare Westcott Papers, F-2094, Vice-president of the Ontario Progressive Conservative Party: Correspondence, 1946–59, file: Loose correspondence, Memo of conversation, Dave Sleesor and Clare Westcott, 24 Nov. 1987; Graham, *Old Man Ontario*, 145–51.

67 AO, Department of Finance Papers, Dominion-Provincial Conferences, 1935–55, box 10, file: Federal-Provincial Relations, 1945–55, George Gathercole, assistant provincial statistician, to Chester Walters, 27 July 1949. It was advisable that this be done "through informal talks with a minimum of publicity."

68 The best assessment of Ontario's inactivity in the field of unemployment assistance and the constitutional arguments surrounding its jurisdiction can be found in James Struthers, "Shadows from the Thirties: The Federal Government and Unemployment Assistance, 1941–1956," in Jacqueline S. Ismael, ed., *The Canadian Welfare State: Evolution and Transition* (Edmonton: University of Alberta Press, 1987), 3–32.

69 AO, Cabinet Office Papers, RG 75–12, container 1, file: Cabinet agendas, 1947, no. 2, Council agenda, 15 May 1947, part I, item 16(a), Re: Old Age Pensions.

70 NA, Robertson Papers, vol. 29, file: Conference of Fed.-Prov. Governments, Dec. 1950 – correspondence re. Agenda, Frost to St. Laurent, 3 Feb. 1950.

71 AO, Department of Finance Papers, Dominion-Provincial Conferences, 1935–55, box 15, file: Untitled, federal-provincial conference, 1950. "Committee on Old Age Security," 6 Dec. 1950.

72 Ibid., Federal-provincial relations correspondence, container 1, file: Confidential notes on Dec. 1950 Conference, "Constitutional Amendment to provide for 'Contributory' Old Age Pensions," n.d.

73 AO, Cabinet Office Papers, L.R. McDonald, Secretary of Cabinet series, RG 75–42–1–85, container 9, file: Federal-Provincial Old Age Pensions. Frost to Goodfellow, 10 May 1951. These points are made in much greater detail in James Struthers, "Family Allowances, Old Age Security, and the Construction of Entitlement in the Canadian Welfare State, 1943–1951," in Neary and Granatstein, eds., *The Veteran's Charter and Post–World War II Canada*, 179–204.

74 AO, Cabinet Office Papers, L.R. McDonald, Secretary of Cabinet series, RG 75–42–1–85, container 9, file: Federal-Provincial Old Age Pensions, Frost to Goodfellow, 10 May 1951.

75 The means test was used at the discretion of each provincial government,
so Frost's solicitation of George Davidson and Paul Martin was to no
avail. For an overview of Canadian pension policy, see Kenneth Bryden,
Old Age Pensions and Policy-Making in Canada (Montreal and London:
McGill-Queen's University Press, 1974), 103–28. On another suggestion
to make the national program more useful, Ontario followed its own
advice and later so did Ottawa. In 1952 Ontario introduced a pension
for handicapped persons over the age of eighteen as a supplementary
component to the means-tested pensions available for the five years prior
to turning seventy.

76 NA, Department of National Health and Welfare Papers, RG 29, vol.
1372, file: 1–1, Memo, "Health Insurance and Ontario," Davidson to
Martin, 5 Aug. 1955; Malcolm Taylor, *Health Insurance and Canadian
Public Policy: The Seven Decisions That Created the Canadian Health
Insurance System* (Montreal: McGill-Queen's University Press, 1978),
124–25; Robert Bothwell, Ian Drummond, and John English, *Canada
Since 1945: Power, Politics and Provincialism*, rev. ed. (Toronto: Univer-
sity of Toronto Press, 1989).

77 *Proceedings of the Federal-Provincial Conference, 1955: Preliminary
Meeting*, 19.

78 Taylor, *Health Insurance*, 126–27.

79 As early as 1949, federal officials had been concerned about the leadership void in federal-provincial affairs and talked about the need to
"recover the initiative" (NA, St. Laurent Papers, vol. 84, file: Conferences
– Dominion-Provincial, vol. 1, Personal and Confidential, J.W. Pickersgill
to St. Laurent, 19 July 1949). They were still concerned about ensuring
"the retention of the initiative by the federal government" in 1955 (NA,
Department of National Health and Welfare Papers, vol. 1372, file: 1–1,
Davidson to Dr. Jackson, 20 Sept. 1955).

80 AO, Department of Finance Papers, Federal-Provincial Relations Correspondence Files, 1950–62, RG 6–115, box 4, file: 1955 Conference –
Preparatory Committee – 3rd Meeting, 4–6 July 1955, "Meeting of
Provincial Health Officers and Advisors, July 4 1955," submitted 13 July
1955.

81 NA, Department of National Health and Welfare Papers, vol. 1374, file:
Health Insurance, Committee Meetings, 1955, "Informal Discussion
Concerning Health Insurance," 25 Aug. 1955.

82 AO, RG 3–24, Office of the Premier: Frost, Premier's Correspondence, box
7, file: Dom.-Prov. – Conference, Sept.–Oct., 1955, St. Laurent to Frost,
2 Sept. 1955.

83 Queen's University Archives (QUA), Grant Dexter Papers, vol. 19, file:
Health Program, no. 183, Memo, 16 Sept. 1955.

84 AO, Office of the Premier: Frost, Premier's Correspondence, box 7, file:

Dom.-Prov. – Conference, Sept.–Oct., 1955, St. Laurent to Frost, 29 Sept. 1955.

85 QUA, Dexter Papers, vol. 7, file: Correspondence, 1955–56, Dexter to Tom Kent, 3 Oct.1955.

86 Taylor, *Health Insurance*, 131. Of course, the participant, Malcolm Taylor himself, might be expected to overstate the positive reaction to the proposals he had drafted.

87 *Proceedings of the Federal-Provincial Conference, 1955.*

KARINE HÉBERT

Between the Future and the Present

Montreal University Student Youth and the Post-war Years, 1945–1960[1]

As World War II drew to an end, the students of the Université de Montréal and McGill University once again began gradually to participate in a number of extracurricular activities that had been suspended during the conflict. For example, after a five-year absence, the Université de Montréal's evening of drama and comedy, the Revue Bleu et Or, was reborn from the ashes, under Jean-Louis Roux's creative direction. At McGill, university athletics, which since 1940 had been limited to intramural competitions, recovered its pre-war dimensions as intercollegiate Canadian athletic associations were reconstituted.[2] However, while at one level the willingness of students to re-engage in pre-war activities signified a return to normalcy, profound changes had in fact unsettled university life. The very parameters of student existence had been radically transformed: enrolments in university courses were substantially higher than in the 1930s; across a number of academic disciplines, women were attending university in far greater numbers; veterans, especially at McGill, took advantage of federal assistance programs to begin or continue their university education; and research, which even in the 1930s had carved out a significant niche, was now accorded a greater priority in Canadian universities. More significantly, the war itself, because of its global character, had stimulated an increasing awareness of international issues among students, who, when suddenly faced with the new reality of ideological diversity, felt an increased affinity with their counterparts in other countries. The cornerstone of this new internationalism was the conviction that the war had created the conditions for the building of a new world order, an ideal anchored upon a common search for peace undertaken by university youth in all countries. At war's end, while this new world existed only in blueprint, university students, like many adults in their society, exalted this reconstructed international order as both a national and an international imperative in which all must participate.

This essay aims to investigate a number of themes central to the social and cultural experience of post-war university students. First, it seeks precisely to define the status that public discourse ascribed to students in the post-war period. More importantly, however, it endeavours to analyze the way in which students appropriated an identity and language of youth both to demand a greater role in the task of national and international reconstruction and to launch a questioning and revision of the student status accorded them by the wider society. These issues have been examined through the lens of two Montreal university communities that together reflect the overriding cultural duality of Quebec's metropolis: the Université de Montréal, a francophone, private, and officially Catholic institution, in both its administration and its pedagogical ethos; and McGill University, English-speaking and Protestant, which although private, was administered by secular elites and financed by large corporations as an essential auxiliary to the Anglo-Protestant culture of the anglophone elite of Montreal.

In a study of the historical experience of youth, university settings offer a number of advantages. First, they provide a stage where the participants are clearly identified, since on the one hand, administrators and professors, occasionally seconded by parents and governments, embody authority and represent the adult world, while, on the other, male and female students are associated with youth. Such distinctions held true even in the more diverse university environment of the immediate post-war period, where returning veterans injected a certain maturity into the student body, which, however, still consisted largely of young men and women recently graduated from high schools and *collèges classiques*. While many of them legally attained adulthood during their university careers, they continued to be viewed as youth. According to the ideology that held sway among many educators at this time, one of the principal characteristics of the youthful stage of life was that it was a preparatory and formative period, and that university students were at the final and critical stage of their professional training.[3] Second, the university setting allowed both adult authorities and youth to produce a varied but accessible discourse. Despite some official constraints, students enjoyed sufficient freedom of expression to publish newspapers, present briefs to governments, and engage in the investigation of social and economic conditions.[4] However, it must be recognized at the outset that these sources are not representative of the entire student body but, rather, reflected the views of an activist minority engaged in student politics and who participated in university associations or wrote for student newspapers. The significance of this minority lies in the fact that their activities diffused new ideas which animated campus intellectual life. On the other side, university authorities produced their own discourse, one that appears in correspondence, official university publications, speeches, and occasional addresses.[5] The confrontation that took place between these two bodies of discourse allows an analysis of how students and university authorities conceived the place of youth in society. In light of the way in which students defined and deployed the concept of generation or the title of "young intellectual worker," we can also see how students developed a self-identity and, in this way, forged an awareness that they formed a specific group in post-war society.

YOUTH: GUARANTEE OF THE FUTURE

A discourse on youth that identified it as the guarantor of the future life of both the nation and the church was already in existence at the beginning of the twentieth century. This discourse survived largely unchanged during the first half of the twentieth century, and presidents, professors, and students at both large Montreal universities shared the fundamental belief that youth constituted tomorrow's elite. Reflecting in 1895 on the mission of the university to the nation, Father Filiatreault affirmed, "More than ever, ideas rule the world, and it follows from this that an institution that trains on behalf of the nation a generation of men who know how to think holds the future of society in its hands [Plus que jamais ce sont les idées qui mènent le monde. D'où il suit qu'une institution qui prépare au pays une génération d'hommes sachant penser est une institution qui tient entre ses mains l'avenir de notre société]."[6] In 1912 Édouard Montpetit, future director of the École des Hautes Études Commerciales, then at the outset of his career, addressed the following paean to the students: "You are the future, this is the theme of the discourses of philosophers and the songs of poets. You see the approach of life and you are already aware of the cares, should I say, rather, the distressing pangs of responsibility [Vous êtes l'avenir: tous les philosophes vous le disent, tous les poètes vous le chantent. Vous regardez s'approcher la vie et vous savez déjà les soucis, j'allais dire les angoisses de la responsabilité]."[7] What is striking about Montpetit's phraseology is that he did not reckon that students were full participants in the world of adult life, although he described them as being on its threshold. This idea was also present in the many addresses of McGill University authorities, especially at annual graduations, as they sought through these occasions to explain to the students that it was now the moment to enter the world and to assume the responsibilities for which their studies had prepared them. Among many such speeches, that of Principal Currie at the 1924 convocation admirably expresses this notion: "Many of you will be going out into the world to assume the full responsibilities of citizens, to do in earnest the work for which you have been fitting yourselves."[8]

Student representatives themselves regularly evoked the tenets of this discourse, reiterating on a number of occasions their status as a future elite, of a generation upon whom the future rested, and generally echoing the rhetorical flourishes of their elders: "And we who are the youth, who are still equipping ourselves, who have not yet entered our careers, the practice of our professions, and who look to the future; we, the student youth, what do we think of life? [Et nous qui sommes la jeunesse, qui préparons toujours notre équipement, qui ne sommes pas encore entrés dans la carrière, dans la pratique de la profession et qui regardons l'avenir; nous la jeunesse étudiante, que pensons-nous de la vie?]."[9] Near the end of World War I, a McGill student maintained, "The least we can do to-day is to put forth our best efforts and insure as far as possible the bequest of famous years to the generation of students which will be called upon to lead not only McGill, but Canada, during the era of reconstruction."[10] Such sentiments would be expressed again, almost unaltered, at the end of World War II.

Because the war effort enjoyed overwhelming support at McGill University, with some 5,570 current and former students enlisting in the armed services,[11] the challenge of reconstruction was more acutely felt by students there than at the Université de Montréal. Indeed, the attitude to be adopted towards reconstruction was an issue of fundamental importance for McGill's vigorous young principal, the Englishman F. Cyril James.[12] In his estimation, an enduring reconstruction ultimately rested upon an education that respected the twin principles of citizenship and democracy. "Democracy," he wrote, "depends for its existence on men and women who think for themselves, men and women who vote after they have appraised policies as well as personalities, men and women who are willing to assume public responsibilities in local and national government, men and women who have the skill and the wisdom to contribute a reasonable quota to the national income."[13] The obligation to actively participate in the process of reconstruction was even more incumbent upon those students who had escaped military service by continuing to pursue their academic studies, because only in this way were they deemed fit to assume their responsibilities and justify what many thought to be a privileged existence. Thus at the end of 1944 the McGill Student Executive Council organized a preliminary conference to prepare for the full congress of the Canadian Youth Commission which had been called to assemble in February 1945. An editorial in the *McGill Daily* exhorted students to think about the type of world they wanted to emerge from the war: "Now, with the end of the war approaching, the time is ripe for students to discuss and prepare plans, carefully considered and sound, for the world which soon will be largely theirs ... Your only justification for being at a university during a time of war has been to study, and to learn, in order that you might offer this opinion and assist in carrying it out."[14]

Although certainly present at the Université de Montréal, this discourse of reconstruction was modified in this context because its connection to the war effort enjoyed somewhat less support in the French-speaking university setting. A number of commentators argued that concentration on the war effort must not adversely affect students because they were themselves essential to society. In an article published in *Quartier latin*, Guy Beaugrand-Champagne responded to a piece that had appeared in the University of Toronto student newspaper, the *Varsity*, which had questioned the necessity of keeping the university curriculum intact for the duration of the war, arguing that only those whose education was vital to the war effort should be allowed to continue their studies, all others being forced to enlist in the armed services. By contrast, Beaugrand-Champagne asserted the position that students, in whatever discipline they were enrolled, had a key social role to play from the perspective of post-war reconstruction: "While we recognize that soldiers are immediately engaged in fighting the enemy, workers and civilians are engaged in the same struggle, and our contribution as students is just as crucial, even though it is directed to preparing a more-or-less distant reconstruction. We do not claim any privileges; we can only be deprived of our essential condition of student if our society is faced with an immediate, overriding, and certain danger [On reconnaît que non seulement le soldat combat, mais aussi l'ouvrier et le civil. Très bien, leur action est immédiate, parce qu'elle doit l'être; mais la nôtre, parce qu'elle prépare, espérons-le, une reconstruction lointaine, doit être considérée comme très importante quoique médiate. Nous ne jouissons d'aucun privilège; notre condition nécessaire d'étudiants ne peut nous être supprimée que devant un danger immédiat, souverain et certain]."[15]

YOUTH: STRENGTH OF THE PRESENT

With the end of hostilities in Europe and the Pacific, reconstruction became a reality, and students evinced an increasing awareness of the need to translate the oft-repeated pre-war discourse of anticipation into concrete terms, demanding that they be permitted an active role in the shaping of post-war society. There was, however, some disagreement on the means to be adopted in realizing this imperative. Some continued to hold to the older ideal that it was sufficient merely to undergo a proper preparation for future responsibilities by taking their studies seriously. Students who adhered to this position believed that their views would not be listened to until they had effectively entered adult life. At both Montreal universities, while there was widespread realization of the fact that a considerable number of young people desired to play a more active role in society, there was a continued adherence to a future-oriented discourse. Students themselves regularly referred to their future social roles to advocate greater rights and advantages such as scholarships or reduced public transit fares. But a number of students in the post-war period began to elaborate a parallel language that called into question more general adult definitions of youth and, in turn, the particular characteristics assigned to students. They enunciated, in fact, a new self-perception and a new, more critical appraisal of the student condition: "The mentality of the university student is framed by an unconscious acceptance of the condition of a legal minor. University students feel like minors, because they are treated as such by their parents, professors, and employers. Students are never considered in light of what they really are, but in terms of what they are going to become ... Under the present dispensation, the profession of student carries with it no wider responsibility [La mentalité universitaire se caractérise par un statut de minorité inconsciemment consenti. L'universitaire se sent mineur. Il est traité comme tel par ses parents, ses professeurs et ses employeurs. On ne le considère jamais comme ce qu'il est, mais pour ce qu'il deviendra ... Le métier d'étudiant dans les circonstances actuelles ne comporte pas de responsabilités]."[16] Increasingly, students aspired to be recognized as fully empowered advocates of their own condition, and on this basis, they demanded acknowledgment of their rights and privileges. In other words, students balanced uneasily between the future and the present, because even those who most forcefully sponsored the idea that students had an actual role to play in society did not entirely reject the older notion that youth was a factor in reconstruction, a guarantee for the future. However, the very questioning of youth and student identity had large implications for the whole issue of citizenship and inclusion in a democratic civic order.

It would seem that the new student position, that which attributed a concrete and immediate social role to youth, thus identifying it as an actual social reality, was evident in the post-war period and more forcefully articulated at the Université de Montréal, despite the currency of more traditional language that connected youth to the future.

At McGill the issue was not framed in these terms; there, a generational discourse was superimposed upon the traditional definition of youth. But for students at both institutions, the essential was to situate oneself according to a framework that enabled the individual to relate to the wider society.

For one part of the student population, the notion of participation advanced in current debates was directed by the expectation that they would be the leaders of tomorrow's society, and that from this standpoint they had the right to speak and be consulted: "We are all together now and we must think the thoughts and lead the life that will one day make the Canada of tomorrow ... The responsibility is ours now!"[17] This was the type of discourse prevalent at McGill for nearly the entire period under study. With their gaze firmly oriented to the future, students there did not, however, minimize their sense of responsibility to their own institution, to the wider Canadian society, still less to the international order. But for them, these responsibilities remained close to the conventional definition of the student – young men and women undergoing an apprenticeship – and their overriding sense was that it was this preparation that constituted their primary obligation. This task was, however, not merely confined to academic education, since extracurricular activities were regularly presented as important components of this apprenticeship, as sites where students could develop their leadership skills. In this respect, student associations were upheld as the ideal method of education for citizenship. During the annual elections for the Students' Society, a 1946 *McGill Daily* editorial exhorted the students to cast their ballots, explaining, "Only in this way will you be performing your duty and exercising your rights as undergraduates and worthy future citizens."[18] One student's reply to the editorial conveys an apt picture of this emerging discourse of citizenship: "We are not citizens of tomorrow, but student citizens of the Canada of today, whose importance is just as great as that of our fellow citizens in all walks of life."[19] Such comments, which invoked the active and actual participation of students based upon their status as citizens remained, however, fairly isolated at McGill, and although present in the immediate postwar years, it did not re-emerge until after the mid-1950s.

Thus students at McGill continued to legitimate their status through reference to their future social role. According to this schema, graduation marked the end of one stage and the recognition of a new role in which social status was a function of the training the individual had received. Year after year the university authorities repeated this message at the May convocation. Students themselves were not indifferent to its substance and often appropriated its central themes: "Convocation is the time of transition for the student. He comes from the somewhat cloistered atmosphere of the academic world, where ideas matter – to the practical world, where action matters"; and further, "graduation is the time for the student to stop receiving and start contributing – now is the time for the graduate to justify the undergraduate."[20] Along the same lines, one *Daily* editorialist presented the graduating class of 1952 somewhat negatively as "profiteers" and exhorted students to pay their considerable debt to society as soon as they had graduated: "College is the freshman year in the university of life. This puts college graduates in a superior class. For this privilege, the student has been dependent upon the community, obtaining his education at the expense of others. He has spent four unproductive years and when he graduates he must repay his debt by doing some constructive work for the community which has supported him."[21]

It was significant that this type of discourse always included a warning: students must not overreach themselves and especially should not play at being adults. In denouncing the political agitation in which the Department of External Affairs of the Student Executive Council of McGill University (SEC) had recently engaged, one of the *Daily*'s editorials left little room for doubt concerning the fact that university students had not attained the status of adults: "McGill students are in the general sense young men and women involved in the difficult process of becoming mature and reasonable persons ... We should above all keep in mind that we are students. We are in the main, at McGill to learn. The SEC is not McGill's answer to Parliament and should not act as such." And even more dismissively, "Little girls flouncing about in their mother's high heels not only look silly but are remarkably liable to trip and fall on their youthful noses."[22] From this standpoint, the student was emphatically not a full-fledged adult who enjoyed the full panoply of civic rights, but a person undergoing a period of training and waiting. However, acceptance of this social position by students was a direct function of how they perceived the future: when it appeared murky, the future-oriented discourse could be turned in a much more conflictual direction. At times, students felt trapped between two incompatible ideals: those of the protected environment of the university and of the bustling "real" world outside academe: "The student of our era is still living in an Ivory Tower, it is true, but his views and opinions are not confined to matters only with his small society. Within the confines of the University today we are comparatively safe and secure, but unlike the princess of old, or the scholars of past centuries, we can look out on the exterior world and see the society that we will be forced to live in as soon as we have served our time in the Ivory Tower."[23]

Generally speaking, when McGill students reflected on the subject of their identity, they did not move outside the boundaries outlined by their predecessors, nor did they contest adult prescriptions of the image of the ideal student. It should be understood, however, that this is a description of the official position subscribed to by the Students' Society of McGill and the editorial policy of the *McGill Daily*. Dissident voices surely existed, given the example of the previously cited open letter in which one student advocated full citizenship rights. However, the fact that such opinions were rarely expressed by official student representatives suggests that students as a group, if they called their identity into question, did not challenge the fundamental category of youth as prescribed by adults. It must be recognized, nevertheless, that the concept of education then in vogue at McGill was a variant of that more generally current in Anglo-Protestant educational circles, which defined the primary goal of education as the training of free and responsible individuals, and in consequence, students were given a certain degree of initiative in their own education. As outlined by student journalist David Grier, "[t]he fundamental mission of the University especially, and of education generally, is to teach tomorrow's citizens to think for themselves."[24] What is significant about this statement is that Grier repeated almost word for word the declaration of Chancellor Gardner, who at the beginning of the academic year had adumbrated his concept of the university's role: "the turning out of graduates who are trained to think for themselves and whose thinking is a product of the truly educated mind."[25]

In the final analysis, students at McGill enjoyed a certain autonomy that in some ways conditioned them to accept the systems of authority already in place. For example, the student association was given responsibility over the internal disciplining of its members. However, the university administration did not hesitate to intervene informally in making public its own position regarding certain events. Even on those rare occasions when student governing bodies did not take the views of the administration into account, there were mechanisms in place to bring student associations to heel. By and large, however, students seemed to share the prescribed adult goals regarding the overriding purposes of university education, and what official contestation did occur usually occurred discreetly. More tellingly, at the end of the 1950s, just as McGill students were beginning to join with other Quebec university students in a wider campaign of social activism, an article in the *Daily* attempted to explain why it had taken so long to arouse this more politicized awareness: "In the comparatively tranquil political scene of this continent, students are insulated through a tradition of democracy from the necessity for extreme action in defence of their rights. This has probably led to the lack of vibrant interest in national student unity and in asserting the importance of students as a social force."[26]

A substantially different context characterized the Université de Montréal. Students who arrived there found themselves with a markedly greater margin of liberty than they had experienced during their secondary education in the *collèges classiques*, but they still operated in a Catholic institutional setting that was directed by the clergy. As Nicole Neatby explains, university education rested upon Catholic doctrines, an injunction that was more publicly adhered to in the postwar years in the face of the communist menace. The Catholic attempt to manage students was overt and was expressed, among other ways, through the presence of a chaplain in the student association. The student newspaper, *Quartier latin*, was also tightly controlled, for according to its constitution, the university rector (president) or his delegate was designated the official censor. However, censorship was not regularly applied by the authorities, and it occurred only when students were deemed to have stepped outside acceptable bounds of expression, an instance of which happened in January 1950, when the rector took severe steps to curb articles that had criticized the university administration and the Catholic religion: "Attacks on University officials are prohibited, and no article touching upon religion or morals can be published without approval in advance by the rector [Défense d'attaquer les Administrateurs de l'Université, défense de publier aucun article touchant à la religion et à la morale, avant de l'avoir soumis au recteur]."[27] In March, faced with the collective disobedience of the entire editorial board of *Quartier latin*, the rector reiterated his position: "Henceforth, any article scheduled for publication in *Quartier latin* must be submitted to me for vetting before being sent off to the printer [Dorénavant, tout article destiné au *Quartier latin* devra lui [le recteur] être soumis avant d'être livré à l'imprimeur]."[28] On this occasion, the rector threatened to suspend the publication of the newspaper if his edicts were not respected. This response stood in contrast to the situation at McGill, where a censor's scrutiny over the moral tenor of articles was not written into the *Daily*'s constitution. As a general rule, students there were self-governing in this respect.[29] However, the principal became involved on a number of occasions when, in his estimation, the reputation of the university appeared compromised by student publications.[30]

The climate that prevailed at the Université de Montréal appeared to be more constraining than that at McGill. However, in spite of these tighter official controls, "disturbing" elements had an impact on the student body, especially in the aftermath of war. In particular, these centred upon intellectual currents emanating from France, mainly those of the Catholic left as represented by the magazine *Esprit*. For some of these young people, according to Gérard Pelletier, such ideas constituted a revelation, because they offered them a way to understand that "Christianity was not, in and of itself, hostile to innovation or to modern values, that its intersection with human history did not take the form of a backward-looking anachronism but of a sustained movement towards the future [la pensée chrétienne n'est pas, par nature, hostile aux innovations ni aux valeurs du monde moderne, qu'elle n'explore pas l'Histoire les yeux braqués sur le rétroviseur mais dans une démarche soutenue vers l'avenir]."[31] The presence of progressively minded professors in the university, coupled with the palpable emergence of new ideas in French Canada, most notably evident in the refurbished Montreal daily *Le Devoir*, now directed by Gérard Filion and his team of editorialists,[32] also convinced students that they possessed an intellectual space in which they could question imposed adult and clerical authority. In other words, Université de Montréal students found themselves in the immediate post-war years in a cultural setting torn between the values of tradition and progress, a position that was potentially uncomfortable to occupy. It was in this context that a new concept of student status emerged among young people at the Université de Montréal, that of the "young intellectual worker." The existence of this idea provided for the actualization of youth, the adoption of an attitude based upon a complete assumption of responsibility that allowed students to claim an active role and the full status of citizens in French-Canadian society.

In order to understand how such a concept emerged, it is necessary to consider the ongoing relationship that Université de Montréal students forged with their counterparts in France and other European countries. The war fostered a new self-awareness among European students, who engaged in a process of questioning their place in the reconstruction of their societies. It was the Grenoble Charter, drafted by the Union Nationale des Étudiants Français (UNEF) in 1946, that first officially promulgated the concept of the "young intellectual worker" as the new definition of student identity. Because of its very novelty and significance for student life during the ensuing years, this idea requires further analysis. At the end of the war, French students found themselves bereft of any organizing principle; indeed, the UNEF, their national association, had been discredited by its silence during the conflict. Although the UNEF escaped overt accusations of collaborating with the Nazis, it had not distinguished itself by participation in the Resistance. As an association that aspired to represent all French students, it thus required a new source of cohesion in order to regain their full confidence.[33] In 1946 French students held a congress at Grenoble that aimed at rebuilding a national student union and at establishing a new definition of the social status of the student. While a number of influential dissenting voices continued to be heard within the French student community, the Grenoble congress marked an important change in attitudes. By defining the student as a "young intellectual worker" (*jeune travailleur intellectuel*), the charter sought to socially "situate" students, to confer upon them a specific place and active role in a reconstructed French society:

Art. 1: The student is a young intellectual worker.
Rights and duties of the student as a young person
Art. 2: As a youth, the student has a right to benefit from special foresight on the part of society in the physical, intellectual, and moral domains.
Art. 3: As a youth, the student has the duty to integrate himself into the wider group of world and national youth.
Rights and duties of the student as a worker
Art. 4: As a worker, the student has a right to work and leisure under the best possible conditions and to be guaranteed material independence, both personally and socially, through the free exercise of union rights.
Art. 5: As a worker, the student is under the obligation to acquired the highest technical competence in his discipline.
Rights and duties of the student as an intellectual
Art. 6: As an intellectual, the student has the right to pursue the search for truth and to that freedom which is its essential precondition.
Art. 7: As an intellectual, the student has the duty:
To define, propagate, and defend the truth, which implies the duty to share and participate in the progress of culture, and to elucidate the sense of History;
To defend these freedoms against all oppression, this, for the intellectual, constitutes the most sacred calling.[34]

The charter, by insisting in this way upon the rights and duties of students, sought to fully integrate them into society. On a more collectivist level, it sought to confer the powers of a trade union upon the UNEF, in order to galvanize it out of its pre-war corporatist mentality, which had been denounced by two participants in the movement as characteristic of an era where "conflicts were quietly resolved in the background, so long as students were well behaved and presented their requests politely [(o)n résoudra les problèmes, entre soi et bien tranquillement, à condition que l'étudiant se tienne sage et demande poliment]."[35] Although the grafting of the new approach onto French student culture did not occur without contestation, it did gain a growing number of adherents during the years immediately following the proclamation of the charter. Grouped in the UNEF, the student associations gained a forum for discussion and a more effective channel for presenting their demands, one that was increasingly recognized by the adult authorities of French society.[36] Because the leaders of the UNEF envisioned it as a trade union devoted to securing the welfare of its members, they advanced a number of policy demands, such as mutual benefit schemes and social security. Thus in 1957 the charter's definition, "which explicitly used the term worker to describe students, placed them within that active community upon which the life of the nation depends. Prior to this, economists had considered students as forming a part of society that lived off the labour of others and ranked them on a level with children and the elderly. This definition aimed to identify the student with the active segment of society [en employant à dessein le mot de travailleur pour qualifier l'étudiant, le place au sein de la communauté active qui fait vivre la nation. Alors qu'auparavant les économistes rangeaient les étudiants dans cette partie de la société qui vit du travail de la population active, à l'égal par exemple des enfants et des vieillards, cette définition vise à placer l'étudiant dans la fraction active de la société]." Such recognition "implied that students had the right to obtain the material equivalent of the work they had provided [implique que l'étudiant a le droit d'obtenir la contre-partie (sic) matérielle du travail qu'il fournit]." In this way, two French student activists in the student union movement argued that the student's work "has economic value and constitutes a most precious intellectual investment [a valeur économique et constitue un des plus précieux investissements intellectuels]."[37]

Students at the Université de Montréal appropriated and adapted the concept of the "young intellectual worker." It was mentioned for the first time in *Quartier latin* in 1944, in an article by the Belgian Jean de Brouckere,[38] who commented upon wartime developments in French and Belgian student culture. In his estimation, the student community had taken a great leap forward by joining the ranks of the Resistance and, in so doing, affirming an association with working-class organizations and, indeed, with all workers in their collective struggle against the enemy: "What a happy indication that a new turn of events is occurring to see these young intellectual workers taking action along the lines set forth by their comrades in so-called manual trades. During these terrible years, all workers have been brought together in a common realization of a profound community of aspirations and interests [C'est un heureux symptôme que cette action des jeunes travailleurs intellectuels, si conforme à celle menée par leurs compagnons des métiers dits manuels. Tous les travailleurs auront été unis durant ces années terribles par une communion profonde d'aspirations et d'intérêts]."[39] In 1946 the idea of the "young intellectual worker" reappeared on the student horizon at the Université Montréal, this time to stay. Gérard Pelletier, in his capacity as travelling secretary of the Fonds Mondial de Secours aux

Étudiants, had been introduced to the new "labour and social" (ouvrières et sociales)[40] orientation of the French student environment, and in an interview with *Quartier latin*, he reported that "as far as student youth is concerned, there is currently occurring a vast effort to integrate it into the nation. Students themselves have reacted against that dangerous isolationism that prior to the war had led them into a rigid and superficial intellectualism. Student youth desires to reconnect with the working masses [(e)n ce qui concerne la jeunesse étudiante, il se fait un énorme travail pour l'intégrer à la nation. Les étudiants eux-mêmes réagissent contre l'isolationnisme dangereux où avait conduit, avant la guerre, un intellectualisme rigide et superficiel. La jeunesse étudiante veut reprendre contact avec la masse]."[41] Always interested in ongoing developments in the student world, Pelletier returned to the theme the following year, this time as covering the labour beat. He congratulated the editorial team of *Quartier latin* for following in the footsteps of their French counterparts and for "publishing the clear-sighted weekly paper of the young intellectual workers [universitaires (qui) publient l'hebdomadaire lucide des jeunes travailleurs intellectuels]."[42] Flattered, Jean-Marc Léger, the lead writer, used the occasion to publicly affirm the new orientation of the newspaper[43] and to explain his own views on the university student's place in society: "Thank God that the actual tendency of *Quartier latin* is not a sterile dilettantism but flows from an awareness of the responsibilities that devolve upon the university student in today's world. Because their origins are with the people, students must give themselves to the people to assist them in their ongoing struggle for material and spiritual welfare [La tendance actuelle du *Quartier latin* n'est pas, Dieu merci, la manifestation d'un dilletantisme stérile mais le résultat d'une prise de conscience des responsabilités de l'universitaire dans le monde contemporain. L'universitaire venu du peuple doit se donner au peuple pour l'aider dans sa lutte pour le mieux-être matériel et spirituel]."[44]

However, direct references to the Grenoble Charter in *Quartier latin* were not evident before 1952. One student, Gilles Lortie, unreservedly accepted the concept of the "young intellectual worker," but he noted the difficuly of framing a student unionism appropriate for Canada because, in his estimation, the general conditions of university life were not the same as those in France. The major difference revolved around the fact that the Canadian university system was private while, by contrast, the French one was public:

It goes without saying that the circumstances that have defined the transformation of the student movement in France do not exist in Canada and probably never will exist in such a definitive manner. However, the same state of mind will one day exist, and at that time, students must adopt a full awareness of their social role and what they represent for the worker and the civil servant. They will no longer be able to lapse into their eternal status of spoilt children, in blissful ignorance of the fact that, like them, other young people have the right to benefit from higher education. A well-defined student unionism will compel them to see the problem, and when they have grasped its significance, they will be brought to envision the democratization of the University.[45]

[Il va sans dire que les circonstances qui ont présidé à la transformation du mouvement étudiant français n'existent pas au Canada et qu'elles n'y existeront probablement jamais d'une façon aussi cruciale. Cependant, le même état d'esprit régnera un jour et alors les étudiants devront prendre conscience de leur rôle dans la société et de ce qu'ils représentent pour l'ouvrier et le fonctionnaire. Ils ne pourront jouer éternellement leur rôle d'enfant gâté sans penser que d'autres jeunes pourraient bénéficier comme eux d'une meilleure éducation. Un syndicalisme étudiant bien compris leur fera voir le problème et quand ils en auront bien pris conscience, ils penseront tout normalement à la démocratisation de l'Université.]

What is apparent here is one of the fundamental objectives of student unionism: the democratization of university education, an issue that would progressively acquire more importance in the Quebec student environment, particularly following the debates on university finance that aroused considerable discussion during the ensuing years.

It was with these Canadian and especially French-Canadian national particularities in mind that the Association Générale des Étudiants de l'Université de Montréal (AGEUM) officially adopted the notion of the "young intellectual worker" when it presented its brief to the Royal Commission of Inquiry on Constitutional Problems (Tremblay Commission) in 1954–55.[46] The brief began with the following justification: students could participate in this far-reaching national debate because they were "in fact young intellectual workers who, by virtue of the education they had acquired before entering university, possessed the ability to pursue, in a more personal and autonomous manner, a critical analysis of the conditions that characterized their society and to elucidate the underlying principles and laws [véritablement un jeune travailleur intellectuel car, par la formation acquise avant son entrée à l'université, il est en mesure de poursuivre d'une façon plus personnelle et autonome son analyse critique des réalités qui l'entourent et d'en dégager des principes et des lois]."[47] In this way, the AGEUM conferred a specific expertise upon students, a necessary precondition to advancing the claim that students' work must be recognized. Thus it followed that "(t)he student is a young intellectual worker whose labour is absolutely essential to the full development of society. This work, however, requires that those who pursue it must be able to do so in an atmosphere characterized by complete freedom. The student's contribution to the common good, even though it may at times appear obscure, is no less real than the services provided by workers in other domains [(l)'étudiant est un jeune travailleur intellectuel dont le travail est absolument nécessaire au plein développement de la société. Mais ce travail exige que celui qui s'y livre puisse le faire dans une atmosphère d'entière liberté. Son apport au bien commun, pour être parfois plus obscur, n'en est pas moins aussi réel que les services rendus par d'autres dans des domaines différents]."[48] In other words, the student was now situated in reference to society, and "he can now demand to be recognized as a useful member of the social body, with the same rights as those who practise a trade or profession [il peut donc exiger d'être reconnu comme un membre utile au corps social, au même titre que ceux qui exercent une profession ou un métier]."[49]

Through their student association, the Université de Montréal students affirmed their status as intellectual workers. However, they also considered themselves as youth, and from this standpoint, a number of advocates sought to forge links with young people of other classes. According to the AGEUM representatives, because students were young people privileged by their education, they had a responsibility to put themselves in the front line of defence of the interests of all youth. With this end in view, one of the representatives of the AGEUM preached the necessity of a united youth and suggested that students could be the interpreters between young people and civic authorities:

Students no longer constitute an isolate caste: on the contrary, they are as essential to the movement of the nation as are workers and employers. For students, this entails a social responsibility of which our associations have a particular duty to be increasingly conscious … At the beginning of this article, we identified the defining characteristic of student culture: youth. Far from excluding students from public issues, this quality compels an engagement with their highest task: to be in the forefront of youth, an imperative that directs student associations to lobby public authorities for policies that will advance the interests of youth. In this way, student associations proclaim their solidarity with all young people.[50]

[Le monde étudiant ne peut constituer une caste isolée: il est au contraire un rouage de la population autant que le monde ouvrier et le monde patronal. Il y a donc pour les étudiants une responsabilité sociale et cette responsabilité, nos associations ont le devoir d'en être de plus en plus conscientes … Nous avons indiqué au début de l'article l'une des caractéristiques du milieu étudiant: la jeunesse. Loin d'exclure les étudiants des problèmes publics, cette caractéristique les engage vers une tâche éminemment louable: celle de se porter à l'avant-garde de la jeunesse … Les associations étudiantes interviennent auprès des autorités compétentes pour une politique en faveur de la jeunesse. Les associations étudiantes se déclarent solidaires de tous les jeunes.]

Finally in 1961, the AGEUM sponsored the drafting of a "Charte de l'étudiant universitaire" that reiterated many of the prominent themes articulated in the Grenoble Charter, adapting them to the experiences of Université de Montréal students. This new charter rested on the following general principle: "The student possesses all the rights and assumes all the duties of a *free citizen* and *a youth*, who by performing *intellectual labour* in a *university setting*, is apprenticed in a professional training which will eventually enable the student to serve society [L'étudiant possède tous les droits et assume toutes les obligations d'un *citoyen libre* et *jeune*, faisant par un *travail intellectuel*, au sein d'un *milieu universitaire*, l'apprentissage d'une profession par laquelle il doit servir plus tard la société]."[51] This document added to the qualities of youth, worker, and intellectual those of free citizen and member of the university community. However, the new charter aptly expressed the ambivalent position occupied by the student in society and also illustrated that the attempt to actualize this status raised contradictions. On the one hand, the charter insisted upon the fact that the student was a citizen, a worker, and an intellectual, but on the other, the placing of the student's youth in the foreground indicated that intellectual work only had value based upon what the student would become following the stage of apprenticeship. Thus it was difficult to surmount this inherent ambiguity between present and future, as students did not succeed in demonstrating that the work of the young intellectual was in fact immediately productive for society, even though they realized that this recognition was necessary to the acquisition of a definite social status. Indeed, students themselves were not blinded by these ideals, as some reflected bitterly that their work was held to be of little account: "Without a house, a car and without a salary, the 20th-century man is not considered a man … How does society really regard us, we who are without money and power … We represent society's living potential … but in the future [Sans ameublement, sans auto, et sans salaire, un homme au 20e siècle n'est pas considéré comme un homme. Sans argent et sans puissance … que représentons-nous aux yeux de la société? … Nous représentons le potentiel vital … mais de l'avenir]."[52]

It must also be recognized that the discourse on youth proffered by the authorities of the Université de Montréal was not fundamentally different from that of their counterparts at McGill, and they reacted neither to the new identity presented by the students nor to the concept of the "young intellectual worker." Father Llewellyn, the student chaplain, published an article in *Quartier latin* that explained to students that their training was oriented towards the future: "Student of the Université de Montréal ... In this context, you are still at the stage of formation and training. In your daily activities, we can already see the type of service you will render to the world tomorrow [Carabin de l'U de M ... Dans le cadre de l'Université, tu en es encore à la période de perfectionnement et d'entraînement. De ta conduite d'aujourd'hui, on peut conclure déjà au service que tu rendras demain au monde]."[53]

YOUTH: GENERATION OR CLASS?

During the post-war years, students at the Université de Montréal and McGill University pursued their efforts to develop a group consciousness, a cultural process whose origins lay earlier in the century. However, this was not undertaken in a concerted manner and there were a number of differing ways in which group identity was articulated. Université de Montréal students explored a new terrain of identity: they began to define themselves as a distinct social class and sought to establish links with the working class. McGill students never referred to the concept of the "young intellectual worker" during the post-war years. They chose another way to express their identity and advanced the notion that they were a generation, understood as a feeling of contemporaneousness[54] that they hoped they shared with other young people the same age, but especially with other students. There was considerable self-questioning about what characterized their generation,[55] and they reacted to the rather unflattering descriptions that newspapers or magazines occasionally directed towards young people. Whether contemporary opinion referred to a "silent generation," a "waiting generation," or a "nonsense generation," there was no lack of descriptive phrases to decry American youth during the 1950s. It should of course be remembered that the great majority of these descriptions emanated from the more conservative cultural climate of the United States, which during this decade had wide-ranging repercussions on university campuses.[56]

The rather negative assessment presented in a 1951 *Time Magazine* survey, entitled "Portrait of the Younger Generation," gave rise to a series of reflections on the part of McGill students. This survey treated the attitudes and values of young Americans aged eighteen to twenty-eight, and put forward a harsh assessment of the younger generation, which was described in the following terms: "silent, fatalistic, security-minded, conservative, grave, morally confused, tolerant of almost everything and blaming no one for its troubles."[57] Interestingly, these were attributes normally imputed to adults or to the elderly and not to young people, from whom society expected enthusiasm and questioning and criticism of previous generations.[58] In short, such a portrait was not flattering to a youth generation that seemed to have lost its way. Faced with such accusations and comments, which they believed were inaccurate, some students began to question both the very existence of the generation and its validity as a category of analysis. For example, in an open letter to the *Daily*, one student wondered whether there was any unifying feature to his generation: "ours is a complex generation, made up of a kaleidoscope of people and types, ambitions and tastes. We can never even attempt to apply the same label on the young advertising executive making his way on Peel Street, and the young miner on the picket lines, fighting for his union in Timmins; the student wandering among the riches of the libraries, and the soldier on his way home from Korea, older and wiser."[59] The article continued in this vein by stating, "No label will stick on us," without ever calling into question the implicit belief that whatever differences existed, a set of common problems forged links among young people. However, in the student's opinion, surveys failed to encapsulate such a fragmented entity as his generation. To return to the *Time Magazine* survey, Louis Eddy, another editorial writer, criticized both its results and its methodology.[60] Eddy maintained that those surveyed by *Time* were not representative enough to cast the entire youth generation as silent, confused, and conventional. However, in so doing, he made no distinction between young Canadians and young Americans, suggesting that his critique of the *Time* survey was a defensive posture, stemming from the feeling that Eddy believed his own generation had been targeted. At the beginning of the next academic year, another editorial firmly equated the youth of the two countries: "While *Time* was referring to youth in the United States, it was generally agreed that much of what they had to say applied to the younger generation in Canada."[61]

Despite these criticisms of the methods that *Time* had used in conducting its survey, most agreed that the accusations directed at the younger generation carried some weight, as demonstrated by the large number of articles that appeared in the *Daily* subsequent to its publication. Among other issues, the writers of these articles sought to expose the roots of the supposed silence of youth: was it because they had nothing to say or, rather, because they did not wish to express themselves? Most opinion converged around the second explanation, concurring that the young generation was quiet because it lacked self-confidence, that either its concerns were of interest to no one or that it had all been said before, with no apparent result. All of these findings were aimed at exhorting young people to express themselves openly, otherwise they might well deserve the epithet "lost generation": "Are we another Lost Generation?

We may be just that, if we don't come out and say what we think about the society we are to inherit; if we don't hold and express opinions about the problems that face it today. For our own sakes, we must shrug off the compulsion of silence that seems to grip us."[62]

These American initiatives to understand the younger generation were not limited to *Time Magazine*'s description of the "silent generation." The *New York Times* spoke equally vividly of an emerging generational shift, what it termed the "beat generation,"[63] while the novelist William Styron coined the term "waiting generation." In the face of these divergent analyses, one McGill student proffered his own rather negative assessment of his generation's experience: "We've been called the silent generation, or the waiting generation. We're neither. We're effete, the indifferent generation. We're the generation of small men, small hopes, small achievements. We're not even disillusioned; we've never had any illusions. If we're silent it is because we have nothing to say. But we're also a very sad generation. We're perhaps as monotonous as the age in which we grew up, and ours is the age of proletarian democracy. It is dull and uninteresting. It is an age of mass-men. It is neither repulsive nor very attractive."[64]

The prevailing finding from all the American surveys was that youth was silent, conformist, and conservative. However, not everyone readily accepted this generalization and endeavoured to find an explanation for it. According to one McGill student, although his generation was indifferent because the world in which it lived was one of disenchantment and disillusion, he did not characterize the situation as entirely hopeless, pointing instead to the high level of student participation in a conference organized by the Student Volunteer Movement – to which the Student Christian Movement of Canada was affiliated – at the University of Kansas during the Christmas holidays. This writer's hopefulness stemmed from the fact that the students who spoke at the 1952 congress, whether they came from the United States, Canada, Japan, Germany, China, Africa, or one of the other forty countries who sent delegates, all shared a vision of the world and were convinced that "a significant and fulfilling 'modus vivendi' must be religiously oriented."[65] In other words, the world could be saved so long as world youth could join together to find a common understanding among nations. Returning to the theme in 1957, a number of students explained the conservatism and conformity of their generation by the particular conjunction of historical events, citing especially the threat of a new world war, and thus the sense that the future was absent, to account for the reaction of post-war youth. According to one editorialist in the *Daily*, youth's seriousness and need for security could not be blamed; rather, these were evidence of a new maturity apparent among the younger generation, a maturity that had been thrust upon it by the concatenation of historical events, but proof, nonetheless, of the fact that youth was not simply withdrawing from mainstream society.[66] Reacting to the same accusations, another student journalist reached the following conclusion: "The thirties may have been a lost generation, but they had a lot of fun. In the fifties we are faced with another lost generation, a product of the Age of Anxiety, young people who are not quite sure where they will end up, but are living in the same atmosphere of fear that now encircles the globe."[67]

The conviction of forming a generation was generally linked to a sense of opposition to other generations. The generation of the 1930s, categorized as a "lost generation," was now grown to adulthood, and it was against that generation that the youth of the 1950s defined its own identity. Communication between these two generations was difficult, and reading the editorials of the period would lead one to believe that the two groups were complete strangers to one another, the fissure between them developing from the sense that the values of the older generation had no relevance for the younger:

If we mention sex, their squirming embarassment generates discomfort in us. So silence. If we wax idealistic, they reply with Wise-Old-Man cynicism which is both unanswerable and unacceptable. So silence. When we listen to them as professors delivering a fervent lecture whose aim is to involve us in their philosophy of life, we cannot become involved because somewhere in the back of our minds we know that they belong to the generation which has failed frighteningly and therefore whose philosophy must be defective no matter how eloquently it is expressed. So we sit in classrooms, silently, with stupid faces, and take notes. They are aliens. So silence.[68]

The sheer volume of this generational questioning reveals that, particularly at McGill, student youth during the 1950s devoted considerable attention to probing their self-identity and the image that they projected to the wider society. At the end of 1957 a *Daily* editorial expressed the matter particularly eloquently: "When history departments of the future will look back at this period of history, what will be the comments they will make about it [the younger generation]. Will we be the Lost generation or the Silent generation or the Beat generation or the non-sense generation, or the Good or the Evil or the Naïve or the Doomed? What are we? What are we doing in this world? Is there anything which is important to us? What do we believe? if we believe anything."[69]

At the Université de Montréal, this explicitly generational discourse was less evident, despite the fact that it had formed a principal component of youth identity during the Depression, when students portrayed themselves as a sacrificed generation, a sentiment that was amplified by the threat and onset of war. As late as 1944, Fernand Seguin published an evocative article describing his generation, holding the previous generation accountable for the war, and calling upon his elders to assume their responsibilities to assist the younger generation:

Young people aged twenty to twenty-five belong to the interwar generation ... Those years when we asked our fathers for a scooter or a bicycle coincided with a complete collapse of the stock market, so that for us, our growing up has been a materially and emotionally arduous exercise, rather than a walk in the park. Thus, already exhausted, we have arrived at that stage when young men are gearing up for the leap into life. A further nasty surprise was held in readiness for us: just for our own personal pleasure, our elders kept a lovely little world war in store, telling us that it would be the perfect occasion for us to display the benefits of our manly education and to celebrate martial virtues ... In short, if the ripe apples had adopted the motto of "let's help out youth," the green apples would exclaim less often "make way for youth."[70]
[Les jeunes de vingt à vingt-cinq ans appartiennent à la génération de l'entre-deux-guerres ... L'âge où nous demandions à notre papa de nous acheter une trottinette ou un bicycle, coïncida avec la dégringolade des valeurs boursières, de sorte que notre jeunesse a été une marche, une course, mais jamais une promenade sur roulettes. Aussi, sommes-nous arrivés essoufflés à l'époque où le jeune homme prend son élan pour sauter dans la vie. Une surprise nous y attendait: on nous avait réservé, à notre usage personnel, une gentille petite guerre mondiale, histoire d'exposer les bienfaits d'une éducation virile et de célébrer les vertus martiales ... Bref, ne croyez-vous pas que les raisins verts crieraient moins souvent: Place aux jeunes! si les raisins mûrs adoptaient la devise: Aide aux jeunes!]

This type of hard-edged generational consciousness was blurred during the years between 1945 and 1960, surfacing on a few occasions, such as in 1952, when under the threat of a nuclear world war, the future appeared more ominous than ever before. André Lefebvre, in an editorial entitled "Pessimism or Realism," exposed his vision of the future in the following terms: "What a stark contrast between two generations! How the perspectives differ between those born about 1880 and those who appeared on the scene around 1925! ... Without falling under the spell of an illusion, our parents still had the possibility to discuss reasonably precisely the road to follow in pursuing a definite goal ... As for us, we simply lack horizons [Quel contraste frappant entre deux générations! De celle qui voit le jour autour de 1880 à celle qui paraît vers 1925, comme les perspectives diffèrent! ... Sans trop d'illusions, nos parents avaient la possibilité de discuter la route à suivre vers un but entrevu avec une netteté raisonnable ... Quant à nous, nous manquons simplement d'horizons]."[71]

Like their McGill counterparts, students at the Université de Montréal engaged in self-questioning about the peculiarities of their generation, and some reached the sad conclusion that all generations were destined to resemble their predecessors and replicate their experiences, that none would contribute any real solutions to humanity's problems: "Before us, in an unremitting series of ten-year cycles, generations of students have succeeded one another, and with the enthusiasm of youth, each swore to transform its society as soon as they could. And yet the same old problems have remained unsolved. Each new generation, like its predecessor, has been guilty of a lie. Their zeal has died with age. And now, it is our turn. There is nothing that would lead us to believe that we will be any better or any worse than those who have preceded us [Avant nous, de dix ans en dix ans, les générations d'étudiants se sont succédées. Et avec l'enthousiasme de la jeunesse, chacune avait juré de transformer son milieu dès qu'elle pourrait y jouer un rôle. Et pourtant les vieux problèmes sont restés sans solutions. Chaque génération nouvelle, comme sa précédente, a menti. La ferveur mourait avec l'âge. Et maintenant, c'est notre tour. Rien ne laisse prévoir que nous serons pires que ceux-là, ou meilleurs]."[72] However, in 1957 Julien Aubert, editor-in-chief of *Quartier latin*, evinced a greater combativeness and commitment in proclaiming the merits of his own generation. The message he delivered to the previous generation was "Watch out, you old people, for what happens over the next few years. Young people will not hesitate to account for your deficiencies ... Revolutions happen swiftly, but are prepared over the long term." Thus in his estimation, youth is "fed up with being polite, and among them, respect for authority is wearing thin [Prenez garde! Vous les vieux, prenez garde aux jours qui viennent. On pourra alors décharger bien des choses sur des épaules en loques. Les révolutions se font en un jour mais se préparent de longue haleine ... tannés d'être polis, le respect de toutes les autorités commence à peser lourd]."[73]

In other words, when Université de Montréal and McGill students used the term "generation," they shared a certain standpoint. They placed themselves in opposition to the previous generation, those who had fought in the war and who, in their opinion, had not succeeded in building a lasting peace. Part of their generational sensibility was to adopt the mantle of the new defenders of world peace. Moreover, they accused their elders of not listening to them and considering their views. However, this generational consciousness was more overt at McGill where it was sustained in part by American media surveys to which, significantly, francophone students never referred. For Université de Montréal students, generational consciousness was coupled with a growing desire to define themselves as a social class, and this constituted one of the strikingly new ideas that characterized Quebec student culture during the 1950s. Added to this self-description as a social class was the development of a social conscience. During the process of questioning their identity, Université de Montréal students turned their gaze towards Europe, and especially to France, to appreciate how their overseas comrades were able to forge a place in the post-war social order. Their discovery of the concept of the "young intellectual worker," a notion which, as previously explained, rested upon a sense of difference between the classes in modern society as well as upon a well-developed social conscience, provided an answer to this search for identity, as demonstrated by demands for the democratization of the university and the building of bridges to the working class.

Although certainly drawn to the idea of the "young intellectual worker," Université de Montréal students were also aware of other elements of French student culture. To the question of what was the student's place in society, they advanced the claim that they constituted a social class. As early as 1945, *Quartier latin* referred to students as a class in announcing a forthcoming congress of the Jeunesse Étudiante Catholique that was to include all of Quebec's university and college youth. This congress, organized around the theme of "The Student," declared as its purpose the fostering of awareness of the student's profession and the articulation of a public expression of student pride. Its promoters justified the resort to the idea of class in the following way:

The student class is born of the need to coordinate the efforts of students in their search for a fundamental humanism. It states its ambitions, its ideal, its concerns in a collective consciousness whose necessary sentiment is pride. Our profession is noble and worthy in its immediate aim: the harmonious growth of the person ... Because the student class cannot exist without the multitude of individual students, its pride cannot be expressed without calibrating its capacities as a function of the number and diversity of its members. To rise to an awareness of this common strength, the necessary consciousness of the sentiment of pride, student youth must group itself together.[74]
[La classe étudiante, née du besoin de coordonner les efforts des étudiants dans leur recherche d'humanisme intégral, résume ses ambitions, son idéal, ses préoccupations dans une conscience collective dont un des sentiments nécessaires est la fierté. Notre métier est grand et digne dans son objet immédiat: la croissance harmonieuse de la personne ... Comme la classe étudiante ne peut exister sans la multitude des individus étudiants, sa fierté est impossible si elle ne constate pas ses capacités à cause du nombre et de la diversité. Pour prendre conscience de cette force commune, conscience nécessaire au sentiment de fierté, toute la jeunesse étudiante doit se grouper.]

However, those who articulated this type of language also acutely realized that it was difficult to arouse a class-consciousness among students who were aware that both their status and their time at the university were temporary. Under such conditions, mobilization of class sentiment was difficult and remained restricted to a minority: "the university as a society has no existence. There is no student class and as a group, students are incapable of acting. If student leaders wish to galvanize their constituency into action, it is up to them to make the advances, and it falls to them to convince these students that they are an important and active social group, because left to itself, the student class will be stillborn [(l)a société universitaire n'existe pas. Il n'y a pas de classe étudiante. Comme groupe, les étudiants ne peuvent pas agir. Si les chefs étudiants veulent avoir les étudiants avec eux, ils doivent faire les avances, il leur faut donner à ces mêmes étudiants l'occasion de se concevoir comme groupe important et agissant de la société parce que, comme tel, il n'a jamais eu la chance de vivre]."[75]

Despite all these difficulties, some Université de Montréal students attempted to develop a class-consciousness at both local and national levels through the National Federation of Canadian University Students (NFCUS).[76] Attempts to develop a national student union arose from the Quebec university environment, but found little resonance among anglophone students, who viewed them as European imports that were ill-adapted to the North American context:

In post war years the concept of NFCUS as a "trade union" of students developed, in an attempt to impose the European theory of national student unions onto the Canadian scene. The attempt has led a number of people to take a rather expensive farce with absolute seriousness ... At its best NFCUS has and can not represent any unified view as being that of "Canadian students." The Canadian student comes from a variety of regional, family and educational backgrounds. The North American educational system has led him to believe that his education is a training for life in the community as a whole. He is already in many ways a part of that community, reflecting its opinions and views.[77]

It was not until the academic year 1961–62 that the elected representatives of the Students' Society of McGill made direct reference to the notion of social class.[78] On the other hand, during the 1950s, Université de Montréal students, despite resistance from national student bodies, continued to explore ways in which to define youth identity around the idea of social class. At the end of the 1950s, if the official statements of the AGEUM provide any indication, the decisive step seems to have been taken. Thus the AGEUM's Comité d'Éducation, formed in 1958 to deal with questions of education and to affirm the student position in the debate, stated that "university students form ... a well-defined social class (much like the professional class or the working class), and in this sense, they must on occasion state their demands like a bloc or social unit. Students must take positions on these issues because no one else can really do it for them [(l)es étudiants universitaires forment ... une classe sociale bien définie (tout comme la classe professionnelle, ou la classe ouvrière) et en ce sens, ils doivent à l'occasion s'affirmer en tant que bloc ou unité sociale. Il faut que les étudiants prennent position car personne ne peut le faire vraiment pour eux]."[79] In a similar vein, in 1960 the AGEUM presented a brief to the Commission Provinciale des Universités, an opportunity for representatives of the student class to observe the fact that "the student group has become increasingly self-aware of its responsibilities and social obligations. It feels rising within itself a tremendous desire to integrate itself with the progressive forces in our society and a firm will to assume the direction of its own affairs [le groupe étudiant a pris davantage conscience de lui-même, de ses responsabilités et de ses obligations sociales. Il a senti naître en lui un grand désir de s'intégrer aux forces progressives de notre société et une volonté bien arrêtée de prendre en main la conduite de ses propres affaires]." In their estimation, students, because they were a progressive social force, had a particular responsibility "to propose new solutions and unbiased perspectives. More than any other class, students are able to defend noble causes and fundamental freedoms [de proposer des solutions neuves et les points de vue désintéressés. Plus que toute autre classe, elle est en mesure de défendre les nobles causes et les libertés fondamentales]." Thus for them, youth had become a social actor whose views could not be avoided, and "no government could legitimately assure social progress without drawing fully upon the energies and strength of youth, especially those of university youth [aucun gouvernement ne saurait vouloir véritablement assurer le progrès d'une société sans vouloir y associer à part entière les énergies ct lcs forccs dc la jcunessc, surtout celles de la jeunesse universitaire]."[80]

Whether from ideological conviction or from a more strategic attempt to enlarge the basis upon which to elaborate a class-consciousness, students envisioned an association with the working class. In so doing, they demonstrated that their concerns had moved beyond the limits of the university itself to extend to the entire society. Equally, students revealed that their privileged position went hand in hand with a breadth of spirit and a vigorous social conscience, a combination that made possible the articulation of statements such as the following:

We live in an era, on a continent, where all is ruled by dynamism, the spirit of enterprise, the sense of wide open spaces, the taste for creation and all things new, and we are withering inside structures, formulas, and an atmosphere of 'conservatism' that only a minority has been able to challenge. Workers have hitherto comprised this minority. What are we waiting for to join them, to support them in their struggles, to discuss those demands that do not exclusively concern the working class? What's keeping us from whipping ourselves into shape? Students are not treated any better than workers. We have interests in common. Compared to students in other countries, our social status suffers from underdevelopment.[81]

[Nous vivons à une époque, sur un continent, où tout commande le dynamisme, l'esprit d'entreprise, le sens du grand air, le goût de la création et du neuf, et nous séchons dans des structures, dans des formules, dans une atmosphère de "conservatisme" contre laquelle seule, une minorité, a entrepris la lutte. Et ce sont les ouvriers. Qu'attendons-nous pour nous joindre à eux? Pour les appuyer dans leurs luttes, pour discuter de leurs revendications qui ne concernent pas uniquement la classe ouvrière? Qu'attendons-nous pour nous dégourdir? Les étudiants ne sont pas mieux traités que les ouvriers. Nous avons des intérêts communs. Notre statut social est en retard sur celui des étudiants de beaucoup d'autres pays.]

It was from this perspective that Jean-Marc Léger instituted the Équipe de Recherches Sociales in 1947, a group whose main objective was to introduce students to contemporary working-class issues. The popularity of this organization proved that it answered the intellectual probings of the student community, and during meetings and colloquia, crowds numbering up to a hundred students, Léger recalled, came out to hear Gérard Picard, Gérard Pelletier, Jean Marchand, Gérard Filion, and André Laurendeau. Nor was the Équipe de Recherches Sociales content to limit its activities to the discussion of working-class conditions; in 1949 the group decided upon a concrete demonstration of unity with workers by participating in events such as the Asbestos Strike. On this particular occasion, it organized a subscription campaign on behalf of the miners at the Université de Montréal, and approximately 150 students went to support the strikers on the picket lines.[82] Such support was also evident through the sending of telegrams to the major protagonists in this labour conflict: the strikers received a message of unreserved support and Mgr Charbonneau was congratulated by the students. Premier Maurice Duplessis was not so fortunate; he received a telegram worded as follows: "Honourable Prime Minister, Most recent meeting Équipe de Recherches Sociales de l'Université de Montréal – stop – We have sent a message of sympathy to the asbestos strikers and congratulations to Mgr Charbonneau – stop – We regret that we cannot do the same for your government. Équipe de Recherches Sociales, Université de Montréal."[83] It must of course be underscored that the university authorities were unimpressed by this student activism and went to great lengths to ensure that the telegrams were not published in Montreal's daily newspapers. However, *Le Canada* published the story before receiving Rector Maurault's request to suppress it. The opposition to Duplessis, which at this time existed in embryonic form, became more widespread, especially after the provincial elections in 1956. [84]

Nationalist concerns also lay at the heart of the formation of the Équipe de Recherches Sociales, and this implies that the association of students with the working class was not merely a tactic employed to secure material advantages. It indicated that there existed a social conscience that wanted to marry class and nation. For Jean-Marc Léger, the founder of the Équipe de Recherches Sociales, French Canadians in 1948 found themselves faced with "the problem of a tragic division between the working masses of the nation and those who attend university, and we are confronted with the imperious task of re-establishing communion ... But even beyond these interests of a universal character, there is another issue at stake for us: the majority of our ethnic group is made up of workers, so that if we were to lose these people, we would be consenting to the loss of our nation, which will not be saved by intellectuals whose impotence has already been amply demonstrated [problème d'une division tragique entre la masse ouvrière de la nation et le groupe des universitaires, nous nous retrouvons avec le devoir impérieux de travailler à rétablir la communion ... Par delà ces intérêts de portée universelle, il s'en trouve un autre en jeu, pour nous: la majorité de notre groupe ethnique se compose maintenant d'ouvriers en sorte que perdre ceux-ci, c'est consentir à perdre la nation – celle-ci ne sera pas sauvée par des intellectuels dont l'impuissance n'est plus à démontrer]."[85]

It is this perception that explains why, at the end of the academic year 1947–48, *Quartier latin* published a special issue entitled "The University and the Nation" (L'université et la nation). In this way, the editorial team led by Camille Laurin[86] hoped to galvanize youth by informing them about the great social questions of the age, the most pressing of which was the condition of the working class. In so doing, the editors hoped to scandalize orthodox opinion and, in the ensuing fireworks, demonstrate that they were not voices crying in the wilderness. In short, the special issue contained many articles dealing with working-class questions: one article exposed the scandal of silicosis in the mining town of Saint-Rémi d'Amherst; as well, an article by Gérard Pelletier called upon professors and students to climb down from their ivory tower and join the workers. Pelletier used the occasion to appeal for greater democratization and openness in the university, exhorting academics, on the one hand, to interest themselves in the realities of working-class life, while, on the other, he urged them to democratize the university by making it more accessible to young workers who were excluded from higher education because of financial considerations. Out of this concern arose the idea that greater openness to the working class would permit the emergence of a far more diverse group of youth, one not simply limited to students. During the 1950s this idea became a major element in the demands of the Quebec student community, and it was around this issue that, for the first time, collaboration between francophone and anglophone students crystallized.

In 1958 students from all Quebec universities[87] joined forces to indicate to the provincial government and the wider community that higher education was a key priority for the development of the province and that all young people, whatever their social origins, had the right to pursue an education according to their aptitudes. Although these guiding principles were not completely novel for Quebec's student population, in 1958 the province's universities were facing a particularly acute situation as a result of the financial crisis that had affected them for a number of years. Following an edict from Duplessis, they found it impossible to accept the federal subsidies due them, but they had been systematically starved by the provincial premier who consistently refused to allocate them statutory grants, preferring to dispense funds on a discretionary basis. To compensate for this lack of revenue, some universities such as McGill decided to increase tuition fees. Students reacted to these developments, which directly affected them, and the presidents of the university student associations joined to form the Association of Student Councils of the Province of Quebec, which then sent a brief on student living conditions to Duplessis. The student presidents demanded an interview with the premier to discuss the issues raised in the brief, as well as the state of university finances. They came up against the insult of a flat refusal from Duplessis, and in response, student leaders decided to show him that he had to respect the province's democratic process and that he could not cavalierly dispense with their opinion.[88] They resolved to make public their disapproval of the premier's conduct and organized a one-day strike to be held on 6 March 1958.[89]

This strike involved two overarching objectives: first, to ensure that universities had adequate and stable finance; and second, to give all young people the opportunity to gain a university education. Students of the Université de Montréal and McGill University agreed on these objectives, and they jointly signed the newspaper *L'Étudiant du Québec*, which was published during the strike. This bilingual publication insisted upon the democratization of the university through articles with such titles as "Do your children have a right to an education?

Should this be a matter of money or a question of talent? [Vos enfants ont-ils droit à l'éducation? Question d'argent. Question de talent]," and "Students cannot be bought [Les étudiants ne sont pas à vendre]," and on the question of university finance it ran articles such as "Statutory grants [Octrois statutaires]."[90] However, beneath the agreement on these fundamental objectives, differences persisted. On the issue of university finances, McGill students based their arguments on the fact that the money had already been provided by the federal government, and that the province should be more flexible in allowing universities to accept these funds, to which it should add statutory grants.[91] Université de Montréal students were far more insistent on provincial responsibility in education. In fact, the difference between the two groups of students boiled down to divergent standpoints on the national question: for each, higher education was a matter of national interest, but the nation to which they referred was not the same one – Canada for McGill students[92] and Quebec for those at the Université de Montréal. The second objective, the democratization of the university, had wide support among students, but they disagreed over the means. All agreed that because of financial circumstances, young people did not all have an equal opportunity to attend university. Socio-economic surveys on both campuses had pointedly revealed the under-representation of working-class youth.[93] But how to provide universal access to knowledge? At McGill a system of repayable loans enjoyed considerable support: "The system of education on credit has much in its favour. It is in the best traditions of self-help and should be seriously considered by the many interests so anxiously mulling over ways and means of financing education."[94] At the Université de Montréal, a system of non-repayable grants was preferred, as expressed in the student brief presented to Premier Duplessis a few weeks before the launch of the strike.[95] In the final analysis, the one-day strike that occurred on 6 March 1958 enabled students from Laval, Montréal, McGill, Bishop's, Sir George Williams, and Sherbrooke[96] to collaborate and to demonstrate that, despite differing political and ideological positions, they formed a group capable of being mobilized for a common purpose. More significantly, however, by insisting upon the democratization of the university in the name of all Quebec youth, they demonstrated that the mobilization of youth was now possible.

From the end of the war to the close of the 1950s, students of the Université de Montréal and McGill University questioned the place they occupied within society. All believed that youth, of which they formed a part, had a role to play at local, national, and international levels because of the fundamental qualities they possessed. Youth, for example, were described as a factor in forging a lasting peace, because they had had no political interests or personal assets to defend.[97] Thus students were induced to take positions on issues of international order, such as the invasion of Hungary by Russian troops, desegregation in the United States, and the wartime deportation of the Japanese by the Canadian government. However, they were brought up short by one overriding realization: in North America, students and youth in general did not enjoy the prestige that they were accorded in Europe, in communist countries, or in the developing world, where, they believed, students were esteemed vectors of progress and, as a consequence, their opinions were given careful consideration.

In their quest for social status, for an answer to their questions regarding their own identity, students drew upon a number of sources. Those at McGill turned mainly to their American counterparts,[98] who sought to show that in a society marked by conservatism and McCarthyism, they represented a generation that incarnated the values of the future. McGill students took up and adapted this form of generational questioning. Without discarding their status of student based upon a traditional understanding of youth, they interpreted their passage through university as a period of training, the final stage before attaining a firm foothold in the adult world. As such, they regarded themselves as force for the future, as a generation still undergoing preparation. At the Université de Montréal, while the same generational questioning was certainly present, students looked, rather, to France to find answers. In this way, the path of student unionism premised upon the concept of the "young intellectual worker" presented itself to them. By attempting to position students as a distinct social class, such an approach claimed a greater social role for student opinion. Thus, despite being physically separated by Mount Royal, students at the Université de Montréal and McGill University shared common difficulties. Their quest for identity was constantly suspended between the future and the present, but the answers they provided to such questions effectively demonstrated the impact of divergent cultural influences.

NOTES

1 This essay was translated by Michael Gauvreau. It has benefited greatly from the financial support of SSHRCC and FCAR. I would especially like to thank Fernande Roy, Pierre Trépanier, Brian Young, and Julien Goyette for their discerning comments. A number of themes treated here are analyzed in greater detail in my thesis, "La construction d'une identité

étudiante montréalaise (1895–1960)" (PhD diss. [histoire], Université du Québec à Montréal, 2002).

2 *Old McGill*, 1941, 215; ibid., 1946, 248.

3 Such views involve the substance of the debate surrounding "youth" as a social category, in which biological age is not held to be the fundamental criterion of inclusion or exclusion. Other considerations, such as marital status, economic dependence upon parents, and whether an individual is still in school have an important influence upon definitions of youth as a social category. For example, a married male worker aged twenty with a steady job and a child is not considered to be in the same category as a single male university student who relies upon his parents for financial support. The worker can claim adult status, while the student would be placed in the category "youth."

4 The two principal student newspapers of the period were consulted during the research for this paper. The Université de Montréal student weekly, *Quartier latin* was exhaustively analyzed for the entire period covered in this article. The *McGill Daily*, a paper published by McGill students, was systematically sampled by consulting two issues per week and by reading the editorials of all the other issues. As well, the archival collections of the student associations of the Université de Montréal and McGill University were systematically studied. Furthermore, I paid particular attention to briefs and memoranda prepared by the student associations and presented to various governments and university administrations.

5 The university records, especially those of the general secretary and the university president, of the Université de Montréal, and those of the office of the principal and chancellor, as well as the Senate Secretariat, of McGill were selectively targeted, especially those records providing information on the relations between the respective administrations and their student bodies. In the researching of specific events, personal papers from the archives of the two universities were also examined.

6 Archives de l'Université de Montréal (AUM), Secrétariat général, D35/413, 1895, 4, Father Filiatreault, "L'oeuvre universitaire."

7 "Un écho de notre banquet," *L'Étudiant*, 1:5(8 fev. 1912), 49.

8 "The Principal to the Students," *McGill Daily* (henceforth cited as *Daily*) 13 (27 March 1924): 1.

9 Themis, "La vie," *Quartier latin* (QL), 11 (20 déc. 1928): 6.

10 "Answering the Call," *Daily* 17 (9 Oct. 1917): 2.

11 R.C. Fetherstonhaugh, *McGill University at War, 1914–1918, 1939–1945* (Montreal: McGill University, 1947), 130.

12 Principal James also chaired the Dominion Advisory Committee on Reconstruction, established by the federal government to plan the return of veterans and avoid a post-war depression. However, political tensions

forced the dissolution of this committee in 1943, although James continued a strong personal interest in these issues. See Stanley Brice Frost, *McGill University: For the Advancement of Learning,* Vol. 2, *1895–1971* (Kingston and Montreal: McGill-Queen's University Press, 1984): 230.

13 McGill University Archives (MUA), RG2, C187, f. 6495, F. Cyril James, "The Foundations of Tomorrow's Dream: An Address by Dr. F. Cyril James, Principal and Vice-Chancellor of McGill University to the Ottawa Valley Branch of the McGill Graduates' Society," 25 Jan. 1944, 6.

14 "Silence Is Not Golden," *Daily* 34 (14 Feb. 1945): 2.

15 Guy Beaugrand-Champagne, "Étudiants d'Amérique. Les étudiants sont privilégiés?," *QL* 26 (17 déc. 1943): 2.

16 "La mentalité universitaire," *QL* 39 (11 oct. 1956): 2.

17 "United We Stand," *Daily* 35 (1 Oct. 1945): 2.

18 "Don't Wait – Vote!" *Daily* 36 (11 Oct. 1946): 2.

19 James Friedman, "Letter Forum," *Daily* 36 (16 Oct. 1946): 2.

20 David Grier, "A Time of Transition," *Daily* 42 (22 May 1953): 2.

21 Eddie Kingstone, "Valedictory," *Daily* 41 (22 May 1952): 2.

22 "Youthful Noses," *Daily* 45 (6 Mar. 1956): 2.

23 Arthur Wienthal, "From the Ivory Tower," *Daily* 42 (3 Nov. 1952): 2.

24 David Grier, "Censorship and Education," *Daily* 42 (16 Jan. 1953): 2.

25 MUA, RG1, c.22, f. 695, B.C. Gardner, "Inaugural Address," 6 Oct. 1952.

26 "Our Mailbag and Student Unity," *Daily* 47 (10 Feb. 1957): 4.

27 AUM, Secrétariat général, D35/1411, Recteur Olivier Maurault à Pierre Perreault, directeur du *Quartier latin,* 30 jan. 1950.

28 Ibid., D35/1411, Olivier Maurault, "Avertissement du recteur," 4 mars 1950.

29 Before 1949, there seems to have been a system of student censors in existence, since there were references to the fact that articles had to be submitted to a member of the Student Executive Council before publication. After that date, approval of articles was done internally by the Managing Board of the *McGill Daily.* See Clyde Kennedy, "Unpopular Rules," *Daily* 39 (9 Dec. 1949): 2.

30 The most well known of these occurred in 1942, when a special issue devoted to the Business School occasioned the suspension of the *McGill Daily* by Principal James.

31 Gérard Pelletier, *Souvenirs: Les années d'impatience, 1950–1960* (Montréal: Stanké, 1983), 143. It should be noted that this current represented by the Catholic left was not entirely novel, as the founders of *La Relève* were already strongly marked by the personalism that had developed in France during the 1930s.

32 From 1947 *Le Devoir* was managed by Gérard Filion, and André Laurendeau held the position of lead editorial writer. The views held by *Le Devoir* moved in a more socially progressive direction. See Julien

Goyette, "Gérard Filion et André Laurendeau: convergences et diver-
gences," *Cahiers d'histoire au XXe siècle* 10 (automne 1998–hiver 1999):
110–18.

33 Michel de la Fournière et François Borella, *Le syndicalisme étudiant*
(Paris: Seuil, 1957), 27.

34 The charter is reproduced in de la Fournière et Borella, *Le syndicalisme
étudiant*, 54, and in *QL* 35 (11 déc. 1952): 6.

35 De la Fournière et Borello, *Le syndicalisme étudiant*, 43. These authors
(40) explain the corporatist mentality as an "attempt to respond rapidly
to a number of student needs; this was done in a largely ad hoc manner,
with an emphasis upon the initiative and 'resourcefulness' of individuals
compensating for the lack of an overall plan of action [de répondre rapidement a un certain nombre de besoins des étudiants; ceci se fait de façon
improvisée, l'initiative et la 'débrouillardise' suppléant l'absence de tout
plan d'ensemble]." The aim of the corporatist movement was to assist
students, but it lacked a union strategy and an analysis of the deeper
causes of socio-economic problems faced by students (ibid., 43).

36 In 1948 the UNEF's lobbying of the French government secured tangible
results, since students gained a health insurance scheme administered by
their own associations. See A. Belden Fields, *Student Politics in France: A
Study of the Union Nationale des Étudiants de France* (New York: Basic
Books, 1970), 28.

37 De la Fournière et Borello, *Le syndicalisme étudiant*, 94.

38 Jean de Brouckere was, however, not himself a university student. Joël
Kotek, in *La jeune garde: La jeunesse entre KGB et CIA 1917–1989* (Paris:
Éditions du Seuil, 1996), 53, identifies him as one of the leading spirits
behind the World Congress of Youth.

39 Jean de Brouckere, "Résistance universitaire," *QL* 26 (4 fév. 1944): 6.

40 Pelletier, *Les années d'impatience*, 32. Pelletier was a journalist who was
well known for his sympathetic attitude to trade unions. In later years he
became a federal politician and was, with Pierre Elliott Trudeau and Jean
Marchand, one of the "three wise men" of the Liberal Party.

41 Jean-Marc Léger, "En causant avec … Gérard Pelletier," *QL* 30 (14 oct.
1946): 2. Léger is a well-known nationalist. As a journalist and diplomat,
he was a pioneer of the concept of an international "francophonie."

42 Jean-Marc Léger, "Où l'on parle du 'Quartier latin,'" *QL* 30 (21 nov.
1947): 1.

43 The editorial team was in fact directed by the editor-in-chief, Camille
Laurin. The highly "social" orientation of *QL*, however, did not secure
everyone's support. During the following years, the editorial position was
not quite so overt.

44 Jean-Marc Léger, "Où l'on parle du 'Quartier latin,'" *QL* 30 (21 nov.
1947): 1.

45 Gilles Lortie, "Syndicalisme étudiant au Canada," *QL* 35 (11 déc. 1952): 6.

46 AUM, AGEUM, P33/E1.11, "Mémoire de l'Association générale des étudiants de l'Université de Montréal présenté à la Commission royale d'enquête sur les problèmes constitutionnels," 25 fév. 1954.

47 Ibid.

48 AUM, AGEUM, P33/E.1.11, "Résumé du mémoire de l'Association générale des étudiants de l'Université de Montréal présenté à la Commission royale d'enquête sur les problèmes constitutionnels," 25 fev. 1954.

49 AUM, AGEUM, P33/E.1,11, "Mémoire de l'Association générale des étudiants de l'Université de Montréal présenté à la Commission royale d'enquête sur les problèmes constitutionnels," 25 fév. 1954.

50 Yves Papillon, "Pour une doctrine étudiante," *QL* 42 (10 déc. 1959): 12.

51 AUM, AGEUM, P33/H.1.1.9, Louis Bernard, Jacques Guay, Yves Papillon et Michel Pelletier, "La Charte de l'étudiant universitaire," 23 mars 1961, 1; emphasis in the original.

52 "Les étudiants: une classe a part," *QL* 36 (17 sept. 1953): 4.

53 Le père [abbé Llewellyn], "Trahisons," *QL* 31 (16 nov. 1948): 1.

54 On generation understood as a concept of contemporaneousness, see Raoul Girardet, "Du concept de génération à la notion de contemporanéité," *Revue d'histoire moderne et contemporaine* 30 (avril–juin 1983): 257–70.

55 McGill students were not the only ones to engage in self-searching about their generation. Indeed, at the end of the 1950s a group of students opposed to nuclear weapons founded the Combined Universities' Campaign of Nuclear Disarmament, and the Montreal branch of this organization created the magazine *Our Generation against Nuclear War*, which during the 1960s became *Our Generation*. See Cyril Levitt, "Canada," in Philip G. Altbach, ed., *Student Political Activism: An International Reference Book* (New York: Greenwood Press, 1989), 420.

56 Philip G. Altbach, *Student Politics in America: A Historical Analysis* (New York: McGraw-Hill Book Co., 1974), 116.

57 The results were reported by Eddie Kingstone, "This Ailing Generation," *Daily* 41 (2 Nov. 1951): 2.

58 In both universities reference was made to the notion that if youth was not radicalized between sixteen and twenty would be utterly fossilized by age forty or sixty. At McGill, an article entitled "Black Shadow of Fear" (*Daily* 46 [24 Jan. 1957]: 2) expressed the matter as follows: "The French statesman Clemenceau once remarked, 'Anyone who isn't radical at 16 has no heart, anyone who is still one at 60 has no head.' We seem to be a heartless generation." At the Université de Montréal, similar language was in evidence. Jean Dionne, the Quebec regional president of the National Federation of Canadian University Students declared, "I think

that at age twenty we have some things to say, some criticisms to offer, and while these at times may be awkwardly expressed, it is important that we be able to write freely. If we follow this guideline, there is a faint chance that at age forty we will not be complete dead losses [Je pense qu'à vingt ans nous avons des choses à dire, des critiques à faire, qui certaines fois sont peut-être malhabiles mais il est important que nous puissions les écrire librement. À partir de ce principe, il y a quelques chances qu'à 40 ans nous ne serons pas encore trop crétinisés]." (AUM, AGEUM, P33/H1.13.6, 1958).

59 Earl Kruger, "The Unclassified Generation," *Daily* 43 (2 Oct. 1953): 2.
60 Louis Eddy, "On Portraying Youth," *Daily* 41 (6 Nov. 1951): 2.
61 D.G., "A Compulsion of Silence?" *Daily* 42 (1 Oct. 1952): 2.
62 Ibid.
63 One of the main characteristics of the beat generation was its withdrawal from mainstream society. As Anthony Esler explains, "for the young generations of the 1950s, beat or button-down, there was only one solution: find someplace to hide." See Esler, *Bombs, Beards, and Barricades: 150 Years of Youth in Revolt* (New York: Stein and Day, 1971), 226.
64 Claude-Armand Sheppard, "The Paradoxical Generation," *Daily*, 43:50(21 Jan. 1954), 2.
65 Nino Goaltieri, "Age of Disbelief," *Daily* 41 (15 Jan. 1952): 2.
66 "Security or Maturity?" *Daily* 47 (21 Nov. 1957): 2.
67 "No Sense of Adventure," *Daily* 46 (18 Feb. 1957): 2.
68 "The Silent Generation," *Daily* 47 (10 Oct. 1957): 2.
69 "We are the ——— Generation," *Daily* 47 (Dec. 1957): 4.
70 Fernand Seguin, "Les raisins verts et les raisins mûrs," *QL* 27 (5 nov. 1944): 8.
71 André Lefebvre, "Pessimisme ou realisme," *QL* 34 (7 mars 1952): 2.
72 Jacques Mackay, "Notre generation," *QL* 35 (11 déc. 1952): 2.
73 Julien Aubert, "Les Canadiens français, quêteux professionnels," *QL* 40 (12 déc. 1957): 2.
74 Guy Beaugrand-Champagne, "Congrès étudiant," *QL* 27 (23 mars 1945): 1.
75 Gilles Duguay, "Sommes-nous des écœurants?," *QL* 40 (26 sept. 1957): 6.
76 In French, this organization was known as the Fédération nationale des étudiants universitaires Canadiens, or FNEUC. On the question of student unionism, Cyril Levitt explains that this position was "first advanced by students in Quebec, who in turn were influenced by the student syndicalist and New Working Class theory expounded by the Union nationale des etudiants de France." See Levitt, "Canada," 423.
77 Jim Robb, "NFCUS, a Proven Failure," *Daily* 44 (7 Feb. 1955): 2.
78 MUA, RG8, c.14, f.87, Howard Roseborough, Department of Anthropology and Sociology of McGill University, and Kurt Jonassohn, Department

of Sociology of Sir George Williams University, "Memorandum from the Students' Society of McGill University," 1961–62: "At the same time it is necessary to clearly define the student's place in society and to give him a solid sociological basis. As long as the student feels that he must continually apologize for or defend what others consider to be a parasitic position, the public attitude towards education will not change."

79 Statement of André Gareau, director of the Comité d'Éducation, reported by Yves Carrière, "De grands projets au Comité d'éducation," *QL* 42 (3 mars 1960): 8.

80 AUM, AGEUM, P33/E.1.17, 1960, AGEUM, "Mémoire de l'AGEUM au Gouvernement de la Province de Québec, re: Commission provinciale des universités."

81 J.B., "Sous la botte de Peron, la lutte contre les étudiants," *QL* 37 (10 mars 1955): 8.

82 Jean-Marc Léger, *Le temps dissipé: Souvenirs* (Montréal: HMH, 2000), 122–3.

83 AUM, Fonds Olivier-Maurault, P7/A189, "Les étudiants ne félicitent pas Duplessis," article tiré du *Canada*, 9 juin 1949.

84 Nicole Neatby, *Carabins ou activistes? L'idéalisme et la radicalisation de la pensée étudiante à l'Université de Montréal au temps du duplessisme* (Montreal and Kingston: McGill-Queen's University Press, 1999), 189–190.

85 Jean-Marc Léger, "Pour rétablir le dialogue: Le rôle de l'Équipe de recherches sociales," *QL* 30 (16 mars 1948): 4.

86 Camille Laurin is best known as the architect of Bill 101, the charter of the French language, one of the most important achievements of the Parti québécois government of René Lévesque.

87 Students from the universities of Montréal, McGill, Laval, Bishop's, Sir George Williams, and Sherbrooke collaborated over the course of several months. All students participated in the strike of 6 March 1958, with the exception of those from Sherbrooke, who withdrew from the coalition at the last minute under pressure from the university administration.

88 On both campuses, Duplessis's attitude was considered an insult and served as a catalyst. See AUM, AGEUM, P33/B.1.1.15, "Procès-verbal de la réunion spéciale du Conseil de direction, Rapport de la réunion des universités du Québec," 20 fév. 1958; Louis Donolo, "Donolo Reports: Campus United in Student Executive Council Support," *Daily* 47 (3 Mar. 1958): 1.

89 For a more complete description of events surrounding the launch of the student strike, see Neatby, *Carabins ou activistes*, 145–52, 166, 224–9; and for an overview of the question of university finances, particularly from the McGill perspective, see Frost, *McGill University*, Vol. 2, 247–53.

90 *L'Étudiant du Québec* was published by the NFCUS's Quebec division and
    represented 22,000 students.

91 In fact, before a federal conference on higher education, a *Daily* editorial
    writer explained, "[T]hat money is the most basic need is common knowl-
    edge and, as far as Quebec is concerned, the question of acceptance of
    federal grants is of paramount importance." See "Blueprint for Progress,"
    Daily 47 (17 Feb. 1958): 4. Returning to the issue in November 1958,
    another editorial quoted the words of Roy Heenan, the SEC president:
    "There is at present four million dollars in trust for McGill in an Ottawa
    bank – four millions which we need desperately. Not accepting this money
    was a serious mistake, we cannot afford to refuse any help at this time."
    See "The President's Letter," *Daily* 48 (3 Nov. 1958): 4.

92 Here the McGill students were in complete agreement with Principal
    James, who, since the beginning of the 1950s, had frequently declaimed
    upon the national importance of higher education for Canada. See MUA,
    RG1, c.1, f.1, F. Cyril James, "Education: A National Problem," 1 June
    1950.

93 The first such survey was undertaken in 1953 among Université de Mon-
    tréal students. See Jacques-Yvan Morin, "Le problème social et l'Univer-
    sité: Esquisse d'un dilemme," *QL* 35 (19 mars 1953): 4; Claude Bélanger
    et Luc Cossette, "La condition financière des étudiants de l'Université de
    Montréal," *QL* 35 (26 mars 1953): 4. In 1958 the student associations of
    both universities collaborated in drawing up the "Mémoire des universi-
    taires à Monsieur Duplessis," which contained a socio-economic analysis
    of student life in Quebec. See *QL* 40 (27 fév. 1958): 2; MUA, RG1, c.5,
    f.102, NFCUS, "A Brief on Government Aid to Higher Education," Jan.
    1958.

94 "Credit's the Thing," *Daily* 47 (15 Jan. 1958): 4.

95 AUM, AGEUM, P33/E.1.12, 1958, Les 21,000 étudiants des universités de la
    province, "Mémoire des étudiants des universités de la province de
    Québec sur les conditions matérielles de l'enseignement universitaire en
    cette province."

96 Although the Sherbrooke students did not participate in the strike itself,
    they were involved in the initial planning sessions.

97 A.T., "International Understanding," *Daily* 37 (27 Nov. 1947): 2.

98 It is interesting to note in this context that Britain was not the ultimate
    reference-point for McGill students after World War II. Henceforth, the
    United States would be the central terrain of cultural comparison.

MICHAEL GAUVREAU

The Protracted Birth of the Canadian "Teenager"

Work, Citizenship, and the Canadian Youth Commission, 1943–1955

"The age of adolescence in this northern clime," acidly observed the Queen's University historian Arthur Lower in 1955, "is supposed to run from about 12 to 16. In our wisdom, we Canadians have discovered a method of prolonging it to 18, 19 and in certain cases, 20 years of age." Reflecting upon the fact that for the first time, more than half the Canadian adolescents aged fourteen to seventeen were actually in high school, Lower identified "this undue prolongation of adolescence" as the principal symptom of a mass culture he so despised, one dominated by "softness – our sentimentalism."[1] What is surprising about this tirade is that Lower, a persistent advocate of raising the intellectual standards of Canadian youth, harshly castigated the increasing propensity of Canadian young people to opt for a lengthy high school education, rather than entering the workforce at age sixteen. However, his sarcasm directed at "elderly adolescents" sprang from his fear that through prosperity and a rising standard of living, Canada in the mid-1950s was rotting from within, the principal culprit being an American-style "teenager" culture, one anchored in the high school and posited upon a conscious separation of youth from the world of adults, in which young people's conformity in clothing styles, sexual relationships, musical tastes, patterns of leisure, and consumption stood at sharp variance with, and in some ways rejected, adult values. This increasingly rigid separation of "teenager" and "adult" cultures, Lower fulminated, amounted to "a betrayal of our society" and could only be countered by swiftly moving adolescents into adult patterns of work and responsibility, "either devoting their time to sterner training or earning their living."[2]

At one level, Lower's diatribe against the Canadian teenager could be read as but the increasingly shrill and ineffectual attempt by cultural conservatives to stem what was by the 1950s a cultural riptide of American values, products, and practices that dominated the entire Canadian social scene outside the universities and bastions of "high" culture.[3] However, what his commentary reveals is a public sensibility that regarded the "teenager" as a very new and recent phenomenon in mid-1950s Canada. The notion, well established in the United States by 1940, that there was a fundamental cultural difference between adolescent teenager and adult[4] was one that took nearly two decades longer to develop in Canada. The classic image of the teenager stood in sharp contrast with a range of public attitudes and policies regarding "youth," which had since the mid-1930s sought to reduce the distance between adolescents and adults. The fundamental consideration shaping Canadian post-war attitudes to youth was not a generalized wartime prosperity, but the Great Depression, in which massive numbers of young Canadians between the ages of sixteen and thirty had experienced prolonged unemployment and dependency, either on families or on the relief provided by public agencies.

Beginning with a series of joint federal-provincial youth training schemes during the latter stages of the Depression and culminating with the Canadian Youth Commission, established in 1943, government, educational, business, and religious leaders in Canada formulated an age definition of "youth" that encompassed those aged between fifteen and twenty-five,[5] thus effectively denying the existence of teenagers. More tellingly, throughout the 1940s, Canadian attitudes and policies on the subject of youth were premised, not upon the notion of young Canadians as consumers of a leisure culture or out of a preoccupation with regulating the private sexual conduct of adolescents,[6] but upon establishing a firm equation between productive work and citizenship. In this dynamic, "adolescents" were defined economically, psychologically, and politically as immature "dependents" whose lack of training and work opportunities rendered them as, at best, unfit for civic life in a democracy and as, at worst, volatile "masses" to be preyed upon by unscrupulous demagogues or potential dictators. And because of this preoccupation with work, the public discourse surrounding youth in the immediate post-war era focused almost exclusively upon the socialization of young men. "Youth," defined as those either working productively or being trained to enhance their skills in the workplace, were considered the wellspring of renewal and creativity in a society in which the post-war period was widely regarded as a new departure in social and cultural values. This spirit of renewal, however, could only be concretized by those whose work and willingness to assume family responsibilities marked them both as potentially responsible citizens and on the road to an emotionally mature adulthood. It was the emphatically "public" qualities of youth as producer and citizen, rather than the "private" nature of the teenager as consumer of leisure and personal relationships, that defined the attitudes of Canadians between the end of World War II and the early 1950s.

The waning years of the Depression in Canada marked the beginning of a wholesale reversal of two dominant attitudes regarding the place of young people in society. Relying upon late-nineteenth-century psychological theories, social reformers of the Progressive Era sought to enact legislation and create institutions that effectively removed the adolescent from the adult world. Two key corollaries accompanied this underlying imperative. First, definitions of delinquency and conformity tended to centre around fears of precocious adoption of adult modes of behaviour by young people, especially those outside the urban middle classes, and second, youth organizations in a number of countries tended to elevate adolescents as a spiritual and moral force for renewal and rebirth that was superior to a "decadent" world ruled by adult values.[7] It was this second, more spiritualistic current that firmly established generational conflict and the emancipation of youth from family and "bourgeois" society as a cultural metaphor in both Canada and a number of western European countries between 1890 and the middle years of the Depression.[8] However, after 1935 a particular conjunction between an awareness of the economic impact of the Depression on young people and a growing fear of the overly close ties between notions of generational conflict and the rise of fascist dictatorships operated a significant change on the mindset of Canadian government policy-makers and youth organizations. By the post-war period, a series of attitudes and policies were in place that sought to blur the lines between youth and adulthood by defining policies which would inculcate in young people a model of "productive" behaviour that would encourage early adoption of the qualities of the economically and civically responsible adult.

In a background study prepared for the Canadian Youth Commission in 1943, Irene Baird evoked the notion that the Depression in Canada was "almost wholly a record of defeat" and that the hundreds of thousands of jobless young men who lived through it constituted a

"lost generation."[9] Though written during a period of relative optimism as the wartime Canadian economy successfully generated high
levels of production and full employment, Baird's harsh assessment
stated what had in fact since 1934 become the orthodoxy concerning
the Depression's impact on Canada's young people. Present in most
late-Depression and wartime writing was the stark dichotomy between
the promises of "opportunity," by which prior to 1930 an expanding
settler society had smoothly bridged the transition of young people
from adolescence to adult responsibilities by integrating them into a
perpetually expanding economy through the values of "thrift, hard
work, honesty, and God-fearing pioneering,"[10] and the "stunning dis-
appointment"[11] of the Depression, in which a contracting economy
forced hundreds of thousands of young people into a twilight world of
prolonged childhood dependency. "Reared in the philosophy of opportunity," declared youth leader Norman Levy in 1937, "it was
inevitable that young people should enquire why the doors of life have
been closed to them in vast numbers."[12]

What so preoccupied a number of government policy-makers, religious leaders, and educators was the sheer magnitude of the youth
cohort that found itself mired in this state of dependency, despite indi-
cations that, while the Canadian economy as a whole seemed to be
showing signs of recovery by the late 1930s, persistently high levels of
youth unemployment constituted a "permanent" social crisis. Writing
in 1939, A.G. Watson observed that out of 3 million young people in
the fifteen to thirty age group, there were 455,000 without gainful
employment and a further 75,000 "homeless transients," a situation
that constituted a "state of national emergency."[13] The realization
that the Canadian economy was persistently failing to absorb 10 per
cent of the "youth" category spurred the Canadian Youth Congress,
from its inception in 1935, to adopt a broad definition of youth as
constituting all those between the ages of sixteen and twenty-six, and
to call for a Canadian Youth Act and a permanent youth commission,
whose role would be to design and fund systems of vocational training and guidance and plan public works and enterprises that would
focus on apprenticeship training in trades, professions, and agriculture.[14] Although the response of Mackenzie King's federal government
to these promptings was far more modest, it was becoming an
accepted orthodoxy of public policy by the end of the 1930s that a
high level of youth unemployment constituted a "permanent" feature
of industrial economies, with the prospect of "mere subsistence living
for a large section of the population."[15] In a brief submitted to
Norman Rogers, the Liberal minister of labour in 1939, the Canadian
Youth Congress stated that the new schemes of vocational training

were not "temporary and short-term activities, but ... a permanent part of the work of educating the younger generation and helping them to take their place in the community and the working force of the nation."[16] The significant aspect of this development was not the size of the federal youth appropriation, which was in fact quite niggardly, but the consensus among youth leaders and government officials that "youth" now constituted a very significant temporal span in the life of the individual. Under the conditions of the Depression, and without a series of state initiatives, there was the very real prospect that more and more young Canadians could spend literally ten years of their lives as adolescent dependents, unable to acquire sufficient income or work skills to mediate the transition to the responsibilities of adult work and citizenship.

The premise of these programs was occupational training – the belief that young people participating in programs that enhanced their education and technical skills would escape the cycle of unskilled, low-paying jobs which exposed them to the ravages of unemployment.[17] However, the direction of these federal youth policies was not simply dictated by demographic or economic concerns. A conjunction of gender and psychological imperatives identified what was in fact the central issue underlying all writings on youth unemployment. As bluntly stated by a report of the federal Department of Labour in 1939, "the increasing length of dependency for young people ... has been greatly accentuated during the past seven years." What most alarmed youth workers and policy-makers was the fact that "the extension of the age of dependence has been entirely among boys and young men. Girls have actually increased their earning power in the period."[18] Studies undertaken during the last few years of the Depression thus tended to fixate on one particular group of young people: unemployed males. A survey conducted by the Ottawa Youth Federation in 1938 drew a composite picture of thousands of young men in their early twenties who had left school at sixteen in search of work, their "education incomplete," and who had been unable to retain steady employment. "While [they] may still have hope for the future," concluded the report, young men in this position had "little to anticipate but unemployment" and were "just approaching that state of mind where [their] unfortunate situation will cease to concern [them]."[19] Irene Baird's influential 1939 novel *Waste Heritage* drew a bleak yet compelling vision of a society that marginalized so many of its potential young male workers by labelling them "transients." Her warning that "it was possible for a man to be a citizen of Canada and yet to belong nowhere" evoked the insidious psychological mood of hopelessness and irresponsibility, the "sweat smells and the lack of privacy and the comfortable acceptance of bum status" that infected young men unable to find work.[20] It was not surprising that among a group of youth workers and policy-makers whose horizons by the late 1930s had become almost totally preoccupied with the work of male breadwinners as the foundation of civic order and entitlement to welfare benefits, the problem of male dependency would be of over-riding concern.[21]

The fundamental consideration that underwrote most discussions of "dependency" among Canada's male youth was that the prolonged unemployment occasioned by the Depression severely curtailed the smooth assumption of adult responsibilities among this segment of the population. More specifically, lack of work had a detrimental impact on the age of marriage and precluded normal family formation, and thus an older process of integration of young men into society by which they became responsible heads of families. In the minds of educators, youth workers, policy-makers, and civic leaders, this "dependency" of male youth thus carried with it deleterious social, moral, and psychological consequences. "When one realizes," observed a study of female labour undertaken by the Canadian Welfare Council in 1937, "the number of idle young male dependants in urban and rural homes and ... young males 'on their own' in work camp, hostel or farm placement, one realizes that just as the War cut a lean blank across the young life of the last generation, so has the depression frustrated the foundation of young family life for thousands of young Canadians to-day."[22] At one level, those educators and activists who studied Canada's young people during the 1930s were aware that this male dependency was an aspect of a longer process in which adolescents tended to spend more time in school. In a study published during the late 1930s, J.E. Robbins stated that the Depression-era adolescent spent on average two years longer in school than his counterpart of 1911. However, what troubled these observers was that this increased education did not translate into steadier or higher-paying work as young men left the family to become self-supporting. As Robbins demonstrated, even before the economic downturn, there had opened a continuous gap of 1.75 years between the age of leaving school and the age when a young person was able to be self-supporting, an extended period of dependency only further exacerbated by the Depression. This, in turn, had serious consequences, the most telling of which was a loss of independence among men and boys, which translated into an "unusual fall in the marriage rate" among young people aged twenty to twenty-four.[23]

It was precisely around the question of marriage and its links to the public values of work and citizenship that the anxieties of Depression-era youth activists and policy-makers tended to converge. According to their vision, in which work and citizenship formed a symbiotic whole, the economic incapacity of many young Canadian males to marry and form families was in fact the very mark of their social and psychological adolescence. Thus they traced the connection between youth unemployment, low-paying jobs, the belief that many young men were becoming reconciled to the necessity to postpone marriage, and what they identified as a growing lack of civic values and loyalty among young male Canadians, a situation that awakened fears for the very survival of a liberal-democratic political order. The Canadian Youth Congress held in Winnipeg in 1939 posited a firm connection between what it termed "[s]ecurity of employment, opportunity for family life ... and the making of a good citizen."[24] A study published by the Ontario YMCA in the late 1930s, with considerable input and advice from the Reverend C.E. Silcox, head of the Social Service Council of Canada, opened with the composite portrait of John Smith, a twenty-four-year-old white-collar employee who left high school at age seventeen. Despite working for six years, Smith was essentially an adolescent dependent because he was not yet self-supporting and lived with his parents, unable to even contemplate the prospect of marriage and beginning a family for another five or six years.[25]

Postponement or prevention of marriage as a result of poor male economic prospects, in turn, carried with it dire social consequences, the most visible of which was, in the sober language of the federal Department of Labour, "a very material increase" in the number of illegitimate births.[26] Surveys of attitudes among both male and female youth noted with alarm the rise in extramarital sexual relations and what was described as a growing tolerance of illicit liaisons. Although quick to absolve Depression-era youth of promiscuity by pointing to the fact that most of these extramarital liaisons were monogamous and the product of frustrated desires to marry, the YMCA juxtaposed this picture with the observation that only a minority of young people reprobated these relations, and it lugubriously concluded, "There is in process a breakdown of the traditional standards of sexual morality."[27] Only one-third of young people under twenty-six surveyed were actually planning marriage, and less than 20 per cent were engaged. Pointing to the "mass psychosis and distortion of human values" that had contributed to the collapse of democracy in Germany, the report posed the question of "whether any society is safe from disintegration or dangerous social conflict if a large group of its members are denied a normal outlet for normal human impulses. Nor is it likely that social harmony and a high level of citizenship can be attained on the basis of thwarted and repressed individual lives."[28] In what had become the mainstream of thinking about Canadian youth by the late 1930s, work occupied the total horizon of any consideration of family responsibilities and civic order. Prolonged unemployment and lack of training in adult male economic responsibilities led ineluctably to sexual delinquency and to the subversion of democratic citizenship.

Thus, by the end of the 1930s, the anxieties of a range of youth workers, educators, and government officials over the widespread unemployment and consequent "dependency" of young men as the causal factor in definitions of sexual delinquency and absence of socialization into civic participation had contributed to the shaping of a new public definition of youth. The central element was the abolition of adolescence as a "separate" and distinct psychological stage in the transition of young people from childhood to adulthood. Under the impact of the Depression, young Canadians were regarded either as dependent "children" whose work was fully integrated into preserving the self-sufficiency of the interdependent family or, if over sixteen, as "youth" being socialized in work camps or federal-provincial training and apprenticeship schemes to assume adult responsibilities.[29] That adult values and responsibilities were ascribed to Depression-era youth was the consequence of a particular definition of citizenship. Canadian commentators of the 1930s retained a vision, current in the late nineteenth and early twentieth century, that "youth" represented renewal and the future. In the face of an international order increasingly assailed by totalitarian dictatorships, it was imperative that such pre-eminently youthful qualities be enlisted in defence of democratic society. However, the 1930s definition rigorously eschewed what had been fundamental to older visions of youth: the sense of difference and separation from the adult world, and with it the possibility of generational conflict based upon the moral superiority of youth. Canadian youth activists were acutely aware of the example of interwar German and Italian youth movements, which had become totally incorporated into the Nazi and Fascist social orders.[30] There, it was believed, a powerful ideology of youth "separateness," the incarnation of a separate youth culture based upon a generational critique of adult, "bourgeois" values, had actually hastened the complete subservience and dependency of youth to totalitarian dictators.[31]

Although some Depression-era youth workers such as the YMCA's R.E.G. Davis, later the executive director of the Canadian Youth Commission, eagerly contrasted adult lack of vision with the "fresh viewpoint and clear-eyed understanding" provided by youth, both mainstream youth organizations and federal policy were principally directed to ensuring that political and social divisions in Canada did not revolve around the issue of age.[32] Thus in 1937 Norman Levy, a key figure in the Canadian Youth Congress, emphatically rejected the idea of "'setting-off'" youth as a special category, arguing instead that youth problems of unemployment and insufficiency of training and education were inseparable from those of the entire Canadian community.[33] Significantly, Kenneth Woodsworth's 1939 assessment of the work of the Canadian Youth Congress and government youth policy was entitled *Canadian Youth Comes of Age*, which juxtaposed the idea that youth stood at the cutting edge of national renewal but implicitly rejected the idea of cultural separation between "youth" and adulthood. In it, Woodsworth confidently proclaimed that "today it is economic depression and the threat to democracy that is rousing a new generation. Youth is building the foundations of a new and richer confederation."[34] However, the report was less self assured when it described the "helplessness and hopelessness" of many young people whose education and training had failed to equip them "for a life's work." Such adolescent dependency, Woodsworth concluded, was inconsistent with the maintenance of freedom and democracy, because the existence of thousands of "disinherited" youth simply created a breeding ground for agitators and demagogues. Youth's loyalty to notions of democratic citizenship, in the final analysis, could only be assured through measures designed to integrate young people into their responsibilities as adults, what Woodsworth described as "their rightful place in our economic and social order."[35]

Established in 1943 as part of the Canadian government's post-war reconstruction strategy, the Canadian Youth Commission ostensibly belonged to a new cultural paradigm. At one level, its surveys and deliberations were governed by optimistic calculations of a consumerist social prosperity achieved through full employment and an expanding social security state. As emphatically stated by the Canadian Teachers' Federation, the Canadian state must assert "the inherent dignity of labor and the right of mankind to work," and in return, "man has a right to expect a fair share of the amenities of life – highest standard of living possible that can be provided by the maximum development of our peace-time economy."[36] And the security afforded by a widely diffused economic prosperity, the Youth Commission believed, would support a new partnership between generations, one that abandoned the authoritarian model of the old patriarchal family in favour of a "democratic home" in which all members would cooperate in securing emotional stability for all individuals.[37] Despite the presence of these new attitudes, what emerged from the Canadian

Youth Commission was less a profound reorientation of public attitudes towards youth than the reiteration and reinforcement of definitions forged during the waning years of the Depression. As articulated
by the commission, citizenship and the survival of post-war democracy
remained firmly anchored upon a productivist ethos, in which educating the responsible male breadwinner to work as the wellspring of both
family formation and civic status retained an overwhelming priority.
And the fact that this attitude continued to inform the thinking of government officials, public educators, and church leaders led to two consequences of central importance to the shape of post-war Canada
between the end of the war and the middle of the 1950s. First,
"youth," in the person of the potential young male breadwinner, stood
at the centre of a participatory vision of citizenship in which democracy was defined in psychological and cultural terms, as a "way of life"
– a realm of values centred on the individual – rather than as a set of
political or institutional adjustments, and was anchored upon home,
school, and church, the traditional institutions of the local community.
Firmly wedded to an ideal of individual responsibility, citizens of such
a democracy were expected to form a solid bulwark against the
enchroachments of a centralized welfare state. Second, the exaltation
of the productivist image of the youth as worker or worker-in-training
dictated a firm resistance to any attempt to define a psychologically or
culturally separate Canadian "adolescence" in the immediate aftermath of World War II.

"[D]uring the years from 15 to 24," declared the author of a background study for the Canadian Youth Commission, "nothing means
more to the great majority of young people than a satisfactory introduction to the world of work. This it is that establishes their status as
adults – a goal to which every normal youth is impatient to reach. It
also opens up new life possibilities, notably the prospect of establishing their own homes, which comes to the fore ordinarily among the
interests of youth in this period."[38] For the commission, the achievements of the wartime production economy opened the possibility of
harnessing the now well established trinity of work–family formation–democratic citizenship to a vision of post-war economic prosperity, in which "freedom from want" could be achieved through full
employment and maximum social welfare, and which would under-
gird a harmonious democratic social and world order of peaceful
cooperation between "free societies of free men."[39] Proclaiming allegiance to the now-fashionable Keynesian economic orthodoxy, R.E.G.
Davis, executive director of the commission, declared that the
governing priorities of domestic economic policy must henceforth be
"full employment; economic stabilization to ensure maintenance of

full employment, plus social security." It was the role of government, in Davis's estimation, to "shoulder greater responsibility for ensuring a stable and high level of national income. It means that government can guarantee to private enterprise that consumption will be maintained at least at some irreducible minimum."[40]

This veritable welter of optimistic rhetoric on the subject of post-war abundance and full employment placed youth at the epicentre of an emerging post-war sensibility that defined the era as one of renewal, marking a decisive break with the traditions of the past. "Youth," stated one study undertaken by the Canadian Youth Commission, "has unlimited reserves of generous enthusiasm and idealism; if these can be mobilized at the critical age – the late teens and early twenties – they can crack the shell of hard-boiled apathy and unconcern."[41] Wartime and post-war attitudes on the subject of youth confidently evoked the articulation of a new "partnership" between Canadian youth and public bodies by which the nation could integrate "a measure of the courage and spirit of adventure" into post-war tasks.[42] However, it was significant that the commission, although it publicly rejected "the traditional paternalistic approach to youth's problems,"[43] found it necessary to reiterate a set of public attitudes derived from the Depression. These sought to firmly constrain any utopian associations contained in the notion of "youth as renewal"[44] by enjoining a thoroughly individualist priority on the absolute necessity of steady work as the precondition to adult self-sufficiency and family formation.

Indeed, the principal fear underlying the background studies and policy calculations of the Christian youth activists, prominent university and public educators from English Canada and Quebec, business leaders, and a scattering of federal civil servants who composed the Canadian Youth Commission[45] was that, although the wartime economy had created a superficial social harmony by providing full employment through "an indirect form of government control," post-war Canada would not possess "the same degree of social and economic unity."[46] Philip Fisher, one of the businessmen principally responsible for elaborating the broad policy outlines of the commission, characterized the ideological division as one between two groups: "on the one hand, those who prefer the authoritarian way by which the many who wish to avoid personal responsibility, hand over power to the few who have an insatiable desire to wield it; or, on the other hand, the libertarians who are jealous of their own and other people's personal liberty and, though ready to delegate authority to individuals as the only practical way of getting things done in an organized world, place bounds to that authority. They also make its continued exercise contingent upon an efficient and social use of it which

must not, however, trespass upon personal liberty more than is necessary to obtain the social results desired."[47] Members of the Youth
Commission thus anticipated that post-war Canada would be characterized by a conflictual ideological climate, and they therefore deemed
it necessary to assert from the outset that the notion of full employment held a distinctly conservative and individualist implication, one
in which "a socially disciplined system of private enterprise," rather
than wholesale government planning or regimentation, held principal
responsibility for the achievement of post-war economic abundance.[48]
Fisher elucidated the fundamental cultural divide of the post-war
period as "a conflict between those who seek high protection for the
individual and those who feel that too great protection for the individual saps initiative and places a premium on improvidence and
incompetence."[49]

It was precisely on the issue of full employment achieved through
"authoritarian" or "libertarian" means that the conservative liberalism
of the Mackenzie King government's post-war reconstruction plans[50]
crystallized around the question of the status of Canadian youth. To
what degree could Canada's young people be trusted to possess the
responsible civic attitudes appropriate to sustaining the "libertarian"
social order envisioned by these prophets of full employment? On the
one hand, it was recognized that the wartime economy had succeeded
in absorbing the 200,000 young people who as late as 1939 had *never*
worked at a gainful occupation. However, such integration was not
regarded as permanent. In what was advanced as a constant caveat to
all the predictions of post-war abundance, the Youth Commission's
economists warned that the concept of full employment "would still
allow temporary unemployment" as workers shifted from one job to
another or were retrained in the period of peacetime conversion.
"[S]ome seasonal unemployment," they concluded, "is inevitable."[51]
The most intractable economic task facing Canada during the post-war
period of transition was the demobilization and economic reintegration of the nearly 1 million young people under the age of twenty-five
and still in uniform who would need civilian work. In addition, the
economy would have to absorb an additional 150,000 young people
who would enter the job market annually.[52] Confronted with these
figures, it was not without reason that the commission soberly warned
that "when the war ends we will face a youth problem of considerable
magnitude," and it declared, "Confidence in post-war Canada is not
without its qualifications."[53]

Two considerations, one structural and demographic and the other
psychological, informed the consensus within the Youth Commission,
which rested upon the notion that Keynesian economic manipulations

to achieve full employment would not dispose of the youth unemployment problem. First, the youth planners relied upon demographic projections that indicated an aging population, with a consequent reduction in demand for the services of young people in the labour market, and thus the continuous widening of the gap already discerned during the Depression between leaving school and the type of steady employment that would elevate young people to adult self-sufficiency.[54] And second, they recognized that the type of modern industry that would sustain post-war prosperity required less physical strength and endurance than education and skill. Young people who followed the traditional pattern of leaving school at an early age would at best secure "blind alley or unskilled" types of jobs, in which workers "receive relatively low wages, work long hours, are the first to be laid off in times of depression and the last to be employed when conditions improve."[55] There could thus be no return to a pre-Depression economic pattern of easy transition from adolescence to adulthood through work, and this charge urgently dictated the elaboration of measures such as raising the school-leaving age to fifteen, the institution of part-time education to age eighteen, proposals for further compulsory military service, the institution of government employment services, improved vocational training, and modernized and extended apprenticeship schemes,[56] all calibrated around the definition of the youth as a "worker-in-training."

However, most troubling to the members of the Youth Commission were the results of studies that revealed the stubborn persistence of a Depression-era psychology among the very group of young people they so exalted as incarnating a new post-war democratic culture. What alarmed them was the existence of attitudes of adolescent "dependency" even among those young people who had secured jobs during the wartime boom. The publications of the commission were unanimous in pointing to the gnawing fear that underlay all post-war visions of full employment and abundance: the fact that Canadian young people had not forgotten the Depression.[57] This situation, however, was viewed in negative terms, because young men had failed to imbibe the "adult" values of personal responsibility and the necessity of proper education and training from their experience of economic catastrophe. Rather, prolonged idleness had bred an enduring habit of "fatalism" as the young Canadian contemplated his economic prospects, which revealed "how little he looks on its coming or prevention as a matter of human responsibility, least of all his own personal responsibility."[58] These they regarded not only as impediments to the fostering of a proper psychological sense of civic participation which rested upon personal responsibility, but as forming the

breeding ground for movements that might enlist unemployed youth
to demand "authoritarian" state planning and government intervention in private enterprise. "Fatalism," by which they meant psychological dependency and an absence of personal responsibility, reduced
the "stature" of the young male citizen to the level of "a pauper." The
overriding fear was that any temporary recurrence of unemployment
would once again re-create the conditions of massive youth unemployment of the 1930s, a situation that would induce many young
men to project their "humiliation and resentment" outwards because
they had not been able to successfully overcome older notions of adolescence which reinforced a sense of separateness and opposition.
"Other types of freedom," concluded one study of citizenship, "will
mean little to him if he is not free to get a job; equality of opportunity will sound like sheer hypocrisy ... A man who has gone through
that kind of bitter disillusionment is psychologically ready for the
demagogue who will tell him that democracy is a lie. Men – especially
young men, in that state of mind flocked to Hitler's party in
Germany's depression."[59] A revival of "adolescent" psychological
styles among the fifteen-to-twenty-four age group, as opposed to the
acceptance of adult work values by "youth," would expose Canadian
democracy to pendulum-like shifts between "radicalism and reaction,"[60] and would seriously compromise the achievement of the
"middle course,"[61] the balanced democracy anchored upon a mixed
economy and the individualist notions of work and private enterprise
to which liberal ideals of post-war reconstruction were so firmly
wedded.

In the final analysis, the Canadian Youth Commission's belief that
"youth" constituted the creative edge of a spirit of renewal that would
enable the country to chart a new direction in the post-war period
ultimately depended upon young people adopting the values and
conduct appropriate to a new breed of democratic citizen. These could
only be fostered by young people imbibing and practising, in work,
family, and civic life, the economic, producer-oriented values of steady
work and personal responsibility. The military struggle, many believed,
was but a prelude to the "Battle of Ideas ... the minds and hearts of
youth will be the fighting ground, and the issue will be the worth and
dignity of the individual."[62] However, the educators, youth workers,
businessmen, and Liberal civil servants who dominated the Youth
Commission believed that these values were not the by-products of
"planning," greater state initiative in the fields of social security, or
institutional reform, because their source was not in the external political order represented by the "state"; rather, they were shaped in the
crucible of the individual personality itself. Democracy, they main-

tained, was less a set of political structures and ideologies than a "way of life," a set of subconscious allegiances and practices learned by the individual citizen through participation in family life, the church, and the organizations of the local community. "Citizenship," concluded the Youth Commission, "must be understood not as an end in itself, and not merely as a means to immediate social ends, but rather as the proper and necessary expression of man's nature within the community of men."[63] In a troubling world of competing ideologies, particularly since many feared that "youth" could be swayed by the extremes of radicalism and reaction, the identification of "democracy" with a "way of life" served an important consensual function. As an ideal, it at once was classless and rendered political values and the civic order ultimately tributary to a private sphere ruled by individual moral choice. Here was a conservative variant of modern liberalism, one that, in the words of Sidney Smith, head of the Youth Commission, counterposed "the supreme and measureless worth"[64] of the human personality to what the commission feared was the tendency of the modern state towards an ultimately dehumanizing bureaucratization and centralization.

"[T]he state," declared the commission in 1948, "is being called upon to assume a greater responsibility for citizenship." In one sense, it might appear that members of the commission were positively associating the wartime creation of a strong state with the urgent desire of Canadian young people for "more opportunity, more equality, and social progress." However, it was clear from the outset that their ideal of citizenship was not oriented to the achievements of the political state in the field of economic planning or social security, for the commission emphatically stated that "government action alone is not enough ... Citizenship requires action on the part of each community as a whole, just as much on the part of each member."[65] Here, in embryo, appeared a new vision of post-war citizenship, one in which the ideal citizen was to be governed at a distance and whose allegiance was enlisted through the decidedly individualist vocabulary of voluntarism, conscience, and civic duty, whose private values and personality must be protected from the encroachments of state planners.[66] The Youth Commission thus adhered to a decidedly limited notion of the modern state, one that placed the primary responsibility on the individual to personally acquire and foster civic values through the cultivation of his or her personality. As the Women of the University of British Columbia stated, they were "unwilling to sacrifice the individuality of the personality to the designs of the state."[67]

Therefore it is not surprising that all discussions undertaken by the Youth Commission on the subject of citizenship in post-war Canada rested upon a careful calculus of state initiative, local community participation, and individual responsibility. Because it interpreted the achievement of citizenship as a partnership between these different elements, the overarching premise guiding the commission cannot be interpreted as a simple conservative anti-statism or as a retreat into the private sphere as the source of values.[68] However, while youth workers and educators fully admitted the need for federal and provincial state responsibilities in the fields of social security planning, they posited a notion of "decentralization" when it came to the promotion and fostering of citizenship itself. "[T]he foundation of citizenship," declared one study, "rests on the initiative of the citizens themselves ... not what government does for them, but in what they do for and with their own government."[69] For this reason, the surveys and reports of the Youth Commission were always alert to signs of "healthy interest in community-wide planning" of matters such as recreation, leisure, and cultural activities among Canadian young people.[70] Indeed, the focus on community initiatives such as recreation was *not* because these were regarded as part of a needs-based expansion of the social security state,[71] but because these activities lay most completely outside the purview of the modern state, in the realm where individual choice was most private and inviolate, where "we have a sense of considerable freedom from compulsion."[72] This was the key corollary of the limited view of "planning" held by the religious leaders, educators, and businessmen who articulated the framework of the commission's ideology. In their estimation, "planning" occurred in the Keynesian realm of fiscal management and public works expenditure as part of the federal responsibilities of post-war economic stabilization.

Indeed, as Philip Fisher, vice-president and managing director of Southam Corporation, stated, community life was impossible "without some form of planning, but extreme planning is the negation of personal liberty." Fisher described the cardinal task facing post-war Canadians as the identification of some proper balance between centralization and decentralization, praising the latter as most consonant with democratic ideals and the preservation of the individual personality. "As authority is decentralized," he concluded, "it spreads out to Provincial Governments, to Municipalities, and ultimately to the individual citizen himself."[73] Democratic planning, maintained Sidney Smith in 1946, "[i]s a really big job, far too big for any one voluntary agency or group of voluntary agencies or any government department to undertake alone,"[74] and consequently, "decentralization" testified to a view of democracy prevalent within the Youth Commission that the state was only one agent that had claims upon the allegiance of "the well-rounded individual."[75] Such a view was emphatically echoed by Quebec's Catholic Action youth organizations, which defined the task of political authority in the modern state as one of "uniting without unifying, grouping without depersonalizing, coordinating without constraining" the initiative of individual citizens.[76] While more distinctly anti-statist social commentators of the post-war period saw voluntary organizations and the state in opposition, the Youth Commission adhered to a far more pluralistic outlook, in which governments, churches, community organizations, and individuals mutually participated in the task of forming the civic personality of modern Canadians.

The Canadian Youth Commission's definition of post-war Canadian society as a pluralistic partnership was founded upon a novel view of democracy that rejected classic institutional, idealistic, or merely political formulations of the term in favour of a predominantly psychological and emotional definition. Indeed, such a view of citizenship did not rest upon a dichotomy between public and private but on an attempt to define a public, non-political, consensual "civic" realm that included family, church, and community organizations which lay outside the political machinery of federal and provincial governments. It was for this reason that makers of post-war youth policy were able to define citizenship in largely emotional, psychological, and affective terms. "The connections between citizenship and religion," stated Irene Baird in 1943, "remain close and deep."[77] During the late 1930s and early 1940s, a number of commentators close to the various Canadian youth movements elaborated a non-political definition of democracy, one that moved the idea away from institutional forms or abstract rights of individual citizens. Emphasizing that the central meaning of democracy revolved around "respect for human personality,"[78] this classless, non-conflictual definition was brought to the fore as part of a wider ideological struggle against totalitarianism and as a response to immediate wartime conditions, where overly forceful assertion of individual and group rights would impede the effectiveness of the war effort. Indeed, the thrust of this wartime language was to carefully navigate the claims of "freedom and order" by limiting and cautiously circumscribing "rights-based" notions of citizenship and insisting instead that citizenship was a set of "privileges" that entailed "responsibilities."[79] Many of these wartime imperatives were then incorporated wholesale into discussions of post-war youth policy and reconstruction, where the recurrent phrase in all discussions of democratic citizenship was that it was a "way of life," "*un cadre réel de la vie*,"[80] in which individual rights were carefully balanced by a reciprocal set of duties and obligations

to the wider community[81] – not merely a set of common political
ideals, obligations, or participation in organized political parties but
"a personal attitude, even a personal commitment." "Democracy,"
declared the Canadian Teachers' Federation in 1943, "is not merely a
form of góvernment but *a way of life*," an attitude that first and foremost must inform not merely politics but all human relationships.[82]
Although their view was individualist in its emphasis on the human
personality as the ultimate wellspring of social and political authority,[83] the members of the Youth Commission clearly subscribed to a
"social individualism," one which insisted that citizenship was essentially a cooperative enterprise that could "only develop in social relations and is fostered best by some kind of organized co-operative
endeavour with others."[84] In the words of George Tuttle, associate
director of research for the Youth Commission, the democratic citizen
was characterized by "a respect for persons (though not in isolation
from their social behaviour), tolerance of differences, equality of
opportunity, flexibility in the face of new contingencies and willingness to accept responsibilities," rather than the narrowly "acquisitive"
type of individualism that was identified as one of the prime culprits
behind the Depression.[85]

Because the locus of democratic attitudes lay within the individual
personality itself, the fostering of democratic citizenship fell, not primarily to the state, but in the sub-political terrain of family, school,
church, and voluntary community organizations that was located
outside the immediate purview of government, the very relationships
and organizations that fully expressed individual creativity and choice.
Because citizenship was primarily a matter of emotional identification
and daily practice, and not simply adherence to traditional ideals, its
acquisition depended upon a type of education that integrated the
"ideas and sentiments fostered by democratic homes, the enlightened
instruction and liberal atmosphere of progressive schools, the social
idealism and moral training offered by the churches, and the emotional
conditioning of national traditions and symbols." These would
combine to train the individual "in the skills of the civilization to
which he belongs."[86] The individual's acquisition of proper civic values
was not, in the estimation of the Youth Commission, a matter of incul-
cation by traditional authority figures but, rather, an activist "learning-
by-doing" in which young people were progressively initiated into civic
responsibility, not directly through politics itself, but through initiation
into democratic practices in families, schools, and churches, those
agencies in most intimate contact with the individual personality.[87] The
family, stated the final report of the Canadian Youth Commission on
citizenship,

must be the first matrix of citizenship at this deepest level ... not so much as a matter of precept as of practice: not lectures, but patterns of feeling and actions are the basic determinants of character. The family has an opportunity, unrivalled by any other institution in our society, to be a complete community. Here values are truly shared. Here the common need takes precedence over private pleasures. Here all feel jointly responsible for the welfare of each, and the common resources are pooled to meet the individual's need. Parents can best prepare their children for citizenship if they themselves meet the demands of the family community in their relations with each other and with their children.[88]

Moreover, the identification of the family, the church, and community organizations as not merely part of the private sphere but emphatically part of the wider public because of their primary responsibility for educating citizens in the activities and qualities of the "way of life" provided, in the minds of members of the Youth Commission, an essential counterweight to the tendency to centralized planning that they believed would inevitably reduce citizens to a state of "dependency" and stultify the flowering of adult personalities.

The immediate post-war definition of democracy as a cultural and psychological "way of life" that flourished within the Canadian Youth Commission provided a firm line of resistance to any attempt to assert an idea of generational opposition based upon notions of a youth culture separate from that of adults. Indeed, the belief that the task of fostering democratic values in the individual fell to a set of relationships and organizations that lay outside the government simply reinforced the economic notion that the "youth" was an adult worker-in-training with the conviction that young Canadians were adult citizens-in-training. In advocating "youth's right to participate in community endeavours," emphatically promoting the lowering of the voting age to eighteen, and pressing for the establishment of a national youth council as a coordinating agency,[89] the Youth Commission moved in a decidedly liberal direction, convinced that the ideological "ferment" evident in post-war Canada opened up possibilities for an enduring conjunction between the creative energies of youth and a sense of renewed confidence in the national purpose.[90] However, the notion of "partnership" most emphatically did not imply "self-determination" or the ability of youth organizations to take an independent line on public questions.[91] According to George Tuttle, "the prevalent view that the solution of the world's problems lies in the hands of youth has within it both falsity and truth. It is false in this respect, that youth is capable of much impatient arrogance, of a lack of adequate knowledge and a lack of balance so that it still needs guidance and information."[92] Writing to F.G. Patten, Colonel William Line, director of Personnel Selection of the Department of National Defence, declared that young people should first be initiated into citizenship practices through activities at the level of the local community. The federal arena, he observed, "is more the responsibility of experienced citizens" because, in his estimation, "youth itself is not particularly competent in the planning operation itself. Youth debates on public issues are all right as exercises in understanding. But debating will not lead to action, and when it stands alone, it lends itself to the vote-getting proselytization of the political demagogue."[93] The concept of a "partnership" between adults and Canada's young people meant in essence a form of training through practice in activities appropriate to the democratic "way of life," with the essential element provided by responsible and sympathetic adult volunteer leadership and guidance – consulting youth representatives in the context of high school student councils, community recreation and leisure activities, and inclusion on committees concerning industrial and educational matters where youth issues were discussed – all to further the aim of "helping them to become more capable and responsible citizens."[94] The intent was to preclude the emergence of "youth movements and youth lobbies" based upon a frustration with and sense of separateness from the social and cultural world of adults. As the 1946 volume *Youth Challenges the Educators* concluded, post-war young people must not be hived off from the rest of the community, for "it would be a bad thing for them to become solicitous about themselves – introverted and regarding themselves as 'problem cases.'"[95]

The central imperative underlying the public attitudes and policy prescriptions of the Canadian Youth Commission was the reinforcement of connection between generations, expressed by the very definition of "youth" as a stage lying between ages ffteen and twenty-four, thus encompassing *both* adolescents and adults within a single set of interrelated economic and citizenship values. These values, though springing from a more private realm of individual emotions and psychological adjustment, were most emphatically linked to a public, civic sphere through the participation of the individual in a democratic "way of life" that included family, religious, educational, and community activities. Moreover, this new definition of democracy was consensual, classless, and non-political, a citizenship ideal that would overcome the serious cultural and ideological tensions that existed within Canadian society and would firmly identify post-war Canadian youth and, more importantly, the nation as a whole with a spirit of renewal and creativity. And to its proponents, the key building block of this post-war consensus was the absolute necessity of resisting the reassertion of interwar politico-cultural ideas of youth that celebrated a separation of generations. This, in the estimation of youth planners, would simply negate their ideal of democratic citizenship by creating a demand for separate government policies to meet the particular needs of youth, an intervention that many believed would thrust the generations apart and re-create a notion of the dependent "adolescent" relying upon state "planning." Such an approach would subvert the Youth Commission's liberal ideal of a non-political, participatory democracy by drawing the state – and with it, the possibility of ideological conflict between the extremes of radicalism and authoritarian reaction – into the consensual world of family, church, and community.

"On nearing adolescence," observed the Canadian Youth Commission in 1948, "the child enters the distinctive world of teen-agers where 'having a good time' becomes an extremely important business ... the bond between the generations is often weakened more than it need be."[96] While, superficially, this might appear to be the first official recognition that an American-style "teenager" culture of language, clothes, and social events separate from the family existed in post-war Canada, a close reading of the commission's thinking about teenagers would suggest that it still conceived of the values of youth as in a continuum with those of adults. This critique of the teenager appeared in a study entitled *Youth, Marriage, and the Family*, consciously designed to promote the commission's new ideal of the "democratic family" as the centrepiece of post-war stabilization. The "teenager" phenomenon, the members of the commission concluded, was in fact restricted to certain urban high schools, and evoked no fundamental opposition between a new consumerist leisure ethic and the productivist civic values inherent in the prevailing definition of "youth." "The young people," maintained the study, "feel that adults generally underestimate their capacities and do not provide opportunities for them to grow into those responsibilities they must shortly assume as adults."[97] Significantly, the assumption that governed public attitudes towards youth was not that this supposed existence of urban teenagers signalled a deep-rooted social crisis caused by the inroads of mass media and consumerist marketing, or that it represented a new "subculture" that would exist permanently on the margins of the adult world.[98] Thus the fundamental assumption underlying the Youth Commisson's efforts remained the Depression-era definition by which young people would be streamed into steady employment through education and training programs. The causes of any teenage rebellion could therefore be ascribed to a temporary inability of governments, community institutions, and families to find a formula that would smoothly integrate male adolescents into the work-derived family and civic responsibilties of adults.

Such a formula was adumbrated in the very definition of the "democratic family," a new concept first articulated during World War II and promoted by the Canadian Youth Commission as the first line of defence in the struggle against a breakdown in generational solidarity. Based on a recognition of the obsolescence of the old notion of the economically interdependent family[99] and on a fear that purely economic definitions of the family would lead to an atomized, materialistic, and acquisitive individualism which would erode wartime democratic ideals of cooperation and solidarity, the concept of the "democratic family" stressed the importance of the family as "a source of emotional satisfaction" and affectional ties that would counteract "the decreasing intimacy of so many relationships outside the home," in which the individual was increasingly considered merely as a unit of economic production.[100] The "democratic family," proclaimed the Youth Commission, comprised a series of more egalitarian relationships between husband and wife and between parents and children, but according to its definition, egalitarianism was not a recipe for individualism. "[T]he family as a group," maintained one study, "tries to achieve emotional stability, to encourage each member to express his wishes and desires and to give sympathetic consideration to them. In a cooperative way family problems are discussed and solved. Younger members of the family are advised and guided rather than commanded."[101]

It should be emphasized, however, that while the central values undergirding the family were emotional and psychological, they were not purely "private," because the family during the immediate postwar period was defined as the institution that first introduced the individual to the "democratic way of life" which extended into other aspects of the civic realm. Because of this continuing bond between the values of the family and the public citizen, notions of "egalitarianism" within the democratic family elaborated by the Canadian Youth Commission were carefully circumscribed to preclude the type of individualism that would lead to the formation of an independent social and cultural world of adolescents. As with the initiation of youth into desirable workplace values and into democratic practice in community organizations, the central issue revolved primarily around the quality of adult leadership and less with the specific values of young people themselves. The new function of the family as the source of emotional satisfaction and security was clearly identified as an "adult" responsibility. As Irene Baird stated, "Family living is essentially a partnership between two generations and of the two it is the parents who have the most searching adjustments to make."[102] What was significant about this declaration was the expectation that as "youth" moved gradually into the adult world through work, marriage, and family formation, they should retain and express some of their "youthful" qualities, thus further blurring the psychological and cultural boundaries between generations. Post-war parents, Baird maintained, should be "a vital, warm-blooded breed; good to look at, easy to live with, fun to have around," a complete contrast to the stern, moralizing authoritarians who only bred youthful desires for independence and rebellion. Thus, in counteracting what she believed was the propensity of adolescents to seek excitement outside the home, Baird enjoined modern parents to "*Open our homes* more than we do and really get to know our children's friends." By stocking a plentiful "supply of cokes" and by holding forth the allure of a "welcoming atmosphere,"[103] the family home would remain the site of intergenerational cooperation, an interdependence based, not upon the family economy, but upon the shared interests and leisure supplied by a new democratic culture of "youth" that spanned a variety of age groups.

Therefore signs of the emergence of an independent youth culture that rejected the intergenerational ideals of productive, participatory adult citizenship through clothing styles, musical tastes, and a more open sexuality clearly troubled those associated with the Youth Commission. Although such behaviour was frequently labelled "juvenile delinquency," the commission's pronouncements were far more understated and less shrill than those of its American counterparts or of more conservative voices in Canadian society, who elevated the problem to the status of a "moral panic," citing a massive breakdown in the structures of institutional control or the influence of the mass media.[104] "No psychiatrists," claimed one report, "will object to a modern jive session, to frankness about sex, to abandonment of some of the formalities of a past generation." The "zoot suit" phenomenon was likened to a "stage," similar to "fraternity years" among upper-middle-class college youth, and it simply indicated the need of modern youth for a sense of belonging and inclusion in a community. Indeed, the phenomenon of "mild rebellion" among youth was precisely linked to the need for "security" and "recognition,"[105] words that go far to explaining the more benign interpretation of juvenile delinquency and youthful independence that prevailed within the Youth Commission. These were not structural problems but temporary, passing symptoms of the breakdown of the obsolete ideal of the authoritarian, economically materialist family, a situation that the Youth Commission staunchly refused to lament. For these more liberal voices, the emergence of the "democratic family," whose very raison d'être was the provision of psychological security, emotional

satisfaction, and training in the practices of the new social individualism for *all* its members,[106] would provide a set of values that its promoters believed was more attractive than visions of an independent
youth culture: a cooperative, harmonious family that would serve as
an enduring source of social stability.

Between 1948 and 1954, most Canadian social commentators
remained reasonably confident that the new democratic family had
successfully forged a new intergenerational partnership. Two sociological studies, one of Anglo Montreal's "Suburban Town," and the other
of "Crestwood Heights," a Toronto suburb, appeared to demonstrate
the existence, not of a separate, antagonistic youth culture, but of a
dominant pattern of "adult directed and approved activity," what the
authors of *Crestwood Heights* termed "dependent interdependence," a
similar acceptance of adult values and way of life.[107] Teenage rebellion,
where it did occur, invariably happened "within the framework of the
general patterns of the culture" and usually involved different career
and work choices.[108] Not coincidentally,[109] these were precisely the
ideas that informed the Canadian Youth Commission's plans for adult-
controlled adolescent socialization under the rubric of the "democratic
family." However, by the mid-1950s, intimations of a new sensibility
were appearing among a number of Canadian educators and commentators. In 1953 *Cahiers d'Action catholique*, a review intended for
Quebec's educators and youth workers, reiterated what had become a
stock-in-trade of post-war Canada's thinking about young people,
stating that "left to themselves, today's students will elaborate a false
doctrinal synthesis on sexuality, love, the roles of men and women,
marriage, and chastity, basing their ideas on modern propaganda and
current slogans." Manifestations of a separate youth culture, centred
around teen dating, were denounced simply as evidence of materialism,
individualism, and Americanization.[110]

The following year, the same periodical ran a series of articles that
were clearly more positive towards what it believed was a new form of
social and cultural values evident among youth. Dating and sexual
exploration among male and female teens, argued these secondary
school educators, should be encouraged and properly educated about,
rather than opposed and deplored, because "the adolescent has his
own affectional life whose normal channels must be opened. An
authentic experience of the affectional life, achieved at the moment of
adolescence, will give him the equilibrium necessary to become an
adult."[111] "The mutual discovery of intimacy by teenage boys and
girls," confided Father Roch Duval, "presupposes that a certain degree
of selflessness has been attained by each. This discovery, then, is a manifestation of the beginning of their integration into society; in the type

of dating practised by teenagers appears a new type of community which entails a certain degree of responsibility and possibilities of development that have been hitherto unknown to the child."[112] What was significant about these articles was their reassertion of the notion of adolescence as a psychological stage distinct from adulthood, based not upon the "public" values of production and civic involvement so elevated by the Youth Commission but on a "private" acquisition of emotional maturity founded on a "self-consciousness" that derived principally from sexual self-awareness and initiation into gender roles defined by sexuality.[113]

The enunciation after the mid-1950s of a psychological definition of youth, centred around the primordial essence of sexuality and the emotions, marked a seismic shift in post-war Canadian culture, and it paralleled the efforts of Protestant and Roman Catholic churches to reconstruct the idea of marriage as primarily a sexual partnership based upon personal satisfaction,[114] rather than a set of economic or reproductive obligations. First, this new concept of adolescence as the key to individual sexual identity sundered the chronological definition of youth as encompassing the fifteen-to-twenty-four age group that had been orthodoxy since late in the Depression, by locating the crucial years for developing sexual self-awareness and cultivating heterosexual relationships in the teen years. In so doing, it implicitly resurrected the old tradition of the moral and spiritual superiority of youth, but this time garbed in the trappings of psychological "authenticity." Second, it enjoined a minimum of adult supervision and control, as it placed the priority on a process of mutual self-discovery by teenagers within a more authentic form of community *outside* the family, whose bounds and norms were determined by adolescents themselves. Parents and educators were confined to providing visible but non-authoritarian models of proper sex roles for teenage men and women.[115]

In a 1959 study of the teenage dating phenomenon, the *Maclean's Magazine* reporter Sidney Katz appeared to echo Arthur Lower's bitter characterization of Canada's "elderly adolescents." Katz argued that the quintessential element of teenage culture, steady dating, promoted sexual promiscuity, but more troubling still, it produced a stifling conformity, a lack of initiative, an obsessive desire for security, and a subversion of the masculinity of young men, who found themselves trapped in what was a largely "female device" to ensure social acceptance[116] and were consequently shorn of their virtues of intiative and sense of adventure. Katz characterized the new breed of Canadian adolescent as a passive consumer of both leisure activities and emotional relationships, and although many of his criticisms evoked the producerist language of the Canadian Youth Commission, his article rested on a number of new assumptions. Although he argued that the obsessive teenage craving for security through "going steady" mimicked the adult "advocacy of health insurance, pensions," it is significant that Katz accepted the notion that there now existed an "adolescent world" which lay beyond the capacity of parents to understand or control. More surprisingly, he quoted without comment the view of one social worker who stated that there was "no harm in premarital relationships for adolescents if the social taboos and fears of conception are banished."[117] The appearance of statements such as "Parents and their children live in two different worlds" at the end of the 1950s, which accepted the existence of a generational divide, should induce us to at least question the conventions of post-war chronology. The appearance of "teenagers," whose leisure, consumption, and sexual practices made them the quintessential cultural icons of the American 1950s, may fulfill a very different explanatory function for Canadian historians. Katz's very linking of teen dating with the supposed sexual utopia of oral contraceptives, what he called "a social revolution in sex behaviour," rather than evoking the cultural climate of the post-war decade, hints at the need to place the birth of the Canadian teenager at the epicentre of the "cultural revolutions"[118] that were to so profoundly alter the mainstream of Canadian society during the 1960s.

NOTES

I would like to thank my research assistants Anna Locke and Kari Theobald for their work during the summer of 2000.

1 Arthur Lower, "Our Elderly Adolescents," *Saturday Night* (SN), 28 May 1955.
2 Lower had always held a low estimate of the intellectual abilities of adolescents, estimating their mental qualities as "practically blank on public affairs," "life viewed as acquisition, rights many, duties few," and devoted to having a good time. See Queen's University Archives, Arthur Lower Papers, box 1, "Correspondence 1943," Arthur Lower to Hon. C.B. Power, minister of defence for air, 24 March 1943. For statistics on Canadian high school attendance, in which 1954 stood as the pivotal year in which 50 per cent offourteen-to-seventeen-year-old adolescents were enrolled, see Wolfgang M. Illing and Zoltan E. Zsigmond, *Enrolment in Schools and Universities, 1951–2 to 1975–6*, Staff Study no. 20 (Ottawa: Economic Council of Canada, 1967), appendix table B-2.
3 The similarity between Canadian and American popular culture throughout the period 1945–67 is the key theme apparent in a recent cultural

history of the post-war period, Doug Owram's *Born at the Right Time: A History of the Baby Boom Generation* (Toronto: University of Toronto Press, 1996).

4 For American definitions, see Grace Palladino, *Teenagers: An American History* (New York: Basic Books, 1994), 5. Palladino notes that by the mid-1930s American teenagers were already considered an age group and not simply a wealthy social class.

5 The Dominion-Provincial Youth Training Agreements, enacted after 1937, defined "unemployed young people" as those aged between eighteen and thirty. See McMaster University Archives (MMUA), Canadian Youth Congress, box 20, file "Youth Training Agreements." Those familiar with 1930s youth movements tended to adopt 16 as the lower end of the age spectrum. See ibid., box 19, Research Files, "Unemployment," A.G. Watson, assistant secretary, Canadian Youth Congress, "Unemployment among Canadian Youth," n.d.; ibid., *Canada Department of Labour, Youth Training Division, The Unemployed Youth Problem – Steps Towards Its Solution*, reprinted from *Canada, 1939* (Ottawa: King's Printer, 1939). Established in 1943, the Canadian Youth Commission defined its mandate as studying "the main problems of young people from 15 to 24 years of age." See Canadian Youth Commission, *Youth Challenges the Educators* (Toronto: Ryerson Press, 1946), "Announcement," ii.

6 This paper thus stands at variance with a recent current of writing on post-war Canadian youth, which tends to uncritically accept that American definitions of the "teenager" were in vogue in Canada as a consequence of wartime prosperity, and that public response was governed by a series of "moral panics" that fixated upon sexual delinquency and sought to repress the freedom of young people by postulating a "normal" monogamous heterosexuality. For the main statements of this literature, see Mariana Valverde, "Building Anti-Delinquent Communities: Morality, Gender, and Generation in the City," in Joy Parr, ed., *A Diversity of Women: Ontario, 1945–1980* (Toronto: University of Toronto Press, 1995), 19–45; Mary Louise Adams, *The Trouble With Normal: Postwar Youth and the Making of Heterosexuality* (Toronto: University of Toronto Press, 1997); Mona Gleason, *Normalizing the Ideal: Psychology, Schooling and the Family in Postwar Canada* (Toronto: University of Toronto Press, 1999); Shirley Tillotson, *The Public at Play: Gender and the Politics of Recreation in Post-War Ontario* (Toronto: University of Toronto Press, 2000); Franca Iacovetta, "Parents, Daughters, and Family Court Intrusions into Working-Class Life," in Franca Iacovetta and Wendy Mitchinson, *On the Case: Explorations in Social History* (Toronto: University of Toronto Press, 1998), 312–37.

7 See John Gillis, *Youth and History: Tradition and Change in European*

Age Relations, 1770–present, 2nd ed. (New York: Academic Press, 1981), 133, 137–8, 151.

8 For well-established European cultural traditions of generational conflict, which flourished in France, Germany, and Italy between 1890 and 1930, see Robert Wohl, *The Generation of 1914* (Cambridge: Harvard University Press, 1979); Luisa Passerini, "Youth as a Metaphor for Social Change in Fascist Italy and America in the 1950s," in Giovanni Levi and Jean-Claude Schmitt, eds., *A History of Young People in the West*, Vol. 2, *Stormy Evolution to Modern Times* (Cambridge, Mass.: Belknap Press, 1997), 281–3. In terms of Canadian attitudes, it must be noted that the notion of generational conflict, while more muted in Anglo-American societies, was an important cultural presence in Catholic Quebec during the 1930s and served as an important component of what new scholarship has termed "the Quiet Revolution." See Michael Gauvreau, "'The Presence of Heroism in Our Lives,'" chapter 1 of *Catholicism Betrayed: Elites, Popular Religion, and the Cultural Origins of the Quiet Revolution, 1931–1971* (Montreal and Kingston: McGill-Queen's University Press, forthcoming).

9 National Archives of Canada (NA), Canadian Youth Commission (CYC), MG 28, I, II, vol. 32, file 7(3a), "Misc. Memoranda," Irene Baird, "Study of Pre-War Citizenship Attitudes among the Unemployed," 29 Dec. 1943. This was precisely the view adopted by Claude Ryan, national secretary of Quebec's Catholic Action movements. See Claude Ryan, "Un congrès sur la jeunesse," *Vie étudiante* 13 (jan. 1947); Archives de l'Université de Montréal (AUM), Fonds Action catholique canadienne (ACC), P16/O4.26, "Canadian Committee on Youth Services," "Brief to the Royal Commission on National Development in the Arts, Letters and Sciences," June 1950.

10 NA, CYC, vol. 31, file 3(3a), Employment Correspondence, Col. W. Line to F.G. Patten, 27 March 1944; MMUA, Canadian Youth Congress, box 19, "Unemployment," *The Unemployed Youth Problem*, 6.

11 NA, CYC, vol. 68, file 43(5a), "Youth 1939–1944," D.L. Ritchie, *Youth and the Machine Age* (The Machine Age Series, Published by the Social Service Council of Canada), 6.

12 MMUA, Canadian Youth Congress, box 16, *Canadian Youth Act Manual*, Jan. 1937.

13 A.G. Watson, "Half-Million Canadian Youth without Employment," *United Church Observer*, 1 June 1939. By comparison, British youth unemployment during the 1930s also remained intractable, not moving below 150,000 for the fourteen-to-seventeen age group until the beginning of World War II. See Bill Osgerby, *Youth in Britain since 1945* (Oxford: Blackwell, 1998), 7.

14 MMUA, Canadian Youth Congress, file CYC Congress, Clippings 1936, John Boyd, "Youth Charts a Course" [*Advance*].

15 For the creation of the joint youth training schemes, see James Struthers, *No Fault of Their Own: Unemployment and the Canadian Welfare State, 1914–1941* (Toronto: University of Toronto Press), 165–6. For the notion that significant levels of youth unemployment were "permanent," see NA, CYC, vol. 32, file 7(3a), "Misc. Memoranda," National Council of Young Men's Christian Associations, "Statement to National Youth Employment Committee," Dec. 1936; MMUA, Canadian Youth Congress, box 1, file "CYC Correspondence, undated," R.E.G. Davis, secretary, Personnel Division, National Council of YMCAs, "Guiding Youth in a Transition Period: Some Suggestions for Leaders of Young People," 4 Dec. 1934.

16 MMUA, Canadian Youth Congress, box 15, file CYC, Fourth Congress, Winnipeg 1939, "Brief Submitted to the Federal Minister of Labour, Mr. Rogers, on March 3rd, 1939." For a similar conception of youth training schemes by Catholic social reformers, see Archives Nationales du Québec à Montréal (ANQ-M), Fonds Jeunesse ouvrière catholique, P104/104, "Belle Victoire de la J.O.C.," 23 avril 1937.

17 NA, CYC, vol. 30, file CYC 36, Frame of Reference, "Dominion-Provincial Youth Training Programme"; Edith Lewis, "Youth Training – a Solution to Unemployment," *United Church Observer*, 1 July 1940.

18 MMUA, Canadian Youth Congress, box 19, "Unemployment," *The Unemployed Youth Problem*, 6–7; ibid., box 24, "Publications Received – Miscellaneous," J.E. Robbins, *Dependency of Youth*, n.d.; Kenneth Woodsworth, *Canadian Youth Comes of Age* (Toronto: Ryerson Press, 1939), 5.

19 NA, CYC, vol. 68, file 44(5a), Youth Councils, 1938–39, "Report of the Unemployment Survey Conducted by the Ottawa Youth Federation, Nov. 21–26, 1938," 22 Feb. 1939.

20 Irene Baird, *Waste Heritage* (Toronto: Macmillan, 1939), 220; NA, CYC, vol. 32, Baird, "Study of Pre-War Citizenship Attitudes among the Unemployed."

21 For an analysis of the increasingly male-centred direction of federal and provincial welfare policies in the late 1930s, see Nancy Christie, *Engendering the State: Family, Work, and Welfare in Canada* (Toronto: University of Toronto Press, 2000), 196–248.

22 MMUA, Canadian Youth Congress, box 19, Research Files, "Women," *In Home and Office: In Factory and Shop* (Ottawa: Canadian Welfare Council, 1937), 18.

23 Ibid., box 24, Robbins, *Dependency of Youth*.

24 Ibid., box 15, file CYC, Fourth Congress, Winnipeg, 1939, "Report of the Chairman of the Fourth Canadian Youth Congress."

25 Ibid., box 18, Research Files, "Marriage," *Youth's Eye View of Some Problems Connected with Getting Married* (Toronto: Ontario Young Men's Council of Young Men's Christian Associations, n.d.), 1.

26 Ibid., box 19, *The Unemployed Youth Problem*, 9; ibid., box 24,
    Robbins, *Dependency of Youth*; ibid., box 18, Research Files, "Mar-
    riage."

27 Ibid., box 18, *Youth's Eye View of Some Problems Connected with
    Getting Married*, 22–3; ibid., box 19, *In Home and Office: In Factory
    and Shop*, 18. The theme of extramarital yet monogamous relations
    between young unemployed men and young women was featured in Irene
    Baird's *Waste Heritage*. Frustrated by his inability to secure work and
    marry Hazel, a young Vancouver woman he met in the hostel canteen,
    Matt Striker, the central character, actually engages in an illicit sexual
    relationship with her. However, his own personal morals remain quite
    traditional, as he expresses moral outrage and physical violence against a
    prostitute who tried to approach his chum, Eddie. See *Waste Heritage*,
    63, 96, 97–8, 137.

28 MMUA, Canadian Youth Congress, box 18, *Youth's Eye View of Some
    Problems Connected with Getting Married*, 18, 20; ibid., box 1, R.E.G.
    Davis, "Guiding Youth in a Transition Period."

29 For the persistence of the notion of the interdependent family as a policy
    imperative during the Depression, see Christie, *Engendering the State*,
    153–4. For the work camps, see Struthers, *No Fault of Their Own*;
    Laurel Sefton MacDowell, "Relief Camp Workers in Ontario during the
    Great Depression of the 1930s," *Canadian Historical Review* 76 (June
    1995): 205–28.

30 For recent studies of the German and Italian youth movements in this
    period, see Alexander von Plato, "The Hitler Youth Generation and Its
    Role in Two Post-War German States," in Mark Roseman, ed., *Genera-
    tions in Conflict: Youth Revolt and Generation Formation in Germany,
    1770–1968* (Cambridge: Cambridge University Press, 1995), 210–26;
    Dagmar Reese, "The BDM Generation: A Female Generation in Transi-
    tion from Dictatorship to Democracy," in Roseman, ed., *Generations in
    Conflict*, 227–46; Peter Stachura, *The German Youth Movement,
    1900–1945* (London: Macmillan, 1981); Passerini, "Youth as a
    Metaphor for Social Change." .

31 NA, CYC, vol. 31, "Employment Correspondence," Col. W. Line to F.G.
    Patten.

32 Armour Mackay, "Canadian Youth May Determine the 1939 Election,"
    SN, 5 Aug. 1939; MMUA, Canadian Youth Congress, box 1, Davis,
    "Guiding Youth in a Transition Period."

33 MMUA, Canadian Youth Congress, box 16, *Canadian Youth Act Manual*,
    Jan. 1937; Norman Levy, "Youth's Effort."

34 Woodsworth, *Canadian Youth Comes of Age*, 18.

35 Ibid., 15.

36 NA, CYC, vol. 61, file 8(5a), "Education, Part 3, 1940–1944," *Report of*

the C.T.F. Reconstruction Commission, Adopted by the Canadian Federation of Teachers at Annual Convention, St. John. N.B., Aug. 10–13, 1943, 9.

37 Ibid., vol. 40, file 7C3F, "Part II: Are We Educating for Citizenship?"

38 Ibid., vol. 30, file CYC 36, Frame of Reference, "The Canadian Economy in the Post War World," n.d.

39 CYC, *Youth and Jobs in Canada* (Toronto: Ryerson Press, 1945), 53; NA, CYC, vol. 65, file 28(5a) Reconstruction(1), 1942–43, Robert B. Bryce, "Basic Issues in Postwar International Economic Relations," *American Economic Review,* supplement, 32 (March 1942), 181; ibid., vol. 65, file 28(5a), R.E.G. Davis, "Economic Reconstruction in the Post-War World," paper read to the Association of YMCA Secretaries, Cleveland, Ohio, 19 May 1942.

40 NA, CYC, vol. 30, file CYC 36, Frame of Reference, "Minutes of the meeting of the committee on National Economic Policy, held in Dr. Keenleyside's office ... Dec. 15, 1944," R.E.G. Davis, "Suggested Outline: Post-War Economic Policies." Also present at this meeting were influential government economic advisers such as W.A. Mackintosh, J.F. Parkinson, and John Deutsch. For the impact of Keynesian ideas on the reconstruction policies of the wartime Liberal government of Mackenzie King, see Doug Owram, *The Government Generation: Canadian Intellectuals and the State, 1900–1945* (Toronto: University of Toronto Press, 1986), 294–5; Christie, *Engendering the State,* 271–3.

41 NA, CYC, vol. 40, "Prospects of Citizenship for Young People," *Youth Speaks Out on Citizenship* (Toronto: Ryerson Press, 1948), 102, quoted a lengthy extract from German sociologist Karl Mannheim's *Diagnosis of Our Times,* in which he stated that "the specific function of Youth is that it is a revitalizing agent."

42 CYC, *Youth and Jobs in Canada,* 223.

43 *Accent on Action: A Report of the National Conference of Agencies Serving Youth* (Ottawa: 1946), 7.

44 NA, CYC, vol. 40, "Citizenship Report," part 1: "Vaporous indeed many of their ideas may be, and inarticulate. But they are not crying for the moon. They want changes, but they do not expect utopia – far less."

45 The CYC was chaired by Sidney Smith, president of the University of Manitoba and later president of the University of Toronto and secretary of state for external affairs in the 1957–58 Conservative cabinet of John Diefenbaker. The vice-chairs were Liberal senator Lomer-Mercier Gouin and H.L. Keenleyside of the Department of External Affairs. R.E.G. Davis of the YMCA and George Tuttle of the United Church of Canada were respectively director and associate director of research.

46 NA, CYC, vol. 30, Davis, "Suggested Outline."

47 Ibid., file C307, Frame of Reference, Philip Fisher, "The Political Scene."

48 Ibid., Fisher, "The Political Scene"; ibid., "Minutes of the Meeting ...";
    Davis, "Suggested Outline: Post-War Economic Policies."

49 Ibid., Fisher, "The Political Scene."

50 For the strongly conservative, free enterprise bias of the federal Liberals'
    reconstruction policies, see the analysis in Christie, *Engendering the
    State*, 270–90.

51 NA, CYC, vol. 30, file CYC 36, Frame of Reference, "Legislation."

52 CYC, *Youth and Jobs in Canada*, iv.

53 NA, CYC, vol. 40, "Citizenship Report"; ibid., vol. 31, file2(3a), "Employ-
    ment Report, Comm. #2," "Youth Employment."

54 Ibid., vol. 31, file 2(3a), "Employment Report Comm. #2"; ibid., vol. 30,
    file CYC 36, "The Canadian Economy in the Post-War World"; Dr Sidney
    E. Smith, commission chairman, "An Interpretation of the Canadian
    Youth Commission," *Accent on Action*, 17; AUM, Fonds ACC, P16/O4.26,
    "Report of the First Annual Meeting and Workshop Session of the Cana-
    dian Association of Youth Serving Organizations," Montreal, 2 June
    1949, Dr Eugene Forsey, "The Problem of Youth Employment."

55 NA, CYC, vol. 30, "Legislation."

56 Ibid., vol. 31, "Employment Report, Comm. #2."

57 CYC, *Youth and Jobs in Canada*, iii.

58 NA, CYC, vol. 40, file 7C3F, "Prospects of Citizenship for Young People";
    ibid., vol. 65, file 28(5a), "Reconstruction(1), 1942–3," Stuart Chase,
    "Man Is a Working Animal," *Survey Graphic: Magazine of Social Inter-
    pretation* 32 (May 1943): 151.

59 Ibid., "Prospects of Citizenship for Young People"; CYC, *Youth and Jobs
    in Canada*, 223.

60 NA, CYC, vol. 40, file 9C3F, "Citizenship," John Webster Grant, "Youth
    and Citizenship."

61 *Accent on Action*, 7.

62 NA, CYC, vol. 61, file 8(5a), "Education, Part 3, 1940–1944," Dr Sidney
    E. Smith, "Foreword," *Education, the Keystone of Democracy: Report of
    the Reconstruction Committee of the Canadian Teachers' Federation*,
    Aug. 1943, 2.

63 CYC, *Youth Speaks Out on Citizenship*, 107.

64 NA, CYC, vol. 61, file 8(5a), "Education, Part 3, 1940–1944," Dr Sidney
    E. Smith, "Foreword," *Education, the Keystone of Democracy*, 2.

65 CYC, *Youth Speaks Out on Citizenship*, x.

66 For a discussion of these priorities in the Australian context, see Nicholas
    Brown, *Governing Prosperity: Social Change and Social Analysis in Aus-
    tralia in the 1950s* (Cambridge: Cambridge University Press, 1995), 99.

67 NA, CYC, vol. 40, file 9(3F), Citizenship, "Citizenship," Brief submitted by
    the Women of the University of British Columbia; ibid., "Prospects of
    Citizenship for Young People."

68 For the anti-statist current among Canadian post-war conservatives, see Nancy Christie, "'Look Out for Leviathan'," in this volume.

69 NA, CYC, vol. 40, "Prospects of Citizenship for Young People."

70 Ibid., "Citizenship Report."

71 Here I dissent from the argument advanced in Tillotson, *The Public at Play*, which sees community recreation initiatives as central to the elaboration of the post-war Canadian welfare state. Tillotson (13) identifies as "communitarian" and "socialist" concerns by recreation promoters to constrain state expansion. In reality, this rhetoric was deeply conservative and focused on the preservation of the individual personality, a fact recognized by Tillotson herself (15) in her identification of Premier George Drew, an arch-conservative, as one of the main promoters of community welfare initiatives.

72 CYC, *Youth and Recreation: New Plans for New Times* (Toronto: Ryerson Press, 1946), v.

73 NA, CYC, vol. 30, file C307, "Frame of Reference, Printed Matter," Philip S. Fisher, "Memorandum"; ibid., vol. 61, *Education, The Keystone of Democracy*, 9; Frank P. Fidler, "War Strikes at Our Homes," *United Church Observer*, 15 April 1943.

74 Sidney Smith, "An Interpretation of the Canadian Youth Commission," in *Accent on Action*, 25; ANQ-M, Fonds JOC, P104/181, "Jeunesse et politique nationale."

75 NA, CYC, vol. 40, file 9(3F), Citizenship, "Citizenship," Brief submitted by the Women of the University of British Columbia.

76 Claude Ryan, "La Fédération provinciale des mouvements de jeunesse," *Jeunesse canadienne*, jan. 1948: "Unir sans unifier, grouper sans depersonnaliser, coordonner sans nuire"; ANQ-M, Fonds JOC, P104/181, "Le civisme et la jeunesse."

77 Irene Baird, "We Fail When Youth Says, 'What Now?'" *SN*, 7 Aug. 1943; NA, CYC, vol. 61, *Education the Keystone of Democracy*, 30; ibid., vol. 40, "Report of the Committee on Citizenship and Morale."

78 NA, CYC, vol. 64, file 25(a), Minority Groups, 1939–43, Claris Edwin Silcox, general secretary, Christian Social Council of Canada, *The Challenge of Anti-Semitism to Democracy* (address delivered before Canadian Clubs in western Canada, Jan. 1939, published by the Committee on Jewish Gentile Relationships, Toronto), 6; MMUA, Canadian Youth Congress, box 22, "Publications Received, Canadian Association for Adult Education," R.S. Lambert, *Do You Deserve Democracy? A Letter to a Young Canadian Citizen, Food for Thought*, 9 (Nov. 1940); ibid., Jos. McCulley, headmaster of Pickering College, Newmarket, Ont., *Youth in a World in Transition* (ca. 1938); ibid., *Education: Bulletin no. 3. Youth Makes Tomorrow: A Programme of Thought and Action* (Ontario Committee of the Canadian Youth Commission, n.d.).

79 NA, CYC, vol. 41, Citizenship Briefs, Beryl Truax, "Training for Citizenship in Canadian Schools"; ibid., vol. 61, Sidney Smith, "Foreword," *Education, the Keystone of Democracy*, 2.

80 Ibid., vol. 39, file 4(3F), "Citizenship Report, 1946," George Tuttle, "The Democratic Way with Youth"; ibid., vol. 41, Citizenship Briefs, Beryl Truax, "Training for Citizenship in Canadian Schools"; CYC, *Youth Challenges the Educators* (Toronto: Ryerson Press, 1946), 41; NA, CYC, vol. 66, file 32(5a), Religion 1931–33, 1941–44, Professor H.S. Elliott, "Religious Education and Religious Growth," World Conferences Y.M.C.A., Toronto, 1931; Jean Hunter Morrison, SCM secretary, University of Toronto, "Students Must Choose," *United Church Observer*, 15 Sept. 1941; J.M. Paton, "Youth Must Be Educated for National Service," *SN*, 26 Oct. 1940; AUM, Fonds ACC, P16/04.52, "Commission canadienne de la jeunesse," "Rapport sur le Civisme."

81 NA, CYC, vol. 40, file 9C3F, "Congrès Provincial Congress," 27–28 janvier 1945, Université de Montréal.

82 Ibid., vol. 61, *Education the Keystone of Democracy*, 71; ibid., vol. 40, file 9C3F, "Report of the Committee on Citizenship and Morale."

83 Ibid., vol. 40, file 7C3F, "Prospects of Citizenship for Young People."

84 Ibid., vol 41, Citizenship Briefs, Malcolm Young, "Citizenship Attitudes of Industrial Youth"; AUM, Fonds ACC, P16/O4.26, "Report of the First Annual Meeting and Workshop Sessions of the Canadian Association of Youth Serving Organizations," Montreal, 2 June 1949, Dr George V. Haythorne, "What Citizenship Means to Youth"; CYC, *Youth Speaks Out on Citizenship*, 105–7.

85 NA, CYC, vol. 39, Tuttle, "The Democratic Way with Youth"; ibid., vol 41, Truax, "Training for Citizenship"; ibid., vol. 40, "Prospects of Citizenship for Young People."

86 MMUA, Canadian Youth Congress, box 22, *Education: Bulletin no. 3*; NA, CYC, vol. 39, file "Citizenship Youth Commission Report."

87 NA, CYC, vol. 41, Truax, "Training for Citizenship"; ibid., vol. 40, "Prospects of Citizenship for Young People"; ibid., vol. 66, file 32(5a), Religion 1931–33, 1941–44, "Concerning Religious Instruction in the Public Schools: Yorkminster Discussion Group"(1941); ibid., vol. 61, *Education, the Keystone of Democracy*, 71–80; ibid., vol. 40, "Are We Educating for Citizenship?"; CYC, *Youth Challenges the Educators*, 26.

88 CYC, *Youth Speaks Out on Citizenship*, 104–5.

89 NA, CYC, vol. 40, file 7C3F, "Citizenship Report."

90 Ibid., vol. 39, "Citizenship Youth Commission Report"; ibid., vol. 40, file 9C3F, "The Canadian Youth Commission"; Fernand Jolicoeur, chef du secrétariat de l'Action sociale du diocèse de Joliette, "La jeunesse ouvrière," in *Les Semaines sociales du Canada, 1946: La jeunesse* (Montréal: École Sociale Populaire, 1946), 150.

91 *Accent on Action*, 7; NA, CYC, vol. 40, file 9C3F, "Citizenship," Squadron Leader Gregory Vlastos, "Youth Faces the Future."

92 George Tuttle, "A Commission Is Set Up to Study the Problems of Youth," *United Church Observer*, 1 Dec. 1944.

93 NA, CYC, vol. 31, file 3(3a) Employment Correspondence, Col. W. Line to F.G. Patten, 27 March 1944.

94 Ibid., vol. 40, file 93F, "Report of the Panel on Citizenship," Hamilton & District Youth Conference, 6–7 May 1944; CYC, *Youth and Recreation*, ix.

95 CYC, *Youth Challenges the Educators*, 23; Sidney Smith, "An Interpretation of the Canadian Youth Commission," 25; NA, CYC, vol. 61, *Education, the Keystone of Democracy*, 88–9; Dr H.M. Cassidy, "Planning for Youth at the Provincial Level," *Accent on Action*. According to Catholic Action leader Claude Ryan, "Une bonne partie de nos désirs repose en effet, sur la volonté des adultes, qui ont plus d'experience, qui voient plus loin, et qui nous font souvent attendre" ("Jeunesse d'aujourd'hui," *Jeunesse canadienne*, nov. 1946). The commission's view was not unanimously accepted, however, as there existed a counter-view of the separateness of youth and adults particularly evident among those youth leaders such as Gérard Pelletier active during the 1930s. See, for example, Reginald Boisvert, in "Affaire de Famille?" *JEC*, 11 (juillet-août 1945), who argued, "Le monde étudiant est un." See, for further analysis, Gauvreau, "'The Presence of Heroism in Our Lives.'"

96 CYC, *Youth, Marriage, and the Family* (Toronto: Ryerson Press, 1948), 21.

97 Ibid.

98 For an analysis of these two concepts, which underlay post-war American definitions of juvenile delinquency, see James Gilbert, *A Cycle of Outrage: America's Reaction to the Juvenile Delinquent in the 1950s* (New York: Oxford University Press, 1986).

99 For the erosion of the ideal of the interdependent family among both federal welfare policy-makers and sections of the working class during the 1930s, see Christie, *Engendering the State*, 153–4, 246–7.

100 CYC, *Youth, Marriage and the Family*, 27–8; W.J. Gallagher, "The Christian Family Faces the Post-War World," *United Church Observer*, 1 May 1945. Recent studies by Valverde, "Building Anti-Delinquent Communities," and Mona Gleason, "Psychology and the Construction of the 'Normal' Family in Postwar Canada, 1945–60," *Canadian Historical Review* 78 (Sept. 1997): 442–77, have suggested that the "democratic family" idea was simply empty rhetoric and amounted to nothing more than a reassertion of conservative, patriarchal, and authoritarian family relations, a somewhat surprising conclusion for two scholars so devoted to Foucauldian concepts of discourse. It should be recognized at the

outset that the "democratic family" was, first and foremost, an ideal and not intended as a description of reality. A more rigorous application of Foucault's method would suggest that, while family practices may have remained patriarchal, the language of the "democratic family" amounted to a significant shift in the way in which the discourse of social agencies, media, churches, and governments conceptualized the nature of the marriage, family authority, and patterns of child rearing, which amounted to a significant change in *public* attitudes rather than individual practices.

101 NA, CYC, vol. 40, file 7C3F, "Part II: Are We Educating for Citizenship?"; ibid., vol. 62, file 14(5a), Family Life 1942–44, M'Ledge Moffett, *Youth Looks at Marriage: A Guide for the Study of Marriage and Family Life* (New York: Association Press, 1942), 33–5, 46; Sidney Smith, "An Interpretation of the Canadian Youth Commission," *Accent on Action*, 18.

102 NA, CYC, vol. 41, file Citizenship Briefs, Irene Baird, "The Home – Its Influence on Citizenship Attitudes of Youth."

103 Ibid.

104 Here my analysis diverges from that offered by Valverde, "Building Anti-Delinquent Communities," and Adams, *The Trouble with Normal*, 53–82. The purpose of this essay is not to deny that such conservative attitudes towards juveniles existed, but simply that they were far from being hegemonic. For the American post-war "panic," which stressed the subversive and violent influences of mass media, see Gilbert, *A Cycle of Outrage.*

105 NA, CYC, vol. 67, file 41(5a) YMCA, "'Teen-Aged Youth' – With Special Reference to the 15–19 Year-Old Young Men Who Have Left School and Are Working at Full-Time Jobs," 1 Nov. 1943; Jean Tweed, "Is This a Solution for Juvenile Delinquency?" *SN*, 25 March 1944. One post-war article even commended the much-maligned comic books for teaching proper civic values. "Dick Tracy," stated Ruth Hobberlin in 1946, "stresses the importance of law and order," while she noted that Mussolini and Hitler had banned comics such as Superman and Flash Gordon because they were protectors of minority groups. See Hobberlin, "Why Blame Comics, Movies, etc., for the Young's Delinquency?" *SN*, 16 Nov. 1946.

106 "What Can We Do about Juvenile Delinquency?" (address delivered at a meeting of the Ontario Federation of Home and School Associations, Royal York Hotel, Toronto, 12 April 1943) in NA, CYC, vol. 61, *Education, the Keystone of Democracy*, 76, 83, 94.

107 John R. Seeley, R. Alexander Sim, and Elizabeth W. Loosley, *Crestwood Heights* (Toronto: University of Toronto Press, 1956), 112–13; Frederick Elkin and William A. Westley, "The Myth of Adolescent Culture," *American Sociological Review* 20 (1955): 682.

108 Seeley, Sim, and Loosley, *Crestwood Heights*, 114.

109 The sociologist John Seeley, the principal author of *Crestwood Heights*, had undertaken a number of research studies for the Canadian Youth Commission.

110 "Problèmes de vie sentimentale des étudiants canadiens," *Cahiers d'Action catholique* (CAC), 154 (juin-juillet-août 1953): 283: "laissés a eux-mêmes, les étudiants actuels s'élaborent une fausse synthèse doctrinale sur la sexualité, l'amour, la femme et l'homme, le mariage et la chasteté à partir de la propagande moderne et les slogans en cours."

111 La Rédaction, "Presentation," "Les voies du cœur en éducation," CAC, jan.-fev. 1954, 129; Agatha E. Sidlauskas, "L'adolescente et son premier amour," ibid., 135–8.

112 Roch Duval, "La fréquentation des adolescents," CAC, jan.-fev. 1954, 148: "La decouverte de l'intimité qui peut s'établir entre un adolescent et une adolescente présuppose un certain degré d'alterité atteint par l'un et l'autre. Cette découverte est une manifestation d'un commencement d'intégration à la société; par ce genre de fréquentations propres aux adolescents apparait un nouveau type de communauté qui comporte un degré de responsabilité et des possibilités de développement inconnues jusqu'ici dans la vie de l'enfant."

113 Sidlauskas, "L'adolescente et son premier amour," 137; Sœur Gabriel-Lalement et Sœur Marie-de-Sainte-Jeanne-Louise, "L'Adolescence, cet âge riche," CAC, oct. 1953, 35–40.

114 For the Protestant churches in the post-war period, see Nancy Christie, "Sacred Sex: The United Church and the Privatization of the Family in Post-War Canada," in Christie, ed., *Households of Faith: Family, Gender, and Community in Canada* (Montreal and Kingston: McGill-Queen's University Press, 2002); for the Catholic Church, see Michael Gauvreau, "The Rise of Personalist Feminism: Catholicism and the Marriage-Preparation Movement in Quebec, 1940–1966," ibid.

115 Sidlauskas, "L'Adolescente et son premier amour"; John Nash, "It's Time *Father* Got Back in the *Family*," *Maclean's Magazine*, 12 May 1956; ANQ-M, Fonds Jeunesse étudiante catholique, P65/3, Maurice Lafond, "Cours sur l'Action catholique," 1951; ibid., P65/SS2, SSS1, D4/2, André Juneau, "Le problème de la J.E.C. des jeunes," ca. 1955. It should be noted in this context that Mary Louise Adams dates much of the sex advice for teens to a period just after 1954; on the other side of the coin, fears of homosexuality tended to become more prevalent when individual self-identity was defined as a product of sexuality. See Adams, *The Trouble with Normal*, 83–106.

116 Sidney Katz, "Is Going Steady Ruining Our Teen-Agers?" *Maclean's Magazine*, 8 Jan. 1959.

117 Ibid.

118 In this context, it is not without significance that Arthur Marwick's
     recent *The Sixties: Cultural Revolution in Britain, France, Italy, and the
     United States, c. 1958–c. 1974* (Oxford: Oxford University Press, 1998)
     posits the beginning of the culture of the 1960s in the waning years of
     the 1950s decade. See also Katz, "Is Going Steady Ruining Our Teen-
     Agers?"

DENYSE BAILLARGEON

"We admire modern parents"

The École des Parents du Québec and the Post-war Quebec Family, 1940–1959[1]

In a similar way to English-speaking North American societies, Quebec during the 1930s and 1940s was confronted by profound economic and social transformations that aroused considerable anxieties around the subject of the family and its ability to deal with the "modern" world. These apprehensions induced the Catholic Church to undertake a number of initiatives to attempt to rechristianize the family,[2] but they also led to the formation of the École des Parents du Québec (ÉDP), an association of lay people that aimed to solidify the family by diffusing new methods of education and defending the interests of the family in the public realm. While this organization was less widely diffused than the Service de Préparation au Mariage, launched by the Jeunesse Ouvrière Catholique in 1939, the ÉDP nonetheless marked one of the first attempts undertaken by the new francophone middle classes, trained in the social sciences, to compete with the church on a terrain that the latter had historically monopolized. As a number of historians have observed, the place occupied by the laity in Catholic Action movements eventually eroded the power of the clergy and turned the Catholic vision of marriage towards more secular notions of family and conjugal relationships.[3] However, at the beginning of the 1940s, the activists in these associations remained loyal to the notion that the church was still competent to dominate the terrain of family relations, an idea that the ÉDP was the first to contest.

Founded in December 1939 at the prompting of Claudine-S. Vallerand,[4] an educator who operated a private kindergarten that followed the active learning method,[5] the ÉDP attacked the prerogative of the schools, then controlled by the church, to play the pre-eminent role in child rearing. Denouncing the system of boarding schools, where young people lived for many years in physical separation from their families, the ÉDP aimed to "return to the family its former prestige" (redonner à la famille son prestige)[6] by convincing parents to reclaim a role that they had abdicated to teachers, who were usually clergy. In contrast to the affirmations of the Franciscans, who founded the magazine *La Famille* in 1937, the ÉDP was insistent on the fact that it was not within the competence of the "Church as teacher" (l'Église enseignante) to organize and group families. Rather, it was up to those primarily responsible for children – namely, the parents – who were best placed to identify their needs.[7] To the claims by the church that it possessed competent expertise on questions of family and education because of its divine mission, the ÉDP counterposed the findings of psychologists, who insisted upon the overriding importance of the parent-child relationship in structuring the human personality and thus denied the church's pretentions that it could act as the trustee of, or even the substitute for, parents. The "discoveries of modern psychology," which it promoted, thus served as a platform in an attempt to free the family from clerical tutelage. If the ÉDP was ultimately unable to act convincingly as a representative of families, it nonetheless contributed to the diffusion of new standards of childhood education, both among its own members and in the wider public. An analysis of its public statements and of the correspondence that it carried on for six years in the Montreal daily *Le Devoir* demonstrates that its goal of family emancipation rested upon the defence of democratic values which presupposed an increase in parental, and especially maternal, responsibilities towards children. At the same time, however, it articulated a new vision of childhood based upon respect for the integrity of each individual, and it encouraged the cultivation of greater intimacy between generations. In linking education to the training of future citizens, the ÉDP also inaugurated a public debate on these issues. While the church always attempted to command respect by virtue of the fact that it was the only advocate and guide for parents and because it had occupied practically the entire discursive space on these questions, the ÉDP promoted the emergence of a rival public discourse, including one from mothers themselves.

SCHOOL FOR PARENTS

Two articles signed by Claudine Vallerand in the *Revue dominicaine* at the end of the 1930s allow some insight into the origins of the ÉDP.[8] These articles reveal that the founder of the ÉDP had very little regard for the school in the process of child rearing and she had many criticisms of an educational system that, in her estimation, was affected with sclerosis. Thus, in "École et foyer," Vallerand opened with a statement that the chief purpose of the school was not to form the child but to instruct, and contrary to what parents and teachers believed, it had never possessed this "magical power."⁹ In fact, she maintained that each moment of a child's life was a stage in the process of formation, so that each child was, by the time of entering school, already influenced and conditioned by a host of lived experiences: "We are convinced," she unequivocally maintained, "that it is impossible for teachers to compensate for what is deficient with our children, or to undo what has been achieved. *And in most circumstances, this is immensely reassuring to us.* [Nous sommes ... convaincus ... qu'il est impossible aux maîtres de refaire chez nos petits tout ce qui est mal fait, ou de défaire ce qui est réussi. *Et ceci nous est d'un grand réconfort dans bien des circonstances*]"¹⁰ Furthermore, she declared that children's "natural" setting of life was the family, in which they spent most of their time,¹¹ and not the school, and it was thus in the family where they must learn "to adapt and integrate themselves, [because] it is there that they prepare themselves for that most serious and complex role of citizen which they will be called upon to play in adult society [à s'adapter, à s'intégrer, [car] c'est là qu'ils se préparent au rôle plus grave et plus complexe de citoyen qu'ils seront appelés à jouer dans la société adulte]."¹² Thus Vallerand concluded that "if education must be reformed, and it was high time that it happened [s'il doit y avoir des réformes en éducation, et il est grand temps qu'il y en ait],"¹³ such reforms "must first occur ... within the bosom of the family [elles doivent naître d'abord ... au sein même de la famille]" through an enhanced awareness by parents of their "responsibility towards [their] children and towards [the] nation" and by a thoroughgoing reform of their "methods of education."¹⁴

According to Vallerand, reforms of the school system could only be accomplished after and in answer to the needs and expectations of parents, and only under this condition could the school "retain the right to collaborate in the appropriate manner in the education of our children [conserver le droit de collaborer dans la mesure qui lui revient à l'éducation de nos enfants]."¹⁵ Alluding to the "obsolete attitudes" prevalent among parents and teachers on the subject of education, she condemned the "daily dose of moralizing" (moralisation quotidienne) and the "sermonizing" (prêches) that went on in school, and she asserted that parents had "the right to require that the school adopt an up-to-date attitude towards our children, until it can formulate a better approach [le droit d'exiger de l'école qu'elle adopte envers nos enfants l'attitude de notre époque, en attendant qu'elle puisse en concevoir une meilleure]."[16] In concluding her article, Vallerand insisted upon the need for an intelligent school, by which she meant one adapted to the needs of a modern society, in what pertained both to curriculum and to pedagogical methods, and open to all facets of life and the world: "A school that does not have the courage to face life's realities, a teacher complacently abstracted from all the world's problems," she added, "should not have the right to cooperate in educating our children [Une école qui n'a pas le courage de faire face au réalisme de la vie, un maître qui se complaît dans un détachement total des problèmes du monde, ne devrait pas avoir le droit de coopérer à l'éducation de nos enfants]."[17] In another article explaining the objectives and methods of her kindergarten, Vallerand went even further in openly refuting the notion that a religious vocation constituted a badge of competence in a teacher: "You will allow me to underscore," she stated, "that the religious vocation alone does not infuse a person with knowledge [On me permettra en passant de souligner que la vocation religieuse à elle seule, ne confère à personne la science infuse]."[18]

What these articles illustrate is that Vallerand wanted her position to be completely understood. The firm tone of her articles – her barely veiled criticisms of the school system and its teachers, most of whom were nuns or brothers, the constant use of the possessive (*our* children), the reiteration of parental rights, the relegation of the school to the status of a collaborator of the family (rather than the reverse) – permits no doubt as to the meaning of her message: that the school must stop considering itself the exclusive institution in the child's formation and that parents must cease to passively prop up this myth. In fact, she believed that parents must urgently realize that the development of the nation depended upon the worth of its future citizens and that, consequently, the upbringing of the latter was a serious responsibility incumbent upon parents. Vallerand's articles expressed the core of the ÉDP's program: to awaken the responsibility of parents to the training of their children by making them understand the primary and fundamental aspect of their role of educator and to counter the "prejudice" that "the school forms the human being in collaboration with the family [l'école form[e] l'homme en collaboration avec la famille]."[19]

Thus the ÉDP was established in order to induce parents to assume the primary place in the education of their children, thus "preserving the rights of the family over the child."[20] Its first objective was to establish a "mutual school of educators, composed of fathers and mothers who wanted to take on their family, social, and national duties and determined to seek mutual enlightenment for themselves [école mutuelle d'éducateurs, composée de pères et de mères désireux d'assurer leurs responsabilités familiales, sociales et nationales, et décidés à s'éclairer mutuellement],"[21] but the ÉDP also intended to diffuse new educational models throughout all social classes in order to break, as it bluntly expressed the matter, the vicious circle of "incompetent parents, mediocre children; mediocre children, incompetent parents."[22] As a result, it sought to rely upon the advice of childhood education experts, especially psychologists, and to reach an audience that extended beyond its own membership. In addition to a series of courses and lectures that it organized each year and the magazines that it published – *Nos enfants*, distributed between 1940 and 1942 as a supplement to the Franciscan publication *La Famille*, and *L'École des parents*, followed by the *Revue de l'École des parents* (1949–59), intended solely for its members[23] – from 1943 onwards it broadcasted a program called *Radio-Parents* on the Radio-Canada network, where it answered questions from the public. A second radio program, *Le théâtre de Radio-Parents*, launched in 1950, dramatized the problems faced by an "average" family of four children, whose father was a clerk in a hardware store. According to the ÉDP itself, the choice of a "lower middle class" family was a deliberate one: this lower-middle-class was considered most representative because it combined certain traits characteristic of both the bourgeoisie and the working class, thus increasing the program's audience.[24] Finally, with the complete support of Germaine Bernier, editor of the women's section of *Le Devoir* during the 1940s and 1950s, the ÉDP maintained an ongoing correspondence in the daily between 1948 and 1955, an activity that will be analyzed later in this essay. Although *Le Devoir* was read mainly by an elite, the fact remains that the ÉDP was able to reach an audience beyond its actual membership, and through its radio programming and its contribution to the rural magazines *Paysanna* and *Terre et foyer*, it even reached people from the lower classes of Quebec society.

The ÉDP was thus able to diffuse its message fairly extensively, but without a list of its members, it is difficult to determine what type of parents this new educational institution drew into its ranks or how many of these people actively contributed to its operations.[25] The composition of its first board of directors, formed of several teachers, a doctor, a psychologist, a lawyer, and their "wives," clearly reveals, however, that impetus for the organization came from the middle classes.[26] From her standpoint, Claudine Vallerand sought to assemble a certain elite around her project because, in her estimation, "in the difficult and tragic moments of history, it is only such an elite that knows how to react, it alone has the capacity to draw the multitude of the orthodox along in its wake [dans les moments difficiles et tragiques de l'histoire, elle seule sait réagir, elle seule peut entrainer à sa suite l'armée des biens-pensants]."[27] However, her plans for the ÉDP rested upon a fairly broad definition of who in fact constituted the elite:

From my perspective, it [the elite] has nothing to do with social rank, wealth, culture, or erudition. What constitutes it is nobility of soul, the natural capacity of a human being to rise above himself to generously embrace the common good, a future for all. We rest all our hopes upon this elite. If we can recruit it among all classes of those in society who are active, devoted, and anxious to serve, our action will encompass the whole spectrum of improvement.[28]
[Elle (l'élite) n'a rien à voir avec le rang social, la fortune, la culture, ou l'érudition. Ce qui la constitue, c'est la noblesse d'âme, la capacité naturelle d'un être de s'élever au-dessus de lui-même pour embrasser généreusement le bien commun, l'avenir de tous. Sur cette élite, nous fondons tous nos espoirs. Si nous pouvons la recruter dans toutes les classes de la société active, devouée anxieuse de servir, notre action embrassera alors le champ immense du bien.]

Such a definition was in fact fairly close to that of Catholic Action, which aimed to form a sort of "enlightened" vanguard in each of the social settings where it was active, including the working class. One of the primary strategies of groups such as the JOC or the LOC was to identify persons endowed with those human and spiritual qualities that would enable them to be leaders who would then help to bring "illumination" to those most immediately around them. From their perspective, belonging to a particular social class was not an obstacle to being recruited into the movement: to futher its aim of penetrating all social environments, the church had need of male and female collaborators drawn from all social strata. Similarly, for the ÉDP, it was of central importance to rally all those of goodwill, for it was only in this way that it could hope to make its ideas known and accepted. Further, it was the only way to advance its claim to be a representative institution: even though the ÉDP concentrated upon parent education, it also envisaged becoming, over the long term, an effective pressure group. "If we are still a school," declared the organization in 1950, "we want also, in a larger sense, to act as the advocate for families and in order to do this, we need the weight of numbers behind us [si nous sommes encore une école, nous voulons aussi pouvoir parler au nom des familles en général et, pour cela, il nous faut le nombre]."[29]

The existence of a second École de Parents, founded in Quebec City in 1943 (L'École des Parents *de* Québec), this one subordinate "to the authority and doctrine of the church,"[30] perhaps accounts for why the École des Parents *du* Québec felt the need, at the beginning of the 1950s, to claim the status of sole representative of parents in the public realm. However, from that date, the ÉDP certainly encouraged the formation of affiliates outside Montreal so as to extend its core of leaders and influence. At the beginning of 1949, within the framework of the ongoing chronicle of its activities in *Le Devoir* that it had undertaken a few months previously, the ÉDP published a series of articles that sought to explain its origin and purpose, and where it insisted that its objective was always to "serve the needs of all parents, without distinction of class or social setting [desservir tous les parents, sans distinction de classe ou de milieu]," that since its formation, it had "scrupulously sought ... to remain accessible *to all parents* [scrupuleusement tenu ... à rester accessible *à tous les parents*]" and that its founders had aspired from the beginning "to launch a vast movement, a mass enlistment by all the parents of Quebec [de lancer un vaste mouvement, une levée en masse de tous les parents du Québec]."[31]

The intention of the ÉDP to orient itself towards a form of political action did not simply indicate that there was a struggle for legitimacy brewing between the two organizations; rather, it revealed a wish to have the problems facing the modern family publicly discussed and to influence public authorities to take action on behalf of families. For the ÉDP, as for a number of other groups who worried about the fate of the family, society during the 1940s and 1950s evinced "materialism and decadence" and was "organized against the family and the child."[32] To effectively fulfill their role to adequately prepare the younger generation to face the challenges of the future, parents needed "a society within which they and their children will be recognized as human persons worthy of respect ... a society based upon the moral law, imagined and organized by parents, and directed towards the complete flowering of the child's personality [une société au sein de laquelle eux et leurs enfants seront reconnus comme des personnes humaines dignes de respect ... une société basée sur la loi morale, pensée et organisée par les parents, en faveur de l'épanouissement intégral de l'enfant]."[33] The achievement of such a reorganization of society could not be accomplished without the uniting of parents "of all classes, social settings, and diverse professions [de toutes les classes, de tous les milieux, des professions les plus diverses]," because "in a democratic nation" only an association that "represented the whole of society" could influence the political order.[34]

The ÉDP was convinced that grouping individuals, whether parents, employers, workers or even feminists, into organizations directed to the defence of particular interests would contribute to the enrichment of democracy, because these groups would allow the expression of legitimate interests which without such institutions might be stifled: "It

is through these [associations] that social life flourishes in a well-func-
tioning democratic society, because their very existence enables the
citizen to overcome the rigidities of the system and the stifling constraints of conformity [C'est par elles [les associations] que la vie s'é-
panouit dans une société démocratique bien comprise, hors de l'esprit
de système et des cadres étouffants du conformisme]."[35] The ÉDP reckoned that the mere right to vote or membership in a political party was
an insufficient guarantee for the effective expression of the popular
will. True citizenship was a function of participation in organizations
that could, far more effectively than individuals, act to defend their
rights and interests in the political realm and even obtain the recognition of "the right and the competence to collaborate in managing the
affairs of the nation [le droit et la compétence de collaborer à la gestion
des affaires de la nation]"[36] from the state itself. From this standpoint,
in which democracy and participation were equated, being a parent
represented a focal point of identity that transcended class divisions.
"Love of children," stated René Vallerand in a speech delivered to the
first annual meeting of the Fédération canadienne des écoles de parents
in 1953,[37] "is perhaps, of all cultural influences, that which is most
powerful in creating social harmony [L'amour pour les enfants est
peut-être de toutes les influences, la plus créatrice d'harmonie]."[38] Like
the maternal feminists who earlier in the twentieth century justified
their social involvement through the claim that, despite class differences, women were united by a common concern for children,[39] the
leaders of the ÉDP advocated a type of "parentalism," basing their call
for parents to unite in groups and engage in political action on a sense
of common responsibility to promote the welfare of all children: "It
[the parent association] is premised upon this deep and acute feeling of
being both mother and father to one's own children and to those of all
other parents and *at the same time* to desire the greatest good for one's
own and others [Il (le regroupement des parents) suppose ce sentiment
profond et aigu d'être à la fois père et mère de ses propres enfants et
de ceux de tous les autres parents et de vouloir *en même temps*, pour
les siens et les autres, le plus grand bien]."[40]

   The ÉDP, in its attempt to rally parents to its ranks and by asserting
that families should present their demands to the state on questions
such as housing, the reform of the school system, and fiscal policy, conveyed the message that the church either did not hold or no longer held
the necessary expertise to represent families; nor did it possess, as it
had often claimed, the competence to deal with their problems. In a
society that had become more complex, and even hostile to the family,
it was better to dispense with such intermediaries and use the machinery of the democratic system in order to be heard. Despite these efforts,

the ÉDP was never able to mobilize a group of adherents large enough to transform itself into a pressure group; however, it nonetheless paved the way for the Fédération des Unions de familles, which succeeded it at the end of the 1950s and became a key reprsentative in dealing with the Quebec government in the 1960s, even securing the creation of a ministry of the family.[41] During the two decades in which the ÉDP was active, its efforts were more concentrated on the education of parents, in order to provide them with greater competence in the training of better citizens.

MAKING NEW PARENTS AND NEW CHILDREN
FOR A NEW SOCIETY

For thousands of Quebecers, World War II brought a return of economic prosperity. However, the leaders of the ÉDP, in common with the nationalist, religious, and intellectual elite, interpreted this rising standard of living as going hand in hand with a weakening of morality and the consequent aggravation of family problems. "More than ever," claimed the ÉDP manifesto, "child rearing poses a problem, as hygienists are concerned about the physical debility of youth; undisciplined behaviour troubles family peace; the morality of childhood is in decline; the authority of teachers is called into question; people complain that young people arriving at the stage of earning their own living lack courage, initiative, perseverance, and social sense [Plus que jamais, l'éducation des enfants pose un problème, les hygiénistes s'alarment de la débilité physique des jeunes; l'indiscipline trouble les familles; la moralité de l'enfance est en baisse; l'autorité des éducateurs est compromise; on se plaint que les jeunes, le moment venu de gagner leur vie, manquent d'audace, d'initiative, de persévérance, de sens social]."[42] In this cultural environment, families were increasingly preoccupied with securing a rising standard of living through the progress of science and technology, and they adhered to a lifestyle centred on consumption. This, in the estimation of the founders of the ÉDP, constituted a major obstacle to the family's ability to fulfill its central role in preparing children for the future. As a result, these family activists portrayed the future in highly ominous terms: "In the post-war world," claimed Germaine Bernier, whose opinions echoed the views of the ÉDP, "life will be more difficult than in any previous era. Only those of strong and competent character will be able to look out for themselves and to grasp their own destinies. The others will perpetuate the generations of derelicts, whose growing number is directly proportional to the degree of material progress [Dans le monde de l'après-guerre qui sera peut-être plus difficile à vivre qu'aucune autre époque ... seuls les caractères forts et les compétents pourront se débrouiller et prendre leur sort en main. Les autres vont continuer les générations d'épaves qui sont de plus en plus nombreuses, semble-t-il, à mesure que le fameux progrès matériel s'intensifie]."[43]

Wartime "material progress" thus represented a threat for the family insofar as it seemed to sap the moral fibre of both parents and children. The immediate post-war years did not ease such worries, since the family now appeared to be literally invaded by a host of external influences, especially by the media, which were viewed as competing with parents for authority: "The family circle once had a protective and directive power that was not even subject to discussion; but today, not only do external influences function at the same level as those of the family, but the former actually penetrate into the family circle through the radio, the newspaper, and magazines of all descriptions."[44] Families, when faced with this "modern world" literally "bubbling" with ideas, were compelled more than ever to make intelligent choices,[45] and in order to adapt to change without losing certain fundamental values, thus avoiding social disorder, they were expected to rely increasingly upon the aid of "experts." Because post-war society seemed to contain so many currents of innovation, it required a new style of parents so that the rising generation could adapt in a "healthy manner" (sainement), in other words, without lapsing into anarchy. Therefore, one of the ÉDP's most important self-assigned tasks was the making of competent new parents by instructing them in the fundamentals of "modern psychology."

According to Mona Gleason, the war and post-war era marked a favourable conjuncture in the rise of the profession of psychology both in Canada and in North America generally.[46] For those who lived through it, this period appeared dominated by an acclerating pace of technological and social change, which they believed were sources of instability and social tension, and by political insecurity engendered by the Cold War. To absorb all these changes, to preserve democracy and arrest the diffusion of subversive ideas – namely, Communism – as well as to sustain continuing economic development through consumption, North American society relied upon a stable family, one satisfied with its lot and able to produce zealous citizens committed to democratic ideals.[47] Psychologists, because they claimed to understand the characteristics of a "normal" personality, one that was well adapted to this democratic society and the means to be followed in cultivating such a personality, seemed to hold the key to both individual and collective well-being. By insisting upon the importance of the family and family education for elaborating healthy, mature, and balanced personalities and upon the primary role of mothers in this task, psychologists promoted a specific family type: the nuclear family, founded upon clearly defined gender roles. Such families were considered essential to the stability of post-war society.

The leaders of the ÉDP, whether they themselves were psychologists or simply called themselves "educators," relied heavily upon the psychological theories of their Anglo-Canadian and American counterparts to legitimate their intrusion into the family under the rubric of specialists and advisers. The ÉDP defined itself as a group of parents who had "raised themselves above their legitimate concerns as parents to a wider concern for the improvement of education in our society [élevés au-dessus de la légitime préoccupation de leur propre rôle de parents jusqu'au souci plus large du relèvement de l'éducation chez nous]."[48] In other words, the ÉDP had conferred upon itself a mandate to galvanize parents into an awareness of the importance of their responsibilities and to train them to become more competent in their role. From this perspective, while the ÉDP did not overtly claim the status of "expert," it sought to diffuse their ideas. However, in the context of Quebec, where religious belief was still widespread, this project required a number of accommodations that coloured the "psychological" discourse promulgated by the ÉDP.

In the estimation of the ÉDP, there was no doubting the fact that if parents were to blame for deficiencies in their children's education, they were also in a position to remedy these problems, so long as they were properly led and instructed.[49] To fulfill this educative duty, which had become extremely complex, it was no longer possible to improvise, nor could one rely solely upon tradition or "Providence," or simply adopt a laissez-faire attitude in the hope that crises would pass. Faced with the new problems posed by child rearing, parents must firmly reject the prescriptions of the past which were deemed obsolete, and resolve to "learn" the skills of parenting. This meant preparing themselves through familiarization with the "methods" and "techniques" of "modern" education adapted to new social conditions, a training that they could easily acquire because of the sheer variety and accessibility of this type of information.[50] In short, if modernity threatened the family, it could also, by offering parents the appropriate conceptual tools and theories that would ensure better child rearing, prove itself to be a powerful ally in assuring the family's preservation. If "modern" methods of communication contaminated the inner life of the family, they could also, following the example of the ÉDP itself, become the major vehicle for the wide diffusion of these new psychological ideas, thus inoculating the family against the very dangers that the new media incarnated.[51]

The ÉDP was convinced that defective practices of child rearing stemmed from the fact that parents were basically ignorant of the very nature of the child. Therefore the psychologists attached to the organization devoted a good deal of energy to rooting out what they termed certain "prejudices" and to propagating a new concept of childhood and of parent-child relations that, in their estimation, represented the key to successful parenting. Founded upon what they confidently termed "the discoveries of modern psychology," this vision rested upon a definition of the child as a being in perpetual evolution, different from adults, who had reached maturity, but nonetheless possessing an individuality and a separate personality that adults had to accept and respect.[52] Reversing an older notion of family relationships that had been propagated by the church, the ÉDP affirmed that children had rights, especially the right to achieve freedom, and that parents had obligations towards them, especially the duty to learn how to recognize the different stages of childhood development in order to adequately address each individual child's specific psychological needs.[53] As Thérèse Gouin-Decarie, one of the pioneers of psychology in Quebec, explained, a good knowledge of the basic elements of early childhood psychology would allow parents to know "who exactly the child is, what are his immediate needs, what he is capable of, what can be required of him, and what should not be asked of him [ce qu'est cet enfant, ce dont il a besoin aujourd'hui, ce dont il est capable, ce que l'on peut exiger de lui, ce qu'il ne faut pas lui demander]."[54] By being more cognizant of the characteristics of childhood and of the specific features linked to each stage in the child's development, parents would now be able to raise their offspring with a precise knowledge of their limits and capacities, giving them sufficient freedom to realize their potential. Armed with this knowledge, they would be able to avoid being excessively severe or overly demanding, and of equal significance, the new psychology would remove the lurking stigma of failure from parents by now defining certain types of disobedient behaviour as entirely normal. For the wife of psychologist Georges Dufresne, herself trained in this discipline, it was infinitely more reassuring for a parent to know "that children [are] normally stubborn, independent and ungrateful during certain periods of their growth [que les enfants (sont) normalement entêtés, indépendants, ingrats durant certaines périodes de leur croissance]."[55] Thus the knowledge of infantile personality development provided by psychology was proffered as a way of defusing tense family situations that might prove to be distressing and calming the apprehensions of parents. However, the definition of precise rules of behaviour for each stage of childhood had the effect of inducing parents to trust a normative framework to measure the value of their educational methods, which could easily foster greater parental anxiety when their children did not seem to be following the "normal" trajectory and could make parents feel guilty for the "failures" (ratés) that this developmental standard now allowed them to identify.

However, the new psychological theories promoted by the ÉDP were themselves not free from contradictions. For example, they affirmed, on the one hand, that all children without exception went through certain stages – "we don't skip grades here, [on ne saute pas ses classes ici]"[56] averred Claude and Manon Mailhiot, the hosts of the Radio-Parents broadcast – a premise that of itself presented a homogenized image of childhood. On the other, they maintained that each child possessed his or her own personality, different from those of his or her siblings. In addition to acquiring a proper understanding of the guiding principles of "modern psychology," parents were urged to closely observe each of their children, to adapt their educational methods to each child so as to ensure the full development of his or her personality.[57] This was an enterprise that had to be undertaken from the moment of birth, for according to post-war psychologists, the early years of life were the decisive period for the healthy and balanced development of the child. As a zealous defender of family education, the ÉDP strongly endorsed this idea: "It is primarily the home that forms the emotions, the spirit, and the body of the child," stated the Le Devoir chroniclers of the ÉDP's activities.[58]

In common with post-war psychological experts, the ÉDP thus considered that environment, rather than heredity, shaped the character of the child. This belief allowed the organization to state that it was possible to change the results of a child's upbringing by modifying parental behaviour and by transforming the nature of the parents' relationships with the child.[59] The child's environment was thus considered the key factor, responsible for both the "successes" and the "failures" in education; indeed, it was regarded as more responsible for deficiencies because according to the statistics reported in the ÉDP's magazine, "strong personalities are from 60–80 per cent the product of their environment ... the rest is their own individual contribution [les personnalités fortes sont déjà (sic) 60% à 80% leur milieu ... le reste étant leur apport personnel]," while "weak personalities ... are 90–99 per cent the products of their family environments [personnalités faibles ... sont 90 à 99% leur milieu]."[60] The term "family surroundings" (milieu familial) most often meant the mother, assigned primary responsibility for child rearing. In the estimation of the ÉDP, so important was the mother's contribution to the child's personality that her role as an educator must at all times take precedence over household chores.[61] More than ever, women were asked to identify with their maternal role, regarded by post-war psychology as the principal dynamic of the social adaptation of their children; as well, social problems such as juvenile delinquency or a "defective" (faussée) sexual education, prime evidence of individual maladaptation, were attributed to failures in maternal education.[62] If childhood experts were prepared to revolutionize educational methods, they were far from advocating fundamental changes in parents' gender roles. Indeed, what they promoted was in fact a reinforcement of traditional women's roles. While it is true that fathers were called upon more and more to involve themselves with the family in order to ensure that boys developed well-balanced personalities,[63] these expectations did not move outside traditional conceptions of male identity. According to the psychological categories of the ÉDP, fatherhood should be expressed through a "manly" love for one's children, a tempered exercise of authority, and a punctilious fulfillment of household tasks.[64] Both the psychologists and the ÉDP reckoned that only women possessed natural predispositions for child rearing; however, because they rejected the notion that this quality was instinctive, they believed that women could never completely develop these aptitudes without being taught by specialists.

The importance that was attached to childhood stages of development and the emphasis placed upon the need to respect the individuality of children and to their right to "a happy childhood, ... free from those emotional upsets so harmful to their psychological equlibrium [à une enfance heureuse, ... exempte de ces chocs affectifs si nocifs à l'équilibre psychologique],"[65] in turn enjoined parents, especially mothers, to display a great deal of patience, consideration, understanding, flexibility, and self-discipline in their relationships with their children.[66] The progressivist notions of education that underwrote the new concepts of childhood and parent-child relations presupposed that parents themselves would exemplify the highest virtues but, above all, that they would hold their authoritarian instincts in check in order to create a "democratic" family atmosphere characterized by tolerance and freedom. "In former times," observed psychologist Charles Gill, "the adult's authority over the child and the adolescent was implacable and dominating. It was the age where the strongest ruled; there was little place for give-and-take, for different viewpoints between the generations. Parents arbitrarily imposed themselves ... Happily, we have realized that domineering, 'breaking the child's will,' and making oneself feared are grievous errors [Autrefois, l'autorité de l'adulte sur l'enfant et l'adolescent était implacable et dominatrice. C'était la loi du plus fort. Il n'y avait pas de place pour des échanges humains, des points de vue différents d'une génération à l'autre. Les parents s'imposaient brusquement ... Heureusement, on s'est aperçu que dominer, 'casser les caractères,' et se faire craindre, c'était une erreur]."[67] These excesses of parental authority were regarded as extremely serious "errors" in a post-war climate where psychological studies equated authoritarianism with the very indoctrination and dictatorship that had characterized those fascist regimes which were blamed for causing World War II, and which continued to sustain the totalitarianism of the Soviet bloc.[68] By contrast, the defence of democracy required that the family rest on the foundation of democracy. Future citizens, psychologists argued, must be introduced at an early age to democracy's principles and mode of operation, so that they would learn to exercise their fundamental freedoms in harmony with the values of discrimination and restraint.

The ÉDP's promotion of a less rigid family education, however, did not imply that the individual was freed from all restraint, and its psychologists were always concerned to make clear that freedom did not mean licence, disorder, or undisciplined behaviour.[69] Rather, as Charles Gill expressed the matter, freedom was the product of an interior sentiment: "The child who is truly free experiences inside himself the awareness that he can act, decide, think, and create freely without any morbid fear of being criticized, blamed, or rejected [L'enfant véritablement libre éprouve intérieurement qu'il peut agir, décider, penser et créer librement sans crainte morbide d'être critiqué, blamé, rejeté]."[70] A more liberalized system of child rearing thus must encourage the development of creativity and judgment, qualities essential to the exercise of citizenship; but of equal importance, the child must learn to understand to "be bound by the demands of his parents, of society, and at any given moment, to the demands of his moral conscience [soumettre aux exigences de ses parents, de la société et le moment venu, aux exigences de sa conscience morale]."[71] The child's initiation into freedom within the bosom of the family thus also included an apprenticeship in respect for the social order. In contrast to the tenets of traditional education, post-war psychologists maintained that discipline must be exercised with the objective of assuring "intellectual, social, emotional, and moral maturity [l'épanouissement intellectuel, social, affectif et moral]"[72] of children and was not something that could be simply imposed from outside. The flowering of the individual personality in fact demanded that children be allowed to "collaborate" in their own education in order to freely accept the rules of behaviour laid down by parents, so that these duties would not become a source of frustration that could lead to revolt.[73] The interiorization of obedience was therefore a key component of the preparation for life in a democratic society, for as the ÉDP affirmed, "the individual is subject to orders during his whole life [car, toute sa vie, il faut se soumettre à des ordres]."[74] "If the child learns to obey for the common good of the family," concluded one psychologist, "he will become a good citizen ready to collaborate for the common good of the collectivity [Si l'enfant apprend à obéir pour le bien commun de la famille, il deviendra un bon citoyen prêt à collaborer au bien-être de toute la collectivité]."[75]

Despite its language, which evoked freedom for children, the ÉDP, like many post-war psychologists, did not reject the idea of parental authority. In its estimation, the pairing of freedom and authority or freedom and discipline did not constitute a dichotomy: the two attitudes were in fact perfectly compatible insofar as each sought to form self-disciplined adults, able to "act properly without supervision [de se bien conduire, en dehors de toute surveillance],"[76] and aware of the constraints that life in a democratic society placed upon individual freedom. The ÉDP was most emphatic about the concept that children should not simply be allowed to do "whatever they wanted" (n'importe quoi), but that parents should guide them in an apprenticeship of freedom, which always presupposed a certain measure of authority.[77] The ÉDP psychologists nonetheless imposed limits upon parental authority. In order for it to attain its goals, the flourishing of the human personality through the acceptance of constraints, parental authority should rely upon love and affection that were both tangible and unimpeachable, and it not be exercised in a vengeful manner, capriciously or dictatorially, but according to the rules of justice and fairness, always considering the age of the child and the gravity of the misdemeanour.[78] "The parent who loves well always punishes well [Qui aime bien châtie bien]," was in many ways the essence of the ÉDP's message: "In the first instance, the child must have a true feeling of being loved and accepted for what he is by his family. Otherwise, any type of constructive discipline is compromised. How can children who are disappointed, neglected, and disturbed 'give of themselves,' renounce or sacrifice anything ... they can do so only if they are moved by the desire to please their parents or by fear of losing their emotional security [L'enfant doit avoir en tout premier lieu le sentiment très vif d'être aimé, accepté tel qu'il est par les siens. Autrement, tout travail de discipline vraiment constructif est compromis. Comment l'enfant déçu, négligé et angoissé pourrait-il 'donner,' renoncer, sacrifier quelque chose ... s'il n'est pas stimulé par le désir de plaire à ses parents ou par la crainte de perdre sa sécurité affective]."[79] Parents' love was thus presented as the essential and overriding condition for the acceptance of discipline by their children,[80] but it was important that this discipline be exercised in a humane manner so that children would submit themselves voluntarily to authority: demands for blind obedience, failure to explain the reasons that lay behind orders, attempts to "break" the child's personality, severe punishments meted out for trivial errors or omissions, and chastisements that were public, degrading, or humiliating were all types of parental behaviour that were rigorously proscribed.[81] Even if a number of dissident voices existed, it can be stated that the ÉDP psychologists and most of its leaders disapproved of corporal punishment, since they deemed it overly severe and demeaning. From their standpoint, parental despotism could only foster contempt,[82] revolt, or complete rejection of all legitimate authority and could even produce anti-social behaviour: "We must refrain from corporal punishments because these create animosity and can awaken in the child a predisposition for cruelty, feelings of revenge, or anti-social tendencies [Il faut épargner les punitions corporelles qui font naître l'animosité et peuvent susciter chez l'enfant le goût de la cruauté, les sentiments de vengeance, les tendances anti-sociales]."[83] These new principles were advocated essentially to protect the democratic social order; however, at the same time, they worked in favour of a greater respect for the individual child, for a more open expression of emotions in the family, and for intergenerational harmony.

From the standpoint of those who adhered to a more orthodox Catholicism and accepted the unconditional authority of the church, even the mitigated liberalism of the ÉDP's psychological theories, which assigned a central place to the development of the indiviudal personality, could appear threatening. In Quebec during the 1950s, the church as a whole, if the conflicts that studded the history of the Catholic Action movements provide any illustration,[84] was certainly not inclined to favour democratic behaviour. Indeed, it might easily interpret calls for tolerance, freedom, and the rights of children as sanctioning criticism, insubordination, and rejection of the clergy's teaching. More fundamentally, because the new psychology stressed the self-realization of the individual, it posed a serious challenge to Catholic dogma because it seemed to call into question the "supernatural" destiny of humans, their sanctification only with reference to God, and the utility of the canons of morality. How, then, to reconcile this secular psychological vision of human beings with the precepts of Catholicism? How to harmonize the freedom of individuals with the necessity of obedience to the will of God? Such questions could not simply be ignored by the ÉDP leaders and psychologists, who, although critics of the church hierarchy, were nonetheless Catholic faithful. Both from profound conviction and to calm fears among their prospective audience, they thus sought to demonstrate that belief and psychology could work together.

The ÉDP therefore constantly reaffirmed that moral training was the principal objective of child rearing and that, in this respect, Catholic psychologists diverged from the views of their Protestant colleagues:

we are a long way from sharing the opinion of Protestants, who claim that the moral education of the child is nothing more than a psychological given and that moral education is justified solely by the achievement of a balanced personality. On the contrary, we assign to those spiritual elements placed within us by the sacrament of baptism a preponderant role in the acquisition of moral virtue. However, on the other hand, we cannot ignore natural law: in effect, our task is to better prepare the entire human psyche to exploit the spiritual resources that it already possesses."[85]

[nous sommes loin de partager l'opinion des protestants qui prétendent que cette éducation morale de l'enfant n'est qu'un fait psychologique et que si on arrive à former des personnalités équilibrées toute l'éducation morale sera réussie par le fait même. Au contraire, nous reconnaissons aux facteurs spirituels déposés en nous par le Baptême une place prépondérante dans l'acquisition des vertus morales. Mais nous ne pouvons pas, d'autre part, méconnaître les lois naturelles: en effet, il importe de préparer toute la psyché à mieux exploiter les ressources spirituelles latentes qu'elle possède.]

Thus for psychologist Charles Gill, as for Father Irénée Lussier, the ÉDP's chaplain, himself a trained psychologist, and for most of the leaders of the ÉDP who pronounced on this subject, psychology could promote the acquisition of a truly Christian moral sense. They maintained that once the individual had attained a psychological equilibrium, it would become easier to receive God's grace. "Grace operates more effectively ... on a healthy human psyche [La grâce opère mieux ... sur un psychisme sain]," declared Charles Gill, thus summarizing what many within the movement believed. The understanding of infantile psychology by parents would also enable them, in a more enlightened way, to initiate their children to religion taking into account their level of psychological development and understanding of "supernatural" phenomena. In fact, the teachings of psychology, which, in the estimation of the ÉDP were based on respect, love, and understanding, brought the individual closer to God: "The discoveries of psychology concerning the development of the moral sense are precious if they are deployed in conjunction with a Catholic mentality. They can only contribute to a better training of the type of Christian that we envision, by making God progressively more evident to the individual child [Les acquisitions de la psychologie sur l'évolution du sens moral sont précieuses si on les utilise selon notre mentalité catholique. Elles ne peuvent servir qu'à mieux former ce chrétien que nous avons en vue. Elles rendent Dieu de plus en plus évident]."[86]

Psychology could thus assist the burgeoning of religious sentiment in the child. However, the ÉDP was equally convinced that in order to be truly attractive to children, religion itself had to be reformed. More specifically, it insisted that Catholicism had to abandon its overly austere and authoritarian aspects, especially its tendency to assign guilt and to place undue stress upon human sinfulness, and henceforth insist upon the goodness and love of God.[87] This change implied a kind of "psychologizing" of the child's relationship with God. Just as the parent-child relationship must be founded upon love and respect in order to foster the individual's freely chosen obedience to authority, so children's belief in God and their relationship with him had to be nourished by a more attractive representation of the divine character which would induce the individual to give free assent to Christian moral teachings and Catholic dogmas. What the ÉDP hoped to instill in the child was something more than a surface religiosity or a set of conformist religious practices; rather, it hoped to foster a true and deep religious feeling, up to the level of a mature and autonomous individual, a religion made in the image of the self-disciplined citizen that the child would one day become.

Following this logic, René and Claudine Vallerand went so far as to state that it was their contemporaries' religious dependence on the clergy, far more than psychology, that constituted an obstacle to the development of religious sentiment. In an article published in 1951, they in fact admitted that the type of "popular education" that they promoted involved certain dangers, but that any possible deviations would more likely come from parents animated by superstitious forms of belief, because they were more likely to relinquish shallow religious convictions in order to follow new gurus. "There is always the danger," warned the Vallerands, "that parents who are less learned in their faith will endow science with powers that it does not possess. Those families that in former times prostrated themselves at the foot of the cross and placed unquestioning trust in the Virgin Mary will no doubt think that experts and psychologists possess all the efficacy that they no longer believe prayer has [Il y a, entre autres ce danger que des parents plus ou moins instruits de leur religion, accordent à la science des pouvoirs qu'elle n'a pas. Des familles qui, autrefois, se jetaient au pied de la croix et s'abandonnaient dans leur confiance dans la Vierge Marie, en viendraient peu à peu à croire, que le spécialiste, le psychologue possède des pouvoirs que la prière n'aurait plus]."[88] From their perspective, the antidote to this credulous mentality lay in psychology itself, for it alone could ensure the development of balanced and mature personalities, and thus of adults who were able to achieve a true faith. Fully confident in their new "science," the leaders of the ÉDP did not intend to retreat from the terrain of religion and morality. Rather, they tended to implicitly blame the church for requiring an unquestioning faith, thus encouraging servility among the faithful and a low level of religious sentiment.

THE ÉCOLE DES PARENTS ADVICE COLUMN: A FORUM FOR MOTHERS

At the end of 1948, the ÉDP inaugurated an advice column in the daily *Le Devoir*, thus opening a forum for mothers to express their worries on the subject of child rearing. By the time it was wound up in the spring of 1955, the "École des Parents Clinic" had received more than 220 letters, which provide an opportunity to study the attitudes of this group of women towards education, the problems that they experienced in raising their children, and the ways in which they attempted to resolve them. Moreover, the existence of these letters both serves as a measurement of the extent to which the ÉDP's psychological theories had penetrated a certain segment of Quebec society[89] and affords an opportunity to observe how the ÉDP reacted to the concrete situations presented by the experiences of its audience. The nature of the advice provided suggests that the experts, in the interests of getting their message across, did not hesitate to blame mothers, but that they often had to face debate and contestation from a number of their correspondents.

For the most part, mothers wrote in to describe the difficulties that they were encountering with children under twelve, and because they believed that these children exhibited severe behavioural problems. An analysis of the motives that induced women to write to the clinic shows that in over 40 per cent of the cases (98/227), they were worried about the attitude, actions, bad manners, or "misdemeanours" (délits) of their offspring. Lying, stealing, crying or temper tantrums, jealousy, laziness, refusing to eat or sleep, impoliteness, aggressive behaviour, violence, or hyperactivity constituted the main reasons that led mothers to ask for advice. If we add to this category the 19 letters that complained, in a more general way, about disobedience, it is apparent that maternal anxieties were primarily centred upon questions of comportment, or to adopt their language, on the "faults" that they wanted to "correct."[90] Viewed as a whole, this body of letters reveals mothers frequently at their wit's end, completely exasperated by the behaviour of their children and thus not inclined to be lenient: "My seven-year-old is a liar," one woman confided. "He never owns up to what he has done wrong, and he stubbornly holds out when we confront him with the evidence. Furthermore, he is a sneaky little hypocrite [Mon fils de

7 ans est un menteur. Il n'avoue jamais ses torts et s'obstine contre toute évidence. Il est de plus hypocrite et sournois]."⁹¹ Another mother declared, "My little boy aged eleven has a very nasty fault: he is lazy and hot-headed [Mon garçonnet de onze ans a un bien vilain défaut: il est paresseux et emporté],"⁹² while still another stated, "Our four-and-a-half-year-old son is proud and extremely stubborn [Notre petit garçon de 4 ans et demi est orgueilleux et très têtu]."⁹³ One woman went so far as to say, "I feel that God is testing us by giving us children [J'ai l'impression que Dieu nous éprouve en nous envoyant des enfants]."⁹⁴ If some wrote to reassure themselves on the soundness of their child-rearing methods, often because their circle of family and friends disagreed with the "soft" techniques they had chosen to follow at the ÉDP's direction,⁹⁵ in the majority of cases women had recourse to the clinic's psychological advice as a last resort. Indeed, most mothers confessed that they had already tried everything to try to change their children's behaviour, from gentleness to a range of punishments, to a gamut of promises and threats, and finally to blows, without any visible result.

These letters, signed "worn out mother," "tearful mother," "worried mother," or "anxious to do well," testify both to a profound desire to educate their children well, and to an at times morbid fear that they would "turn out badly" (ne tournent mal). The belief that character traits were laid down in childhood was apparent in many letters – a sentiment that the ÉDP had itself encouraged by insisting on the importance of the first years of the child's life – as well as a traditional vision of childhood and education, one founded upon parental authority and the idea that children should be "trained" (dressés) from a very early age to act well so that they did not acquire any evil tendencies. One mother, for example, was alarmed by the lies her six-year-old daughter was telling. She explained that while at this stage, this "fault" did not appear terribly serious, she feared "that she will acquire vicious habits [qu'elle prenne ainsi le chemin du vice]."⁹⁶ In many cases, these maternal worries also expressed a need to meet the expectations of family and friends: the fear of being described as a bad mother, the humiliation of seeing one's children behaving in a disagreeable or anti-social manner, frequently induced women to write. But their letters also revealed a set of exaggerated and unrealistic expectations that exposed a complete misunderstanding of, or indifference to, the basic principles of psychology. Many correspondents, for example, complained that even their very young children did not immediately or fully obey them, while others were alarmed that their three-year-olds already exhibited a "contrary spirit" (esprit de contradiction) and said no to everything. In general these mothers had the following expectations of their two-year-olds: that they have proper table manners, that they be polite and sociable with strangers and guests, that they get along with their siblings, that when called upon to do small chores, they drop their games without any crabbiness, that they understand directions the first time they were told – in short, that they should behave at all times in an exemplary manner. These women's list of complaints regarding the "faults" of their children and their own inability to secure obedience was also suggestive of a tension between their role of mother and that of wife and homemaker. How, in effect, could women keep a clean and orderly household "with children always getting underfoot"[97] (avec les enfants dans les jambes), a question asked by one correspondent. How could mothers "keep children quiet" (faire tenir les enfants tranquilles) while they sewed and cooked, to say nothing of carrying out a thorough spring cleaning? How to calm them down before father arrived home from the office and avoid his grumpiness or reproaches?[98] This recounting of child-rearing problems illustrated that the task of harmonizing women's responsibilities with societal expectations concerning their role as wives, mothers, and housekeepers was particularly harassing and stressful. It was thus not surprising that many women invoked either the precarious state of their health or their fragile nerves to explain their impatience with their children, the slaps or spankings that they were forced to administer, and the urgency with which they sought a solution to the problems of child rearing.

The stories these women told of their difficulties and the way in which they sought to resolve them aroused a twofold response from the clinic's psychological experts. In most cases, they began by reassuring mothers, informing them that their children's behaviour and reactions were "perfectly normal" when the age of the child was taken into account. Basing their advice on the theory of "developmental stages," to which they referred constantly, they explained that the "negativism" exhibited by two- and three-year-olds was merely the sign of a personality that sought to affirm itself, that the tall tales told by four- and five-year-olds did not mean that these children were liars but, rather, that they were normally endowed with a vivid imagination which expressed itself, that the rough behaviour of older children towards younger ones was simply a manifestation of jealousy, not the mark of intrinsic maliciousness, and that furthermore, agressiveness and disobedience indicated a child's normal desire for autonomy. Thus parents who worried over their three-year-old received the following answer: "In looking over the details of your letter, it seems that your worries … amount to this: (1) he says vulgar words, (2) he does not listen and is stubborn, (3) he hits and bites his little brother, (4) finally, he is nervous, yells and stomps about when he doesn't get what he wants. Dear parents, we assure you that there is nothing here that should alarm you. Every one of these character traits is typical in a normal child aged three [En relevant les détails de votre lettre, il ressort que ce qui vous inquiète ... se résume à ceci: 1) il dit des mots vulgaires 2) il n'écoute pas, il est têtu 3) il bat et mord son petit frère 4) enfin, il est nerveux, crie et danse, tant qu'il n'a pas obtenu ce qu'il demande. Nous vous assurons chers parents, qu'il ne saurait y avoir là sujet d'alarme. Chaque trait de caractère mentionné se retrouve chez l'enfant normal de 3 ans]."[99]

However, once the experts had established that the child was completely "normal," the advice took on a more accusatory tone, especially when the childish behaviour described by the mother seemed to transgress the limits established by the standards of psychology. Women were then enjoined to reconsider their techniques of child rearing, which, according to the columnists, had only aggravated the situation. Could not the child's exaggerated "negativism" be interpreted as a sign that the mother was simply contradicting the child to show who was right and who was wrong? Did jealousy not emerge from the fact that the parents appeared to have abandoned the older child in favour of the baby, indicating that they had not taken care to prepare the older child before the arrival of a younger brother or sister? Might four-year-olds who told tall tales be seeking parental attention because they lacked it? Were lies, aggression, and hyperactivity not the products of exaggerated parental desires for perfection or demands for good manners, or, worse, did they not result from overly severe punishments, such as slappings and spankings?

Those mothers who wrote in to receive encouragement and advice and to find a solution to their problems often found themselves duly lectured by the experts. While they sought a way of modifying the behaviour of their children, they were asked to look for the root of the problem, to undertake an examination of conscience, and to change their own practices and attitudes – in other words, to become themselves psychologists. For example, to one mother who complained that her oldest son, aged eleven, was uncouth, disobedient, temperamental, authoritarian, and selfish, the columnists emphasized that it was highly possible that this child's aggressive behaviour emanated from jealousy towards his younger siblings, and they called upon the mother to evince more affection, while at the same time giving the older child more freedom.[100] Another woman, who expressed a series of dissatisfactions with her two children, was summarily warned about the dangers of an overly demanding perfectionism: "you should adopt a less rigid attitude towards your children, one that is less demanding and less perfectionist, because they display no deep-seated faults

[devant vos enfants, qui ne révèlent en somme aucun défaut bien sys-
tématisé, vous devriez adopter une attitude moins rigide, moins tendue
vers la perfection, moins exigeante]."¹⁰¹

Those women whose educational methods were deemed traditional
and authoritarian found themselves subjected to a public scolding by
the ÉDP columnists. For example, one of these mothers admitted to
being often impatient with her two-and-a-half-year-old son because he
cried, wet his bed during the night, and did not seem able to eat
without assistance. She stated, "[My husband] does not seem to
approve of my severe approach, but I cannot relinquish it because this
child of mine seems to be more difficult to raise than others. I would
like him to grow up to be a good citizen, one who loves, obeys, and
consoles his parents. We give him good clothes, comfortable surroundings, and proper medicines. Isn't all this enough? [(Mon mari) n'a pas
l'air d'approuver ma méthode sévère que je ne puis abandonner car
mon enfant me paraît plus dur à élever qu'un autre. Et je voudrais en
faire un bon citoyen, qui nous aime, nous obéisse et nous console.
Nous lui donnons de bons vêtements, du confort, des toniques. N'est-
ce pas que c'est assez?]" The answer given to this mother was brutally
frank: "What you are giving him ... is not sufficient ... In addition to
all this, children must be given ... affection and security, which alone
can ensure their emotional equilibrium. And how can you satisfy these
needs ... if you act so thoughtlessly towards him? [Mais non ... ce n'est
pas assez ... L'enfant doit recevoir en plus ... l'affection et la sécurité
qui assureront son équilibre émotif. Et comment pourriez-vous satis-
faire ces exigences ... si vous agissez envers lui avec si peu de pondéra-
tion?]"¹⁰² Another woman wrote in declaring that she was unable to
control, either gently or by resorting to blows, the temper tantrums
thrown by her daughter, aged six. The ÉDP psychologists answered in
this way: "You should begin by trying to reform yourself, not your
little girl [Ce n'est pas votre fillette que vous devez commencer par
réformer. C'est vous-même]."¹⁰³ A third, the mother of six who
"admitted" having a "soft spot" (un faible) for her older child, whose
behaviour had become completely intolerable, was severely chastised
for disregarding the *equal* rights of her children to parental tenderness
and fairness.¹⁰⁴ Finally, another mother wrote in to ask whether it was
"possible to get my girls, aged two and one half and one and a half to
listen to my orders"; she was admonished to completely revise her
goals of education and to abandon the idea of disciplining very young
children: "Madam, your success in educating them will be judged not
by the fact that you have taught them to obey you, but if you have
enabled them to behave well by following only the dictates of their
conscience. This is the final end of education ... Obedience requires a

certain maturity that your little girls do not yet possess ... You are merely wasting your energy if you try to impose upon them the standards of conduct appropriate to older children [Vous les aurez bien éduquées, madame, non si vous leur avez appris à obéir, mais si vous les avez rendues capables de se bien conduire, d'après les seules dictées de leur conscience. Ceci est le terme final de l'éducation ... L'obéissance ... réclame une certaine maturité que ne peuvent absolument pas posséder vos fillettes ... N'essayez pas de leur faire pratiquer les vertus d'un âge plus avancé, vous vous fatigueriez en pure perte]."[105]

By minimizing the problems encountered by mothers who were desperately attempting to combine their household tasks with child rearing, the ÉDP sought above all to popularize the principles of psychology, which emphasized that parents must respect each child's individual rhythm of development, to be more patient and attentive, less demanding and authoritarian, and most significantly, that their love for their children be expressed in tangible ways, through kind words and encouragement. In fact, the ÉDP identified the absence of affection or its demonstration as the primary cause of defective parent-child relationships and, moreover, as the source of physical ailments such as bedwetting, sleepwalking, and stammering.[106] By contrast, the psychological experts deemed that displays of affection and tenderness were quasi-magical solutions to emotional and physical problems. Increased love and attention, in the estimation of the ÉDP, must emanate essentially from the mother. If the organization accorded fathers an important role in child rearing, it was most insistent on the fact that the paternal role was quite specific: "We have stated over and over again in this forum, that education is a task that is accomplished by the *parents*, and each one must bring to bear aspects which, while different, require a good deal of self-sacrifice and love. The mother is always at home, but the father must, through his authority and firm tenderness, have a presence in the household [On l'a dit et redit dans cette tribune, l'éducation est une œuvre qui se fait par les *parents*, chacun doit y apporter sa large part qui est différente, sans doute, mais qui requiert beaucoup d'abnégation et beaucoup d'amour. La maman est là, toujours présente, mais le père doit habiter la maison lui aussi, par son autorité et sa ferme tendresse]."[107] In other words, because of his work outside the home, the father would have to be content with leaving a certain impress upon the atmosphere of the family, rather than directly intervening in its day-to-day functioning. In addition, the expression of paternal tenderness was always balanced by an aura of authority that precluded him from expressing his feelings too overtly. Indeed, according to the ÉDP, it was only when the children became older that the father should take an active part in their education, mainly to guide them in their dealings with the world outside the family: "He should, depending on the age of the children, take an interest in their games, their schoolwork, their friends, their leisure activities and evenings out [Il s'intéresse, suivant l'âge des enfants, à leurs jeux, à leurs études, à leurs amis, à leurs loisirs, à leurs sorties]."[108] While the ÉDP experts certainly encouraged men to develop closer relations with their children, they nonetheless recognized that doing so might prove difficult for them. Thus, when one young mother lamented her husband's indifference and hostility towards their new baby, the columnists advised her to "give him psychological support" (porter psychologiquement) for a time, because in their estimation, "women learn maternity more readily than men do paternity [les femmes apprennent plus rapidement la maternité que les hommes la paternité]."[109]

Whether in reference to their children or to their husbands, it was thus incumbent upon women to change their attitudes and to be the psychological prop for their families, even in extreme circumstances, without first attending to their own needs. The ÉDP emphatically reprobated those women who stated that they wanted to leave husbands who were rude, "coarse" (indélicat), or frankly abusive. Even though the organization condemned such behaviour, they considered that women must bear up under their troubles, because the presence of both parents was necessary to foster a balanced psyche in the children.[110] In a similar vein, they opposed the cohabitation of parents with grandparents or other relatives in the same household, advising those women who wrote in on this subject not to consider this solution, even when the family's financial situation was precarious. Likewise, they urged women who complained about sharing accommodations with their family or in-laws to rapidly extricate themselves from this situation. The nuclear family, in the opinion of the ÉDP experts, was the best environment in which to raise children, for "the law of nature, like Christ's own law, requires that once a woman establishes a home, she has created a new cell which, in order to progress, must live openly, breathe, act, and grow freely. This is why we never recommend that families sustain overly close connections with another family, for in such situations, individuality of thought and action cannot be respected, and conflict becomes inevitable [la loi de la nature, comme la loi du Christ, demande que, lorsqu'une femme établit un foyer, elle crée une cellule nouvelle qui, pour progresser, doit vivre au grand air, respirer librement, agir librement, croître librement. C'est pourquoi il n'est jamais recommandable qu'une famille évolue en contact trop étroit avec une autre famille. L'individualité de pensée et d'agir ne peut plus être respectée et les heurts deviennent inévitables]."[111] Psychologists were especially concerned that parents put grandmothers gently in their place when they tried to offer advice on children's upbringing, because they were deemed too elderly to effectively care for children, and, more tellingly, they were utterly ignorant of modern educational methods and inclined to spoil youngsters.[112] However, the ÉDP was utterly confounded when a grandmother wrote to expose a real-life case of parental neglect; as she reported the matter, she felt powerless because she did not belief that she had the right to interpose herself between her daughter-in-law and her two-year-old grandchild, who was shut up in her room all day. "As you yourself so aptly express the matter," the columnists remarked, "you are only the grandmother [Comme vous dites si bien, vous n'êtes que la grand-maman]." In this case, they had to reaffirm their own advice, but they advised the grandmother to do all she could to "indirectly" offer this little girl love and attention.[113]

It is, of course, impossible to determine how the mothers who wrote in to the ÉDP Clinic received the proffered advice or whether they put it into practice. When women went against the opinion of their circle of family and friends and attempted to apply the methods recommended by experts, the ÉDP naturally encouraged them to stay the course, advice that may have reaffirmed their determination. In these particular cases, the intervention by experts may have contributed to a greater sense and autonomy among some women. The ÉDP's language also had a reassuring side, insofar as it maintained that the childish behaviour described by mothers was completely normal. However, as we have seen earlier, these soothing statements were frequently accompanied by reprimands and exhortations to mothers to change their attitudes. Undoubtedly, some of them, upon reading the answers to their questions, felt disappointed or experienced a strong sense of guilt.

The debates that were carried on in the ÉDP's advice column also revealed that some women were critical of psychology and its new methods of child rearing. One mother was so distressed by her girl's jealousy of her little brother, which was carried on to the point of physical abuse despite the increased attention the mother gave the older sibling, that she expressed her skepticism in the following terms: "I am still awaiting the wonderful results that you have promised me ... It is very nice to know that Jacqueline's attitude is normal, and I would very much like not to give in to my impatience and punish my daughter for her conduct. However, in the meantime, I would like to preserve Jacques's limbs intact and to release him from Jacqueline's tyranny [J'attends toujours les heureux résultats que l'on m'a promis ... C'est très joli de savoir que l'attitude de Jacqueline est normale, je veux bien continuer de ne pas céder à mon impatience qui me porterait à punir ma fille. Cependant, je voudrais bien aussi que Jacques conserve tous ses membres et qu'il ne soit pas trop longtemps l'objet de la tyrannie de Jacqueline]." When pressed on the matter, the ÉDP was constrained to say that the techniques it prescribed were "easier to settle on paper than to apply in daily practice [plus facile(s) à régler sur le papier qu'à pratiquer au jour le jour]."[114] In a letter entitled "I'm mad at psychology" (J'en veux a la psychologie), another woman bitterly repented adopting the clinic's counsel in sending her child to kindergarten, where he was extremely miserable: "[The kindergarten teacher] tells me that Paul is a problem child, that he is sulky, inhibited, and will always have difficulty in adapting to new situations. I was always pleased to have my two little boys with me. After this awful experience … I am now always second-guessing myself, something I didn't do before, and I have become overly demanding and a worrywart. It is no longer fun to raise children [(La jardinière) me dit que Paul a un caractère difficile, qu'il est boudeur, qu'il est inhibé, qu'il aura toujours de la difficulté à s'adapter à de nouvelles situations. J'ai toujours eu du plaisir avec mes deux petits gars. Depuis cette vilaine expérience … je m'observe continuellement et je les observe d'un œil critique, ce que je ne faisais pas avant. Avec tout cela, je deviens exigeante et tracassière. Et ce n'est plus du tout amusant d'élever des enfants]." This final comment revealed that some women considered psychological theories, far from an inducement to developing closer relations with their children, a real hindrance. The ÉDP passed over the mother's criticism in silence but, in a parting shot, could not resist blaming her by telling her that her son perhaps lacked the necessary maturity to adapt to kindergarten.[115]

In the fall of 1954 there occurred another debate on child rearing methods, this one involving many correspondents. This time, one woman who signed herself "disgusted mother" (maman revoltée) addressed her remarks directly to the readers of the advice column, rather than to the "experts." Her long letter touched off a noisy polemic, for in it she explained how she had completely spoiled the education of her oldest child by following "to the letter" (à la lettre) the prescribed regime of 1930s psychologists, which recommended that parents raise their children in a rigid and systematic manner, with no demonstrations of ill-timed affection. A "specialist" had now informed her that her son, aged ten, craved affection like a child of four, which prompted her to say,

In concluding this tale, I read in a newspaper that at a conference of psychologists, it had been decided that it was necessary to completely alter the method that was in vogue ten years ago, and that mothers had to display affection to their children ... because this is what makes them develop normally. My God, I was disgusted by reading this! ... What you are saying is that I should throw out every book, treatise, and school that tries to guide our conduct. I eagerly await your opinion, but I know that you will simply find a way to blame us ... in fact, my reason for writing to you ... is not really to elicit your opinion but those of the readers of this column. To each his own and the responsibility is ultimately my own, because if I am the one with the real experience of raising children, I wonder if the *écoles de parents* really have the common sense to do the same.[116]

[Pour tout finir, je lis dans un journal qu'à un congrès de psychologues, on a décidé qu'il fallait changer la méthode d'il y a dix ans, qu'il fallait que la maman montre de l'affection à son petit ... que c'était cela qui faisait développer l'enfant normalement. Dieu! que j'ai été révoltée en lisant cela ... C'est donc dire que je fiche par terre tout livre, tout traité et toute école qui viendront essayer de nous dicter telle ou telle conduite. J'attends votre opinion, mais je sais que vous allez trouver des choses pour nous donner des torts ... mais si je vous écris ... ce n'est pas tellement pour avoir votre opinion, mais celle des lecteurs de cette chronique. À chacun son métier et je m'en rends compte. Car si j'ai l'expérience pratique d'élever des enfants, je me demande si les écoles de parents abondent toujours dans le sens pratique.]

A month later, the ÉDP answered this woman, publishing a volley of fifteen letters mailed in by mothers, a few married couples, and two fathers. Taken as a whole, their contents indicate less a total rejection of expert advice than a pattern of generalized skepticism. Four mothers claimed that they had experienced the same thing as "disgusted mother," with much the same result, encouraging her to completely ignore the prescriptions of the psychologists, whom they described as "people with an armful of diplomas but no children [des gens avec beaucoup de diplômes et pas d'enfant]."[117] Most correspondents, however, recognized that the advice had a certain level of usefulness, even if, at worst, as one couple somewhat humorously contended, it enabled parents to vent their spleen at others.[118] More seriously, while the majority rated psychology as good, mainly because it taught "parents not to be always on their children's cases [à ne pas crier sans arrêt après les enfants]" these letters nonetheless urged mothers to reserve judgment, and many claimed that "disgusted mother"'s only real mistake was that she had insufficient trust in herself. "The blame in all this," concluded one couple, "attaches not so much to the theorists who set forth the data of their science to the educators but, rather, to the latter, especially when they set aside common sense, judgment, and the intuition of mothers and fathers in order to follow the theorists blindly and rigidly [L'erreur dans tout cela, n'est pas tellement du côté des théoriciens qui énoncent les données de leur science aux éducateurs … mais bien de la part de ces derniers quand ils renoncent au bon sens, au jugement, à l'intuition maternelle et paternelle, pour suivre aveuglément les théoriciens avec rigidité]."[119]

Following this debate among the readership, Monique and Georges Dufresne, who conducted the ÉDP Clinic, felt the need to clarify their own position in the matter. In an answer serialized in several issues, they began by underscoring that the rigid advice that "disgusted mother" complained of had never, in fact, been given by psychologists but, rather, by pediatricians whose objective was to prevent the transmission of disease at a time when many young children died from contagious illnesses. Thus this advice did not rest upon "the scientific findings of infant psychology (des connaissances scientifiques en psychologie infantile)," even though the Dufresnes recognized that "some people were persuaded to justify it by appealing to psychological concepts [certains se sont laissés allés à les justifier sur le plan psychologique]."[120] Since the 1930s, there had been a number of significant developments in "psychological knowledge," and because it was now established upon objective empirical observation, it offered "proven theories" that were not subject to alteration. However, readers of the column had to beware of ascribing "magical powers" to psychology, because there were still many aspects unexplored by research. In the estimation of the Dufresnes, parents who consulted psychologists were more to blame than the expert professionals, because in their haste and confusion, they often refused to listen to the words of caution expressed by the latter.[121] In this way, mothers were asked to adopt a more prudent approach. According to the Dufresnes, and in contrast to what many letter writers had claimed, maternal intuition was not a sufficient qualification for child rearing, since this intuition was frequently clouded by other, less noble sentiments that could affect a mother's judgment. Psychology, by contrast, stood above this natural response by offering a more objective, and thus more enlightened, perspective, but it did not possess the power to resolve all difficulties.[122] In the final analysis, it was the judgment with which Providence had endowed mothers that constituted an essential source of child-rearing wisdom.

By one standard, this debate had allowed the experts to justify themselves and to reaffirm the validity of their knowledge. However, by another, the decision of the ÉDP to publish the letter of "disgusted mother" and a few others that advanced criticisms of their theories, shows that the clinic viewed itself both as a site where mothers could bring their worries and as a forum to challenge expert advice.[123] In both these instances, and even when the experts reprimanded mothers, it can be argued that the clinic enabled the public expression of maternal cares and probably contributed to breaking down the isolation of women and even to forging feelings of solidarity among them. Indeed, many women who wrote in claimed that they regularly read the advice forum and in explaining their own problems, they frequently referred to situations described in other letters.

CONCLUSION

Through its work and writings, the ÉDP acted as the interpreter of a psychological discourse that affected the wider North American society at the same time and aimed, as a number of historians have stated, at transforming family relationships by adapting them to the social, economic, and political context of the post-war years. According to this analysis, psychological theories infused a democratic spirit into the family, one suited to training citizens by instilling them with liberal values. This cultural project relied heavily upon the efforts of women, and consequently, it reinforced their maternal identity by thrusting increased responsibility for forming new citizens upon mothers. These elements were clearly evident in the language of the ÉDP. As we have seen, the close association between the education of children and their citizenship training, as well as the links established between the goals of education and the widening of parental responsibility – especially that of mothers – strongly infused the whole of its public rhetoric. However, its ambition to transform the vision of childhood and the parent-child relationship had other goals, and thus more ambiguous consequences. From the moment of its foundation, the ÉDP rested upon the belief that the church had arrogated to itself a function that it could not perform, and this view explains the organization's strong desire to put an end to its "meddling" (ingérence) by restoring to parents the "autonomy" that they had far too readily abdicated. From this perspective, it can be argued that, first and foremost, the ÉDP strove to substitute its own expertise for that of the clergy, psychology serving as a means of "emancipation" (affranchissement) because it provided "scientific" demonstration of the fact that only parents could establish a meaningful, affectional relationship with their children and thus accomplish their education in the full sense of the term. However, the new psychological theories compelled the ÉDP to distanced itself from the traditional idea of the family, in which the interests, wishes, and individual needs of children had to be put in abeyance in order to ensure the solidarity and reproduction of the family social cell. As defined by the ÉDP, modern society was considered less a grouping of families[124] than an assembly of citizens, whom parents had been called upon to form, not simply for the benefit of the family but with reference to an overarching common good. This new social calculus dictated that children be treated as individuals who enjoyed certain rights and a measure of autonomy.

The new status assigned to children of course contained its own share of ambiguity, and it presupposed that women would renounce other identities and, indeed, any prospect of self-fulfillment (épanouissement) outside of the maternal role. Significantly, however, maternity was presented by the ÉDP not only in terms of duty and constraint, or as a "blessed slavery,"[125] (esclavage béni) added on top of a destiny to which they passively submitted, but as a profession whose exercise involved learning precise rules. Beneath the normative character of this discourse, there lurked the idea that child rearing was a function of such social importance that it could only be carried out by women who were real "professionals." In this way, the psychological theories promoted by the ÉDP can be read as a new form of female indoctrination, but they can also be interpreted as an enhanced recognition of a wider social function for maternity. At the very least, as the letters written to the ÉDP Clinic testify, these theories not only put child rearing on the public agenda but also opened the door for women to participate in these debates, even allowing them to contest the scientific pretensions of the experts.

NOTES

1 This essay was translated by Michael Gauvreau. The research upon which it is based was undertaken with the support of a SSHRCC General Research Grant through the Université de Montréal. My deepest thanks go especially to my research assistant, Vincent Duhaime, for unearthing the correspondence of the École des Parents.

2 For a list of these family organizations, mostly founded by the Catholic Church between 1937 and 1966, see Marie-Paule Malouin, *Le mouvement familial au Québec: Les débuts, 1937–1965* (Montréal: Boréal, 1998), 147–50.

3 Jean Hamelin, *Histoire du catholicisme québécois*, Tome 2, *De 1940 à nos jours* (Montréal: Boréal, 1984); Jean-Pierre Collin, *La Ligue ouvrière catholique canadienne, 1938–1954* (Montréal: Boréal, 1996); Lucie Piché, "La Jeunesse ouvrière catholique féminine: Un lieu de formation sociale et d'action communautaire," *Revue d'histoire de l'Amérique française (RHAF)*, 52 (printemps 1999): 481–506; Michael Gauvreau, "The Emergence of Personalist Feminism: Catholicism and the Marriage-Preparation Movement in Quebec, 1940–1966," in Nancy Christie, ed.,

Households of Faith: Family, Gender, and Community in Canada,
1760–1969 (Montreal and Kingston: McGill-Queen's University Press,
2002), 319–47.

4 Vallerand, in fact, aimed to create an affiliate of the French École des
Parents, founded by the author Verine in 1930. However, the outbreak of
war ended their correspondence and, effectively, the project itself. See
Malouin, *Le mouvement familial*, 32; *Le Devoir*, 10 jan. 1949, 5.

5 Claudine Vallerand was one of the first hosts of children's television programming at Radio-Canada: her program, *Maman Fonfon*, was first
broadcast in November 1955.

6 "Ce qu'elle attend de nous," *L'École des parents* (*ÉDP*) 1 (août 1950): 16.

7 Louis Pronovost, "Arriverons-nous à temps?," *ÉDP* 1 (nov. 1950): 2.

8 It should be noted that the archives of the ÉDP have been destroyed. The
articles published by Vallerand in the Dominicans' magazine (this was
probably the most progressively minded male religious order of the
period), the magazines published by the ÉDP itself, and the articles and
correspondence in *Le Devoir*, which paid a good deal of attention to its
activities and where the ÉDP maintained an ongoing record of its activities, as well as a psychological "clinic," form the principal sources upon
which this study is based.

9 Claudine-S. Vallerand, "École et foyer," *Revue dominicaine* 45 (oct.
1939): 132.

10 Ibid., 139; italics mine.

11 In support of this argument, she referred to the Claxton diagram, reproduced in the article, which illustrated through a graph composed of black
and white squares the respective roles of family and school in the education of children: the latter was only assigned 7 of the 105 squares. See
Vallerand, "École et Foyer," 139.

12 Ibid., 136.

13 Ibid., 138.

14 Ibid.

15 Ibid., 140.

16 Ibid., 141.

17 Ibid., 142.

18 Claudine-S. Vallerand, "À l'intérieur d'une maternelle," *Revue dominicaine* 46 (fév. 1940): 68.

19 "Ce qu'elle attend de nous," *ÉDP* 1 (août 1950), 16.

20 *Le Devoir*, 4 déc. 1940, 5.

21 Malouin, *Le mouvement familial*, 33; *Le Devoir*, 4 déc. 1940, 5.

22 Malouin, *Le mouvement familial*, 33; *Le Devoir*, 28 nov. 1940, 5.

23 According to Malouin, disagreements occurred between the Franciscans
and the leaders of the ÉDP, which would explain the disappearance of the
supplément *Nos enfants*. See *Le mouvement familial*, 41–6.

24 "Ce que l'École a accompli," *ÉDP* 1 (sept. 1950): 15.

25 In 1949 the ÉDP claimed 1,000 members throughout Quebec. See *Le Devoir*, 21 fév. 1949, 5.

26 In Catholic Action circles (JOC, LOC) the ÉDP was identified with, and criticized for, a type of elitism. On this aspect, see Malouin, *Le mouvement familial*, 36.

27 Claudine-S. Vallerand, "Ce que donne l'École des Parents," *Relations* 1 (mai 1940): 134.

28 Ibid.

29 Jeanne Boulizon, "L'union fait la force," *ÉDP* 1 (mars 1950): 3.

30 "Nos mouvements de famille," *La Famille* 15 (déc. 1951): 664, cited in Malouin, *Le mouvement familial*, 79.

31 *Le Devoir*, 10 jan. et 17 jan. 1949, 5; italics in original.

32 *Le Devoir*, 17 jan. et 21 fév. 1949, 5.

33 *Le Devoir*, 28 fév. 1949, 5.

34 *Le Devoir*, 21 fév. 1949, 5.

35 *Le Devoir*, 21 déc. 1949, 5.

36 Ibid.

37 Despite their differences, the École des Parents de Québec and the École des Parents du Québec, along with their affiliates, joined in the spring of 1953. See Malouin, *Le mouvement familial*, 79.

38 René Vallerand, "Les parents se donnent la main," *ÉDP* 4 (oct. 1953): 7.

39 For a definition of maternalism, see Molly Ladd-Taylor, *Mother Work: Women, Child Welfare and the State, 1890–1930* (Chicago: University of Illinois Press, 1994), 3. For maternalist currents in Quebec, see Karine Hébert, "Une organisation maternaliste au Québec: la Fédération nationale Saint-Jean-Baptiste et la bataille pour le vote des femmes," *RHAF* 52 (hiver 1999): 315–44.

40 *Le Devoir*, 28 fév. 1949, 5.

41 Denise Lemieux, "Le mouvement familial issu de la Révolution tranquille 1960–1987: Une action sociale et politique au nom des familles" (communication presentée au Congrès de l'Institut d'histoire de l'Amérique française, Montréal, oct. 2000).

42 "Manifeste de l'ÉDP," cited by Germaine Bernier, *Le Devoir*, 21 oct. 1944, 5.

43 Germaine Bernier, *Le Devoir*, 19 jan. 1944, 5.

44 Germaine Bernier, *Le Devoir*, 18 oct. 1947, 5.

45 René et Claudine-S. Vallerand, "Nous admirons les parents modernes," *ÉDP* 2 (juin 1951): 3.

46 Mona Gleason, *Normalizing the Ideal: Psychology, Schooling, and the Family in Postwar Canada* (Toronto: University of Toronto Press, 1999).

47 On these questions, see Mary Louise Adams, *The Trouble with Normal: Postwar Youth and the Making of Heterosexuality* (Toronto: University

of Toronto Press, 1997); Doug Owram, *Born at the Right Time: A History of the Baby Boom Generation* (Toronto: University of Toronto Press, 1996).

48 This view was outlined in a historical sketch of the ÉDP, cited by Germaine Bernier, *Le Devoir*, 24 fév. 1942, 5.

49 Manifesto of the ÉDP, cited by Germaine Bernier, *Le Devoir*, 21 oct. 1944, 5.

50 *Le Devoir*, 21 oct. 1944, 5.

51 *Le Devoir*, 18 oct. 1947, 5.

52 Manon et Claude Mailhiot, "L'enfant: une définition," *ÉDP* 1 (nov. 1950): 6.

53 See, for example, the series of charts published in the magazine after April 1952 on the normal development of the child. See also Charles Gill, "Évaluons nos enfants," *ÉDP* 3 (avril 1952): 5–7.

54 Thérèse Gouin-Décarie, "Le bébé cet inconnu," *ÉDP* 3 (jan. 1952): 21–4.

55 "Ce que la psychologie m'a apprise," transcription of an interview by Jeanne Grise Allard with Monique Dufresne, *ÉDP* 6 (juillet 1955): 5.

56 Mailhiot et Mailhiot, "L'enfant: une définition," *ÉDP* 1 (nov. 1950): 7.

57 Ibid.

58 *Le Devoir*, 26 nov. 1949, 6; "Puissance de l'ambiance familiale," *ÉDP* 3 (août 1953): 11–14.

59 Gleason, *Normalizing the Ideal*, 24.

60 "Puissance de l'ambiance familiale," *ÉDP* 3 (août 1953): 11.

61 "Tu vas pleurer pour quelque chose," *ÉDP* 3 (fév. 1952): 6–9.

62 See, for example, Thérèse Gouin-Décarie, "L'enfant devant la vie," *ÉDP* 3 (mars 1952): 16. On the construction of heterosexuality as normal in the post-war period, see Adams, *The Trouble with Normal*.

63 See, for example, *Le Devoir*, 15 jan. 1953, 2, where the ÉDP columnists warned a mother against giving her boys an overly feminized education.

64 Vincent Duhaime, "À la recherche du père québécois: le discours du mouvement familial et l'expérience des pères, 1945–1965," (thèse de MA (histoire), Université de Montréal, 2000), has analyzed the post-war discourse on fatherhood.

65 Mailhiot et Mailhiot, "L'enfant: une définition," *ÉDP* 1 (nov. 1950): 6.

66 Irénée Lussier, "Il a son caractère," *ÉDP* 2 (jan. 1951): 8–9; Gouin-Décarie, "Le bébé, cet inconnu," 21–4.

67 Charles Gill, "La liberté," *ÉDP*, 2:12(nov. 1951), 23.

68 Gleason, *Normalizing the Ideal*, 104.

69 Gill, "La liberté," *ÉDP* 2 (nov. 1951): 21; Laurette Toupin, "Il a été puni," *ÉDP* 1 (août 1950): 27–9; C. Vallerand, "Formation du caractère," *ÉDP* 4 (oct. 1953): 27–8.

70 Gill, "La liberté," 23.

71 Ibid.

72 Ibid.

73 Ibid.

74 "Pourquoi il importe d'obéir," *ÉDP* 6 (juillet 1955): 20.

75 Ibid.

76 Rolande Major-Charbonneau, "Autorité et liberté," *ÉDP* 6 (mai 1955): 3.

77 Ibid.

78 Gleason, *Normalizing the Ideal*, 97.

79 Gill, "La liberté," 24.

80 "La colère," *ÉDP* 2 (jan. 1951): 12; Mme Guy Boulizon, "On s'amuse en famille," *ÉDP* 1 (avril 1950): 18–23.

81 Toupin, "Il a été puni," 30; "Pourquoi il importe d'obéir," 20; P.B.P., "Ont-ils droit à leurs idées?" *ÉDP* 7 (mai 1956): 5; "On ne devrait jamais permettre," *ÉDP* 1 (mai 1950): 16.

82 Major-Charbonneau, "Autorité et liberté," 3.

83 *Le Devoir*, 29 nov. 1949, 5.

84 Hamelin, *Histoire du catholicisme québécois*, 2: 122.

85 Charles Gill, "L'éducation morale," *ÉDP* 2 (fév. 1951): 11–12.

86 Ibid., 17.

87 Laurette Toupin went so far as to state that God was the greatest of all psychologists because he had "believed that it was wise to maintain the most impressive regime of moral sanctions since such a system would help his children to conquer, often in spite of their natures, the supreme reward [cru sage de maintenir le plus impressionnant des systèmes de sanctions en vue d'aider ses enfants à conquérir, bien souvent comme malgré eux, la suprême récompense]." See Toupin, "Il a été puni," 29.

88 Vallerand et Vallerand, "Nous admirons les parents modernes," 2.

89 The information contained in these letters does not permit a precise socio-economic delineation of the mothers who wrote in, but if we bear in mind the readership of *Le Devoir*, we can suggest that the majority of them belonged to the elite, at least in an intellectual if not an economic sense. A few allusions to straitened family budgets or to inadequate housing demonstrate, however, that not all the women were married to members of the upper middle class. Their geographical location was not always specified, nor was the number of children. However, while women resident in Montreal with families of three or four children seemed to have formed the majority, many letters were mailed in from the Quebec and the Saguenay regions, and even from smaller towns. Some of the letters mentioned having a large number of children (between 5 and 8).

90 Among the other letters, approximately 10 dealt with problems of physical health, 20 recounted marital or family problems that were detrimental to child rearing, 24 dealt with dating and problems at school, and 47 touched upon other subjects, such as children's relationships with their

friends, difficulties between a brother and sister, allowances, leisure, and more general questions concerning infant psychology. Even though the ÉDP had strongly insisted in its magazine on the importance of the sexual education of children, only 12 letters were concerned with this issue, perhaps an indication that mothers were still uneasy with this aspect of child education. Except in relation to this latter theme, mothers wrote frequently to recount their disappointments with their boys: of 227 letters, 56 concerned girls and 85 boys, while 86 mothers wrote to express concerns about all their children or neglected to mention their sex, something that occurred most frequently in letters seeking advice on problems relating to infants less than one year old. It should be noted in conclusion that while some letters touched upon many issues at the same time, they have been classed in the above-mentioned categories, depending upon their major theme.

91 *Le Devoir*, 28 mars 1949, 4.

92 *Le Devoir*, 26 avril 1950, 4.

93 *Le Devoir*, 31 mars 1951, 4

94 *Le Devoir*, 9 oct. 1951, 4.

95 See, for example, *Le Devoir*, 19 avril 1949, 5; 4 mars 1950, 5; 11 avril 1950, 5; 5 nov. 1951, 2; 8 juin 1954, 6.

96 *Le Devoir*, 23 mai 1951, 2.

97 *Le Devoir*, 28 mars 1951, 2.

98 *Le Devoir*, 7 fév. 1951, 5. See also 6 avril 1950, 5, and 12 déc. 1950, 2.

99 *Le Devoir*, 7 déc. 1949, 5.

100 *Le Devoir*, 6 avril 1949, 5.

101 *Le Devoir*, 17 mai 1949, 5.

102 *Le Devoir*, 15 jan. 1951, 2.

103 *Le Devoir*, 18 oct. 1950, 5.

104 *Le Devoir*, 17 oct. 1953, 5.

105 *Le Devoir*, 27 mars 1953, 5.

106 *Le Devoir*, 18 nov. 1949, 7.

107 *Le Devoir*, 17 oct. 1953, 2; emphasis in original.

108 *Le Devoir*, 12 jan. 1952, 2.

109 *Le Devoir*, 7 fév. 1951, 2.

110 *Le Devoir*, 18 fév. 1950, 5. See also 28 fév. 1950, 5, and 22 avril 1954, 6.

111 *Le Devoir*, 20 fév. 1950, 5.

112 See *Le Devoir*, 9 oct. 1948, 4; 25 fév. 1950, 5; 23 oct. 1950, 5; 8 nov. 1950, 2; 19 déc. 1950, 2.

113 *Le Devoir*, 13 avril 1950, 5.

114 *Le Devoir*, 27 avril 1949, 4.

115 *Le Devoir*, 13 nov. 1952, 2. Another correspondent referred to this letter when she criticized kindergartens in her own letter of 29

November 1952, 2. A further exchange of this type had occurred earlier in a column that pointed out the risks of spoiling children by rocking them to sleep. See *Le Devoir*, 22 oct. and 3 nov. 1951, 2.

116 *Le Devoir*, 18 oct. 1954, 6.

117 *Le Devoir*, 11 nov. 1954, 6.

118 Ibid.

119 *Le Devoir*, 13 nov. 1954, 6.

120 *Le Devoir*, 20 nov. 1954, 7.

121 *Le Devoir*, 23 nov. 1954, 6.

122 Ibid.

123 Was it mere coincidence that the ÉDP Clinic seemed to stagnate after this debate, before being finally abandoned in the spring of 1955?

124 On this subject, see Denise Lemieux, "L'enfance dans la société et le roman québécois" (thèse de PhD [sciences sociales], Université Laval, 1978.

125 Fadette, quoted in Andrée Lévesque, *La norme et les déviantes: Des femmes au Québec dans l'entre-deux-guerres* (Montréal: Boréal, 1989), 57.